Independent Spirits

History Workshop Series

General Editor

Raphael Samuel, *Ruskin College, Oxford*

Already published

Village Life and Labour
Miners, Quarrymen and Salt Workers
Rothschild Buildings
East End Underworld
People's History and Socialist Theory
Culture, Ideology and Politics
Sex and Class in Women's History
Living the Fishing
Fenwomen
Late Marx and the Russian Road
Theatres of the Left 1880–1935
Poor Labouring Men
Making Cars
Language, Gender and Childhood
The Worst Street in North London
The Enemy Within

Routledge & Kegan Paul
London and New York

Logie Barrow

Independent Spirits

Spiritualism and English Plebeians,
1850–1910

To
Nina and Derek Barrow
– two differently independent spirits

First published in 1986
by Routledge & Kegan Paul plc

11 New Fetter Lane, London EC4P 4EE

Published in the USA by
Routledge & Kegan Paul Inc.
in association with Methuen Inc.
29 West 35th Street, New York, NY 10001

Set in Linotron Bembo
by Input Typesetting Ltd, London SW19
and printed in Great Britain
by T.J. Press (Padstow) Ltd
Padstow, Cornwall

Library of Congress Cataloging in Publication Data

Barrow, Logie.
  Independent spirits.

  (History workshop series)
  Bibliography: p.
  Includes index.
  1. Spiritualism—England—History—19th century.
2. Spiritualism—England—History—20th century.
3. Labor and laboring classes—England—History—19th
century.   4. Labor and laboring classes—England—
History—20th century.   5. Middle classes—England—
History—19th century.   6. Middle classes—England—
History—20th century.   7. England—Religion—19th
century.   8. England—Religion—20th century.
9. England—Intellectual life—19th century.
10. England—Intellectual life—20th century.   I. Title.
II. Series.
BF1242.G7B37   1986   133.9′0942   85–28170

British Library CIP data also available

ISBN 0–7100–9883–9 (c)
     0–7102–0815–4 (p)

Contents

Illustrations

Abbreviations

(Places of publication are London unless otherwise stated)

A Plea	J. Skelton: *A Plea for the Botanic Practice of Medicine,* 1853
BJHS	*British Journal for the History of Science*
BL	J. G. H. Brown: *The Book of Life, or the Fields of Death,* 1859
BM	British Museum Library
BMRA	British Medical Reform Association
BNAS	British National Association of Spiritualists
BST	*British Spiritual Telegraph*
Cause	J. G. H. Brown: *The Cause of the Present War,* 1855
CJ	*The Community's Journal; or, standard of truth. Useful Knowledge, void(sic) of fiction . . .*
CS	*Christian Spiritualist*
DLB	*Dictionary of Labour Biography*
DNB	*Dictionary of National Biography*
EJ	*Eclectic Journal and Medical Free Press*
FMA	J. Skelton: *Family Medical Adviser,* 1852, Leeds
FP	J. G. H. Brown: *Fulfilled Prophecies; or the passing signs of the end, as foretold in Ancient and Modern Prophecy; together with the future fate of India and the world; as described in modern divine revelation,* 1857
GR	*The General Record and Successive Review*
HN	*Human Nature*
ILP	Independent Labour Party
IR	J. G. H. Brown: *Important Relations from the spirits of Emmanuel Swedenborg, the Swedish Spiritualist . . .* 1857
LB	*Lyceum Banner*
Light	J. G. H. Brown: *Light of the World . . .* (a 97-word title), 1859
M. and D.	*Medium and Daybreak*

Message	J. G. H. Brown: *A Message from the World of Spirits* . . .
NR	*National Reformer*
PMMN	*Phreno-Magnet and Mirror of Nature*
ROMG	*Robert Owen's Millennial Gazette*
SBR	*Dr Skelton's Botanic Record and Family Herbal*
SC	*Secular Chronicle*
SDF	Social Democratic Federation
SMM	*Scriptural Monthly Magazine*
TW	*Two Worlds*
UM	*Universal Magazine*
YST	*Yorkshire Spiritual Telegraph*

Acknowledgments

Quantitatively, most of this book is about the culture of self-educating British people of humble birth during the nineteenth and early twentieth centuries. Fundamentally, though, it is also part of an argument about when and how widely knowledge can be accessible, and about how assumptions on accessibility sometimes interact with the content of such knowledge. The argument surfaces particularly during chapters 5 and 6 (and, with hindsight, chapter 4), but has underlain the writing of this book right through from the preconceptual stage. It has been an unpleasant companion. It brings no direct comfort to any political viewpoint.

Indirections are said to find directions out but, with the writing of at least this book, their speed is as wasp-like as their motion. This particular wasp is thus laden with debts. In 1971, Eric Hobsbawm raised a few good jokes but, mercifully, no direct veto when a student, purportedly crawling after a doctorate on Robert Blatchford and the *Clarion*, winged a fat chapter on spiritualism. I often wonder whether I would be so tolerant. Positive reassurance came when Dorothy Thompson seemed interested by a five-minute monologue; when Sheila Rowbotham and Sharon Collins arranged to hear a much longer one; and when Hermione Harris, on their recommendation, commented on my typescript. The enthusiasm of Stephen Yeo, and then of Raphael Samuel and Gareth Stedman Jones added my revised chapter to the editorial files of *History Workshop*. Although this journal's editors held to an unprecedentedly 'Collective' work-rhythm, I would be slick not to mention the two who sacrificed the most of their time: Anna Davin, particularly for her robustly sensitive subbings, and Jane Caplan for her almost telepathic attunement to the message behind a depressive style.

Parts of this book are indebted also to interest shown at various history workshops, at two meetings of the Society for the Social

History of Medicine, at seminars in Cambridge, Braunschweig and Roskilde on social history, at the Wellcome Institutes for the History of Medicine at London and Cambridge, at the Ecclesiastical Historical Society and the Social History Society. It is also indebted further to discussions and correspondence with Ulrike Becker, Roger Cooter, David Goodway, Jimmy Grealey, Marjorie Hanlon, Ruth Harris, J. F. C. Harrison, Preben Kaarsholm, Gustav Klaus, Niall Martin, Alex Owen, Roy Porter, Ruth Richardson, Gareth Stedman Jones, Barbara Taylor, Perry Williams, Hanne Zech and Reinhold Zech. None of the people named have seen or discussed more than one or other part of this book. And even on this scale, few can be accused of having been accessories after the fact.

Earlier versions of small parts of chapters 5 and 6 were printed in *History Workshop*, issue 9, 1980, and of chapter 7 in *Studies in Church History*, number 19, 1982, reproduced by kind permission of the Ecclesiastical History Society.

Among public librarians – without whom nothing would begin to become possible – I owe most thanks to the particularly hard-pressed staff at the British Museum, to Mr Travitt of Grimsby, Mr Ian Dewhurst of Keighley and Mr Stephen Best of Nottingham. Similarly to their colleagues in Darlington, Huddersfield, and Manchester. I am also grateful to Mr Wesencraft, keeper of the Harry Price Collection in London University Library, to the offices of the *Two Worlds* in London and of the Spiritual National Union. In the case of the last two, as of spiritualist readers generally, I hope they find this book stimulating, even though our assumptions diverge as fundamentally as ever.

Nothing would be possible either without good typists, of whom I am certainly not one. Mine have been Julie Winkler-Greher and Dorle Heinrich, who have been consistently amazing.

I am grateful to the British Library for permission to reproduce illustration nos 3, 4 and 18 from the *Lyceum Banner* and illustration nos 5 and 6 from *The Medium and Daybreak*. I am also grateful to the Headquarters Publishing Company for permission to reproduce illustration nos 1, 2, 7–17, 19, 20 and 21, from their publication *The Two Worlds* (still in print).

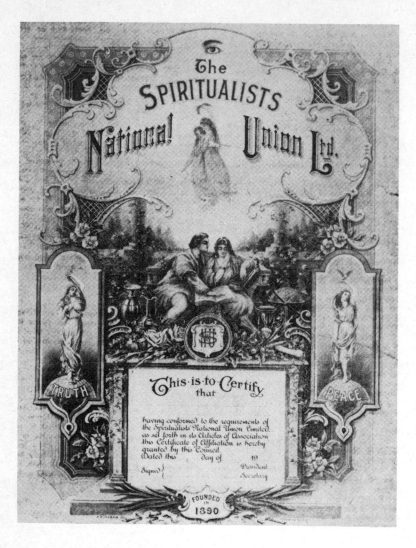

Charter of the Spiritualist National Union On the whole, spiritualists were not noted for their organisational ability, but the SNU remains their longest-lived grouping.

Chapter 1   *Germination*

A   American beginnings

Spiritualism, as a belief, centres on purported conversations with the 'spirits' of physically dead people. Such beliefs have occurred in many or most periods and cultures. But the start of spiritualism as an 'ism' is always dated to precise incidents, at Hydesville near Rochester in upstate New York during 1848. From these 'Rochester rappings', support spread quickly for the spiritualist version of these events throughout the USA. In America, the spiritualist movement 'seems to have reached a highwater mark around 1854–55'.[1] In the mid 1850s it suffered a widespread 'recantation movement' (as contemporaries called it); but it survived, and remained a strong current there. The basic history of American spiritualism can be scanned in a number of recent and often highly readable books.[2]

I am not setting out to stick my hooves into ground as well ploughed as this. But a few aspects are worth comparing or contrasting with their English equivalents. In general, much has been said about the pliably pentecostalist temper of upstate New York before and during these decades – about its status, in other words, as a 'burnt-over district'.[3] Yet, however swiftly spiritualism spread through such areas (whether sparsely log-cabined, or migration- and industry-based boom-towns like Rochester), it also had a largely similar history in the very different environment of the East-coast cities. In other words, it spread more broadly than the revivals. And in any case, Rochester itself was not merely 'the most thoroughly evangelised of American cities', but also 'among the few cities outside the old seaports that supported free-thought newspapers' and where the birthday of Tom Paine, the English-born deist, could be openly celebrated during the mid 1830s.[4] Perhaps, in general, the upstate environment and the urban, whatever their physical differences, had certain social and intellectual overlaps: the geographical and social mobility was, during these decades, intense even by American standards. So there was particularly little to undermine interest among Bostonians or Philadelphians in developments which had originated at or towards the frontier of settlement.[5]

Any contrasting of the American environment with the English involves what anthropologists currently call 'culture contact'. As Nelson notes,[6] there are two aspects of Amerindian cultures which may possibly have influenced the growth of spiritualism: Shamanism and the belief in guardian spirits. We can also note that Indians were important among the early teachers of Samuel Thomson, the pioneer of a system of medical herbalism[7] which, as 'medical botany' or 'Thomsonianism', had an impact before and during the period of spiritualism's arrival in England, often among the same sort of people and in similar geographical areas (as I will note later).[8] Nelson also notes[9] a similarity with certain African beliefs in spirit possession. Given that these certainly resurfaced sooner or later in Haiti, Brazil and elsewhere, they were presumably not unknown among those slaves (or their descendants) who had happened to be sold to English-speaking owners. Not only in ex-French New Orleans were 'many coloured persons . . . found among the mediums',[10] but also elsewhere in the South, fear of spiritualism's social implications was probably one factor in the hostility shown by white mobs and by some legislators. Recently, Peter Linebaugh has argued loud and long that blacks contributed to a political radicalism, common to much of the lower classes in all the, at least English-speaking, countries around the Atlantic basin.[11] Linebaugh's claims may, for all I know, be somewhat excited, but they remain exciting. Further, if Africans and their descendants can at last even be argued to have contributed to the political culture of other poor people, why not (conceivably) also to the religious too? (And if Africans, why not Amerindians, likewise?) True, Protestantism may be a less fertile ground than the Catholicism of New Orleans – or, say, of seventeenth-century Spanish-speaking Colombia[12] – for direct kinds of syncretism (a word denoting a combination of previously disparate beliefs). But can it – particularly at its extreme fringes – rule out indirect kinds? Arguably not. The last two sentences may therefore apply somewhat to England too.

And there are other senses – quite apart from Linebaugh –

in which the differences between the USA and England were, particularly during this time, ones of degree more than of kind. Firstly, in both countries there was often a widespread passion for self-education. In many north-eastern states of the USA (including New York), adult literacy during the early–middle nineteenth century is said to have topped 95 per cent; and there was also a massively successful 'lyceum' movement or 'Association of Adults for the Purpose of Mutual Education'.[13] (Later, 'lyceums' was to be the name of spiritualist Sunday schools, particularly for children, on both sides of the Atlantic.) This educational passion was not necessarily allied with political and religious radicalism; but often it was. And even when it was not, it could still encourage coolness towards any intellectuals associated with the upper classes. Thus autodidacts (those who make their education their own concern, irrespective of social superiors) are particularly likely to hunger for new world-systems, or to build their own. Some vaunt their down-to-earthness even while flapping around on wings of speculation or special revelation.

A minor and (for once) perhaps overwhelmingly American variation on such tendencies was the detailedness with which Andrew Jackson Davis – the founding seer of American, and later indirectly of plebeian British, spiritualism – described the landscape of the 'Summerland' or next world. Here, he often gave not only the topographical measurements – suitably imposing – but also the names. It was sometimes unclear who told him these: they sound vaguely Latinite – though, in a somehow infantile way, not quite. All these visions, we are told, were dictated in a trance. Davis, 'the Poughkeepsie seer', had had little formal schooling; most of his upbringing had been in a recently settled area which remained a major corridor for fresh settlers on their way through westwards. If Welsh-speaking Indians were still a respectable hypothesis among even the likes of Thomas Jefferson, then the mundane geography of many settlers (and of those dreaming of following them) could be equally speculative.[14] Thus Davis's celestial geography may, in part, have echoed the geographical meditations and plain rumour-mongering of generations of settlement-minded people, many of them very autodidact. If so, Davis combined the hunger of visionaries the world over for new worlds, with the hunger of many would-be settlers for new landscapes.

Another difference of mere degree between the USA and

England is the presence of a number of sects whose beliefs overlap with and had foreshadowed some of spiritualism's. The Shakers' communities (eighteen of them, comprising about 6,000 members during the sect's peak in the 1850s) were all in America,[15] though Shakerism had begun in Britain and continued to recruit there through the nineteenth century, as we will see. Another sect which had originated in visions but which, like the Shakers, had sought organisational stability by discouraging further such revelations was the Swedenborgian. Swedenborg himself (1688–1772) had apparently[16] been against founding a new church at all and, during the nineteenth century as much as before, some of those who more or less accepted his teachings retained their positions and posts within older organisations – including occasional Church of England, Unitarian and other clergymen. But the Swedenborgians' 'New' or 'New Jerusalem' Church was, by the early nineteenth century, a stable though minor feature of the religious landscape in both England (as we shall see soon) and New England. A further current which contributed to spiritualism and which had some early adherents on both sides of the Atlantic was Unitarianism (or the belief in one God rather than in a Trinity). In the long run, many Unitarians tended to evolve towards a universalist position (or the belief that all people were saved – i.e. in some way evolved – after death). One spiritualist who remained officially a Universalist was the Reverend J. M. Peebles, a much-travelled American Unitarian who for decades was friendly with English plebeian spiritualists and who sought to strengthen their links with American Shakers.

B   England and Keighley

In 1853, David Richmond returned to Britain. He was by now (as we shall see during chapters 5 and 6) a middle-aged autodidact craftsman who had gone through various phases of communitarianism (including Owenite) and religious belief (including deist) on both sides of the Atlantic. He had been in America since 1842, and a Shaker since 1846. He was hardly the first person of such a background to join the Shakers.[17] He claims[18] that this group had attracted him by its 'spirituality'; but possibly he was also attracted not only by their communal life-style but also by their asceticism:

J. M. Peebles
A busy link between American and British spiritualists. Peebles
had earlier left the Universalist ministry when his congregation
objected to his spiritualism. Sometime professor at the Eclectic
Medical College in Cincinnati, he edited a succession of
spiritualist periodicals and authored numerous pamphlets,
including one against vaccination. He visited Britain not only
as spiritualist but also as sympathiser with the Shakers.

he himself had been teetotal since 1836 and vegetarian since 1841.
Richmond had quickly learnt of the Rochester rappings and had
visited the family in whose house they had been heard, the Foxes.
What seems to have been going on in relation to his 1853 trip is
that he had persuaded the Shakers to allow it (and, for all we
know, to finance it) as a 'mission' for Shakerism but that, once he
felt free of them, he missionised more – or more directly – for
spiritualism. True, he sometimes attracted attention by donning
the Shakers' 'peculiar garb'. But this may have been no more than

a gimmick: he would have known how uneasy they were about further 'revelations from the spirit'.

Richmond's list of contacts (at least as he remembered it 32 years later) seems to have been weighted heavily towards current and former followers of Robert Owen – the now very aged pioneer of communitarianism, socialism, religious 'infidelity' (which, during the 1850s, was being renamed secularism) and much else. Richmond's first meeting was in his natal town of Darlington,

> by invitation of secularistic teetotallers. At Keighley was the next Secularistic Society who listened to [his] Gospel, and embraced spiritualism. London was the next Secular Society, at the City Road Rooms [the then H.Q. of London secularists, where he argued with their current leader Holyoake, and their future one, Bradlaugh] and also at the Secularist Rooms in Whitechapel, and afterwards at Middlesboro' [sic] by invitation of the Secularists.

The prominent individuals whom he visited also included Lloyd Jones (an Owenite and cooperator) and Robert Owen himself. Owen had been converted to spiritualism shortly before meeting Richmond.

We can glean some idea of what Richmond attempted, in at any rate the larger gatherings of secularists, from the case of Keighley – a middling-sized textile town in Pennine Yorkshire. Here, 'getting the Secularists of the town together, he did not leave them till he had turned them [no proportion mentioned] into Spiritualists, in some degree by his own mediumship, but largely by their own sitting in circle under his guidance.' 'Table manifestations', we are told, 'were obtained through mediums in the body of the audience by [sic] Richmond who delivered an explanatory address.' He was subsequently to be known among Keighley spiritualists as 'Father David', and officiated on more than one occasion as their founder.[19]

But the reason why Keighley allows us such glimpses is simply that it seems to have been by far David's most successful port of call. Why is unclear. So, even, is why it attracted him in the first place. True, he had lived in Leeds and Bradford during the late 1830s, the time when he became an Owenite. And there is a very vague assertion by at least one local historian that Owenism had

Members and officers of the Keighley Lyceum

The officers of the Sheffield (Attercliffe) Lyceum

not been forgotten in and around Keighley.[20] At any rate, when Richmond approached David Weatherhead, the outcome was this spectacular-sounding 'demonstration'. It took place in the radical citadel, the Workmen's Hall. 'Weatherhead became convinced of the truth of spirit intercourse and at once became a keen convert.'[21] Possibly also, Richmond discerned his potential: David Wilkinson Weatherhead had been 'connected with every radical movement in Keighley in the first half of the 19th century'. He had been one of the key local leaders in the Ten Hours movement, of the attacks on the new workhouses, and of Chartism; in 1843 he had been imprisoned for leading an agitation against the payment of dues (tithes) to the Church of England.[22] His prison had been York Castle. Two years earlier, he had led 'a triumphal procession . . . to meet Feargus O'Connor' here, on this great Chartist's release.[23] Weatherhead had been personally close to the Tory Radical, Richard Oastler, and probably felt in a similar position now towards O'Connor. He was, in addition, a pioneer teetotaller. This may be one reason why, whether or not his own parents had been lowly,[24] Weatherhead's grocery business was, by 1839, large enough for him to fund the £300 needed for the building of the Working Men's Hall.[25] And Richmond was fortunate not only in his choice of his first major convert but also in timing the event: as recently as 1851, Weatherhead had 'lost a beloved son.'

Like its American beginnings, spiritualism's arrival in England has been written about in a number of recent books.[26] Their narrative is usually different from the one just given. It deals, firstly, with the arrival of three female mediums during 1852 and 1853 from the USA; secondly, with their success among some middle- and upper-class people (with Owen among the former) in London; and thirdly with the positions, for or against, taken up by a number of leading men. For our purposes, Owen was undoubtedly the most significant convert. I have argued this in an earlier piece on the matter. But I may have oversimplified the picture in at least Keighley.[27] Nelson is no more than exaggerating when he describes the spiritualism of 'the 1850s and 60s' as 'almost entirely a matter of private meetings in the homes of believers and investigators'.[28] Such privacy seldom encourages historical recording (though it does not always preclude it). Consequently, even the basic chronology and geography may be oversimplified. Thus Nelson[29] and others speak of 'an epidemic of table turning and tapping spread[ing] across the country' from London. Now successes such as Richmond's at Keighley do sound like the kind of occasion which is sometimes compared to an epidemic. But Nelson himself mentions a British medium demonstrating before no less than Queen Victoria during 1846, i.e. six years prior to spiritualism's official arrival from America[30]: there were, in other words, older and partly native traditions involved, and their chronology remains unclear. In chapter 3, we will try to peer through a particularly startling – but still opaque – window into these, in Nottingham. Again, Nelson admits[31] it is hard to know whether his 'epidemic' was 'a result of the work of [the] American visitors or of the influence of mesmerism from Europe.' As we will also see later (in chapter 4, Section C), mesmerism had, by the early 1850s, had a wide and continuous impact in Britain among people of all classes and most viewpoints for some fifteen years. And there had been many other tendencies. For, very broadly, we should talk less in terms of lines of descent than of points of blur and of tension between, say, Owenism, herbalism, Swedenborgianism, mesmerism, Methodism, Chartism and other isms.

And the Keighley area – whatever its degree of primacy in the chronology of spiritualism – is also where we can see many of these at work least obscurely. The area as a whole (which we can call England's North-West-and-Pennine one) seems to have had relatively sizeable minorities – often artisan – who, during previous decades, had shown interest in Swedenborgianism and in older, similar, mystical traditions such as Behmenism (i.e. the ideas of the seventeenth-century cobbler Jacob Boehme). One historian speaks of 'the numbers of people who studied Jacob Boehme's writings . . . and who were well read [both] in the Catholic mystics' and in the Protestant, as being 'particularly large', 'above all, in the North around Manchester and Bolton'.[32] The same could also be said for interest in – very differently – Owenism. And, just over on the eastern side of the Pennines, 'the Quakers, Methodists and [Swedenborgians]' are all remembered as having 'established meeting houses [in Keighley] before they claimed national attention'.[33]

Admittedly, we have noted Owenism as, it seems, less than spectacularly strong, although perhaps present. But altogether, there seems no full explanation of why this particular town earned its reputation as the cradle of British spiritualism. The town and its surrounding semi-industrial settlements seem indeed to have been almost unique during the 1850s and 1860s in showing much sign of durable spiritualist organisation.[34] 'In Bradford, Bingley and other Yorkshire towns', joked a posh periodical during the early 1860s, 'there are [secularists], once notorious for believing nothing, now equally notorious for believing everything.'[35] The *Westminister Review*'s sneers would have bewildered any spiritualist, but its geography remained less wild. Directly or indirectly out of that session at the Working Men's Hall came also Britain's longest-lived early venture in spiritualist journalism, the *Yorkshire Spiritual Telegraph* (1855–7) whose successor the *British Spiritual Telegraph* (1857–9) also remained more Keighley- than London-based.[36] According to all sources, Weatherhead was the main financial backer during these years.

The sneer about 'believing nothing' hinted transparently that these Northern spiritualists had been Owenites: for decades, Owen's rejection of Christianity had been the main aspect of his thought emphasised by his opponents and, for more than one decade, by many of his followers (as I mentioned). How literally correct was this hint? Certainly the *YST/BST*'s editors and contributors seem to have been noticeably interested in Owen's doings and to have assumed a knowledge of his doctrines. But this went with doctrinal openness to any radical position. Thus the paper could also publish expressions of class feeling which would have been too bitter for Owen's own taste. The very first item of the very first issue roundly attacked the 'aristocracy' and the 'middle classes' as deceivers and exploiters of what it called 'the working community'. This item took the form of a poem, reported to be from the spirit of that democrat Robbie Burns (who, as a spirit, seems to have been working overtime in the Keighley area during these years).[37] Perhaps, therefore, when the now late Feargus O'Connor arrived 'according to promise' and gave even a rather boring communication, we can imagine the circle at the Keighley Working Men's Hall to be sitting on the edge of their chairs.[38] And they must surely have been glad of spiritual support for the ailing Chartist movement: certainly, on a later occasion, Feargus wafted back, declaring how 'gladly' he would 'lay down all my heavenly treasure . . ., if I could be the means of forwarding the . . . Charter, or, of completing my plans in the Land scheme, [though] for anything else I would rather be excused.'[39]

Even while the *British Spiritual Telegraph* was based officially in London, its content emanated, as before, disproportionately from Keighley. The same seems to apply to its editorship.[40] By the late 1850s, Keighley had 'several circles [meeting] regularly, some once a week, and some oftener'.[41] The doctrinal balance within or among them is hard to discern precisely. In other words, the *Westminister Review* was anyway oversimplifying. Certainly the editor of the *Yorkshire Spiritual Telegraph*'s second number described himself as 'a Christian'; but he at once disclaimed any belief in the Devil and in a material hell.[42] Certainly again, one circle was said to consist of 'Christian Spiritualists'[43] but, in this context as we have just seen, the label could mean many different things. On one occasion, the 'group of Spirits' which spoke 'at the Room of the Christian Spiritualists . . . purported to be John, and Charles Wesley, St Paul, Emmanuel Swedenborg, Andrew Combe [the phrenologist], St John, St Matthew and a number of others'. And the 'communication' itself 'was given in consequence of a short discussion which had taken place among some of the friends at a circle in the Working Man's Hall . . ., through some remarks in a communication asserting the Divinity of Christ'.[44] Possibly, the latter circle, which other sources suggest was made up of former 'infidels' (i.e. probably Owenites, more or less), had been unsympathetic to such 'remarks'.

But such generalisations may have been no more than approximately true: after all, 'upwards of four hundred persons'[45] were said to have been in this Hall at the time. (The word 'circle', apparently, could not always be taken as implying intimacy.) And during these years at least, some prominent theologian-spirits used these occasions to un-say some of their most distinctive and abrasive opinions. Thus, on the same vastly attended evening, Luther denounced his doctrine of justification by faith. 'For verily, I say unto you' – he was adopting the language of the King James Bible – 'it matters not what you believe, or what your neighbours believe, but those who love what they conceive to be good, and whose actions are guided thereby, this is the safest passport to a high state of happiness.' From a very different corner of the normal theological ring, 'Thomas Paine' had, only a fortnight previously, asked 'to unsay three things in the Spirit that I said in the flesh, namely – That Christ is God supreme; and the Bible is the Word of God; and Prayer is accepted.'[46] In the same vein, a couple of years later, a Midlands (Dudley) medium reported to the *BST* her amazement at seeing Tom in the same elevated sphere as Luther and Wesley:

> I asked is that the man who wrote that book. I mean the Age of Reason. My Spirit friends replied, Yes. I said, I did not expect to see him here. My Spirit friend [sic] said I know you did not; you will often be disappointed in this respect here.

Whether the word 'disappointed' hinted fairly at her previous level of tolerance is hard to say. True, Wesley had already addressed her in the 'thou'/'thee' form, whereas she had addressed him as 'you': an asymmetry that might, for all we know, imply respect on her part and perhaps allegiance. But on the other hand she had just had her protestations for justification 'by prayer' as against by 'purity and good works' slammed down with a loud 'No!!'.[47] All these unsayings were anything but consistent, but they could encourage an emphasis on common denominators: on what united rather than divided.[48]

If openmindedness was one lubricant to acceptance of spiritualism, or even a precondition for it, then the editor of the *Yorkshire Spiritual Telegraph*'s first issue need hardly have been surprised

> that persons making a profession of religion [had] been by far the most difficult to convince . . ., while a great many of those branded by them . . . infidels, have shown a spirit of honesty and enquiry which does them great credit . . . It must appear that a system of dry creeds must give way to one of working religion.

As we shall see, plebeian autodidacts of any religion or none were particularly likely to demand to experiment for themselves. Thus, once they had begun converging on a partly religious terrain as spiritualists, their common interest in a 'working religion' might become more important to them than their exact theology (which, as we shall see, also helped them to limit the problem of incompatible, implausible, unsympathetic – otherwise called 'lying' – spirits). Some hoped to outgrow theology altogether. Thus the *YST* noted with approval an American ex-revivalist, to the effect that 'the early history of Baptists, Methodists, Presbyterians,

Quakers and other sects, shows that spiritual manifestations were once common amongst them, but were ultimately strangled and slain by their creeds.'[49] For such spiritualists, as we shall see, spiritualism was to be a religion but without creed. Meanwhile, though, as spiritualists, both Christians and others found that their more or less common Christian upbringing tended to resurface untidily in some of the 'communications' they received.

This was the untidiness of openness. As the *YST*'s editors remarked in their opening address to readers, reports were coming in, not only from Keighley but 'from all the surrounding villages . . . of circles being formed – of strange communications received'.[50] Locally and during the mid 1850s in other words, Nelson's word 'epidemic' may possibly be accurate; and spiritualism's propagation would hardly be helped were the new journal to try to impose some uniformity of opinion. The editors in this address seem to have seen themselves as Christian, but only of a very flexible kind. They merely quoted St Paul to 'try the spirits', and hoped 'the day [would] . . . not [be] far distant, when every family will find themselves enabled to hold communion at their own homes, with those who have left the present sphere.' For them, in other words, attempts to impose uniformity were likelier to come from the side of Christian orthodoxy. This is why, only five pages earlier, an editorial sneered at the Christian churches' millennial prophecy of a heaven upon earth: after 1800 years of Christianity, the state of the earth was worse than ever. Only with the arrival of spiritualism, was 'a new era . . . about to commence, which will show us that the mission of Christ was to produce in reality, "Peace upon earth, and good will among [sic] men".' Thus, if the hope was still vaguely millennial, the methods were bittier and more intricate (the family circle) – or, in a word that I will introduce later, 'atomistic'.

This is partly why the milieu of spiritualism in Keighley prevents us measuring the exact role of Owenites or others. From the Owenite side, for example, even the label is tricky. Though the editor of the first number of the *Yorkshire Spiritual Telegraph*, John Garnett, was stated to have been 'an admirer of many of Mr. Owen's social arrangements', 'in theology he was a New Christian' – i.e. as I explained, a Swedenborgian.[51] Nonetheless, Owen was undeniably viewed as far more than merely another prominent or interesting convert or sympathiser. Other papers – American as well as British – were sometimes culled for observations about him.[52] The *YST* advertised and sold one of his major spiritualist addresses in which he announced the millennium. It also filled four of its own pages with extracts from it.[53] Later it gave publicity to Owen's May 1856 and 1857 (birthday) millennial Congresses, and extensively summarised Owen's preliminary address to the earlier one.[54] From his side, Owen also forwarded to the paper at least one address which he had received from the USA.[55] Given all this, and given also the speed with which Owen's own views were – or more often (as I will argue soon) seemed to be – changing, there is only a secondary need to know whether a major portion of Keighley spiritualists can be described as strictly Owenite. Come to that, much of Owen's following could not have been rigidly labelled Owenite, least of all around 1850. Relatedly here, one of the longest 'communications' given in the early numbers of the *YST* concerned the spirit of the feminist communitarian and atheist, Emma Martin. The communication was in the form of a somehow dreamlike narrative of her experiences immediately after her death. Basically this narrative re-enacted (sometimes echoing the King James Authorised Version almost word-for-word) the parable of the Good Samaritan. The difference was that the newly-arisen Emma turned out to be playing the role of the Samaritan while the victim – and guarantor of an accelerated happy ending for her – turned out to be none other than Jesus. (Ironically some newly-arisen Christian spirits passed by on the other side, singing 'Oh when shall I see Jesus'!). Editorially, the *YST* swallowed the story whole, rejoicing that Martin's 'charity for all the human race' had 'made her acceptable into a high and happy sphere': 'Those who were most intimately acquainted with her while on earth' would, it was sure, 'heartily subscribe to this.' Heartily or not, it was implying that at least some of those close to it had known Martin and been moved by her; nor was it exactly scotching the implication that they had also admired the opinions she had held while on earth.[56]

During the 1850s even more than before, the 'Owenite' movement was (as Barbara Taylor[57] has recently made very clear) a nexus of sympathies more than a structured organisation. This nexus involved, among other things, a range of communitarian interests on both sides of the Atlantic. Thus it is not very surprising that one address to Owen, reprinted in the *YST*, should come from a woman supporter of John M. Spear, who figures, in the annals of even early American spiritualism, as eccentric for his invention of a soul-filled world dynamo. She and others proposed to set up a colony whose inhabitants had apparently already 'entered into finer . . . conditions of life through [sic] their . . . inestimable medium, John M. Spear.' This colony would – 'by producing beautiful offspring . . . trained prior to, and succeeding birth, in harmony with the laws of their being' – 'be the deliverer of all nations, kindreds, tribes, tongues . . . Thus, and only thus, shall come that blessed hour when the will of God shall be done on earth as it is in heaven.'[58]

Nationally, as I will argue later, plebeian (or, working-plus lower-middle-class) spiritualism was to prove a particularly rich aspect in the mutation of much of Owenism during the decades around the 1850s. But these years saw broader and, to historians, even better-known mutations, many of which can be summarised as the disintegration of the Chartist movement. And here one aspect was the latter's (as, on a smaller scale, Owenism's) replacement by a number of successor currents. These appealed to particular elements in what had been a Chartist symphony, and sometimes set them into discord with each other. A notorious example here was the Foreign Affairs Committee which the Tory ex-diplomat David Urquhart set up among working men, to study and counter what, in Urquhart's somewhat paranoid vision, amounted to a Tsarist world conspiracy.[59] The West Riding was well represented here; and one of Keighley's keenest activists was Weatherhead. Another was his sometime fellow-editor of the *YST*, Benjamin Morrell.[60] Such involvement brought not necessarily a softening towards Toryism, but rather a tension with the main currents of popular radicalism.

In other respects, though, Weatherhead's own activism was to remain typical of the radicalisms of his time. He had, as noted, been a teetotaller – almost as soon as this agitation had been transplanted from America. Later, indeed, a local temperance writer, when attacking spiritualism, was to claim a warm acquaintance with many of its adherents.[61] There were probably very many other similar overlaps: Morrell, for example, was another prominent spiritualist to be involved elsehwere. He was a pioneer of Cooperation – alongside, he said, 'a few others connected with the Christian spiritualists'.[62]

Still in Keighley, another factor in this rather dishevelled ideological situation was that the arrival of spiritualism put existing groups under pressure. Not surprisingly, the Swedenborgians were one of these. Swedenborg himself had arrived at the more distinct of his doctrines by, he believed, directly viewing the various regions of the next world. The experience of most (though, as with Davis and others, not all) spiritualists was to be less flatteringly direct. But it did have the attractions of freshness and also a certain do-it-yourself quality. I will later associate this quality particularly with what I call the plebeian sciences. Precisely the same openness was what the elders of the New Jerusalem Church (rather like those of the Shakers) feared in spiritualism: it struck at the roots of their doctrinal coherence – hence, given their eccentricity and small size, of their existence. In chapter 9, I will note some indications of the Swedenborgian presence in the North-West and Pennine area. Significantly for Keighley and its more immediate neighbourhood, though, the longest discussion in all the *YST/BST*'s pages was started when a Swedenborgian attacked most of the 'members of the New Church' as 'pigmies' and 'bigots, aping to extinguish the light of heaven, because it happens to shine in the year 1855, and not in the year 1796'.[63] His main opponent digressed, significantly, into an attack, in the name of 'Spiritual Communism', on 'Liberalism', i.e. the economic doctrine of laissez-faire.[64] This discussion provided the only occasion when the *Telegraph* – avowedly at least – broke its own taboo on anything which might directly offend a particular denomination.[65] As it explained later, there were 'in both England and America, . . . those who have been regarded as Beacons in the New Church' who were 'bold defenders of the modern Spiritual developments'.[66] Admittedly, it was, so it said, talking here of those 'whose literary and scientific attainments [were] far above the ordinary standard.'

The Swedenborgians, then, were considered particularly ripe for adherence to spiritualism. But the general situation, particularly in the Keighley area, was rather more complex. 'We find', wrote the *YST*,[67] both 'Clergymen . . . Ministers . . . [and], equally . . . common, . . . members' – 'of the Church of England . . . [and] . . . almost all the various dissenting denominations' who were 'susceptible of [sic] spirit influence.' The denominations listed, included not only 'Swedenborgians' but also 'Quakers, Shakers,

eloquent parts of his harangue had been 'very concerned with death, and thus with religion'.[3] But, both then and much more explicitly during the 1850s, even this related to his approach as a whole.

Even if we 'make allowance' (as he explicitly requests during his 84th birthday-celebrations) for his being 'deaf, and almost blind' as well as for the fact that he 'should' have been 'in his dotage',[4] there is something significant in the twitches of apparent rejuvenation which his acceptance of spiritualism gave to his system of thought. The latter sat as if waiting for its incoherences to be (if we may borrow a metaphor more appropriate to two chapters ahead) electrified. Whether this amounted to renewal, though, was another matter. To some extent, perhaps, renewal was impossible. And perhaps this unrenewability provides another reason why we do not find spiritualists rushing in droves to sit publicly at his feet, however frequently he addressed himself to them and however proud some plebeians were to associate themselves with him implicitly. As we have seen in the last chapter, sectarian discipleship was no part of a Keighley-type strategy. Hence the relevance at this point in our argument of Owen's 'new' or, rather, spiritualist incoherences and rigidities: the more extreme, the more they point up the wisdom of Keighley's humbleness.

By 1853, Owen was discoursing on 'the Future of the Human Race, or, the great, glorious and peaceful revolution, near at hand, to be effected through the agency of departed spirits of good and superior men and women.' Now as before, his great world-transforming factor remained knowledge of a 'truth' which he incorrectly believed he had discovered. 'What, then, is this little grain of mustard-seed, or of truth, which shall . . . overwhelm . . . all mankind?

'It is simply a knowledge that man does not form himself': this was Owen's old determinism.[5] It was this 'truth which [would] rapidly make all things upon the earth consistent, and man everywhere to become a rational being.' For Owen, knowledge of his 'truth' had always been the central agency. Now, however, it was merely one of two. For 'man' was from now on to be 'in daily and delightful communion with his loved and departed ones, and with holy angels, whose every desire is to progress humanity up to excellence and high rational enjoyment'.[6] In other words, spirit agency would soon multiply the availability of Owen's 'truth'. And Owen now increasingly used his newly spiritualised doctrine to interpret the ministry of Jesus. As he wrote in the epigraph of his 1853 pamphlet,

> the first coming of this Truth was through Jesus Christ, an inspired medium from his birth, to teach the world the necessity for it to acquire *universal love* and *charity*.
> The second coming of *Truth* is *now*, to teach the world how to *acquire and practice* universal love and charity.

Thus the well-known incoherences of Owenite and other Enlightenment determinisms encouraged on the one hand an appeal to external agency, i.e. (now) to spirits; they also, on the other, inspired a voluntaristic appeal. 'It is now to be ascertained whether the population of the world is to acquire the requisite moral courage now to abandon at once the principle [i.e. denial of determinism] which creates the necessity for the language of falsehood.'[7] Underlying this appeal to human will lay (as always with such as Owen) the crudest reliance on reason: 'Man is not made to resist his own happiness.'[8]

This old reliance, coupled with his new spiritualist confidence, allowed him to add some typically eccentric emphases and to accentuate a few old ones. The former were particularly rife in his concluding speech to his last birthday Congress (of the 'Advanced Minds of the World', this one) during May 1857. They included predictions that, by the end of the Century, 'the English and Irish channels [would] be crossed on dry land, the seas and oceans . . . navigated on islands instead of in ships' and, more rationalistically, that 'the Anglo-Saxon language, improved to the utmost, [would] be taught to all in its purity from birth, and the language will also be the language of truth only'.[9] These predictions vaguely echoed Owen's contemporary, Étienne Cabet, as also the tendency, since at any rate the seventeenth century, to blame England's ills on the 'Norman Yoke'. Perhaps it also echoed the 'land of Cockaygne'.[10] No less vaguely, Owen, in the last number of his *Millenial Gazette*,[11] called for the formation of a 'society of Life or Death', consisting of men and women who would war against the powers of evil. How, was entirely unclear. Owen was also uncertain as to whether he was appealing to 'the superior and most conscientious of the Spiritualists, Shakers, Rappites, Zoarites, Full Socialists or Fourierite half Socialists', or to a 'band of martyrs' who would somehow 'select' themselves 'out of all parties and nations'.

A strategy of his which his spiritualism clearly revived was his appeal to existing holders of power. Deep down indeed, this seems never to have been against his instincts – if we remember, from the 1820s to the 1840s, both his uneasy organisational relationship with most of his followers and his explicit refusal of popular-democratic theory and practice. Throughout, Owen had acted as an exceptional person, a unique escapee from the determinist trap of circumstances, a non-Christian messiah, 'not . . . arguing a case' so much as 'making a prophecy'.[12] This underlines how deeply many Owen*ites* differed from him around this aspect – quite apart from the fact that they themselves, in their localities, often formed part of an interlocking nexus of plebeian activities, mostly radical but of variable nature.[13]

Even more important for us, it underlines how much spiritualism allowed him during much of the 1850s to say his lengthy farewells (as they turned out) to this world in a way which yet again underlined his divergence from most of the people he had influenced – including, not least, from whomever among them were likely to become plebeian spiritualists. Whatever stance they, during the mid-Victorian decades of stability, might evolve towards the millennium (we will return to this in Chapter 5A), his own brand of millenarianism was elitist. It was elitist in the strategic sense that he preferred his 'great change [to] be commenced and carried on . . . by the wise and calm reason of the governing class' rather than 'through the irritated and violent passions of the suffering masses.' In this sense he scolded the latter for their 'ignorant, inexperienced and undeveloped state'.[14] He might, as we shall see in chapter 6, view medical orthodoxy as a conspiracy, but in relation to social ills he was prepared to use a metaphor with medical aspects ('irritation') in order to summon the existing elite in so as to act as doctors. It was elitist also in the even more exclusive, because snobbish, sense that he felt able to claim personal acquaintance with famous personages:

> The most prominent persons who have departed this life within the last half century, who were deeply interested in the improvement of society, . . . were President Jefferson,

Benjamin Franklin, Shelley, Dr Channing, and, for two or
three of the last years of his life, His Royal Highness the late
Duke of Kent . . . The spirits of these parties – all of whom,
except Benjamin Franklin, knew me in life, and were full
converts or favourable

to his system (or so he claimed) – had now returned to reassure
and guide him.[15] True enough, given his long history of disap-
pointments, he could not afford to be anything but optimistic, but
plebeian spiritualists of any age were hardly in a position to be
elitist.

Thus in 1853, Owen could again – almost as around 1820 – be
confident that existing holders of power were the most open to
reasonable appeal. It was this confidence which had once allowed
him a particularly naive optimism that the Christian churches were
on the point of switching to his version of rationalism: it was,
apparently, necessary for his followers merely to 'make the practi-
cability of his [millennial] change . . . plain [to the] constituted
authorities [in Church and State], and they [would] willingly adopt
it'.[16] No wonder that he liked to question his spirit-informants as
to the private opinions of key members of the ruling elite.[17] No
wonder, again, that he reverted also to his comparison (optimistic
or not) of social or ideological change with technological[18]: a
comparison in which the human was reduced to the material, or
perhaps to the 'hands' whom he had employed during his decades
as a pioneer industrialist.

But these and other reversions (or reemphasisings of old
strategy) exemplify again how much Owen had always searched
for some logical crack where he could shatter all opposing arguments, or rather turn them inside-out. Already on some earlier
occasions (as in his 1817 Address[19]), he had believed he had found
such a crack. And during the 1850s, this glad confident morning
returned, this time on spirit-wings. If what he called 'the language
of falsehood' was, by definition, all-enveloping – if it made even
the best-intentioned efforts self-defeating – he, Owen, now had
the tool which would crack it open and turn or transvalue it into
a no less all-pervading 'language of truth'.[20] (With language – as
with the formation of human character and with so much else –
he left no room for interaction.) Admittedly, with spiritualism he
did – even if only for the sake of argument – entertain the possi-

bility that he was mistaken. This would be most unusual and would make spiritualism 'one of the greatest deceptions ever practised on human credulity'. But assuming, conversely, that it was true, then it constituted 'the most important event that [had] yet occurred in the history of the human race'.[21] Owen had always had to base much of his strategic hopes on his preaching, and/or on what we might call the demonstration-effect – i.e. the striking and self-multiplying example – of his followers' activities. The spirits – via the mere fact, let alone the content, of their communications – now promised to combine both. They had 'uniformly' told at least him 'not [to] dispute with' disbelievers in spirit contact: 'for', they add,

> we will adopt means to convince all, without your doing more than stating the facts within your knowledge and experience. The continual increase and reiteration of the facts which we shall make manifest to the population of the world, will gradually and peaceably convert all, and compel them to believe in this new mode of recreating the character of man and of reconstituting society over the whole world.[22]

Owen, needless to say, had for many decades been 'stating the facts' as he saw them; the novelty was merely that they were now to 'increase' via agents far less fallible than his merely earth-bound (and, in their majority, merely plebeian) followers.

And there were other ways, too, in which Owen's 'reiteration' of his message may have begun to seem, to plebeians, not merely patronising but also hollow. Thus Owen's 1857 birthday Congress consisted of a series of addresses, read by or for him, to various categories of the world's inhabitants: possibly few if any members of these categories were physically present to be harangued.[23] True, responses were not recorded, but many pages of this final periodical, *Robert Owen's Millenial Gazette*, were filled with imaginary dialogues between large masses of people. These hardly life-like conversations seem reminiscent of those in Volney's *Ruins of Empire* – but no more than feebly: their main purpose was too obviously to give Owen some final opportunities to catechise the whole human race.[24] Suitably, one dialogue ended with the 'Answer – Amen. So be it!'.[25]

These would be nice words on which to end this chapter, except that Owen is an exceptionally ancient mariner of the ideological oceans and will not allow us to. As we shall see during the next chapter, Owen was not the only social millenarian during the 1850s to see his millennium as imminent. But most plebeian spiritualists differed from this expectation or were at least beginning to. In later chapters, we will recognise one of spiritualism's obvious attractions: that it offered to re-knit directly the threads which physical death had sundered. In a sense, it offered to the living a community with the dead. Usually, so far as one can tell, such a community was not – directly at least – very extensive: it was more a matter of re-establishing contact with one's loved (or at least liked) ones plus, now and then, other extraneous and occasionally exalted personages. This may, for all we know, always have been the staple of spirit-contact. True, during our period as a whole, there were allusions within many contexts to the constant aid given by spirits.

But when Owen talked of the 'aid of the spirits of our departed relatives and friends, who in the world of spirits are also assisted by the sages and prophets of olden time, and of all that is superior among them',[26] his own much shorter timescale transposed such a community of the living and dead to a new and higher pitch. These spirits, he announced in the next sentence, 'all agree[d] that [their] . . . manifestations [were] now made to prepare the public mind for the reformation of the population of the world.' They seem to have been confident of this effect, precisely because such 'manifestations' were 'new and truly wondrous and almost incredible'[27]: unlike later, no one had, apparently, had time to become blasé yet.

But even more important for Owen, this 'Millenial State of human Existence upon the Earth' was merely a preliminary 'to ['the population of the world's] translation into the superior spirit spheres'.[28] For Owen, more vividly than for most later spiritualists, spiritualism and socialism needed each other: indeed, they were virtually symbiotic. At least 'upon Earth', they would bring about what he now described as 'the spiritual social state'.[29] And their strategy also had to fuse the two aspects. Indeed, as I remarked previously, Owen embraced spiritualism with an abandon which underlines not merely his very public and plausible awareness that he was not long for this world, but also the permanence of his incoherences, particularly those of his determinism: crudely put, if environment determined character, how could character improve sufficiently so as not to undermine a radically improved environment? Spiritualism seemed to allow a break-out from such circularities.

An appreciation of spiritualism would, Owen proclaimed, 'create a new character for each' and would thus open a 'plain, peaceful path to an entirely new existence of man upon earth, in which no inferior character will be formed'[30] – such as might have undermined the new earthly existence. Or, as he rephrased the problem a year later, 'Socialism, until united with Spiritualism, [had been] a body without a soul – the true physical machine of society, devoid of its motive power.' (Might he have had his friend J. M. Spear's soul-filled world dynamo vaguely in his mind here, or alternatively the Frankenstein story?) But 'now soul and body can be naturally and most beneficially united.'[31] This was because spiritualism would 'give a new character' not merely to 'each' but also 'to the human race, by which the mind of all will be born again, . . . so as to become fully-formed men and women, knowing themselves and the principles and practices by which to assist to form a superior character for others.'[32]

One of the unconventional facts which the shock and then the guidance of spirit-contact would, he hoped, help people to recognise was the utter harmfulness of conventional marriage. Not that Owen had ever minced words about this. Rather, he now sought to guarantee the improvement of human character, not merely via spirit-contact but also as before, via two subsidiary routes. The first, we might call eugenic (if only of the emotions: 'true chastity consist[ed] in having no sexual intercourse except when God's affinity, or pure love and affection, exists at the time between the parties'[33]). The second (which we have met via Spear's followers) would today be called maternalist. It involved what we might call intra-uterine well-being: 'Fully to reform the world', there would be a need 'to commence with' 'a fully-formed, physical and mental and spiritual infant'; for this, 'the mother [should] be careful in her diet and exercise, and be kept in a placid and happy state of mind.'[34] Similarly, when Address[ing] the Inhabitants of New Lanark during 1816, near the start of his activity as a reformer, he had attributed his own uniqueness – as escapee from the trap of circumstances – partly to 'causes which fashioned me in the womb'.[35] Here too, in other words, 'spiritual' was not merely tacked on to the 'physical and mental'. Rather, Owen's new spiritualism shocked, again, some of his own unconventionalities into new life. And the history of many other communitarians during and after the 1850s, suggest similarly, in America at least.

And there was yet another way in which relations – between the two worlds and within each – were due for reorganisation. Apparently even 'good and kind Spirits' who came 'to give us the best knowledge which they have acquired in both worlds' had, 'by retaining for a longer or shorter period, while in the second world, the early imbibed prejudices of the first . . . tended so far rather to increase than decrease disunion among spiritualists.'[36] Socialism, therefore, would solve not only what we have seen and will discuss later as the problem of lying spirits: rather, socialism would make the flow of aid between the two worlds two-way. In this sense too, symbioses would exist. Again, as we will see, spiritualists sometimes talked of spirits receiving help from the physically living; but Owen looked forward to a time – and that soon – when such help would flow, on (so to say) a global scale. After this, his hope, expressed in the next sentence, that the same process would afford to socialists on earth just as much unity as to spiritualists and spirits, is a relative anti-climax. Rather, again, his crowning hope was that 'the spirits of just men [sic] made perfect [would] assist, guide and direct the way of the full . . . reformation . . . of the race of man, thus preparing, through a new practical religion', not only a 'new earth', but also 'a new sphere in heaven for those thus reformed and regenerated'.[37]

Thus this world was not the only one open to the efforts of reformers. Even more significant, Owen's version, here, of the old apocalyptic vision of 'a new heaven and a new earth' was to be realised by the activism of human beings (whether physically living or dead). When quite a young industrialist, Owen had taken no small part in ushering in one new world; he had spent much of the subsequent four-and-a-half decades trying to bring about a new social world; now he was at least implying a strategy for remodelling the next world, almost before he, let alone his hearers, had even entered it: clearly, spiritualism whetted his old appetite for reform. As he neared his grave, he grew a tail of ever more radically radiant futures behind him.

Previous versions of a 'new Heaven and . . . Earth' had stressed intervention from God – an act conceived of as some shattering irruption from outside the bounds of the humanly knowable. In this scenario, the part of angels and others was very vaguely sketched in, if at all. Owen, implicitly at least, inverted this disbalance. True, we have seen that he was a deist, and thus remained in this sense a monotheist. But his spiritualism gave such ambitious roles – and in both worlds, as we have just seen – to human spirits, as to leave little space to work out a role for the Divine. Spiritualism (in the hands of Owen and many more consistently plebeian adherents) behaved like a democratisation of polytheism. True, God might be mentioned in theory and doggerel as the summit and guarantor of the Harmony of the whole, but vaguely and as if distantly – or as if S/He has floated so high as to leave space for lowlier (though not necessarily lower) spirits to float in underneath. An Englightenment Deism had developed into something else – though we cannot say whether into something reminiscent of polytheism or of Roman Catholic appeal to saints. (When we come to conceivable underground survivals, I am way out of my depth: see chapter 3). Thus, thirty-odd years after Owen's death, when asked by a local journalist whether s/he believed in God – defined (by the journalist) as 'an individual and creating Deity' – one Middlesborough spiritualist replied with a crescendo of heterodoxy: one's

> conception [of God] must differ according to the individuality
> of [one's] mind; but unquestionably spiritualists do recognise
> as one of their fundamental principles that Intelligence and
> Goodness are the ruling powers of the universe. As to whether
> this Being is one or more, I am not aware of any who, with
> any show of reason, claim to be able to speak personally.[38]

It is unclear whether the last sentence was intended as a statement of neutrality in relation to controversies over trinitarianism or polytheism.

We should also note that this spiritualist was speaking just after conducting a funeral. This can symbolise something: spiritualism, in the shortest term, allowed Owen to go on expecting an imminent millennial transformation, even when Owenite organisation was at its weakest. Subsequently, it was spiritualism that encouraged Owenites and other social millenarians to transpose their expectations for reform from this world to the next – to the 'Summerland', as they came to call it. You could look forward to your own arrival *in* socialism after your physical death irrespective of whether you saw the arrival *of* socialism on this earth as imminent (with most people directly influenced by millenarianism), likely or even, for the foreseeable future, desirable.

But to talk of spiritualism after Owen's time is to measure how far we are leaving him behind. Indeed, spiritualists of the Keighley type had, even during the 1850s, already partly done so – or so the previous chapter can be read as suggesting. This was not simply because he was one, whereas they were many. Rather, it was because he was one (would-be) prophet of an impending millennium, and was seeking to mobilise spiritualism directly to help preach this and to bring it about. The next chapter provides an immensely odder example of such a combination, and will therefore have to be longer than this one. But both the next chapter and this exemplify the prophetic and therefore sectarian pitfall which spiritualists of the Keighley type (whatever their various debts to Owen, where any) seem mostly to have avoided. And this is an important reason *why* they were beginning to leave him behind.

Chapter 3 Nottingham and cabala

A Introduction

'The main features of the Bible', the *Yorkshire Spiritual Telegraph* proclaimed, had been 'communicated by spirits'.[1] This, for the *YST*, was an argument against any dogmatic approach to the Bible. But the logic was invertible: it might dignify some 'spiritual' revelation with Biblical status. And occasionally it was so used. One example comes mainly from Nottingham during the 1850s, 60s and, vestigially, early 1870s. At the time, this town was coming to be spoken of as 'the Manchester of the Midlands': local coal-mining and brick-making were expanding; above all, the town's traditional industry, lace, was booming (though with major hiccoughs which, particularly during the years from 1857, must sometimes have felt more like convulsions). The town's popu-lation, during the 1850s (i.e. between the census-years 1851 and 1861), climbed by roughly one third.[2] However, one cannot easily – unless too easily – say how such background details relate to the developments disclosed in this chapter.

The whole episode, here, may appear so surprising as to be forgettable – dismissable as, say, some crass blurring of Ben Jonson's *Alchemist* with some circum-1800 radical millenarian such as Richard Brothers.[3] But to mention *The Alchemist* is to dignify our central actor in Nottingham as a deliberate fraud, which may well be too simple. Thus, if circum-1600 comparisons are in order, then John Dee might be apter. (I will return to this.) Far more important, even were the explanation to include a devaluing element (whether deception, self-deception, whimsicality, insanity or some combination of these), the interest for us would still lie in the materials available. Whether such materials were less constantly available than during Keith Thomas's '16th and 17th centuries' is hard to say,[4] though presumably they were under greater challenge (from the natural sciences). The point is, that mid-nineteenth-century plebeian spiritualists – whether they were directly familiar with such material or just aware, uneasily or not, that it existed – produced a vaguer and therefore more flexible mixture. If we grow impatient at the apparent bizarreness of this episode (and if, say, we dream of leaving its derivativeness to be sorted out by some ideal committee of, perhaps, Mary Douglas, Gershom Scholem and the late Frances Yates) we owe some thanks to spiritualists such as those of Keighley: even amongst those who believed in spirit-contact, they helped keep (or *make?*) such goings-on – which at least some of them were aware of – bizarre. To some extent, therefore, our impatience is one rough and indirect measure of their achievement.

The 1850s opened famously with that celebration of middleclass triumph, the Great Exhibition, and are said to have opened what one historian has called the 'age of Equipoise.' Prophecy and millenarianism, by contrast, are conventionally said to be symptoms of social strain or breakdown, not of equipoise. The least the ensuing chapter will suggest, though, is that however superficial the 'equipoise' thesis may be, prophecy and millenarianism have at least their own rhythms. (Indeed their devotees, self-consciously living through what the Book of Revelation calls 'a time, times and half a time' and thus through times both mundane and supra-mundane, tend to try and bring these two temporalities together by making them simultaneous: rather like some of those historians who bridle at the very idea that persons can live in more than one temporality 'at a time'.) For, millenarianism continued to flourish into the 1850s, in response not merely to social stresses but also, at least as much as before, to perceptions of the world situation. The latter was characterised by a number of events which, given the existing modes of prophecy, were thoroughly open to interpretation as signs of the Last Things: the restoration of the Napoleonic Empire, Britain's alliance with this against the Russian (the actual or would-be persecutor of political saints in half Europe), and the threatened collapse of Britain's Empire in India. These and similar developments occurred while the Continent-wide upheavals of the late 1840s were still a fresh memory, constantly embittered by reports of further repression.

B   The politics of one crystal prophet

During the mid 1850s, John George Henry Brown,[5] a lame ex-soldier who had 'travelled through various parts of the continent of Europe and America'[6] and who had now – despite or because of growing blindness[7] – turned crystal-gazer, did something which ended his obscurity. It made him 'even as the prophets of old'[8] – if only for himself, a few hundred followers and his wife (who is hardly ever mentioned except for making tea for many of them).

Nottingham was already important in the annals of millenarianism. Earlier in the century, the freethinker Richard Carlile had been in contact with even some Muggletonians there;[9] and the Millerites, Southcottians and followers of 'Zion' Ward had all, at various times, been strong there[10] – the latter continuing into at least the early 1840s.[11] In politics, Nottingham's 'long-standing ['revolutionary'] tradition' had helped make it 'one of the staunchest centres of support for the National Charter Association' with a notably 'diverse range of cultural and political activity'. Within this, 'religious modes [had] remained a permanent feature.' True, as early as 'the mid 1840s, the [Nottingham Chartist] movement had lost much of its momentum.'[12] But something of this old configuration was surely symbolised when at least two of Brown's publications[13] were specifically sold at the shop of James Sweet. Sweet, a barber-bookseller, is described as having been, among the Nottingham Chartists, 'the . . . foremost advocate of educational and moral improvement (as well as being a staunch O'Connorite)'; he also advocated teetotallism.[14] From their side, many of the millenarian groups – whether because of, or (as with the Southcottians) despite, their official theology – were also attractive to some people of radical views. Such views were, as we will see in a moment, nothing strange to Brown and his 'Community of the Great Organisation' either.

The latter's social composition seems – so far as is visible – not to have contradicted J. F. C. Harrison's characterisation of one of these earlier millenarian groups as made up 'mainly [of] small tradesmen [sic], artisans and shopkeepers, with usually one wealthier member in each congregation'.[15] Certainly, Brown was able to mobilise sufficient funds to be able to distribute, often free, hundreds of small pamphlets[16] and, by the late 1850s, to publish a succession of decently printed periodicals – of which the first two used up a respectable quantity of ink in subtitles alone.[17] The formal membership – which was centred on Nottingham, Leicester and Loughborough, with two smaller groups elsewhere in Leicestershire and Warwickshire, plus a scatter of members between the Isle of Wight, London and County Durham,[18] and which numbered 'over 330' by 1859 – certainly included two 'gentlemen' (one of whom owned 'a light conveyance'[19]), and someone wealthy enough to manage one donation of £5.[20] But there is more solid evidence that Brown's practice of milking his followers of a few pence, not once a week, but twice,[21] sometimes ran up against absolute physical barriers. Thus non-payers were offered continual membership,[22] and the proprietors of the *Community's Journal* were stated to be 'poor working men'.[23] 'In consequence of bad trade and loss of work' – during the spring of 1859 particularly – 'many of the members were unable to pay regular [sic]': their total contribution during two months at this time works out at an average of less than ten-pence a head.[24] And precisely the same problems persisted for at least a year.[25] This suggests that many of Brown's followers may have been affected by the financial crisis in the lace trade. Perhaps, therefore, his visionary source (whose official identity I will note soon) was not being merely rhetorical when it described anyone accepting Brown's revelations as 'join[ing] the poor'.[26]

Nottingham, in addition, already had a number of 'mediums' who, like Brown, 'were crystal seers'. But these – or so we are told by a suavely abusive spiritualist narrator of the whole episode[27] – had 'soared only to a slight altitude beyond the function of the common fortune-teller'. Possibly, the town was not unusual in this respect: there is no easy way for us to discover how much of the spirit-contact which had been available before the arrival of spiritualism had come camouflaged in the fugitive costume of fortune-telling, or again, how frequently or for how long. In any case, Brown now 'soared' to realms said to be out of the ken of ordinary mortal crystal-gazers – much, we are told by the same source, to their envy: 'he professed to become subject to spirits of a higher degree'. But even this is to hide Brown's light under a bushel: his main correspondent – appearing in Brown's crystal with a scroll ready for transcription – was the Angel Gabriel, no less.

Even sources so exalted stooped not to stylistic freshness. Curiously or not, their grammar and paragraphing were as turgid as Brown's – or even more. What Brown was pleased to call their 'revelations' groaned with 'Thus saith the Lord's; each of the 157 'revelations' in one of his books begins with 'Behold'.[28] The content, too, appealed to a traditional millenarian preoccupation with fire and brimstone. Brown's immaterial informants hardly economised on 'the calamities . . . decreed to fall upon the earth prior to the coming of Christ and His glorious reign'.[29] Typically of such woes, they were imminent: 'far nearer than anticipated'.[30] Indeed, one could 'glean that the latter days [had] already come'.[31] Yet Brown was usually reluctant (or perhaps too canny) to set dates. His followers might print – and, it seems, distribute free – 'thirty thousand to forty thousand large sheets containing warnings to the people shewing the calamities which are foretold to fall on all the nations of the earth'.[32] But when he excommunicated one notably rebellious disciple, a particular accusation was that the man had more than once 'affix[ed] periods to revealed events' and, doubtless more embarrassingly still, had 'nam[ed] places which should be destroyed, which have [sic] already proved false'.[33] In effect, though, this miscreant was merely repeating an earlier mistake of Brown's – though Brown did not labour this implication.[34]

However prudent the ban on date-fixing, the great change was nonetheless imminent. The proofs of this were more enjoyable than the mere details of revelation. In, again, time-honoured tradition, Brown and his followers seem to have licked their millenarian lips at reports of natural calamities and freaks of weather. In a sense, calamities were the same, whether natural or political, whether current or impending: all not only presaged the End but might also comprise it.[35] Similarly, Brown interpreted, on the one hand, what he called 'ancient and modern prophecies' (though what modern ones he recognised other than his own, plus those attributed to Napoleon on St Helena,[36] is unclear) and, on the other, 'the present aspect of the world' in the light of each other.[37]

The word 'aspect' was only very indirectly astrological, if at all. Brown, for the moment, is more significant for being radically political. As he had just explained, British forces were currently (1857) so overstretched defending India against Indians, and involved actually or potentially in China and elsewhere, that the

A

MESSAGE

FROM THE

WORLD OF SPIRITS,

SHEWING THE STATE OF MEN AFTER DEATH;

DESCRIBING THE SENSATION IN THEIR DYING MOMENTS;

THEIR PROGRESS, SUFFERING, AND OCCUPATION THROUGHOUT THE
SPHERES IN THE SPIRITUAL WORLD BEFORE REACHING
ETERNAL REST;

THUS MITIGATING THE DOCTRINE OF ETERNAL PUNISHMENT;

WITH A

SPIRITUAL DESCRIPTION OF EACH HEAVEN;

AND A SERIES OF PROPHECIES RELATING TO COMING EVENTS;

WITH REVELATIONS FROM THE SPIRITS OF

SIR JOHN FRANKLIN, AND OF WILLIAM PALMER;

CONFIRMED BY CELESTIAL REVELATIONS;

DESCRIPTION OF VARIOUS MYSTERIES;

ALSO SPIRITUAL CONDEMNATION OF VARIOUS WORLDLY LAWS, AND THE
REASONS FOR PUBLICATION OF THIS WORK EXPLAINED;
GIVEN THROUGH A CRYSTAL.

BY

J. G. H. BROWN,

AUTHOR OF THE REVELATIONS ON THE WAR, &c. &c.

LONDON:

PUBLISHED BY HOLYOAKE & CO., 147, FLEET STREET;

SOLD BY RHODES, KEIGHLEY; J. CLAY, FLEET LANE, LONDON; AND ALL
BOOKSELLERS.

—

1857.

A taste of Brown

states of continental Europe would surely pounce on an ill-
defended homeland. Thus 'the vaunted pride, hypocrisy, and
deception of England, which, by oppression, has enslaved myriads
of the people of the earth, will shortly pass away.'[38] 'Know ye,
that the hour of invasion is near and that British power is pros-
trate.'[39] Brown had consistently seen events in the world political
arena as clouds in the approaching storm. The war in the Crimea
had quickly plunged him back into the books of Daniel, Ezekiel
and Revelation; sure enough, out he had come clutching a predic-
tion that Russia would ravage the whole world.[40] She and her

allies would invade England. Their temporary victory was to be preceded by a bloody social war, in which the English people – understandably but misguidedly rising up against their oppressors – would be crushed in pitched battle.[41] The Russians would finally be halted at no less a battlefield than Armageddon. And which powers would lead the crusade against them? The question moved one spirit into 36 lines of muddy doggerel: the leaders would be none other than Britain and the USA. Particularly the latter: after the great victory, 'the starry-spangled banner' ('the emblem of the universe'[42]) would be 'mistress over land and seas' and would wave 'from every nation's public building'.[43] We are left unclear as to whether this Anglo-American (or, rather, all-Americanising) triumph amounted to the millennium itself or merely to its preparatory phase – unclear, in other words, as to whether the millennium was to be brought about with the active cooperation of large numbers of, at least, good Anglo-Americans or merely over the heads of all people – both those who were cooperating with the divine plan and those who were not. Sometimes, massive international social conflicts were envisaged, with Britain as their main theatre.[44] At others, 'the wicked and disobedient' would obligingly 'destroy themselves in fear' at all the calamitous natural signs and wonders.[45]

Brown certainly wore the mask of a prophetic observer, but his sympathies constantly burst through. Thus, Ireland had 'long groaned under the oppressive rule of England';[46] and the Indians' resistance to British power made them a 'heroic people'.[47] Altogether, the wealth of England's rulers had been 'plundered from the toiling masses of all nations, especially England'.[48] All major questions were simultaneously ones of national and class oppression. Thus the Americans, in particular, were blemished by slavery,[49] and would have to undergo purification in order to be 'fitted for . . . their important mission'.[50]

Not that Brown was necessarily consistent, particularly over oppressions abroad: he came to pride himself, also, as a – novelist. He was 'Author of "Uncle Ben's Hovel"', which he explicitly entitled in reply to Mrs Stowe's novel, implying – not uniquely – that 'the poor' in Britain were actually even worse off than Uncle Tom in America.[51] Even less consistently, he offered the British government his 'sincerest' support in its resistance to 'the ambitious thirst of Russia for aggrandizement',[52] even while his spirit-informants held out little hope for such resistance. Similarly, one of his disciples fumed at the same government's dilatoriness in sending reinforcements to India by sailing-ship instead of by steam – as if positively hoping for the suppression of Brown's 'heroic people'.[53]

And a certain kind of patriotism cropped up not merely in incidental comments on contemporary politics but also at the level of doctrine. As Harrison has remarked, 'a characteristic of millenarians' was, not only 'to pronounce God's wrath upon the society around them, but [also] at the same time to assure their compatriots that a special role in the coming millennium was assigned to their nation.'[54] And Brown's Gabriel nominated the British 'people [as] decreed by heaven to assist in the overthrow of all evils and oppression'.[55] Brown quickly agreed that 'England . . . [was] set apart by the Creator from all other nations.' So far, England's uniqueness had led it merely into unprecedented wealth and world power which would, in turn, trigger the catastrophes he was prophesying for her. But, even while sneering at the 'duplicity of her wily diplomatists', he suddenly broke into a paean of militaristic praise for the 'valour' and 'gallantry' of the 'sons of Briton [sic]' who, when 'disciplined and [well] led' could 'withstand the shock of any force three times their numbers anywhere in the world'. The tragedy was precisely that, before England could awake to its millenarian mission, 'the vengeance of Heaven' would have to fall 'heavily and terrifically, upon the nation "whose flag has braved a thousand years, the battle and the breeze"'. He was quoting from Thomas Campbell's patriotic poem 'Ye Mariners of England'.[56]

Meanwhile, he and his followers were not only aware that social and international enmities interacted, but also that the oppressed were everywhere in the right:

All Europe is convulsed more or less through the oppression of its rulers, and England . . . is now, as it were tottering beneath the groans [sic] of her oppressed people, while her colonies stagger beneath the weight of oppression.[57]

This was also the main reason his *Community's Journal* gave for the Indian mutiny: true, Russian gold was in some vague way at work but, first and last, 'the people of India, generally, [were] weary of the British yoke'.[58] More generally, 'no sooner does

England [invade] . . . any land . . . than . . . the people of that land become slaves': why, therefore, should 'our rulers expect loyalty'?[59] Repeatedly, the *Journal* poured scorn on *The Times* for minimising the extent of the 'revolt'.[60] Oppression by the ruling classes (at every level from local to international) allowed to the poor and 'the people' the right of self-defence. An example is the *Journal*'s justification for the recourse by Indians to 'any forcible means' in 'expelling their [British] invaders'. To put the matter in a nutshell: were the boot on the other foot, 'what would Englishmen do with the Indians under similar circumstances of invasion and plunder', had these been perpetrated in England?[61] 'Only under circumstances of self-defence' would the English respond: and then they would be doing so as 'the people themselves'.[62]

Brown and his followers always expressed, and apparently expected their readers to share, an implacable hatred of the rich and powerful.[63] Within his political economy, contrasts in wealth were unmistakable evidence of unbearable oppression and exploitation. Riches and poverty related to each other as plus to minus: there was only so much to go round. This analysis – common to most British radicals into the mid-nineteenth-century – is symbolised in one headline of an editorial in Brown's *Universal Magazine*: 'the Luxuries and Extravagances of Royalty, and the Starvation of the Classes who produce the wealth.'[64] The Poor Law and its implementation in local workhouses came in for particular denunciation.[65] So did the bloody crimes of military discipline: Brown was evidently not the only embittered ex-soldier within reach of his sect's publications.[66] And none of these horrors were seen as incidental. They were linked to an economics which attributed most of the ills of humanity to the replacement of, as we might sloganise it, use value by exchange value. This economics was as much primitivist as what specialists would now call 'primitive'. It is a reminder that, behind much of the sympathy for both the 'popular political economy' (as it called itself) of the early nineteenth century and what historians now call the 'moral economy' of that and many previous centuries, there sometimes lay a Biblical intensity – something like what R. H. Tawney has called 'the rage of the open field against the closed', but broader still and at least as old as John Ball of the fourteenth century: 'behind' and, for all we can speculate, more or less continuously underneath.

'Behold!' the Angel Gabriel proclaimed to Brown, 'God hath said that buying, selling, or traffic for gain in the produce of the earth is an abomination to him [sic]. For no man was gifted by Him with the power of claiming . . . any portion of the production of the earth which would enable him to sell to others, and thereby raise himself in wealth above his fellow-mortals in creation.'

'Money was instituted by oppression and this has become an abomination with God; for without money oppression could not attain its desired ends . . . Were there no buying or selling, there would be neither debtor nor creditor.'[67]

This was a stance which sometimes sounded like a millenarian echo of free-trade rhetoric, but which became blurred with an attack on trade of any kind: in *the new era, under the reign of Christ [sic]*', according to Brown, 'the law of merchandise and traffic from land to land will no longer exist; but the earth shall be permitted a free production without tax or tribute; when every land shall furnish its own sustenance, without interruption.'[68] As already implied, the most evil link in the chain of oppression was money. God had commanded every one to labour by the sweat of their brow,[69] but the lawmakers could flout this command. This was because the coinage bore 'their own private marks [a slightly talismanic phrase, perhaps?] and they [paid] the masses for their [the masses'] production according to their [lawmakers'] avaricious disposition.' Exploitation, apparently, was not what we might call systemic, so much as a matter of greed and conspiracy:

one portion of the creation having, by permission of God, for a wise end no doubt, obtained power over their fellow-creatures, they have in defiance of that God, trampled on the rights of the other portion of the human race, and have established laws . . . to disobey which they tell the people will bring . . . eternal damnation.[70]

As the Angel Gabriel summarised the problem, 'no man can accumulate riches and be honest to his neighbour.' The processes which were seen to result were all the deeper for being long-term: 'from the great landowner to the farmer, manufacturer and petty tradesman', all sought to accumulate within a perspective of gener-

ations.[71] No wonder that Brown and the Angel flayed, not only
the (New) Poor Law[72] and the unequal treatment of large and
small debtors,[73] but also primogeniture (i.e. inheritance by the
first-born). The latter allowed accumulation to outwit death.[74]

And this, in a way, can bring our angelic catalogue of ills, to
the question of marriage. Here, too, our two discussants (if we
may pretend to distinguish them) blended radical views with
traditional. For the Angel, the existing marriage-law was yet
another 'abomination' – particularly in making divorce far harder
for poor people than for rich. Originally, marriage had been an
unnecessary institution; but, as Brown commented, because of
'human depravity' it had subsequently become 'necessary [so as]
to protect females'. Thus, here too, 'human laws [were] founded
upon oppression arising from the result of man's ambition.'
However, Brown complained, the Angel had been sketchy in his
account of the historical origin of marriage. This institution had,
in fact, arisen because of the claim by powerful men to seize any
woman irrespective of her emotional links with less powerful men.
Again, we might say, class took precedence over gender, and men
over women. And the two aspects are, in Brown at least, linked:
not for nothing did he advise his followers that 'the head of every
family' should 'make his house his church'.[75] Though they often
called themselves a 'Community', they were not to set one up till
after the millennium. Meantime, though, while aching for this
event, they could presumably comfort themselves with the Angel's
assurance that the inventors and present-day enforcers of marriage-
laws knew these to be wrong and would therefore be punished for
their deceptions.[76]

C   The crisis of the community

With so deep a catalogue of grievances, what should be done? In
mundane terms, nothing at all. There were two main aspects:
withdrawal, and evangelism toward it. In the long run, the grievances and the strategy proved, at least around 1860, an unsatisfactory mixture. (As we shall see later, other ingredients further
compounded the problem.) As to withdrawal, Brown was
adamant that 'no member . . . shall be connected with any political
association; neither shall they [sic] participate in any civic [sic]

demonstration, . . . nor . . . act in defiance of worldly authority, nor connect themselves with religious communities' – i.e., even with such organisations as the Communist Church.[77] All such organisations were doomed as 'of the present day' (even when they were opposed to the latter).[78] Brown's 'Community', by contrast, should keep aloof as 'a people prepared for the Lord'.[79] At the millennium, they would be 'gather[ed] from the four winds of heaven'.[80] And after this event, the Angel Gabriel promised, 'mankind [would] enjoy the comforts which God creates for them, . . . in brotherly love.'[81]

Meanwhile, the members should prepare themselves in two ways: by 'watch[ing] the progress of events' in the light of prophecy[82] (particularly, of course, those given by Brown), and by seeking to convert others. This was to be done by the time-honoured method of 'going from house to house' 'reading [Brown's] revelations' and 'exhorting ['the people'] . . . to flee from the wrath to come'[83] – by, of course, following Brown.[84] This work must usually have been unrewarding or worse – even though at least one such 'missionary' had for a time been 'supported by the Community's funds, with other privileges in the sale of books'.[85]

Thus the narrative of Brown's tiny sect with its grandiloquent pretensions was not a smooth one. The years around 1860 saw its crisis and virtual collapse. Brown more than once claimed to have announced and obeyed revelations made through him even when he had not yet understood some of them.[86] Coming from a self-proclaimed prophet[87] working from a unique eminence,[88] this is perhaps hardly surprising. (What is more interesting, as we shall see later, are the conceptual worlds within which he and his Angels may have been entangled.) But Brown increasingly demanded, from his followers also, a similarly blind commitment. There is evidence, additionally, that they were sometimes intimidated. His complaint[89] that rebels avoided confronting him face to face is possible evidence of this. And he himself noted the 'consternation' and 'emotion . . . exhibited' when his Angel prophetically denounced one rebel.[90] This incident may well exemplify some of the intimidating factors: the denunciation was being transcribed, word by word, via the crystal. This object was, after all, the source of the revelations fundamental to the whole sect and was owned and operated by the sect's founder. Perhaps even in his turgid style, Brown could frighten. Further, he demanded ever more credulity. In the end, the whole angelic brew was deemed by many to have boiled messily over.

Brown had for some time been at the centre of a circle of adherents who met on Monday and Friday evenings for the purpose of receiving his revelations and organising their publication.[91] These disciples were drawn, of course, from the locality. But one of his most consistent efforts was to appoint (or attract?) a circle of twelve adherents, including some from further afield, whose commitment to the Community would be particularly tight.[92] The coming-together of this grander circle was celebrated at a special tea-party during July 1858.[93] Whether or not Brown had originally imagined his twelve as having cultic purposes, their main tasks were revealed some weeks later: they were to 'go forth to the places which heaven [would] direct them'.[94]

And, in formulating its directions, heaven moved in decidedly geometrical ways: 'Behold! I, Gabriel, the angel of the Lord, am commanded to instruct thee, that . . . ye [sic] are commanded to procure an eligibly deciphered map, of not too ancient a date, comprising this land, viz., England; and that thou shalt procure compasses', and carve said land up into (what I think we can describe as) segmentalised concentric circles. The chief settlement within any particular segment (conveniently, they were to total twelve) then became the seat of a ruler of one or other of a total of twelve tribes.[95] Using the same angelic geometry, the rulers were to 'establish the connecting parts of [their] . . . tribes, . . . so that direct communication can be continually kept with the central stronghold or position'. Heaven, like Brown, was paved with military experience. The twelve rulers were, of course, the very same twelve members of Brown's new circle who ('marvel not, for it is decreed') would 'govern and rule the twelve tribes of this and the other nations of the earth, as they shall become successively united, and . . . each tribe shall be named according to its ruler'.[96] Brown had at first been worried that the geometry (in which the point of the compass would be placed at 'Weedon, in Northamptonshire' which was 'said to be the centre of England') would exclude Nottingham from the central circle: worried, because one of his earlier revelations had promised that it 'must become the central stronghold'. Yet great were his 'surprise and delight' when the geometry after all confirmed 'that the divine authority [had] all along been given for the pointing out of this favoured town.'[97] Nottingham's divine favour might be vindicated to all creation, but the angelic geometry generated a weird list of strongholds, in which mighty Tattershall vied with puny London.[98]

And such were the 'directions' under which Brown's adherents were to 'go forth' and disrupt their own lives if not many others'. Most of the twelve are said to have 'left their employments, and at their own expense subsisted for months . . ., subjecting themselves to the taunts, jeers and rotten eggs of the mob.' Soon enough, not surprisingly, 'want stared some in the face'.[99] True, there were peculiar compensations. Each missionary had to 'publicly display to all persons with whom he may meet or converse' – a card. This object, whatever its size, would surely have slowed a few conversations as its number of words exceeded 400; but it did at least list the twelve tribes and their rulers officially. Yet if any privileges were to issue from Rulership, all the others were apparently to accrue after the millennium.

Previously, when times had failed to change, Brown's explanations had been to do, not with events on a world canvas, but with the conspiratorial pressures he thought he discerned behind his sect's failure (despite occasional large crowds in some villages[100]) to grow. They were, firstly, threats to some of his followers' jobs[101] or, more broadly, that 'many of the people, and some . . . booksellers' had been threatened with hellfire if they sold or even read his *Community's Journal*.[102] (Had James Sweet been one of these booksellers, he would hardly have been frightened.) This was seen as anyway no more than a local example of normal ruling-class behaviour, which apparently always amounted to a conspiracy to grind the poor. For example, 'general education' – even the Three R's – had 'in all ages, even as true Christianity, . . . always been opposed by the ruling powers'. Therefore, current educational discussions were merely so much 'mockery of the people'.[103] Whatever plausibility such sweeping negations had had earlier in the century, they were less adequate to more sophisticated ruling-class efforts from the 1840s. Some historians have recently blamed such inadequacies for, to an extent, the decline of Chartism.[104] Brown's second explanation can only be called sour grapes: the reason why 'the poor downtrodden classes of humanity' had received his *Community's Journal* so coldly – even though it had 'boldly . . . advocated the rights of man, both politically and religiously' – was, sadly, that 'early tuition hath [sic] caused them to believe' that any reformers were merely self-interested. Many of the poor were also, most degradingly of all, 'imbecile worshippers of royalty'.[105]

But now Brown's excuses escalated and tangled with his prophecies. Not only were there to be pitched battles between rich and poor, invasion, devastating plagues and such like, but his adherents were also to suffer persecution and then to win many converts.[106] The opposite was to happen.

For whatever reason, his prophecies were becoming dangerously inflated, and were increasingly accompanied by fulminations – from himself and even from the Angel – against rebel adherents,[107] who were alleged to be 'shrink[ing] from the task' and 'imagining [themselves] incapable of performing' it.[108] Already during the mid-1850s, some of his then Circle had, he later discovered, been embarrassed enough by his revelations to try and alter 'their original phraseology'. Brown understandably spluttered at this 'hypocritical' act of 'neglect, disobedience and unbelief'.[109]

When the big schism came, it was triggered at least in part by the new requirement laid on members of the circle to go forth geometrically. During the winter of 1860/61, 'many' of the Nottingham members 'turned their backs upon the cause'.[110] Nationally, these 'estrangements' approached nearly half of the July-1860 'total strength' of 404. (Another factor seems to have been the affairs of the dispensary, which I will mention below.)

There had already been one schism which, apparently, had threatened the organisation's survival less than that of 1860/61. The evidence for this too had been muffled and perhaps (given Brown's seemingly total control of his printed outlets) garbled. In early 1858, Brown had been denouncing one of his till-then staunchest missionaries. One of this man's crimes (naming dates and such like) has been mentioned above; others will be shortly. Brown disowned him as having 'disgraced the cause';[111] but others disagreed. The man was defended by some members in Warwickshire[112] as well as in his own Leicester area.[113] He was usually identified – as all too many of Brown's followers when in print – merely by his initials. But not always: the offender's surname was Cundy.[114] More surprising, there seems to have been no embarrassment that his initials were 'J.C.' There was clearly much, though, that he had, in blatant rivalry to Brown, gone to the length of forming a circle of thirteen with himself, of course, at the head.[115] And all this was no mere peripheral break-away: numerically, Leicester was a very important centre for the Community. Qualitatively also, one of Cundy's subsequent defenders, 'W.W.',[116] had earlier had a series of his visions and prophecies printed in Brown's journal; their style and odder features had generally overlapped with Brown's, sometimes almost word-for-word.[117]

Clearly, one permanent factor complicating the spread and durability of Brown's organisation was his crystal. True, in the short run, it might centre everything satisfyingly on him. But within any other timescale it made peculiar demands on his followers' loyalty, particularly if they did not live near Nottingham. His promotion of some non-Nottinghamites into his circle turned out to be no solution. Probably too late, he realised that by raising twelve of his followers to a level only a little lower than his own semi-angelic one, he had also somewhat undermined his own power to excommunicate them: for they were now numbered among the saved. He then attempted to recover his power by discovering that God (via, of course, Gabriel and himself) still retained the power to cast even the twelve out, if necessary. But this merely catapulted him into a more theological thicket: whereas he had long delighted in emphasising God's unchangeability, he was now making Him seem flexible. True to their often Calvinist and/or rationalist backgrounds, some of his uneasy followers now seized on this inconsistency: they had, they seem to have felt, caught him out at last.[118] This, too, helped undermine his whole position.

Brown's exalted claims for himself – 'the Author [no comma] and Defender of Justice, and the Servant of the Most High', to quote one of many instances[119] – were likely to make any personal foibles of his all the more galling to those below him. And perhaps they were particularly so to the man most immediately below him. Certainly, by 1870 when the remnant was visited by a correspondent of the *Medium and Daybreak*, 'the Great Organisation [had] faded away, and in its stead, but of a more local nature', there had arisen 'the Universal Church of Christ . . . Mr. T. C. Stretton [had] by the "Angel Gabriel" [been] declared "chief ruler of the Church"'.[120]

Thomas Cox Stretton is described in an 1858 Nottingham street-directory as a 'builder', in the 1861 census as a 38-year-old 'lace dresser' and in an 1862 directory as a 'medical botanist'. In between, Brown had also been described as a 'botanist' (a description whose full significance I'll explain soon), so that here too the pattern of Stretton's life converged somewhat with that of the man he succeeded.[121] Whether 'builder' necessarily meant self-employed, Stretton was able to give a donation of £2 (the largest listed) to Brown's botanic dispensary.[122] With his high level of financial commitment, he seems to have combined personal commitment also. In every field he came to act as Brown's second-in-command: he presided over services of worship,[123] and was the only other author (whom Brown acknowledged) of any part of any publication of the sect.[124] By 1858, he was described as 'Secretary' – whether to the 'Community of the Great Organisation' corporately or to 'J. G. H. Brown, Medium' individually seemed not to matter.[125] Among the twelve tribal 'Rulers', his 'District' had centred on Nottingham – the holy metropolis, as we have seen, of the whole sect.[126]

Like, we are told, most or all of Brown's followers, Stretton had been sickened by the contrast between Christianity's ethics and the elitism of its ministers. His own denomination 'for more than eight years' had been 'the General Baptist Church' within which he had risen to 'Sabbath school teacher and local preacher'.[127] His considerable scriptural erudition had now moved into Brown's service: his 'Discussion of Divine revelations, ancient and modern (beginning with the ancient)' was serialised throughout the complete run of the *Community's Journal*.[128]

But whatever Stretton's personal advantages, Brown added to his own (as a tactician of prophecy – one could hardly say strategist) a degree of personal decrepitude which can only have speeded his downfall yet further. Not that we should necessarily place his blindness[129] under this heading: according to one knowledgeable contemporary, poor sight 'generally' coincided with crystal seership.[130] But, into 1870, Brown was to remain memorable for his personal failings. These were said by his successors to have amounted to 'disobedience . . . to "Divine commands"' and to have been portentous enough to have directly caused 'the fall of the "Great Organisation"'. Where specified, though, they seem humdrum. Before receiving his call as a prophet, he 'had contracted low desultory habits'. True, 'under spirit influence' he had 'improved much in moral status'; but 'a spiritual dispensary was established in [Nottingham] to cure the sick by vegetable medicines. The smell of the alcohol used to make the tincture was to [sic] much for the impressible medium. He could not resist the temptation to drink of it, and fell.' Connectedly here or not, he is remembered as having been 'very lame and helpless during his latter years'.[131] Though there seems no evidence, so far, to confirm or disprove any alcoholic aspect in Brown's fall, the occasion is plausible. As we shall see, diagnosis by 'arisen' spirits was a frequent activity, and Brown certainly offered spiritual assistance in 'obtaining prescriptions for every curable disease'.[132]

Officially, Brown's 'General' or 'U.K. Spiritual Dispensary'[133] was established not only as an elementary exercise in Christian charity, but also with the intention of shaming other sects thereby,[134] and of converting any witnesses or beneficiaries of the cures.[135] Despite its typically grandiloquent name, its 'regular subscribers' during five months of 1858/59 provided a total little over £4, while its expenses on 'Spirits, Herbs, Drugs, etc . . . for infusions' amounted to £5 10s exactly. But these months were mainly winter ones when 'herbs and roots' had normally to be bought 'at disadvantage'.[136] And the major expense arose presumably because prescriptions were sent free to anyone giving their 'name, age, and nature of disease' plus a stamped addressed envelope.[137] Predictably, this soon encouraged Brown to claim 'thousands of testimonials from all parts of the country, in the handwriting of individuals of both sexes'. Not only were these cures 'by direction of divine revelation',[138] but the 'tinctures' and other *materia medica* were also 'spiritualised'.[139] These included, in one balance-sheet, £6 7s 6d for '7 gallons' of 'spirits for infusion'.[140] My last two sentences have of course crassly punned on the word 'spirit', but merely so as to suggest how no less negative thoughts may have crossed the minds of some contemporaries, too. During the summer of 1859, Brown did something else which would have been open to cynical interpretation: he moved to a house 'more commodious and better adapted for the carrying out of the dispensary business'.[141] He also declared himself to be the latter's 'managing director'. In his defence here, he protested that 'no one but my wife and myself' had 'done anything in the shape of labour connected with it' – a labour which involved 'the manufacture of the medicine, . . . the packing of parcels' and altogether 'a vast amount of business'.[142] But the more detailed his protests, the more one could marvel at his being sidetracked from the imminent millennium in so routinising a way. Little wonder, therefore, that Brown later mentioned 'the disturbance and discontent which existed amongst the members on the affairs of the Dispensary and other erroneous notions' as the main reason why contributions to the Great Organisation had, during the winter of 1860/61, virtually dried up.[143]

No less significantly, Brown's medical career seems to have tempted at least one of his members into imitating him. The schismatic 'J.C.' (the Mr. Cundy whom we met earlier) seems to have given Brown some particularly sleepless nights by prophesying that he, 'J.C.', would soon have healing powers bestowed on him by the spirits. This, we can hear Brown squeaking furiously, omitted to mention J.C.'s 'former life, in the neighbourhood of Nottingham, in the practice of medicine, and [how] . . . he has seen hundreds of prescriptions, and obtained many through Mr. Brown'.[144] And we have already seen that Stretton, too, followed Brown in the medical line. Obviously, though, the difficulties that Brown or anyone else would have had in nailing a plagiarism multiply uncontrollably when prescriptions are 'obtained . . . through' rival mediums.

D   Other aspects of Brown

Those spiritualists who did not follow Brown would presumably have been embarrassed enough by even these aspects of his Great Universal melodrama. We would already have the makings of a 'spiritual' burlesque on old sectarian themes. But other aspects of Brown's activities raise possibly even older themes. To change metaphors: though we will be sniffing a deeply musty concoction for the brave new spiritualist brew to be nominally associated with, it was surely original for the sheer wealth of ingredients thrown into it. And most of these, spiritualists of the Keighley type seem to have avoided using.

The first thing that must have struck anyone new to Brown would be his style. Mainly, as has become clear, this can be called Biblico-Methody. But this is occasionally blended, unconventionally perhaps, with echoes of something like a fairground barker or patent-medicine patterer. (Whether such a blend – streetvendors' millenary, as we might dub it – was a marriage of incompatibles or within the prohibited degrees, or both these things, is another question.) A good example of this occurs – perhaps not coincidentally – in the opening three pages of possibly his earliest published writing (1855), on *The Cause of the Present (i.e. Crimean) War: The destiny of the nations of Europe; and the Final Termination of the War, with the ultimate tranquilization [sic] of the world, In REVELATIONS given from the Spiritual World through the medium of the CRYSTAL*: a title of modest length, relative to some of Brown's later ones. Correctly, Brown saw his main originality as a spiritualist (and he allowed the word for himself and his followers[145]) as consisting in his reliance on the crystal. True, he was loudly aware that the device itself was far from new – as we are about to note. But in any case, for him to establish his credentials meant establishing its: very soon after opening, he was at full blast.

'I do not hesitate to say, that the crystal is the very medium through which was [sic] seen the visions prophesied and spoken of in the writings of Daniel and Ezekiel, and the revelations of Saint John the Divine; for, I, after a series of years of deep study and practice in the art of working the Crystal, and testing the assertions received through it from the various spirits with whom I have held communication, am compelled to come to this conclusion.' In content, he was separating himself by no more than a semi-colon from the greatest visionaries in Judaeo-Christian orthodoxy. He was also, by the same token, claiming that he was being more open about their method of seership than they had been. In overall structure as well as substance, this blaring and rather long sentence brought us back more or less to its opening claim; thereby, his logical pounding of his own chest also encourages us to listen more closely. True, the same circularity might have discouraged us, but, here too, Brown was ready: he at once switched to threatening and promising. 'In all ages', God had inflicted

> pestilence, famine, and warfare . . . and . . . will continue to do so, until unceasing suffering has compelled the people of the world to acknowledge His divine power, and when His scourge has reached throughout the length and breadth of the universe [a phrase he fondly repeated elsewhere], that kings

and princes shall no longer be known; but that the people shall unite themselves in love and friendship, and with one accord praise His Holy Name.

In the next sentence he began warning against impostors and cheap imitations: implicitly therefore he was neither. Further, having again flattered himself he now, as implicitly, flattered his audience: 'to the thinking and penetrating mind, . . . [fraud] can easily be detected'. Even more significantly for us, this was so 'in this or any other science'.

Here we have a minor instance of the overlap between fair-ground pattering and what I will define as democratic epistem-ology: 'any' science – including fraud perpetrated 'in' it – lay, apparently, open to the untutored but 'penetrating' mind. And this applied also to Brown's 'science' (as he called it) of spiritualism – or perhaps we should say of crystal-seership. 'For', he continued, he had 'always found that the greatest sceptics and unbelievers in the science, [were] frequently the easiest to be convinced.' Why, his very own history provided the best example here: had he not 'himself [once] utterly rejected anything and everything connected with the existence of a spiritual world'? And this launched him into a long narrative, simultaneously vague and detailed, of his change of opinion about the wondrous crystal and, next, of the trials and tribulations through which he had passed in quest of it. Despite its claims, thirty reading-seconds previously, for what we have called its democratic qualities, this object now turned out to be esoteric (there were 'but few that I have heard who can work the crystal and see for themselves') and even snobbish. This snob-bery comes incongruously from an otherwise so consistent hater of the rich and gaudy; the incongruity may suggest the underlying strength of the fairground mode, where snobbery was seldom far-away.[146] 'In the course of ['several years practice', he had] obtained some of the most startling truths, on private matters, for persons in high and distinguished circles of life' (All this inconsistency risks muffling Brown's straightforward tribute, on the same page, to the Chartist journalist, G. W. M. Reynolds as, allegedly, the only non-crystal-gazing observer to have foreseen the current war.)[147]

Still, the main qualities in relation to the crystal seem to have been that its skill was transferable (however arduously) and that it did not involve mere passive reception of messages but could also include a kind of conjuration of spirits. First, as to the transfer-ability, Brown not only declared himself 'glad to afford infor-mation upon any subject connected with the crystal'[148] (that 'ancient but [sic] sacred medium'[149]), but also wrote one book – *The Book of Knowledge*,[150] no less – explaining how best to use it. Of course, as the instructions came from him, they also proclaimed his preeminence once again. But they still embodied a kind of openness – even if, as Brown alleged of his own crystal, they demanded 'several years practice'.[151]

Second, one reason for this arduousness was that the crystal was apparently believed to have some sort of life of its own. Brown himself had at first 'had great difficulty in getting information from it which I could rely upon.' This, he revealed, had been 'in consequence of it having been used for vile purposes'.[152] These vile purposes may not always have been those of their direct users: they may, sometimes at least, have had something to do with the nature of the clientele. Brown linked the nature of the latter, not to fairground fortune-telling, but to his radical bitterness against existing society: 'the use of the Celestial Crystal' had, he complained, been 'for many ages . . . perverted in its general use for the gratification of the selfish . . . desires of those in power.'[153] (Here, for us, he reached a new level in conspiracy-theory.)

Nor did all the misuse of the crystal come from the earthly side in its operation. As we shall see soon, the shape of Brown's spiritual universe was exceedingly complex, and the complexities issued from a fundamental distinction between good (called 'celestial') and bad (called 'aerial') spirits. Thus his 16-page *Book of Knowledge* is said (by a sympathetic reviewer, named 'G.B.', in the *YST*[154]) to have – 'in order to prevent deception' by aerial spirits – stipulated

that all crystals . . . be consecrated by a solemn invocation of God. This was the course [Brown] took himself. He set apart and purified an upper room for the purpose, spread a white cloth on the table in the midst, placed the crystal, a vessel filled with perfumes, and a lighted lamp, fed with olive oil; and then prayed that he might be divested of all evil and worldly desires, and be fitted to stand in the presence of celestial beings. The next step was in another prayer to invoke Almighty God to pour down his holy and heavenly influence upon the crystal, and after this followed a form of invocation to the Arch-angel

Michael that he would permit the guardian angel of such a one to appear. Furthermore, he is particular that the crystal-seer should bare his head and feet, and that on the table the crystal should be placed to the east, the lamp to the south, and the vessel of perfume to the north. He says that the size or shape of the glass or crystal is unimportant, so that the materials of which they are composed be bright and clear; and that a glass of pure spring water, consecrated as before described, can be used as a medium for opening the Spiritual eye.

However brief, this ritual demanded intricate preparations: it makes the hymn-singing and deistic or Christian prayer (which seem to have been most ordinary spiritualists' preferred way of preparing a seance) look threadbare or sparely Protestant by comparison. Whatever the sources of Brown's ritualism (and these, as we will see, must have included the cabalistic), its very elaborateness set the practitioner apart as – if not personally purer – then certainly purifying, if only for its crystal and its messages. But again, he was hardly keeping all this technique secret. Nor was that for conjuring spirits. One of Brown's – at least for non-believers – typically tautologous ways of differentiating between good and bad spirits was that only the former would make themselves visible in the crystal.[155] Another, no less tautological, was that only the former were 'interrogated by humble prayer and supplication, while the [latter were] worked by command'. Consistent with the last phrase, he gave the text of an oath which could be administered to spirits to prevent them deceiving: a deceitful spirit would, Brown assumed, 'himself vanish as the oath is being put', but an honest one would remain clearly in view in the crystal.[156]

But not every way of differentiating between good and bad spirits was circular. Sooner or later, one sure difference was that the latter turned out to have lied. But how sooner? After all, they would even 'give the most sacred assertions in the gravest language on purpose to allure the unwary into their snares of delusion'.[157] Brown was making this observation as a preliminary to his anathematising of 'J.C.'. The reply open to any rebels or cynics was surely obvious: they could apply the same statement to Brown. (After all, not all his massive prophecies gave signs of coming true, whatever he might claim.) And the same could go for when Brown refuted 'J.C.''s own spirit witnesses: 'J.C.', Brown wailed, must be 'well aware' of their dishonesty, 'or all the labours of the Nottingham circle for the last five years have been in vain'. Alas?

However much we see Brown's mode of differentiation as circular, he himself saw it as his central contribution to spiritual enlightenment.

> The errors which [had] found their way into the world through the different spirit circles [had] originated through . . . the mudiums [sic], being unable to prove the identity of the spirits with whom they communicate, and having to rely upon the words of spirits who are wicked enough to personify celestial angels, or departed relatives or friends.

(In passing, this was precisely the orthodox Christian case against all mediumship, as we will see later.) 'But this delusion God', through Brown's books alone, had 'been pleased to dispel.'[158] This put Brown on a summit, communing with 'the highest celestial angel with whom it is possible to communicate'[159]: 'all [other] mediums' would still have to 'pass through the ordeal of experience' and come plodding 'step by step from the lowest to the highest spheres'.[160]

That Brown should stake so much on such tautologous foundations was typical of his whole system. The latter's key feature was, as just noted, the division of all spirits and their spheres into 'celestial' and 'aerial' or, respectively, good and bad. As far as the spheres were concerned, there were seven of each of the two types. Brown claimed to 'give the name and number of each'[161] and, in each, to describe 'their several orders, with the names of the chief rulers of each order' and also 'the appearance of the angels in each order and sphere'. He claimed further to offer 'directions for obtaining the name and order of any individual guardian angel, with a description of the manner of their appearance'.[162] And as far as spirits were concerned, every individual during earth-life had both a celestial one who was 'the prompter of all good actions', and an aerial one who was 'the instigator of all . . . evil thoughts and acts'. Not that all this made the individual into a passive battleground between the two: rather, every individual could progress and, thereby, help not only the aerial spirit but even the celestial to do the same. For, Brown's hierarchy was more evolutionary than in the versions of Christian cabala (a word I define loosely in the next paragraph) common in Europe during and after the Renaissance: both types of spirit were assigned, not so much to guard as to interact with a succession of fleshed individuals for an allotted period, during which aerials step by step evolved into celestials and celestials towards still higher spheres, those of bliss where 'the angelic host of God . . . [had] existed from everlasting to everlasting, without progress'.[163] The whole supply was replenished (more or less at base, depending on the individual's virtues on earth) by former dwellers in the flesh.

If, as I believe must now be clear, we see Brown as partly very cabalistic – at the very least in the limited sense that he was preoccupied with correctly addressing angels within their hierarchies so as to be able to summon them – then we also have to see his cabala as universalist, in the sense (which we have met during chapter 1) that all were ultimately to be saved.

And this brings us to Brown's version of life after death. Here again, he was complicated and also, even more significantly for my overall argument, simply different from most of those spiritualists whom this book is mainly about. True, like most of them, he did believe punishment would be only temporary[164]: this is why I call him universalist. But he did lay far more emphasis on the punishment (in the 'place of progressive purification'). And virtually every narrative, given him[165] by spirits of their experiences at and immediately after death was distinctly unpleasanter than those given via most other plebeian mediums.[166] The unpleasantness was increased by the ignorance of these spirits as to how long their punishment (apparently structured in successive stages, too) would last.[167]

In one yet further way, Brown seems to have mixed the idiosyncratic and the old-fashioned indeterminately: his spiritual cosmology was heavily astrological or at least astral.[168] Thus his 'Message from the world of spirits' came complete with a heliocentric pull-out diagram[169] of the seven heavens. Brown listed the names of the angels, each of which 'ruled' one of these heavens – those, in other words, of the Sun, 'Moon, Mars, Mercury, Jupiter, Venus, Saturn'. These seven heavens were inhabited by the spirits of earthlings, and were also the only ones relevant to fleshed ones on earth – even though he protested his awareness of 'the new planets, namely, Heschel [sic], Neptune, Uranus, and others, [which] . . .

must [all] have some influence over the earth'.[170] No wonder his Angel Gabriel thought Brown would be interested to hear that 'Dr Sibley' really was correct that Dr John Dee, the Elizabethan magus[171] had raised a female spirit.[172] No wonder, either, that one or two authors and publishers of large astrological works sought out Brown's – one imagines, often only patchily available – publications so as to advertise.[173] No wonder, thirdly, that Brown sold at least one of these himself.[174]

Certainly also, Brown was hardly original in combining astrology with millenarianism. As Capp has pointed out, this combination had been cheaply available via chapbooks and almanacks since at least the seventeenth century,[175] and this combination was far richer than merely a shared interest in 'signs and wonders'.[176] True, there might also be tensions between millenarianism (which had a message for the whole community) and astrology (which spoke also to individual clients). But as Harrison (who argues this) points out, the two were associated (for example in their obsession with the near future?), and such an association may still 'be useful in explaining individual cases'.[177] Brown, whatever his broad and indirect significance, can often be dubbed an individual case! Anyway, as we have seen, Brown's cosmology and practice seem to have been even more cabalistic than astrological; and we are about to note millenarianism as anything but strange to versions of cabala[178] (though whether Brown knew this history is another matter).

But in all this, the most frequent probability is that Brown, where not idiosyncratic, was eclectic unawares. And he certainly linked an unusually large number of ideological worlds, however tenuously. In Nottingham he was, as noted, published twice by Sweet, the Chartist. In London, his most frequent publisher was G. J. Holyoake who, in the 1840s, had been famously imprisoned for his Owenite rationalism and was now pioneering its transmutation into what he began naming 'secularism'.[179] Of course, Holyoake also published some plebeian spiritualist works at this time – while himself publicly ridiculing spiritualism.[180] But then (as I shall argue), plebeian spiritualism certainly had rationalist aspects (of which, in themselves, Holyoake would have approved). And we can say the same now about Brown. After all, he conceived not only God as rational and as incapable of self-contradiction; one of his less circular definitions of his 'celestial' (i.e., as we have seen, good) angels was that they 'never contradict themselves'.[181] This was precisely what all rationalists had, over generations, been claiming for reason and science.

And his writings undoubtedly attracted at least one spiritualist of a rationalist bent, who was based as far afield as London. When William Turley, himself probably an artisan, first came across the *Community's Journal*, he generously wrote in to say that, had he and his circle of spiritualists, known 'that an organisation of "Spiritualists" in England already exists', they would 'probably [have] conferred with it before establishing ours'. Now, however, that he found himself 'Sec. Pro Tem' of a 'Spiritualists Union, London', he offered the *Journal* a taste of his rhetoric. This seems rather reminiscent of that associated with the 'Knowledge Chartism' of the 1840s. The 'object' of his organisation was to effect 'a junction of those who hold belief in the capabilities of science for a thorough emancipation of all peoples from want, degradation, and the ignorance which is their cause'.[182] Possibly, Brown's 'Great Organisation' turned out, on closer acquaintance, to be more than he had bargained for. Politically, he seems to have found it a bit extreme – particularly, he felt, in underestimating the prospects in Britain for a peaceful 'revolution of the mind'.[183] His own political views – to judge from a sixteen-page poem he published during 1856[184] – were as Knowledge-Chartist as his prose. He nonetheless contributed to the *Community's Journal* some still quite long rationalist poems,[185] which were also vaguely socialist. The first and best of these – accurately entitled 'Battle of the Intellect' – spent 48 lines on the ways in which the working class was exploited. It looked forward to the abolition of 'competition'; or rather, the latter would simply 'flee away' when 'Private Wealth' had had its day:

> Justice waits, with pearls bedecked,
> All radient [sic] in her intellect . . .
> Honey hence we will collect,
> And taste the flowers of intellect
> . . . Knowledge is a maid, expect,
> Who marries only intellect
> . . . Moral force shall win the fight
> And substantiate the right;
> Courage wins – with self-respect,
> The battle of the intellect.

As we can see from this (relatively) brief quotation, the *Community's Journal* was here hosting something far from millenarian: an idiom whose abstraction and whose implicit definitions of maleness and femininity were, during this period, harmonising the transformation of the communitarian or socialist artisan of the early–mid nineteenth century into the Lib-Lab or, later, often Labourist trade unionist of the next two or three generations. Such effusions are to be found in, say, some 1890s trade union journals.

Of more direct relevance to this stage in my immediate argument, though, Brown was in touch with the group around the *YST/BST*. We have already seen how seriously he was taken by one *YST* contributor. This was reciprocated: Brown penned a long reply.[186] In his own *Community's Journal* too, he queries (gently, for him) the authenticity of some spirits of the Apostles reported in the *BST*: after some 1800 years, he argued, they would undoubtedly have evolved out of our own range.[187] One at least of his longest books was sold in Keighley by Joseph Rhodes who was one of the local group.[188] And Brown spoke of this group's sometime publisher, Benjamin Morrell, as 'our worthy friend'.[189]

This underlines Brown's double significance: for spiritualists and about spiritualism. The two kinds of significance are often hard to distinguish practically, but are still worth separating analytically. Firstly, even had this whole Tattershall oratorio remained unheard beyond Nottingham (and, as we have seen a number of times, it did not), many spiritualists anywhere must have discerned, dimly or not, that they would guarantee making their belief into a laughing stock if they took grandiloquent 'spiritual' utterance too readily as prophetic. That way, as the *Medium and Daybreak's* correspondent put it, they would become mere 'fanatics'.[190] As against such risks, the correspondent saw only one alternative: to understand and follow 'the laws of spiritual phenomena and existence, . . . the inevitable laws of mind and spiritual development': to become, in other word, 'philosophers'. In fact, though, this was not the sole alternative criterion: there was also Christian orthodoxy. But this the correspondent (suitably for a journal edited by James Burns, a spiritualist anti-Christian) did not recognise. Naturally, goings-on such as these at Nottingham would have been seized on both by orthodox Christian spiritualists and heterodox anti-spiritualists. Here, however, the important point is the following. One of the preconditions for spiritualist belief to become and remain stable, was that it should offer logical procedures for relativising – whenever one wished – any particular 'spiritual' revelation without undermining itself. Some of the contortions this could involve will be mentioned in later chapters. Here, though, my point is merely that any knowledge among spiritualists of developments such as Brown's would only have accelerated a momentum which, being an underlying one, is hard to measure. This momentum is part of spiritualism's birth as an ism: a need to have revelation without dogma, hope without excommunications, millennium without collective agonies of strategy or timing – without, in this sense, the pain of history. At this birth, Owenite swaddling-clothes were (as seen in the last chapter) inappropriate. And this development – like Brown's ministry – began during a decade in which 'the restoration of the Napoleonic Empire and the Crimean War . . . stimulated a flurry of millenial-apocalyptic publishing and republishing in the United Kingdom'.[191]

But to return to Brown's more direct legacy. By 1870, it seems to have embodied as much inconsistency as Brown had himself. True, as I have just argued, spiritualists needed (more than they might want to admit) to write such groups off. But for whatever the report in the *M. and D.* may be worth, Brown's successor Stretton and his hearers during 1870 do seem to have been somewhat confused as to the foundation of their belief. On the one hand, the hymn at the start of their service centred, reportedly, on Jesus 'as having "purchased my ransom on Calvary's tree". An elderly, bland, and cultivated gentleman offered a fluent prayer, embodying very old-fashioned theological notions, and asking God to keep them from vain conceits [as well he might, given recent episodes], and to trim their spiritual communications by the "Word of God". After this, Mr. T.C. Stretton, apparently entranced [unlike, as we noted, his predecessor Brown], delivered an address of the usual religious kind.' On the other, 'the published principles of this Church' were 'ahead of this': Stretton, 'in a published lecture, ridicules and controverts the idea of a devil, eternal punishment, etc. He teaches that spirits pass into a progressive state after death, and mankind in earth-life are influenced by good and evil spirits.'

In any case, other Nottingham spiritualists had either grown

A WEEKLY JOURNAL DEVOTED TO THE HISTORY, PHENOMENA, PHILOSOPHY, AND TEACHINGS OF

SPIRITUALISM.

A MONTHLY JOURNAL Devoted to Spiritual Development, Occult Research, and Human Progress.

A WEEKLY JOURNAL DEVOTED TO THE HISTORY, PHENOMENA, PHILOSOPHY, AND TEACHINGS OF

SPIRITUALISM.

tired or perhaps had always ignored this sickly combination of grandiloquence and inner confusion. They, instead, had set up a Lyceum which the *M. and D.'s* correspondent described – as may be predictable in the context – glowingly.[192]

There remains the significance – to us about spiritualism – of Brown and his followers. Here too, we are dealing partly with something which spiritualism tried to distance itself from – though with, as it were, a birthmark which spiritualists must have found far more embarrassing than they did their millenarian one. The embarrassment lurked within Brown's crystal. As we have seen, the *M. and D.'s* reporter implied, deliberately or not, that Nottingham had been unusual in having crystal-gazers – or at least so high a proportion – who apparently found themselves gazing at spirits. But was it necessarily so unusual? After all, the whole research for this chapter was triggered by one stray dismissal of Brown by an anonymous writer in the *Medium and Daybreak*. From the same or earlier periods (we can still expect fewer from the later, presumably – even though, into our century, spiritualist periodicals occasionally advertised crystals for sale), might there possibly be other Browns awaiting disinterral?

Of course, exact replicas of Brown would surely be too much to ask for: an ex-low-church ex-materialist, bitterly hostile to money and trade (seen as among the grandparents of all oppression) let alone toward existing authority in religion, state and workplace; a man increasingly blind who used his vision-receiving-apparatus for long after the start of his ministry (unlike the Mormon founder, Joseph Smith, with his Urim and Thummim), who claimed that his crystal gave him power to see spirits, to diagnose all ailments, to send his followers geometrically hither and yon, to receive angelic revelation and thus to foretell, in graphic detail, imminent and catastrophic social and international upheavals which would culminate in a millennial *Pax Anglo-Americana*. Individually, few of these items were unique to Brown, but in combination (we gasp) surely! Rather, the aspects which may guide us towards a closer estimate of Brown's particular degree of uniqueness are the cosmological and, in some senses, the cabalistic. These are not always, of course, so far from Brown's crystal. And they accentuate the need to know, not only how much, including how 'degenerately', any cabalistic current continued in Britain after, say, the Restoration, but also whether and when any such continuities correspond to any social divisions. How indirect, for example, was any relation between fairground crystal-gazing, and compendiously – crushingly – uncritical, Latinate and costly productions such as Francis Barrett's 1801 *The Magus*?[193] Barrett, at least according to one socially established-sounding writer (one 'L.L.D.') during 1849, was 'the most approved modern author on these occult subjects'.[194]

More broadly, though, one circum-1860 expert on the *Curiosities of Occult Literature* knew of 'numerous rules . . . published and written [i.e. manuscript] for the consecration and charging of crystals, and for the discharge of the spirit when it has communicated with the seer or seeress'.[195] Presumably such 'rules' were variously suitable: some for fairground practitioners, others for salon or study and others indeterminately. At least one such 'written' production – a shakily literate manuscript – is extant from as late as 1879.[196] In terms of indirect conceptual influence, when exactly should we deem John Dee, Robert Fludd and their lowlier contemporaries to have died?

'Possibly' again, when twentieth-century spiritualists closed ranks against persecution for fortune-telling, they were having to deal not merely with victimisation but also, unawares or not, with an aspect of the transition out of their own prehistory. Possibly, therefore, the fairground and quack modes which a later chapter will note in relation to plebeian medicine were as relevant before the 'crystallisation' of spiritualism no less than during, say, the late nineteenth century. Not that spiritualists need feel ashamed of all this. If there has always been 'a significant interplay between the healing and performing arts',[197] there has also been one involving what we might call the spiritual arts too. After all, the need for customers was enough to induce even so bitter an anti-elitist as William Turley into 'respectfully' advertising to 'the Nobility and Gentry' his services as a medium.[198]

As noted, Brown both claimed power to control angels and possessed an admittedly odd but still recognisably cabalistic cosmology. His context, indirect as well as direct, cries out for further research which, let us hope, will swiftly reveal the following speculations as wide of the mark.

First, given that our sources (apart from the caustic article in the *Medium and Daybreak* and a few mentions in the *YST/BST*) are all dominated – and very nearly all written – by him, we need if possible to know far more about his followers and potential rivals. Which tenets of his – the chiliasm, the cabalism, the crystal, the cosmology, the root-and-branch political economy, the anti-imperialism, the Americanism or whatever – attracted them most and least? What, to take something fresh, was the significance for him and for them of his obsession with banners: mainly militaristic or talismanic?[199] Or again, given that the sect appears to have virtually collapsed soon after Brown had made his geometric demands on at least some of his followers, was it the demands which brought the most disillusion or the geometry? If the latter, can the followers (unlike Brown) be said to have been cabalistic at all? What was the turnover in the membership and why? Conversely, how did Brown retain it? How much did he rule by psychological pressure? After all, his language and ritual style were either laughable or intimidating, and we have at least one case of a rebel allegedly breaking down in public.[200] How important was the appeal to mystery and to love of hierarchy, in view of the degrees of initiation implied in Brown's circle of twelve?

Second, and surely no less intriguingly, what were Brown's doctrinal sources? Or at least – assuming he did not simply elaborate his doctrines out of his own head from stray elements picked up either by chance or from compendia such as Barrett's – the problem arises of whether to see him as echoing any earlier currents, however indirectly, distortively and perhaps ignorantly. Were these entirely British, we might be reduced to positing something continuous: some sort of 'occult underground'. (But surely an underground which includes fairgrounds is no good whatever, even as metaphor.) Were these also foreign, we need to know (but presumably never will) both, on the one hand, who Brown came across during his travels abroad and, on the other, whether such foreign influence occurred more while he was in Britain. If it occurred in Nottingham, then the identity of Dr Julien Goldstein (see n. 20) is obviously worth investigating: he does not appear in any extant street-directories of the time. True, Nottingham did have a number of mostly German-born Jews; but the ones we hear of[201] were mostly expansive men of business with presumably little need of, say, cabala let alone the millennium.

Even the barest possibility of a Jewish dimension relates, thirdly, to the nature of Brown's cabala. Is there any point in trying to disentangle possible Jewish and Christian aspects? After all, Frances

Yates and others may have demonstrated the importance of 'Christian Cabbala' into the seventeenth century, but Gershom Scholem has suggested the importance, if only within Jewish culture, of a (very Brownian-sounding) mixture of cabala with millenarianism. (True, Scholem does not see his cabala as involving spirit-raising, as Brown did: his version is not practical in its mysticism.) This mixture surfaced explosively, Scholem argues, in the movement around the seventeenth-century messiah Sabbatai Zevi, which influenced Jews not merely in the Middle East but throughout Europe.[202] (The 'Sabbatian' movement also excited some gentiles, and not always negatively.) This movement is said to have reverberated, though indirectly, through the eighteenth century. True, the alleged reverberations were overwhelmingly within the Jewish community. But Scholem has also argued that at least one post-Sabbatian Jew became involved in French revolutionary politics.[203] My point, here, is to suggest how indirect any Jewish cabalistic influence may have been and therefore how tricky to distinguish from non-Jewish. And if we can say this about late-eighteenth-century Central Europe, how much more, presumably, in relation to one lame old soldier in the mid-nineteenth-century Midlands of England? Worse, there are particular risks here. One is, of falling into history-of-ideas pedigree-plotting, without any attempt at social history (and Scholem is consistent enough to renounce the latter).[204] Another is, when dealing with a mass of loose threads – some splaying forwards from the mid-seventeenth century, others backwards from the nineteenth – of tying them together according to some appealing colour-scheme and dignifying the resultant jumble of knots as a tradition. But all these risks are no excuse for ignorance.

Fourth, if we assume there to be any doctrinal sources of Brown's power over his followers, then one of the likeliest was surely his claim that he, almost alone, could tell whether 'spiritual' communications were really with good spirits or with evil and unreliable ones. There may be some significance (apart, perhaps, from utter cosmic paranoia) in this obsession with – as we might call it – wrong-addressing.[205] Brown's claim was even more ambitious than that of, say, a Catholic priest to absolve sins. After all, what did the power of a deceptive spirit to come between enquirers and God imply about the latter's power (potential or actual) within the universe? It might imply a gnostic or dualistic cosmology – with the whole cosmos divided between a good god and an evil (if not actually created by the latter). Such schemas have a very ancient history – whether directly continuous is another matter. And Brown's general cosmology, as we have seen, was more manifestly dualistic than his interest in wrong-addressing (though inconsistently: it was also evolutionist). Of course, whether any such gnostic echoes turn out to be a matter of chance, of spontaneous recurrence, indirect continuity[206] or a combination of all these, is yet another question.

Wrong-addressing is significant not only in this potentially very long-term sense, but also in one thoroughly local to Brown's followers. It may, plausibly, have appealed to some of those plebeians bewildered by the insecurities of late-1850s Nottingham or wherever. But, if to some, why not to others? Social historiography cannot live by reductionisms alone: they are not even its bread-and-butter (though it often likes to think so).

As argued above, Brown underlines how some of the birthmarks with which spiritualism grew up were millenarian. And we can describe as diffusely millenarian the milieu in which spiritualism found its first plebeian converts. This was a milieu in which a Coventry devotee of Goodwin Barmby's more or less defunct Communist Church could expect sympathy from Brown – optimistically, given Brown's greater reliance on the immediacy of the Lord's coming.[207] Conversely, it was a milieu in which the longest item about Brown in the *YST/BST*[208] may possibly have been penned by Goodwin Barmby himself: certainly the author ('G.B.') was a 'minister of religion' who, as Barmby would have, roundly condemned the 'doctrine of eternal punishment' as simply 'horrid' – who, in other words, had a universalist confidence that all would be saved, some sooner some later. Barmby was by this time a unitarian minister and, as we noted in chapter 1, many unitarians had long tended towards universalism.[209] But whoever this clergyman was, he seems to have had some grounding, not only in the occult, but also in general millenarianism – a grounding broad enough for him to compare the prophecies of Richard Brothers or Joanna Southcott with what he called Brown's 'political' utterances.

But wherever we turn, Brown underlines how the influences with which spiritualism grew up were also more than millenarian – even if most or all of these were so implicit as to be clear to very few spiritualists. Not that Brown can be assumed to be remotely typical of these influences. Rather, he is likely, at most, to exemplify merely how many other currents these might combine with. Our uncertainty here centres on his cabalistic dimensions.

That spiritualism proved attractive despite these obscurer influences was due partly to its reliance on its claim to produce 'phenomena' rather than on trying to use these to generate or confirm particular theologies. Few plebeian spiritualists tried using their 'phenomena' as Brown had used his crystal. True, within their spiritualism, Chapter 5 will detect millenarian survivals at least. But the vagueness of most of them was of a piece with such spiritualism itself.

And the late-nineteenth-century fate of millenarianism brings us, finally, back to politics. For, however much this Nottingham episode may be seen as exotic, it points up in its own way the gathering confusion within much mid-century social radicalism. Politically, Brown's sect was characterised by what we might call not-yet-ness. For example, it described itself as a community (although its members did not live together) and – reminiscently perhaps of Owen[210] – as a 'great organisation' (though it was little of either). It had banners, but not for political action, let alone for military. And this last paradox can be seen as a trivial symbol of the central one. Brown held to an utterly bitter conception of Britain's ruling groups and their state as the crudest, most merciless conspiracy one could possibly devise to oppress the suffering masses. In this, he merely carried to caricatural heights an old tendency in plebeian radicalism. This tendency, given the growing sophistication and complexity of ruling-class policy from at least the early 1840s, has recently been seen[211] as increasingly disabling for any radical movement (not least for Chartism). This disablement Brown consecrated in the name of the millennium: any effort by the masses to try and free themselves would be 'disobedience to the divine will of God'. Surveying in his vision the corpse-strewn desolation to be left by the coming 'civil strife', his only commiseration with the 'starving populations' was that, for bothering to revolt, they had 'perished for their unbelief; and those who have escaped . . . will only be permitted to live, that they may participate in [the] greater tribulations [of Russian-led invasion], as seen in our next Chapter.'[212] In Brown, social millennialism despaired, and became social masochism. Maybe he also plumbs, however indirectly and eccentrically, the depths of some social radicals' confusion around the 1850s.

Chapter 4 The problematic of imponderables

A Introduction

Many spiritualist beliefs and practices were (as remarked in Chapter 1) far older than the word. So why the word? Why bother to have a new one? The superficial answer is, of course, that this was the label given to a particular grouping of beliefs and practices. But this answer is circular. The present chapter will argue, instead, that a neglected factor was confusions, probably more and more widespread through the eighteenth and at least early nineteenth centuries, as to the fundamental nature of matter. For us, the most relevant aspect of these confusions was over the existence – sometimes accepted, sometimes not – of various forces which were not physically traceable (hence my, and some contemporaries', word for them: 'imponderable') except by their supposed effects, often on human beings. Because this aspect is so relevant, I will view these confusions through it alone and will call it the problematic of imponderables. I will focus, in other words, on questions which today would come under physics or chemistry but which, at the time, had other labels. And one question will be as to whether it was possible to divide and subdivide matter infinitely. Perhaps most physics-cultures during any century allow or encourage non-specialist interest in the limits (if any) of material smallness. Our present-day physics culture may be exceptional in making such problems seem, to many people, inaccessible even to the imagination. The one that predominated so resoundingly during the eighteenth and nineteenth centuries, the Newtonian, seemed accessibly consistent and clear. It was neither. True, it compared very favourably with its predecessors. But the gap between claim and reality allowed confusion. At the time, the gravity of such areas was further enhanced by their heavy relation to 'natural theology', i.e. to attempts to allow for or to discern the hand of the Divine, in originating and upholding the physical universe.[1]

Section B relies more than the rest of the book on secondary sources. In using these I have not distinguished systematically between, for example, the two approaches – based on 'ether' (or 'aether' in his spelling) and on 'force'[2] which are said[3] to have been present within Newton's own writings. The point is, that – historical distance apart – if this and other confusions demand crudite disentanglement from historians (and whether or not any such need was seen at the time), their potential for any confusion during the intervening centuries was presumably more than enough for my argument. Again, during the early nineteenth century, the problems I discuss were made more fashionable by the irruption of German idealism and 'Naturphilosophie'.[4] But they were, I believe, not so much transformed as partially overlaid by these – which is why I spend no time on the latter.[5]

Section B will also treat specialists and non-specialists as if they shared the same world of discussion. For our own century, this would be particularly questionable. For earlier centuries, though, the pattern is untidier. Through such worlds there reverberated – more or less distortedly – the uncertainties I am about (leaning on my secondary sources) to delineate sweepingly. Our focus thus demands that we broaden our chronology. As we have also seen already, the mid-nineteenth-century fashion for spiritualism had been preceded by one for mesmerism. The two quickly overlapped (hence section C).

The power of such discussions, I would claim, lay in their suggestive blurring of two deeper interests, both of which were older and were destined also – transformed or not – to outlast them. One interest was in what matter was, hence in what might be where matter, apparently, was not. The other interest was in what our consciousness was or, for most people more alluringly, in where we might be when our consciousness, apparently, was absent (which might mean, elsewhere). The first discussion ranged from, of course, matter's ultimate nature, to its amenability to (or at least penetrability by) spirit or Spirit or spirits. The second ranged from the philosophical formulations of a Hume on the one hand, to individuals' reflections on their personal experience of health and illness on the other. What allowed the two discussions to interfere with each other increasingly was the perturbation of the first by the problematic of imponderables. This perturbation was at least (a phrase to which I will return in section C) as old as Newton, which is why we must briefly start with him. It produced during the eighteenth century more than one active attempt to bring the two discussions into interference with each other. One such attempt was that by the physician and academic, David Hartley.[6] But a yet much stronger force in this direction was the notoriety of Franz Anton Mesmer. In particular, his supposed 'fluid' (whose ancestry he was right to trace partly to Newton) and via which he influenced his 'subjects', was both interplanetary and interpersonal; and it gained entrée to aristocratic and other salons, partly because of some supposed kinship with an already fashionable fluid, electricity. My 'interference', in other words – between areas that, today, for us to speak unhistorically, would usually be as far apart as the arcanest theoretical physics and lay people's ideas about death and psychosomatics – was part of what I like to call the aftershock of electricity.

B   Conceptual background

In this section, as explained, I glance at some developments in science ('natural philosophy' as it was called). Or rather, I squint: searching with one eye for confusions among whomever we may call specialists and, with the other, for further confusions thus encouraged among non-specialists. All such confusions, together, helped predispose people both to view matter as of uncertain status, and to expect to hear of forces which could penetrate it.

I begin with Newton, because the ways in which he was understood all too well or little provide much of the background in this area, even a hundred years or more after 1727, the year of his death. Whether or not some late-eighteenth-century specialists succeeded, variably, in breaking free from him,[7] the widespread nineteenth-century uncertainties about the nature of matter go back at least to the diffusion of his system from the early and middle eighteenth – or rather, to the initial overestimate of his coherence during that period.

Part of this overestimate was an inflation of his deservedly great reputation. The famous quip, 'God said, "Let Newton be"/And all was light', was glib; but glibness has never impaired its memorability. True, it did not quite deify Sir Isaac; but it did promote him to a more or less archangelic sphere. And others did go further. One mid-eighteenth-century writer believed 'Sir *Isaac* [to be] *infallible* in everything that he *proved* and *demonstrated*, that is to say, in all his Philosophy.'[8]

Sir Isaac would have been particularly amazed at being called infallible. Not only was he notoriously tentative (and secretive), but he also consciously – sometimes, as this Newtonian should have remembered, publicly – changed his mind. Even in more or less extant editions of his works, 'there were', as Heilbron has remarked, 'several Newtons'.[9] Thus the Newton of the first (1687) edition of the *Principia* avoided speculation on the nature or origin of gravity. 'To us', he wrote, 'it is enough that gravity does really exist.' But who might be 'us'? Many of his readers were only deducing the plausible, when (in Heilbron's summary) they believed 'gravity to be an innate property of bodies, and to act immediately at a distance'.[10] And the very contradictoriness of this deduction returned them to the questionable nature of the space which could so be acted through. On this, Newton had changed his mind more than once. In particular, in the second (1717) English edition of his *Optics* he asserted (in his typically unassertive way) that space could be acted through because it was not empty: it contained an 'Aetherial Medium'.[11] But this merely raised further questions, notably on the nature of this aether. Its elasticity, for one thing, needed to be stupendous. In this and in other ways, it embodied some of the problems it pretended to explain.[12] Thus Newton had not manoeuvred himself into a stable synthesis nearly as much as most people believed. Rather, he had produced what Heilbron describes as 'a sometimes contradictory world redundantly filled with several aethers, and with particles that act upon one another at a distance.' This world was 'much the same' as one he had formulated in 1675 in a piece which, no doubt confusingly for many of his readers, was not published till 1744.[13]

True, between 1675 and 1717, Newton had sometimes[14] imagined space to be an aetherless, i.e. utterly empty, void. But this solution had been equally unsatisfactory. It had redoubled not least the embarrassing problem of action at a distance – i.e. in Newton's thinking, the problem of how one body could exert force (say gravitational) on another body despite there being no matter through which to exert or transmit such force. Here,

Newton's alternative had been to imagine an immaterial aether which, to him, could only mean God.[15] In this conception, as Westfall summarises it, 'every movement in the world was the immediate effect of God's power'.[16] Of course, this might be welcome among those Anglican theologians who were claiming they could provide the best medicine against both popular 'atheism' and 'fanaticism'. And these august Anglicans had brought Newton much of his initial prestige among non-specialists[17] (before the itinerant 'popular' lecturers took over[18]). But it was an odd conclusion to receive from a writer who, famously, preened himself that he did 'not invent hypotheses'. Ironically, the Newtonian regularity of the universe – which rationalist Anglicans (these ideologues of what became the eighteenth-century political and religious Establishment) were glad to believe excluded anarchic intervention by spirits – was, particularly in this version, dependent on God's permanent involvement. True, if we follow a recent monograph, the doctrine of the 'Communion of Saints' was, around the eighteenth century, 'virtually a forgotten article of the Creed as far as Anglican theology was concerned'.[19] But Newton's cosmology (or that version or part of it in which the physical universe depended on One Spirit) was always open to exploitation by braver or wilder hypothesis-inventors, whatever their religious persuasion, in favour of intervention by spirits, whatever the supposed origin of these.

On the surface, Newton – in whatever version – encouraged specialists to busy themselves with measuring the regularities of the universe and to suspend their worries (or, as he might have said, their 'quaeries') about its ultimate structure.[20] But such pragmatism is hard to sustain through generations – particularly perhaps among non-specialists whose efforts to join in the pursuit of measurement were (even before our own period's esoteric structuring of scientific knowledge) less likely to receive encouragement. Newton himself had suggested much, and had left much for others to infer. He had, for example, sometimes imagined some 'subtle' or, we could say, imponderable forces of very great power. The scale of their operation might seem irrelevantly tiny to lay people; or it might not.

In any case many researchers, during the generations immediately after Newton's death, increased the potential for lay confusion; not surprisingly, they tended to uncover gaps in his legacy (or should we say voids). Subsequently, 'imponderable fluids were the one part of Newtonian matter-theory to survive as an essential part of the new chemistry of the early 19th century.' If, among the knowledgeable, it survived mainly or even merely 'in the guise of caloric',[21] many of the less knowledgeable might be less restrictive. And, whether more or less knowledgeable, itinerant Newtonian lecturers seem to have been important during and after the eighteenth century, though the social details of their impact still seem hazy.[22] Here, the importance of the less knowledgeable is merely that they were often loose conceptually and, second, that – however much we may label them 'lay' – they had at least one specialist by-product: John Dalton (d. 1844), no less. Though Dalton turned out to have shifted much of practical chemistry further away from Newtonian foundations, he preserved some of the looseness. Partly as a result, though he helped considerably to equip 'chemistry . . . with alternative models and methods of demonstrated value, Newtonian aspects lingered on',[23] even among specialists let alone among others. Some late-eighteenth-century incoherences – whether we can dub them Newtonian or not – 'lingered on' too. They involved particularly the flimsiness of matter, the power and even (confusedly or not) the materiality of forces.

Firstly, Newton seemed to legitimise a belief that matter was flimsy, consequently – at least to lay eyes – penetrable, if not simply mysterious. 'Bodies', as anyone could read in the first edition of the *Optics*, 'are more rare and porous than is commonly believed.'[24] Logically at least, this sentence exaggerated itself the more widely it was believed to have been read. Already in 1728, even what Thakcray calls an '"authorized" popularization of the *Principia* and *Optics*' was stating sweepingly that 'all the known bodies in the universe together, as far as we know [sic], may be compounded of no greater portion of solid matter than might be reduced into a globe of one inch in diameter, or even less.'[25] The great Unitarian scientist and political radical, Joseph Priestley, was to take this up, even more vividly, later in the century. Small wonder that a 'belief in the porosity of matter in the universe . . . underlay much later eighteenth-century thought.'[26]

Secondly, by the end of the century, 'the number of fundamental fluids had become an embarrassment. But none of the many attempts to reduce it by identifying fluids apparently distinct or by introducing other imponderables succeeded. Physics ended the century richer in essences than it had begun.'[27] In this context, any less knowledgeable person who argued the existence of yet another imponderable – perhaps a finer one (and perhaps, by another easy conceptual slide, a yet more powerful one) was merely paying to many of the more knowledgeable the compliment of imitation. After all, Newton himself had (in Heilbron's summary) 'conceived that the electrical effluvia might be the backbone of the frame of the world.'[28] Further, he saw his conclusion that 'the smallest particles of Matter may cohere by the strongest Attractions' as necessitated by his theories: in other words, the smaller the size, the greater the force.[29] Admittedly, the smaller the size the less (for long after his time) researchable. But unresearchable processes might still be argued to be having observable effects – whether familiar or (as with mesmerism) seemingly fresh. Here, the admission by Newton himself that it was 'not improbable that there may be more attractive powers than ["gravity, mechanism, and electricity"]'[30] was particularly suggestive. Among physicists, 'the re-revival' of Newton's concepts of the aether was one of 'the immediate causes' of a 'permissive prodigality'. 'Beginning in 1745' – partly because of the publication the previous year (as we saw) of Newton's 1675 formulation – 'all significant British electricians postulated a special electrical matter identical with, or similar to, the springy, subtle, universal Newtonian aether.'[31]

That it was also 'active' and 'non-material' can only have opened the door to yet further muddle. For, thirdly, while some specialists might have become more adept than in Newton's time at grasping the warning by one of them (during 1793) that 'the adequacy of a supposed substance to explain a number of natural phenomena can never prove the existence of such a substance',[32] non-specialists were all too likely to demand clear answers. What were the ultimate forces, substances or whatever? Specialists might be over-whelmingly[33] agreed that ultimates were unattainable; but non-specialists, to the extent that they knew of such a consensus, were going to see it as a loss of nerve in face of the central question in the field. Nature may 'abhor a vacuum'; not so speculation: some non-specialists rushed in. The problematic of imponderables was a licence either to invent or to disbelieve hypotheses, or at least to proliferate forces which often remained even more mysterious than the phenomena they had been invented to explain.

Thus the nineteenth century's greatest elite mesmerist, John Elliotson M.D., was arguing against spiritualism but might just as logically have been arguing for it, when he thanked a reader of his periodical, the *Zoist*, for sending him a quotation from Newton's *Principia*. Here, Newton had spoken of 'a very subtle spirit [i.e. fluid] . . . pervad[ing] solid bodies', binding them together, lying at the root of electricity and of heat, and facilitating all biological processes: 'but', Newton had concluded, there were still insufficient 'experiments . . . to determine the laws of this spirit accurately'. Elliotson clearly assumed his own experiments would have left Sir Isaac slightly less tentative.[34] And another leading mesmerist M.D., John Ashburner (who had translated the eccentrically naturphilosophical Count von Reichenbach,[35] and who later became a spiritualist) was prepared either for any number of imponderables or for them to turn out to be reducible to a very few. Either, for him, allowed license to break into mysticism (and French):

> I do not attempt to establish the identity of these fluids, for the facts daily developing themselves tend to show that [their] distinctive properties are as various as the substances from which they may emanate, and it may be that the great power antecedent to all consequents [i.e. an abstract way of saying God] may ordain the simplicity of one electric, and gravitating with [sic] centrifugal force, evolving an infinite complication and variety of magnetic cohesive and repulsive agencies; the entire system emerging from the *volonté* directing 'La Grande Formule!'.[36]

Ashburner might be happy to gesture towards recent researches by Faraday[37] (himself to become one of spiritualism's bitterest opponents), but his own basis remained imponderable. In the same volume[38] he elaborated 'a theory of sleep' around Newtonian metaphors of attraction and repulsion; he also assumed his readers would wish to follow up references he gave to John Locke's musings on the same topic. Ashburner's labours of translating many hundreds of pages of Reichenbach had not so far helped him away from the seventeenth century. To the extent that Newtonian physics rested, like an inverted pyramid designed by some pragmatist, on an 'as if', imponderables (or, strictly, non-specialist interest in them) added a thunderous confusion of further 'as ifs' and 'why nots?'.

And my metaphor of thunder may itself be useful here. For, probably the most prolific generator of imponderables – for non-specialists and often for specialists too – was electricity. Heilbron sees its 'problems and popularity' as another reason for specialists' own 'fall in standards'.[39] For, it could link the tiniest phenomena to the most awe-inspiring. Its aftershock reverberated ever wider and more distortedly from the early–mid-seventeenth century to the mid-nineteenth. A second quality of electricity was that it could be seen (or misunderstood) as showing that certain fluids or forces could penetrate matter and, at least in this sense, might 'govern' it. It thus opened the door to all manner of conceptual slides: from 'subtlety' to 'power', from force to the immaterial, from overlap to identity, from undisprovable to proved, from unknowables to the Unknown – and for us, particularly, from imponderable to Ideal. Thirdly, its demonstration – even its research – could be participatory or, at least, could take place in front of non-specialist audiences.

This participatoriness will recur in relation to other would-be scientific pursuits from the late eighteenth century into my period. Some of these, such as phrenology (the deduction and direction of character according to the bumps on people's crania[40]) were, in themselves, not analogous to electricity. Others were: mesmerism is the best example, and also the central one. (In a typically imponderable way, its positing of its own subtle force or fluid – usually conceived as permeating the universe – allowed it a penetrativeness, by which it was able to couple with much of phrenology, producing 'phreno-mesmerism'). Mesmerism's impact in France and elsewhere on the Continent outlasted Mesmer's own notoriety there during the 1770s and 1780s.[41] By the early nineteenth century, it was being preached in Britain. Eventually its most consistent preacher was to be Elliotson who, by 1829 when he accepted mesmerism, was already becoming one of the most respected medical innovators and educators of his time. Ironically (for the long term), insofar as his respectability was already becoming suspect, this was for materialism – or at least for his characteristically brusque exclusion of spiritual forces from areas where other medical thinkers still wanted to allow them: 'to call the human mind a ray of divinity appears to me to be absolute nonsense'.

Although these expressions occurred in the margins of a major textbook on physiology which Elliotson was translating and editing, they were consistent also with his support for a materialist reading of phrenology, during his time as founding president of the Phrenological Society.[42] True, into his mesmeric periodical the *Zoist*, Elliotson continued to see his approach as anti-spiritual in this sense, though he still left room for such miracles as the resurrection which, for him, would be merely extra-scientific by definition.[43] But the long-term irony is, surely, that his efforts transmitted and streamlined the problematic of imponderables, and this (via, not least, mesmerism) carried others far from materialism. This provides a further illustration of the slipperiness of this very problematic.

C   Mesmerism

We can now narrow our chronological focus to where it was before. The problematic of imponderables may give part of the ideological explanation for the popularity of certain pursuits such as mesmerism, but why was British interest in mesmerism at its height from the 1830s? After all, at least one mesmerist had crossed the Channel during the 1790s without leaving, apparently, much traceable impact. To answer this question at once: it is really two. Why was the impact so delayed? And why was it subsequently so considerable? Historical answers to both are easy to imagine (if less to weigh). The circum-1800 fear of things French was obviously one factor. Probably another fear was of anything with the potential to subvert religious orthodoxy. The relevance of the latter to political stability was as much emphasised by both conservatives and radicals – during the period of and immediately after the French wars – as at any other time. Perhaps significantly here (just possibly), the first major discussion of mesmerism occurred during the late 1820s – years which saw a relative political relaxation, confusion among Tories (for long the governing party, mainly over Catholic Emancipation) and renewed middle- and working-class radicalism.

The ensuing boom in mesmerism had many of the features of that of phrenology, a doctrinally less disruptive pursuit with which it overlapped in adherents. The debates within and about mesmerism were analogous, and allow some insight into its strength: it seems to have offered an enticing terrain of argument for advocates of various class agendas for ordering, shuffling or levelling the social hierarchy. Within these agendas, issues such as materialism were favourite bones of contention, as was also the question of whether mesmerism could or should be practised by ordinary people, and not merely on them and others.

All these issues related to British mesmerism's historical self-image. Elliotson (whom we met in the last section) did not see himself as the first British mesmerist.[44] And he was happier about the plebeian origins of some of his forerunners than, as we will see, about that of many contemporary practitioners of the art. Earlier, as he readily acknowledged, there had been mesmerists before the word: their line, he would have agreed, stretched back from time immemorial,[45] via seventeenth-century figures such as Greatrakes (an Irish Protestant gentleman),[46] right up to one or two women during the decades around 1800.[47] Subsequently, the start of mesmerism as a fashionable 'ism' in England sprang from the visit to London during 1828 of a Paris-based Irish gentleman named Chenevix, some of whose cures were noticed in one medical journal, but whose only convert was Elliotson (as far as Elliotson himself could remember[48]). The next gospel-bringers from France were 'Baron' Dupotet (or du Potet) during 1837 and, four years later, an apparently less grand M. La Fontaine, who travelled more in the provinces and may have influenced more plebeians. Elliotson – fairly or not – remembered both men's knowledge of mesmerism as being 'limited',[49] and their motivation 'pecuniary'. (He was himself, as it happened, famously above the latter pressure, being at the height of his medical fees during this time.)

It was Dupotet's arrival which seems to have brought Elliotson out as a mesmerist. Or at least, the account in Elliotson's own *Zoist* is unclear as to whether he himself had treated any of his Middlesex Hospital patients (including his later star ones, the Okey or O'Key sisters) mesmerically until about the time of the Baron's arrival.[50] As is well known, Elliotson's own mesmeric activities were to bring his exclusion from the Hospital within two years.

Recent research has also emphasised that many of Elliotson's fellow-physicians were motivated by fear for the reputation, not merely of the Middlesex, but of their whole profession.[51] The latter consideration was also powerful with Thomas Wakley, a surgeon, 'Radical' M.P. and lifelong agitator (via his *Lancet*) for restructuring the medical profession along what we might call middle-class-meritocratic lines. Wakley seems to have seen himself as riding his *Lancet* to rescue the medical profession from two very different ogres: one, the 'aristocratic' colleges of medicine, the other, 'quacks' of any class and kind. In this sense too, his radicalism can be called 'middle' class. Elliotson had once been friendly with Wakley, and certainly continued to share his scorn for whomever could be defined as quacks. His *Zoist*, early in its career, even demanded a 'cessation of public lectures' – so 'completely and entirely' did it believe mesmerism to be, with only 'a few' exceptions, 'in the hands of those whose previous education by no means entitles them to become expounders of its doctrines'.[52] True, the paper did not disguise – in fact it italicised – its belief that '*all the rest of the race have the power*' to produce mesmeric trance; but it demanded that the 'application' of this 'power' be kept 'in the hands of those whose education, calling, and public responsibility, evidently points [sic] them out as of the party to wield' it.

Correspondingly, the *Zoist* presented an appearance similar to that of most medical periodicals of its time: written as if between and for medical gentlemen: those of 'education', in other words. True, its level of jargon (aside from very occasional and 'educated' Greek) seems on the whole quite low. And this – as we shall see at the end of this chapter – allowed it, indirectly and in the long run, to influence plebeians: some of them, too, might feel some 'calling and public responsibility'. But plebeians were hardly the kind of unqualified practitioners and enthusiasts whom Elliotson hoped to influence. Rather, as we shall see soon, his own social leanings were towards elites (whether new or old, was a secondary matter). And the pages of the *Zoist* suggest it did evoke sympathy from such quarters.[53]

These qualities help explain why Elliotson had 'highly approved' an action by the Hospital authorities which, ironically, turns out to have prefigured in a small way his own expulsion: the exclusion of Dupotet. Whether or not the 'introduction to the Middlesex Hospital . . . [which had] allowed' the Baron 'to make experiments upon several patients' had been via Elliotson, Elliotson certainly took him under his wing for a time, when the Hospital's authorities had grown tired of him – or perhaps embarrassed. His own patience had run out only when the Baron – 'with', Elliotson protested, 'great want of propriety' – had advertised, while Elliotson had been on holiday, 'that all poor people who wished to be mesmerised might apply to him at the hospital and . . . be mesmerised by him there.' 'Propriety', in other words, could make Elliotson bristle as instantly as the Committee of the Hospital, who thereupon ejected the Baron. And the latter at once offended again by hiring private rooms (in a fashionable part of town) and 'commenc[ing] daily demonstrations of mesmerism at half-a-crown a head'. This, the *Zoist* later admitted, brought 'several genuine and remarkable cases and . . . very many converts'. But we may well imagine Elliotson sighing with relief when the Baron finally returned in high dudgeon to France after the Doctor had refused to lend him a sizeable sum.[54] For Elliotson as much as for Wakley, what we might call the shopkeeper, hawker and fairground modes were each a subspecies of quackery. And the same two antagonists equally identified quackery with what I will define as democratic epistemology.

More important at this stage, both of them believed quackery – notably, lower-class mesmerists – to be booming. They may well have been correct. One factor certainly strengthening mesmerists of all kinds was that, wherever they claimed to prevent or relieve the pain of surgical operations (let alone to lessen the need for such operations), they tapped what must have been generations of suspicion of interventionist medical practice (let alone of surgical, which is interventionist almost by definition). Where local practitioners of the latter attacked mesmerism, they risked converting the suspicion into fury and directing it against themselves. Some went further and closed the trap on their reputation (among many, even as human beings) by actually glorifying pain. As late as 1842, one elite doctor had stated roundly that even were 'the account of the [patient] experiencing no agony during the operation . . . true, "the fact was unworthy of . . . consideration, because pain is a wise provision of nature, and patients ought to suffer pain while their surgeon is operating; they are all the better for it and recover better!".'[55] Even if ether and chloroform were, as mesmerists claimed, riskier than mesmerisation, they offered to the incipient medical profession an escape from this trap, and were therefore generally welcomed, not least by many of those who had attacked mesmerism.

Presumably, all mesmerists of any class would have reacted similarly to such an irony. But, as we have seen, both Elliotson and Wakley saw plebeian mesmerists as a menace. And, socially, Elliotson claimed to be further from them than Wakley was. That wretch (in Elliotson's eyes) lacked not merely delicacy but breeding itself: 'I had', Elliotson announced (possibly puffing himself up pugnaciously[56] as he wrote), 'a speaking acquaintance with him, . . . but my taste did not and could not allow of any further acquaintance with the man.' In particular, 'I never tasted food or drink under the same roof with him in my life. . . . I never visited him or met him in society, or ever heard of his being in society.'[57] He, by contrast, was definitely in 'society'. He was happy to list the aristocratic and other elite spectators of his mesmeric operations at the Middlesex. And around this time, one enthusiast later recalled, anyone attending a demonstration of mesmerism in Elliotson's 'drawing room', was likely to meet with 'some fifty or sixty of the highest society in London'.[58]

But whatever the cramps of snobbery to be relished at such sessions, all sides could agree to spread the benefits (as distinct from the practice) of mesmerism not merely in the best circles but among all classes. Already, numbers of Church of England and Nonconformist clergymen had discovered or extended what they saw as their ministry of healing, via mesmerism[59] – even though some other upholders of religious orthodoxy attacked mesmerism as the fruit of the devil.[60] And mesmerism's elite patrons went further and organised themselves on the model of those of any other would-be prestigious branch of medicine. In particular, some of them assisted the setting up of infirmaries for the treatment, not least, of the poor. The central example was the Mesmeric Infirmary in London which came into official operation during 1849–50.[61] Unlike its slightly older sister in Bristol[62] – whose mesmeric practitioners were never able to rely on regular payment and which collapsed from 1852 'from dissensions and mismanagement'[63] – the London infirmary boasted at one time 'four paid mesmerists' (though lack of funds was to be blamed for *its* demise during 1870–1).[64] True, Bristol had shared with it the same noble president. But the London one would have borne comparison with any such institution in the capital: at the top, Lord Ducie was replaced at his death by an archbishop (Whateley of Dublin), whose wife herself had mesmeric powers,[65] and then by another Earl.[66] Under the president sat at least three more earls, two MPs, two professors, one bishop (of Oxford, i.e. Samuel Wilberforce[67]), one baron and one dowager lady. The subscribers included the already famous Charles Dickens.[68] And similarly in Edinburgh – for so long the most serious centre of medical education in Britain – the 'Scottish Curative Mesmeric Association' founded itself no less imposingly some years later.[69]

As with any infirmary during and before the nineteenth century and irrespective of the methods used within its walls, the reward of charity was power of various kinds. And the healing relationship which mesmerists were thought, by their enthusiasts, to have with their patients was often itself believed to be convertible into a power relationship. Thus Major-General Bagnold, enthusing an august and noble roomful at one annual meeting of the London Mesmeric Infirmary, predicted as 'not far distant' 'the time . . . when it would be as common for the strong and powerful to give out a little of their superabundant health to the sick and weakly as it is now for the rich . . . to give their surplus wealth to the poor.' Given that mesmerism's central feature, the 'pass' or stroking-motion, was characterised by gentleness (at least as compared with surgical intervention), he also believed it to be peculiarly exercisable by ladies. 'By your nature and your Christian education,' he told them, they were 'ministering angels in sickness and suffering. Are you aware of the powers you possess . . . by a few patient waves of your hands? That in this power you can disperse a mine of wealth to others, and, like the widow's cruse of oil, is inexhaustible?' – and also 'that . . . to the poor [was] often more acceptable than pecuniary relief?.'[70] Whatever the actual or ideal role of women within it, mesmerism was sometimes expected to enhance the normal relations of power and of money – but only informally: to transfigure, not transcend.

Significantly here, this expectation occurred also in a colonial context (as it had also with Greatrakes in Ireland), where the colonisers had a particular need of cultural, including medical, prestige and where the latter was often at its brittlest. Thus at the same annual meeting, 'Mr Lewis, a gentleman of colour' claimed to have 'witnessed [mesmerism's] wonderful effects in Africa . . . and the East and West Indies'.[71] True, the report of his remarks leaves us uncertain as to whether all the 'mesmerists' whom he had 'witnessed' had been of European culture. But the drift of his speech is hardly that they had been operating within any local native tradition – not least since he had mentioned Africa, America and Edinburgh in the same breath, and since the good Major-General had just rejected the only mesmeric effects he himself had observed in India as 'repulsive . . . religious jugglery'. And certainly India – where native healers may increasingly have been viewed as enemies to Western prestige[72] and where one logical response would have been to try 'out-healing' them – saw mesmerism's greatest institutional success on British-controlled territory. To summarise a long and, this time, relatively accessible[73] story, Dr James Esdaile convinced himself of the reality of mesmerism during 1845. A sufficient number of his fellow-doctors[74] and of the rest of Bengal-British officialdom (including, according to Esdaile, the Archbishop of Calcutta, and most clergy of all denominations[75]) were also convinced, for him to be given a small hospital where his effectiveness could be monitored (1846–7). When this experiment seemed successful, Esdaile was promoted to the highest medical post at the governor-general's disposal. The incidents of this episode were much exulted over in the *Zoist* – as also of parts of the sequel, under Esdaile's successor, Dr Webb. (After a few years, though, official opinion cooled – conceivably under pressure, to some extent, from London.[76])

Admittedly, all this is from the 1840s and 1850s: at the beginning of my period. But echoes of the class-content of at least a good part of mesmerism's patronage were audible as late as the mid-1880s. One of these comes via a friend of Sir Charles Isham, a baronet who had stood by mesmerism for decades. The homoeopath Dr George Wyld had, decades previously, discovered in himself a mesmeric power to cure 'the acute and chronic neuralgia of women', which he had avoided developing for fear of incurring excommunication from the medical profession.[77] Now, however, a keen founding member of the Liberal Unionist party (and thus in alliance with the Tories), he conceived what we might call an imponderable plan of campaign to unseat the plebeian atheist Radical, Bradlaugh, from his constituency of Northampton. This was 'to take a house and let it be known' – presumably through Sir Charles, whose country seat was nearby, who had acted similarly for at least one earlier healer[78] and who had now been the first to advocate Wyld's whole initiative –

that I was prepared to see poor women, the wives of the
working classes [sic]; on the ground that, at that time, I could
almost infallibly cure *women* [his emphasis] suffering from
neuralgia, by mesmerism: and as a large proportion of poor,
underfed and overworked women have neuralgia, I, by my
cures, would become very popular in Northampton. Having
also the faculty of calling forth *Clairvoyance* in some women,
I could have refuted the materialism of Bradlaugh by the
elucidation of the spiritual powers of the soul, of which I
believed *Clairvoyance* to produce a scientific demonstration.
By these means I would have gained the confidence and
gratitude of the poor women; and I believed that through the
increased comforts they could thus bring to their husbands, I
should thus have obtained a good many votes . . .

   Those, however, behind the scenes doubted my ability to
defeat Bradlaugh.[79]

(Did they, even, have to stifle some laughter at such a novel
method of, as it was called, 'nursing a constituency'?)

   But if Elliotson and subsequently some of his more august
supporters remained so remote from plebeians, why should I
discuss them here? The answer – quite aside from his fame or
notoriety among people of all classes, and from his exemplifying
how distinct (to use language from my coming chapters) knowledge, method, epistemology and class leanings can be – is that he
takes us far further into the problematic of imponderables. True,
this problematic was something whose role in the shipwreck of
his glittering career he underestimated. His own sociology of medicine was almost null: egocentric and therefore increasingly paranoid.[80] But more important, his tactical position – and this is the
nub for us here – was slippery.[81] And this at a level deeper than
medical propriety: not only did he (as Parssinen, for one, notes)
use the mesmerised Okey sisters to diagnose some of his other
patients, but he and others in the *Zoist* also wrote about cures
involving magnetised or mesmerised water,[82] as well as 'mesmerised gold or silver or other metals . . . or . . . substances'.[83] Again,
no less tricky a topic than clairvoyance (for most purposes) was
to be the only one listed, within the *Zoist's* closing index, under
every volume. Elliotson also opened his pages to many speculations (e.g. by Reichenbach) as to the nature of imponderables,

both familiar and new.[84] Admittedly, because of the widespread perplexities so often generated by imponderables, a medically orthodox periodical, such as the London Medical Gazette could allow for Reichenbach's 'odic force' by reassuring its readers that it was a new idea and that therefore this Baron had 'not . . . written in support of the mesmeric quackery'.[85] But the Zoist was clearly at home with imponderables in general. It was, for example, open to news about the 'discovery' of new ones (as we shall shortly see in relation to 'psychometry') and of spiritualism. Even though Elliotson himself disliked the latter, we have already met one of his most faithful mesmeric colleagues, Dr Ashburner, as a spiritualist.

Equally, at the other extreme, just (as we have noted) as Elliotson himself had long been seen by many of his medical and scientific colleagues as materialistic and potentially atheist[86] so now, sometimes, was mesmerism. True, Elliotson's reply (which I have hinted at) did not change with his acceptance of mesmerism: 'merely . . ., that we cannot separate mind from matter in this life, and . . . [could therefore leave] the rest to God.'[87] But he himself dominated the Phrenological Association of London which, in celebration of his 1842 birthday, heard a materialist address from his fellow-mesmerist Dr W. C. Engledue. He also contributed to the printed version of this address what could have been seen only as a defence of materialism. True, in this defence, he quoted some Christians. But the pamphlet itself was published by a hero of the recent 'War of the Unstamped' (the plebeian radical struggle for a free press), sold from the shops of two more and jacketed between whole lists of atheist, socialist, birth-controlling and other subversive pamphlets. Here, as if not to be outdone by these neighbours, Engledue denounced idealism in science as 'a malignant disease, which [could] only be cured by extermination'. (Ironically for the long run, his and sometimes Elliotson's word for idealism was 'spiritualism'.[88]) Engledue, in other words, went further than Elliotson in being consistently and proudly materialist. And it was from this position that he welcomed what he saw as reinforcement from the facts of clairvoyance[89] and of mesmerism.[90]

Engledue's same 1842 lecture[91] is also one of the first celebrations of the new 'science' of 'phreno-mesmerism' or, as he called it here, 'the magnetic excitement of cerebration'. This method varied from practitioner to practitioner. But, to Engledue and others, the moment of its discovery seems to have felt like the fall of Newton's apple. It involved 'depressing' the phrenological 'organs' (by, say, pressing on them) and 'exciting' them (by, say, blowing on them). Engledue believed that when he himself 'simply applied my finger to the organs . . . and willed that it should become excited,' the effect, 'in the majority of cases, was instantaneous'. All this was done while the patient was 'in the magnetic state'; but it might, when requested, persist afterwards. It could thus, apparently, alter character. Engledue therefore saw the new method as a break-through in the treatment of insanity. In this he was merely following in the footsteps of many phrenologists. But he himself went beyond them too. He had just[92] rejoiced that 'the masses [were] breaking loose from their thraldom and beginning to under-stand their true position' – he was orating during the most active summer in the whole history of any British labour movement before 1926. And he now hoped that, with phreno-mesmeric and similar tools, 'society might be remodelled'.[93] By now, we must agree, we are in a very different political and religious world from the likes of Wyld, Isham or, usually, Elliotson. True perhaps, no science is born carrying the membership-card of any party; but any science issuing from the womb of imponderables was likely to be peculiarly unreliable. This, as we shall see, was to prove significant in the development of many plebeian autodidacts – and is thus for the whole argument of this book.

Part of the slipperiness of imponderables, then, was that they were unstable between extreme idealism and what, particularly in the eyes of orthodox Christians, would have seemed scandalous materialisms. And it was fear of this and other instabilities which, I will now argue, was at the root of related panics too. For example, opponents of mesmerism made much of alleged sexual impropri-eties by mesmerists[94] (as also, later, by spiritualists). Undoubtedly, one could hardly be more emotive than to tell some impressible paterfamilias that mesmerism had 'been over and over again proved to have *a notoriously demoralizing* tendency'.[95] (This was based, of course, on the insensibility induced in the sufferer[96]). And yet the knowledge that ether and chloroform had the same physiological effect – and had even, on occasions, led to sexual abuse – did not prevent their adoption. Mesmerism, even within panics over sexual misconduct, was feared for qualities of its own.

These were to do with indefinability, and in two ways: firstly, it might itself be untraceable and, secondly, it threatened to dissolve all definition. 'Suppose [mesmerism] to be true', one doctor warned: 'and see the consequences. By a single wave of the hand, we deprive the female of all sense.'[97] Sociologists and historians are right to notice that 'a single wave of the hand' hardly required a medical degree or even the amount of knowledge necessary to administer ether or chloroform safely. But we can recognise any 'wave of the hand' as even less traceable than these substances: any misconduct might therefore, arguably, be even easier to conceal. This might seem all the likelier, when mesmerists boasted (or were accused) of being able to influence a patient's behaviour after the 'sense' had, to all appearance, been restored. The same doctor fretted that 'the female' could be 'throw[n] . . . into such a profound sleep that the teeth may be pulled out of her head'. It was not her teeth whose loss accounted for all of his panic, nor was it even her virginity (though he probably believed this to be the weakest part of the social body). It was simply that 'the whole foundations [sic] of society would be broken up, and every fence of virtue and honour would be levelled in the dust!'

Dust stood, surely, not for dirt alone, but for formlessness: the two went together. Here we can note that when, over at the *Lancet*, Wakley came to pen one of the longest polemics in his campaign against mesmerism, the allegation he laboured most was of *conceptual* formlessness. We will see later how this was something which medical orthodoxy alleged against all 'empirics' and which many of the latter often prided themselves on (viewing it, in themselves, as honest reliance on free, untheorised, granular fact). More important here, though, Wakley linked this aspect – mesmerism's 'turn[ing] everything [not least his own discipline of surgery] into quackery' – with his fear of loss of, simultaneously, religion and all barriers. Mesmerism, he cried, 'shuts the eyes in the head and opens the eyes in the stomach, it destroys all sensation, yet induces clairvoyance; and most blasphemous extravagance, it pretends to annihilate distance and time, and to make its victims, prophets!'[98] And since his very next sentence introduced the topic of pain into this context, he implied that even pain had the virtue of defining boundaries. Better pain – particularly when the (male) surgeon was faced with pain in a woman – than its dangerous alleviation by mesmerism: the latter involved 'publicly sacrific[ing] the moral to the physical'.[99] Mesmerism, in aiming to render 'the performance of parturition itself, without pain . . . aim[ed] at quacking surgery as well as medicine'.[100] And he could have instanced these threats to individuality and to orthodox religion from letters which his own journal had earlier received or reprinted from mesmerists and their supporters. 'Yes, Mr Editor,' Dupotet had exulted to him, 'the individual obedient to magnetism . . . ceases, for an instant, to be the same person, . . . and the ecstasy which [the mesmerist] produces calls philosophy and medicine to new meditations.'[101] 'Man', a leading surgeon had meditated, with something like ecstasy, 'was made in the image of God: [mesmeric phenomena] may be partial revelings of the parity of the spiritual nature of the created being to that of his Creator'.[102] Altogether, wherever imponderables were allowed to develop in directions such as the mesmeric, they risked undermining any 'fences' of definition whatever.

There was ample excuse for such fears. There should, for example, be no surprise at this stage in my argument, that the *Zoist*, as early as its third volume, not only printed but warmly commended a long letter from Dr James Rhodes Buchanan. Had this Doctor not left Wakley's side of the Atlantic during his boyhood, he would have been ill-assorted among the cream of 'society' whom we observed in Elliotson's 'drawing room': he was lowly-born, had allegedly been an Owenite (precociously) at the age of 11 and was to remain at least loosely sympathetic to Owenism into the 1890s.[103] Luckily, by mid-century, he was based in Louisville, Kentucky, where his closest associate had recently met Elliotson's friend, Charles Dickens. Buchanan was to become the most ambitious or grandiloquent student of occult 'sciences' during the whole of the nineteenth century. Nor, by now again, should there be any surprise that he should claim a power to invade and disorder his patients' identity.

Buchanan began his letter with relative modesty by claiming he had inverted the normal direction of phreno-mesmeric examinations: instead of 'excit[ing the brain's] functions . . . by touching the different [phrenological] organs of the head with the human fingers', he recommended making the subject 'place his [sic] fingers upon the various parts of my head, from which I wish him to derive an influence.' This was because of a new imponderable: 'each organ radiates its own distinct and peculiar *nervaura*, which when received by another person stimulates in him the corresponding function.' Via this 'nervaura', 'the impressible person' might

> be compelled to act out the character of any organ which you wish to investigate. In some impressibles [sic] the influence transmitted through either hand will affect only half the system, and it will be necessary to bring both of their [sic] hands into contact with your head that they may not experience a one-sided effect!

Without this precaution, he had 'frequently distorted my subjects . . ., making them feel contradictory passions in the two hemispheres, and giving a double expression to the countenance. The most unnatural and terrible experiments' might be made here:

> it is even practicable to split a man in two – to destroy all cooperation between the two sides of the body, by passing the hands along the median line of the head, so as to form an influence between the two hemispheres. The results of this experiment are so frightful that I never dared to continue it, but have always speedily arrested it by touching the organ of Self-possession upon the side of the head (marked upon my diagram, Self-possession).

The last phrase typifies how phrenological specialists could differ about the exact divisions of the brain even while celebrating their own common validity and power.

Buchanan's letter was already becoming visionary. But he now began to base himself yet further on imponderables, by moving onto the terrain of medicine. Here, he made homoeopaths (many of whom prescribed infinitesimally small dosages) seem by comparison almost coarse. He also offered them a link – which many homoeopaths (though, as we will see, not all) would have found embarrassing – with the occult. 'Not only' did an impressible 'constitution' feel 'the influence of the human brain', but 'also of any medicine with which' it was brought into contact. Thus small quantities of medicine placed in the hands of a susceptible subject, will affect him as powerfully as if he had taken it into the stomach. The results [occurred] almost instantaneously. In this manner I have found it practicable to ascertain the exact physiological tendency of any [pure] medicine . . ., by trying it upon healthy subjects, and to discover in what manner each mental or physiological function is affected by any medicine or article of diet. It is not even necessary that the medicine should in all cases be in contact with the hand? [Punctuation in original.] The influence of the medicine which can pass through the arm to the body, can also pass through the intervening substances to the body.' In other words, phrenological 'organs' were not alone in being, each in itself, able (in Buchanan's words above) to 'radiate its own distinct and peculiar nervaura.' Any 'substance' did too. 'Incredible as it may seem, I assure you', 'several subjects' had felt 'distinct medicinal impressions' even while the substance was still in a container. Thus 'the prevalence of impressibility in various degrees account[ed]', he felt, for 'the efficacy of the homoeopathic infinitisimal [sic] doses.'

Buchanan was entirely explicit that his 'nervaura' operated analogously to more familiar imponderables, and was itself a further imponderable. Via this glittering new research-tool, both medicine and diet would be studied on a scientific basis for the first time.

All these claims – which I am only interrupting – might, in their loudness and inconsistency (which I am only excerpting) have embarrassed some readers of the Zoist. But this was where the latter were reading them. More broadly, Buchanan may allow us a window on to the conceptual (as, for the moment, distinct from the religious or social) unease behind much of what one writer in the 1852 Westminster Review called 'physical Puritanism' – behind, in other words, all those movements for individual physical and moral purity (which overlapped with individual independence), such as temperance, homoeopathy, vegetarianism and, soon, antivaccinationism and opposition to the Contagious Diseases Acts.[104] The unease was about boundaries: those between substances and objects as much as those between individuals.[105] It did not necessarily have to be conscious or – as with Buchanan, here – be turned into an occasion of triumph, in order to be powerful. And it can shed some light not only on 'physical Puritanism' but also on any obsession with 'matter out of place' or, equally here, minds: homoeopathy, mesmerism, spiritualism (together with other 'occult' pursuits) and possibly some kinds of so-called hypochondria or malingering. All were characterised by a belief that the smallest might also, for good or ill, be the strongest.

And here too, Buchanan provides a relevant example. For at this point in his letter he excitedly brought in another power – 'most wonderful of all': 'the paper upon which we write receives and retains a sufficient amount of the influence of our minds and bodies, to impart to another a correct concept of them and of the sentiments expressed in our writing.' And at this juncture he announced a new name for what we have seen him identifying as the 'impressible constitution': he called it 'my psychometer'. Buchanan, in fact, is now mainly remembered as having, some four years prior to his *Zoist* letter, founded the 'science' of psychometry. In accordance with this, he is said to have 'declared that the history of the world was entombed in the present'.[106]

Not surprisingly either, he stipulated in the *Zoist* that this new 'fact' 'should never be stated but to those who are prepared to "believe all things possible".' Whatever Elliotson may have felt about this phrase, the fact remains that he allowed it into print. And he could easily have imagined how wryly it might make Wakley smile. Further, Elliotson would certainly be presumed to agree with the sentiments expressed by Professor Caldwell, also of Louisville, in a letter enclosing Buchanan's report: 'We live in eventful times. I firmly believe, and have long believed, that we already perceive the dawn of a new epoch in anthropology [i.e. in the study of 'man'], which, through discoveries in relation to the nervous system (the brain of course included) is destined to throw into "shadows, clouds and darkness" all our previous knowledge in' that field.[107]

The problematic of imponderables, we can now see, helped increase the plausibility of psychological diagnoses and cures in ailments of many kinds. This effect was partly direct, in blurring distinctions between material factors and immaterial. It was also partly indirect: the more the imponderability of some factors was accepted, the less implausible those factors which had never previously been conceived of as ponderable. Thirdly, there may, sometimes at least, have been a practical convergence between the 'passes' of the mesmeriser and the rubbing motions of some practitioners of other styles of medicine, such as some medical rubbers and (as we will sample later) some 'spiritual' healers. Admittedly, the various styles and practitioners might vary very much in the amount of pressure normally used. But even this is not wholly certain. Further, the assumption was sometimes explicit, among some practitioners of any of these styles, that the healer was some kind of battery (we will meet this very word, later) radiating health to the sick: 'having a good stock of health myself', our 'nervauric' acquaintance Buchanan remarked, 'I have rendered much more pleasure and effectual service to the impressible in this manner than by touching their heads.' True, the word 'pleasure' is, in this context, significant – even more so as his previous sentence had boasted how, 'just before I left Boston, I relieved the wife of Dr T (while labouring under profuse menstrual complaints) by placing her fingers upon the upper region of Cautiousness, where lie the organs restraining the sexual functions.' And, as I briefly noted, the allegedly sexual aspects of mesmerism were loudly moralised over by its opponents.[108] But the 'pleasure' apparently experienced by many such patients within such styles of medicine, sounds more often like simple relief from pain. Further, the phrase 'stock of health' can exemplify the broadly holistic tendency of these approaches to well-being.

D   Before and after

During 1843–56, the *Zoist* was by far the grandest entrepot for many of the interests and pursuits that we associate, blinkeredly or not, with the middle and late nineteenth century. The pervasiveness of imponderables (or rather of a problematic around them) was the central conceptual precondition of this achievement. True, this precondition did not stand alone: other sources were recognised as including older – often much older – pursuits. Characteristically, though, the *Zoist* waxed lengthiest on these when their practitioners were gentlemen, such as Greatrakes, and their supporters reputable intellectuals such as Robert Boyle. It was seeking to raise the prestige of mesmerism, not of folklore. Conceptually, in other words, it was capable of bravery (Greatrakes was a controversial memory); but in what it excluded or (such as 'quackery') denounced, its criteria were more social than conceptual. And increasingly its conceptual tendencies doomed it to be outflanked in the area it most aimed to influence: respectable medicine. Thus Elliotson's continued clashes with the latter's representatives – whether self-appointed (such as Wakley[109] or the *Medical Times*[110]) or duly constituted[111] – confirmed mesmerism's notoriety, not its respectability, however many respectable individuals might dare come out in its support.[112] Social respectability could not buy conceptual. More precisely, it was able to do so less and less directly (compared, apparently, with the eighteenth century), and Wakley was busy crying it down further.

Mesmerism suffered, not simply because of Wakley's war on quackery (which was hardly unprecedented, except in its disregard for snobbery and in its ultimate degree of success) nor of the other pressures of medical professionalisation, nor of the suspicion generated by mesmerism's 'seem[ing] to place one person so totally in the power of another.' All these aspects were important,[113] but were not the whole story – least of all the last factor, however intimidating the rhetoric it could produce about sexual purity. It was not merely sexuality's boundaries, nor only its definition (or rather, in relation to respectable nineteenth-century women, its official denial) which mesmerism was accused of threatening. It also, via the problematic of imponderables, seemed to threaten physical definition itself. Of course, there was no compulsion to view this as a threat: most such pursuits implied or trumpeted some new foundation or force or 'ultimate'. But then, again, even were any of these to seem convincing, its physical status might remain minimal: ambiguously in the border-zone between physical and non-physical. This might, however spiritual, be 'dust'.

Thus, something else which imponderables threatened was natural science itself. And this raises two ironies. Both of these bring us to the relationship – or, as I am about to argue, the estrangement – of imponderables from certain 'sciences' that were little more than rejected relics during the eighteenth and nineteenth centuries. First, as we saw in the early parts of this chapter, the problematic of imponderables had been brought forward (though perhaps not clarified) at least partly by people highly knowledgeable in natural science. Secondly, we have seen how the great scientific god to whom so many scientists genuflected, irrespective of how closely they were following him, was Newton. He had indeed long been thought to have banished such uncertainties and, in particular, to have buried alchemy utterly. True, some recent studies[114] have suggested he may have remained somewhat alchemical throughout his most productive years if not beyond. But the history of alchemy, during the rest of the eighteenth century and into the nineteenth, seems to have been one of overwhelming decay.[115] So I am certainly not suggesting some direct grandfathership for imponderables, of alchemy via Newton. On the contrary: whatever his alchemical aspects, Newton obviously brought about a major shift, including in definitions within those areas of physical discussion which were thereby opened to the problematic of imponderables. Dr George Wyld – whom we have already met as a homoeopath, spiritualist and general devotee of imponderables – provides a belated instance of this. During the late 1830s when he had been a medical student in Edinburgh, he and more prominent medical intellectuals had been, he says, 'rivetted' by the experiments in mesmerism and clairvoyance by one John Dove. Dove had soon afterwards moved to London as a scientific journalist; 'strange to say', as Wyld puts it, Dove there

gave up all his mesmeric experiments and devoted all his spare time, for about twenty years, to the study of Alchemy, by means of books and of patient and laborious chemical experiments.

I used to visit him weekly in his suburban retreat, where for hours he would read to me from his MSS, supporting his arguments by passages from the Bible and from the writings of Jacob Behmen . . . Very briefly . . . his theory was, that, by successive distillations of subtle concoctions, an occult spiritual essence might ultimately be reached, a special tincture which could not only convert the baser metals into gold, but transmute the physical, corrupt and decaying man into the Angelic, Immortal and Christ-like Man.

Wyld believed, plausibly, that he was dealing with an isolated conceptual throwback: 'for many years I never met anyone at his house, I seeming to be the only disciple.' His presumably dutiful summary of Dove's haranguings is evidence not only of personal loyalty to the man who long ago had first made him into 'a practical mesmerist' but also, more important, of an intellectual estrangement which symbolises a generations-old divergence:

I used to get very drowsy under the influence of these endless sermonisings, and I often urged him to resume his mesmeric experiments and, by the production of Trance and Clairvoyance, obtain glimpses of the Angelic Man and

Woman, and through their spiritual insights, find a way to the Spiritual Substance of Matter; but he obstinately refused my advice.[116]

What do historians (as compared with their readers and typists) know about yawnings? The two men were evidently unable to appreciate each other's conceptual universes (or, at least, Wyld was).[117] The problematic of imponderables was, whatever else, not alchemical: it was a different – and in so many senses, newer – way of trying to define the indefinite.

And it persisted right through our period at the highest level, particularly among those specialists who concentrated on the 'ether'. (As mentioned on page 68 above, the Newtonian or post-Newtonian legacy has been argued to have had two strands, one emphasising aether, the other emphasising force). True, even if, as we are told, the period 'after 1810' saw 'ether-theologising declin[ing]',[118] this decline was relative. The ether certainly lingered, among some scientists, as an excuse for them to theologise. 'The central character of the late-Victorian ether', Brian Wynne emphasises, 'was its *supremacy* over matter . . . [All] physical phenomena were to be made intelligible as properties of a "Suprasensual" ether.'[119] And suprasensual supremacies were seized by some as an excuse, not merely for theologising, but for spiritualising: Sir Oliver Lodge continued with this, well into the twentieth century.[120] And none of this, either, makes spiritualist scientists such as Sir Oliver or (the very different, partly because more plebeian) Alfred Russell Wallace remotely alchemical.

As to the *Zoist*, its importance went beyond the orthodox or unorthodox gentlemen and ladies for whom it was intended. Over their shoulders it was read by some lowlier-born people too. One example may well be a Darlington-born radical, William Denton. Some time after being ejected from his engineering apprenticeship for refusing, as a teetotaller, his employer's orders to repair brewery-equipment, he was reading 'Elliotson, Esdaile, and Ashburner, . . . Townsend and Deleuze'. He was already a follower of the then ascetic Unitarian (and later, as we will see, successively secularist and spiritualist), Joseph Barker, and was to become a communitarian, feminist and, on both sides of the Atlantic, lecturer on a host of topics, with mesmerism not the least frequent among them.[121] Further, the *Zoist* was also discussed – supportively or not – in other publications, and continued to be. Burns was happy to reprint an obituary of Elliotson from the *Morning Post*[122]: presumably for the information, not that the Doctor had ended as a Bible-trusting Christian, but rather, that the means of his conversion from materialism had been seances with the medium, D. D. Home. No doubt Burns also agreed with the *Post*, that the *Zoist's* twelve volumes 'form[ed] a history of [its] branch of science'.

And mesmeric publications continued to be discussed and resold throughout the nineteenth century. Plebeian spiritualists, like their secularist counterparts, seem often to have made good customers of secondhand booksellers – sometimes for texts whose prices would have burnt holes in many a plebeian pocket. Thus a work by Ashburner was advertised in the *Lyceum Banner* during 1894,[123] and Reichenbach was honourably mentioned by a spiritual healer who, during the years of the *Zoist*, had hardly been born.[124] The same writer had, as we shall see in Chapter 7, been brought to spiritualism via not only phrenology but also mesmerism and phreno-mesmerism. There were many others, in all classes.[125] Old classics were occasionally also serialised. Thus 'Baron du Potet's' *Students' Manual of Magnetism* ballasted seven parts of *Human Nature* during 1877, and another work of his was serialised in the last dozen or so numbers of the *Medium and Daybreak*, during 1895. No wonder one spiritualist mesmerist saw such isms as 'succeed[ing] each other like steps in a ladder'.[126]

Chapter 5 Plebeians and others

A Plebeian dimensions

At one level – as Chapters 2 and 3 have argued – plebeian spiritualism constituted itself by reaction against social millenarianisms such as Brown's or the late Robert Owen's. At another, however, we can still see it as a development not only out of, but also of, such millenarianism. For, as we saw at the end of Chapter 2, the effect of spiritualism on social millenarianisms such as Owen's (though less of course on such as Brown's) was that the 'change called death' came partly to overshadow the reform of earthly society. True, as we shall see soon, it did not fully eclipse the latter, which was often taken as seriously as before. Nonetheless, the price of this shift of emphasis was often that what had been looked forward to as an event (the coming of socialism) was now transformed into a shapeless series of 'changes' affecting individuals. But it was not only among converts to spiritualism that this 'atomisation' (as we might call it) occurred. In an often less doctrinal way, similar processes can be observed during and after the 1840s. Certainly a growing proportion of Owenites hoped to convert the people individual-by-individual. Some emphasised this atomistic strategy so much, that the socialist aim receded into the mists of the future. At an extreme were many of those Owenites who, seeing intellectual liberation (from 'superstition') as a precondition for conversion to socialism, were pioneering the secularist movement. To the extent, therefore, that Owenism influenced the initial environment of plebeian spiritualism, the latter began as a subvariant of that well-known process in which some of Robert Owen's followers re-defined themselves, during and around the 1850s, as 'secularists' or militant atheists: a *subvariant* in that a minority of Owenites including Owen himself also added spiritualism to their existing beliefs. I say 'added' because that is how most of them, quite rightly, saw it; and the fact that spiritualism *was* an addition to Owenite secularism had considerable significance for many people's conception of strategy, as we shall see.

To stay within secularism for one paragraph: secularists were affected by the atomistic origins of their movement, and this in two ways until at least their period of decline in the 1880s. On the one hand, it reinforced the hegemony of those – like Charles Bradlaugh – whose politics were individualist, not socialist. On the other hand, it allowed old Owenites and their younger sympathisers a place within that movement as integral as anyone's. In addition, when we remember that Owenism had been marked by millenarianism as well as by the emphasis on reason, it is interesting that secularist journals such as Bradlaugh's weekly, the *National Reformer* (1860–93), remained open, as we shall see, to many other kinds of millenarian writing – Owenite and other.

Spiritualism, no less than secularism, was in a position to transmit certain elements of Owenism into the so-called 'new' socialism of the 1880s and 1890s. These first two movements in fact overlapped in doctrine, ethos and assumptions. However, their chronologies differ. Secularism's career is the better known: it turned out to be the sole nationally organised plebeian current of opinion to prosper through the mid-Victorian decades (1850–87), though no longer. Spiritualism's organisational growth during the same period was often painful (organisation seems to have been the spiritualists' particular weak point),[1] but, from the 1880s, when secularism was on the decline, spiritualist organisation took off, with the help of the weekly, the *Two Worlds* (1887 on) and the spiritualist lyceums or Sunday schools (of which more in Chapter 6).

Owenism, secularism, spiritualism and the 'new' socialism of the 1880s and after, were relatively small numerically. The last two probably never had more than 10,000 activists each – including the children in the socialist Sunday schools and the spiritualist lyceums; secularism probably never had more than a few thousand visible adherents. But the significance of these movements is that, in their time, they were the ideological groups most controlled by skilled working- and lower-middle-class people: 'plebeian' as against both the unskilled 1890s new unions, and the middle-class-dominated organisations including Methodism (with exceptions, such as the Primitive Methodists). This alone should draw our interest towards them. More than the others, spiritualism carried forward aspects of Owenism. This means, equally important, that it most preserved in the 1900s some of the paradoxes of 'independence': the flexible blend (within mid-Victorian plebeian culture) of what we would call individualism and collectivism. Instead of writing these awkward edges out in the name of organisational and chronological neatness, we ought to try and see whether the shapes have been correctly drawn.

As must be 'crystal' clear, I believe plebeian spiritualism to be an unusually ramifying topic. But there is also a danger of twisting the ramifications and of becoming caught up in them. It is better for a book such as this to make haste slowly. The present section will focus on plebeian spiritualism's politics and on some of its religious dimensions during the whole of my period.

Plebeian spiritualism maintained Owen's hostility to orthodox Christianity – a characteristic which sharply demarcated it from nearly all middle-class spiritualists. But this does not mean that either Owen or the other plebeian spiritualists were atheists: on the contrary, Owen was a deist, believing in one God, while spiritualists believed in a God or Spirit (in addition to the individual spirits with whom they communicated). Thus they saw themselves as upholders of that 'Religion' which, like their own, was 'universal, . . . emotion, . . . goodness, . . . the spiritual', and therefore as opposed to 'Theology' which, like Christianity, was 'creed, form, . . . of the intellect, . . . limited, . . . seeking to regulate the flow of feeling'.[2] Not surprisingly, this marked them off from the secularists, particularly in secularist eyes. From his side, though, Owen continued to believe that he was addressing a single audience of 'socialists, spiritualists and secularists'[3]: and, into the twentieth century, plebeian spiritualists prided themselves as secularists-plus.

Here, then, is a first complication, blurring the contrasts that historians like to make between religion and secularism. And it is only the first of many such confusions of conventional categories that we shall meet. Our subject also mocks the assumed polarity of political rationalism (reliance on reason for changing the world) and millenarianism. Historians admit that the Owenites combined these two beliefs during and after the 1820s. The same historians then write as if this rationalist millenarianism faded with the decline of Owenite *organisation* during the 1840s and 1850s.[4] We now know the story to have been more complex.

After the demise in 1859 of the *British Spiritual Telegraph*, there followed an eight-year gap before the appearance of the next long-lasting plebeian journal, *Human Nature* (1867–77). During the gap, the only approach to an exception was the *Spiritual Times and Weekly News*, which survived through no less than 118 numbers from March 1864 to October 1866. This paper was a mixture in many senses and, in the final analysis, a predominantly non-plebeian one. Its first five numbers sold at 1½d and attempted an unusual format in which an opening page covered spiritualism, while the other three consisted of weekly news – much of it second-hand – selected (or, more often apparently, not) and presented in a manner which would have belonged in almost any weekly newspaper of the period. From number six, though, the format was smaller, eight-paged instead of four, and cost 2d; the content was now devoted much more to spiritualism. In this, spiritualism was seen as vindicating Christianity.[5] Between numbers 6 and 118, little seems to have changed in either content or advertisements. For most of the time, the proprietor was Robert Cooper of Eastbourne,[6] and when his apparently heavy financial support came to an end, the paper evidently found itself to be insupportable, despite attracting donations amounting to £60.[7] Part of this sum may have come from august hands: certainly, donors towards a presentation six months earlier to the editor, had included the Swedenborgian lawyer W. M. Wilkinson, one colonel, the healer Dr Hugh McLeod (who spoke at the presentation itself), the visiting American mediums D. D. Home and Emma Hardinge, Sir Charles Isham (our mesmeric baronet), the widow of the mesmeric professor William Gregory, Dr T. L. Nichols (the American healer, hydropathist and ex-Fouricrite) and the Christian spiritualist writer William Howitt. On the other hand, they also included at least one prominent plebeian spiritualist,[8] whom the paper had already attacked by name.[9] In other words, even while, as we shall see shortly, the lines of cleavage within spiritualism were becoming clear, spiritualists' continued lack of journalistic outlets was still sufficient to help bring them somewhat together for certain purposes.

True, they may have been helped also by the personality of this editor, J. H. Powell (a working-class ex-Owenite who could also

Sir Charles Edward Isham
A friend to mesmerists and spiritualists (not identifiably to
plebeian ones) for half a century. 'A man of simple habits and
artistic tastes, a lover of birds and flowers' (though also a keen
huntsman: *Times* obituary, 9.4.1903), very active as a gardener:
as tenth baronets go, he is undeservedly ill-recorded.

double as both a healer and entertainer in 'Mesmerism and Electro
Biology'[10]). Born in 1830, a second-generation working engineer,
Powell had been blacklisted from the trade after his involvement,
as a member of the Amalgamated Society of Engineers, in the
1852 lockout. By the mid-1860s, his youthful secularism and
radicalism had mellowed somewhat. And the purpose of his
frequent trampings around England and Wales was no longer to
find jobs in mills and railway-works but, instead, audiences for
his lectures on topics such as mesmerism. He had discovered spiritualism during a stay at Eastbourne at the house of Robert
Cooper.[11]
    So far, I have described the main cleavage among spiritualists as
simply over Christianity. Not that respectable spiritualists were
necessarily rigid about theological detail; their main organ, the
Spiritual Magazine yawned at the Church of England's hottest
controversy – over *Essays and Reviews* – that this collection
'contained nothing new or extraordinary'.[12] Rather, the central
issue was over the personality and divinity of Jesus – whom we

have already seen Owen describing as a great medium, thus implying something less than uniqueness. Some Keighley spiritualists had argued similarly.[13]

But this issue also went to the heart of spiritualism. I may, till now, have left an impression that spiritualism was an easy belief. But it was not always easy. 'Spirits' often made statements which their audience found repugnant, inconsistent or conflicting. How was this to be explained? Most of us might question the reality of spirit-communication itself and might also focus on, as we might call it, the unconscious of medium and audience.

In spiritualist terms, however, after some allowance for the receiver garbling the message of the spiritual telegraph-wires, there were two broad answers. One was the orthodox Christian one: we were talking either to saved spirits or to damned lying ones or even to Old Nick in disguise. This orthodox answer was relatively easy to formulate. The alternative answer involved belief in some form of 'progression': all spirits began at the moral level which they had reached while on earth, and proceeded to evolve at their own speeds. This second solution went counter to Christian orthodoxy and still required its own doctrinal formulations. Most of the efforts to supply this need were taking place in the USA, and only with *Human Nature* were they to be made fully available in England. Meanwhile, though spirit-contact might, to sceptical minds, place all who believed in it into one outlandish category, spiritualists were divided at the very core of their belief. This division lay at the root of outbursts of mutual bad temper which would otherwise be incomprehensible to us. Very early on, *Human Nature* accused the *Spiritual Magazine*, of seeking respectability at any cost. As we have seen, the latter periodical's Christianity was not, for the time, rigid, but merely consistent. It sharply retorted that *Human Nature* was a cacophony of 'mormon, Methodist, Shaker, Freethinker, Freelover' intolerances.[14]

The last slur was peculiarly unmerited; true, *Human Nature's* editor, James Burns, might be close to American spiritualism which was often much influenced by so called 'free-love' ideas, but he himself bitterly opposed these – to the extent, later, of cold-shouldering at least one American medium who advocated them[15] – and his opposition was no matter of fear alone but also of his own asceticism, as we shall see in chapter 8. But the mutual exaggerations of these two periodicals about each other remain

James Burns
Main journalist of plebeian spiritualism. Phrenologist. Life-long vegetarian, teetotaller and ascetic. Reached London from Ayrshire as a working gardener. Moved to a temperance publisher, where discovered spiritualism via its literature.
Founded and ran the 'Progressive Literature Agency' (and, in the same rooms, 'Spiritual Institution'), the monthly *Human Nature* and the weekly *Medium and Daybreak*. A key pioneer of British Lyceums.

good rough guides to their overall tendency. They also provide a good indication of how both sides overlapped in their fundamental method. I will come to this later.

Human Nature and its younger sister, the halfpenny-weekly *Medium and Daybreak* (1870–95), were very much the creatures of James Burns (1835–94). He is a crucial figure. Son of an impover-ished and self-educated Ayrshire smallholder-craftsman, he came south during his late teens and found work as a gardener at

Hampton Court. This was a twelve-hours-a-day job, but two of his spare-time activities were to change his life. Firstly, his propagandism for temperance moved a temperance publisher to employ him in his firm (1858). Here (till 1862) Burns discovered some imported American books on spiritualism. (He claims that his religious opinions had been unorthodox since childhood.)[16] Secondly, he began distributing, on foot, numerous 'progressive and reformatory' publications. This built up 'quite a little business amongst the [local] working population'.[17] In 1862, he combined these two aspects within a grandly named Spiritual Institution which soon moved from his current Camberwell home to an address in Bloomsbury (15 Southampton Row). Officially, the Institution was at least half a meeting place, but its function as a literature-depot was much the more important. This function also dovetailed with his papers and with his frequent provincial tours. In relation to all these functions, there are some parallels with Bradlaugh's Free-thought Publishing Company and Hall of Science. There are two more parallels: doctrinal and financial. Burns sought to strengthen his fellow-plebeians by means of a doctrine independent of Christianity (mainly from the American seer Andrew Jackson Davis,[18] who also prescribed the methods for spiritualist Sunday schools or lyceums). He was also adept at tapping rich sympathisers (some of whom attacked his beliefs and actions even while enclosing the money).[19]

Although Burns's impact in London was significant, his provincial one was crucial. *Human Nature*'s circulation is plausibly said – by spiritualism's early historian Frank Podmore – to have been 'chiefly provincial',[20] and Burns's propaganda for lyceums had its main resonance there. True, this pattern simply coincided with his main efforts: in Yorkshire, as early as 1870, he was finding that spiritualism had already 'attained a position . . . not dreamed of by people of the south'.[21] But his importance grows when we remember spiritualists' slowness to organise themselves above the local level.[22] (Even here it had sometimes fallen to him to introduce local pioneers to each other.)[23] By 1887 there were, disproportionately in the north, more than a hundred meeting places to be listed. The paper where these were listed was the inaugural number of the *Two Worlds*, which began as a mainly friendly rival to Burns's *Medium and Daybreak*.[24] To read now, the *Two Worlds* clearly issued from the movement which Burns, despite his prickly ego, had done much to create. The *Two Worlds* was not, unlike Burns's paper, dominated by one person. In social doctrine, whereas Burns's class-bitterness had been rhetorically vivid,[25] that of the *Two Worlds* was broad and stable.

Now, I share a suspicion of histories which present any movement as if it simply 'advanced' – the more so when that presentation has to rely so much on a handful of periodicals connected with that movement. However, this reliance is peculiarly necessary – however risky – in the case of a belief like spiritualism. Supposedly and often in fact, spiritualism's core practice was the home seance (session with the spirits) held among close friends or family members. Seance-reports are frequent in some spiritualist papers; but, not surprisingly, they focus on 'phenomena' not on social information. True, some spiritualists occasionally complain that this key practice was being neglected in favour of public (and potentially more reportable) sessions taken by big-time mediums.[26] But spiritualism's bad image was hardly likely to make non-spiritualist papers report it more objectively either. In general, there is a logical possibility (if seldom more) that significant numbers of spiritualist circles could have met during whole decades without being directly reported in print.

The only clear thing one can say about the geographical pattern of plebeian spiritualism is that it remained predominantly northern and Pennine until the 1900s. This geographical rhythm does not contradict that of secularism, though the latter had a wider London base. And it corresponded very closely to that of Keir Hardie's Independent Labour Party (founded 1893) and with the Labour Churches which, during the 1890s, were virtually the ILP at prayer. The broad ethos of both these institutions was close to that of plebeian spiritualism, and we will also note some overlaps in personnel. The reasons for this geography are trickier than might first appear. Of course, there is the conventional wisdom that, in the north, working people were more nonconformist than in the south: correct enough, though the chapel-going of the many intensified the irreligion of the rebels, so that the north retained a strong secularist presence. In the lives of many plebeians, as we shall see, nonconformity, secularism and spiritualism formed a triangle of tensions.

It may be that those originally plebeian movements which arose outside London became diffuse, socially and ideologically, within

London when they reached it. During the 1900s, this is certainly
true of the Labour Churches and is probably so of the ILP. In the
case of spiritualism we are dealing mainly – so far as the sources
can tell us – with the lyceums which, after being overwhelmingly
northern, gained some presence in London during the decade. The
lyceums, however, may have enjoyed peculiar advantages, among
both children and adults, over orthodox Sunday schools. One of
the most interesting is that they mobilised, as we shall see, a wide
plebeian interest in doing science and medicine for oneself.

SPIRITUALISM, SECULARISM, MILLENNIALISM

'The spiritualists believed that every tub should stand on its own
bottom,' proclaimed one with his feet on a soap-box in Blackburn
Market Place during the late 1880s.[27] This was a typically plebeian
sentiment; and plebeian spiritualists believed themselves to be allied
with secularists against Christianity. But this alliance went unre-
cognised by the other party to it.

Spiritualism's secularist aspect is easy to instance. Like the secularist press, so both Burns[28] and the *Two Worlds* went out of their
way to poke fun at the orthodox religious. To take 1891, the *Two
Worlds* offered articles entitled 'Ecclesiastical Circusdom', 'Clerical
Circusdom' or 'Christianity run Rampant'. Both papers sold some
writings by the American secularist Ingersoll, and the *Two Worlds*
printed some too.[29] It also issued leaflets of its own with titles like
'Bible Contradictions'.[30] Spiritualists, like Owenites, secularists
and other rationalists, tended to view error or unreason as resulting
from a conspiracy by the powerful and priestly to rig the 'environment of ideas' for the majority. 'Modern orthodoxy', for the *Two
Worlds*, was 'a monstrous scarecrow invention of priestcraft'.[31]
'Spiritualists are essentially secularists as well as spiritualists',
declared one adherent,[32] and there are many similar declarations.
Spiritualists therefore viewed secularism as an excellent route away
from superstition. They welcomed secularists to their journals:
even G. J. Holyoake (who, as we saw, had actually coined the
word 'secularism' in the 1850s) contributed one front-page column
during 1902.[33]

Of course, full secularist conversions to spiritualism were even
more welcome. The *Medium and Daybreak* proudly reprinted

through two editions a debate in which a prominent Leicester secularist claimed, 'as a Freethinker still', to see spiritualism as 'the grand [scientific] discovery of the present age'.[34] Similarly, Tom Ellis, Manchester's leading Welsh secularist, disappeared from the *National Reformer* after announcing 'a series of most astounding appearances' at his home, and resurfaced in Burns's papers.[35]

Burns was therefore in step with his fellow spiritualists when, during a two-night debate with Bradlaugh in 1872, he declared his readiness 'to subscribe to every iota' of the principles of Bradlaugh's National Secular Society.[36] And, when Bradlaugh died, he drew fulsome tributes in the *Two Worlds*, plus three memorial meetings among spiritualists in his Northampton constituency, plus other meetings in London (addressed by Burns), Manchester and Liverpool.[37] Seventeen years later a spiritualist paper was reprinting his daughter Hypatia's rebuttals of Christian allegations that he had repudiated his atheism on his deathbed.[38] From the same decades, the biographies of Will Phillips and Ernest Marklew indicate spiritualists' continued attempts to ally with secularism (see below).

From the secularist side, unfortunately, feelings were harsher. Secularists tended to see spiritualism as a threat – all the more so because of its relationship with themselves and their ideas. Holyoake originally pamphleteered against the movement in 1865.[39] During 1871 secularist anxiety was heightened by two developments. Firstly, A. R. Wallace, Darwin's co-discoverer of the principle of evolution by natural selection, declared himself a spiritualist. Wallace was particularly congenial to plebeian spiritualists: not only did he deliberately emphasise what they saw as their scientificity, but he was also clearly one of their number. For despite his recent eminence, he never made any secret that he had been formed intellectually among plebeian Owenites. (A recent historian has plausibly treated him as an import into the later decades of the century from the 1840s,[40] and we might also see him as an import into prestigious scientific circles from the world of self-taught scientists, which I discuss below.)

Also in 1871 came the *Report* of a committee, set up by the semi-respectable London Dialectical Society, to investigate spiritualist phenomena. With some dissent – notably from Bradlaugh and his birth-controlling friend Dr Drysdale – the committee's clearest conclusions were surprisingly favourable. So much so, that Burns was soon issuing his own complete edition of the *Report*.

These events amplified the clamour at every level of the secularist movement. Locally, secularists' discussions on the matter could last as long as five consecutive weekly meetings.[41] More publicly, secularism's mobile artillery, in the shape of its itinerant lecturers such as George Reddalls and Mrs Harriet Law, salvoed against the new creed. Their ammunition was not only doctrinal but also practical. Mrs Law, for example, while rounding on spiritualism as a 'gigantic, superstitious humbug' also claimed to have attended a seance and to have 'investigated largely' in the literature.[42] Reddalls, similarly, went to the trouble of staging 'very remarkable phenomena', which he reported uncritically in Burns's papers and then exposed as 'trickery'.[43] He and others used their skill as conjurors so as to produce bogus phenomena in refutation of spiritualism.[44] He also attacked spiritualism in his own 1870s periodical, the *Secular Chronicle*,[45] and debated against Burns during 1873.[46] Ironically, the friend who was to give a memorial lecture to Birmingham secularists shortly after Reddalls's death, had himself become a spiritualist.[47]

Among secularist leaders I have already noted Bradlaugh as Burns's duelling partner. During this bout Bradlaugh claimed to have been investigating 'more or less the phenomena of spiritualism . . . for the last twenty years'.[48] A year earlier he had numbered the seances he had attended as 'at least one hundred'.[49] His frame of mind during these sessions would surely have been hostile; but at least one other national leader of secularism, Dr George Sexton, differed. Sexton, unorthodox medic, journalist and ex-preacher, claimed to have been introduced to the phenomena of spiritualism by Robert Owen during 1854, and to have studied them appreciatively ever since. In 1872 he announced his acceptance of spiritualism.[50] He richly exemplifies what emerges as a rhythm in secularist leadership: two other instances are the Rev. Joseph Barker (Bradlaugh's fellow-founder of the *National Reformer* during 1860) and Annie Besant (who rose to almost his level of prestige within early-1880s secularism).[51] Sexton, Barker and Besant all began as clerics (or in the latter's case as married off to one), but gravitated into secularism before swinging back into religion – Christianity via spiritualism for the first two or, for Besant, Theosophy (a semi-spiritualist cult which she helped to make fashionable). All three were highly individual, but all gave one particular reason for their tiring of secularism: a feeling that its materialism was boring and 'negative'.

All this competition within overlapping milieux occasionally made secularists ruthless in their attempts to insulate themselves. Thus, 'after a long discussion' at the July 1875 half-yearly meeting of the 'Freethinkers' Benevolent Fund', 'an old Freethinker' who had 'accepted the phenomena of spiritualism', was 'considered . . . as not being entitled to relief'. The resolution, 'that Freethinkers professing spiritualism' should be so entitled was lost by 25 votes to three, even though the applicant was said to find the spiritualist label 'not . . . representative of his views'.[52] But, even if Bradlaugh might wish to see his movement's relations to spiritualism as merely an extreme case of secularists selflessly practising their ethic of toleration,[53] he could not undo the many years' blurring between the followings of the two movements. Even his own London citadel, the Hall of Science, had an unstated number of 'members . . . who [were] believers in spiritualism'.[54] Possibly they overlapped with Sexton in the reasons for their disillusion: 'on leaving the Hall', one ex-materialist reported to the *Medium and Daybreak*, 'I was accosted by several of the old hands, and questioned as to the best means of investigating [spiritualism]. Some of them seem to be heartily sick of these eternal negations.'[55]

Nor were the secularists immune from the millenarianism which, as I will show, remained associated with spiritualism. Within secularism, the main strategic fissure is traditionally seen as having been between Bradlaugh (the hard 'negative' atheist) and Holyoake (the compromiser). Much of this rings true: Bradlaugh's doctrinal and stylistic aggressiveness won him pre-eminence over a rival who repeatedly squandered the advantages of having been martyred for secularism at a time (the early 1840s) when Bradlaugh had still been a child. But again, this oversimplifies not only Bradlaugh himself[56] but also the *National Reformer* and the secularist movement. And one aspect of this weekly's value to the movement was that it tried to relate to those people who were only semi-secularist or only half within the movement. Thereby, it increased the availability of views whose broadness or eclecticism it denounced.

For instance, it carried detailed reports of meetings, even when the speaker was a particularly notorious spiritualist.[57] Away from the meetings-column, the paper ran scores of contributions, particularly during the late 1860s, from R. W. T. Bedingfield, an avowed disciple of James Elishama 'Shepherd' Smith. 'My friend, the late J. E. Smith', as Bedingfield called him, had been through many phases, including one as a leading Owenite journalist and a briefer one as a Fourierite, but the most constant thread in his life had been millenarianism.[58] In writing to Bradlaugh's paper Bedingfield's main object was to bring about an alliance of everyone situated between atheism and broadminded Anglicanism, on the basis of Elishama's peculiar doctrines (which the latter had provocatively – and to Bedingfield's approval – boiled down to: 'God and the Devil are married').[59] To secularists, Bedingfield appealed as a fellow-opponent of priestcraft.[60] Frequently, he simply reproduced or summarised from Elishama's periodical the *Shepherd*,[61] as well as his later works.[62] He also warmly quoted other millenarians.[63]

Even if Bedingfield did once drop what may have been a hint that Bradlaugh himself had some special interest in Elishama,[64] the *National Reformer* gave no less space to other prolific non-Christians of clashing hues.[65] And in any case – to pursue my Bedingfield example fully – he was also allowed to reproduce Elishama's prophecies in Reddalls's *Secular Chronicle* which, of all the secularist journals, was the most hostile to spiritualism. After Bedingfield's death, the *Chronicle* mourned him prominently.[66] The paper also, during the mid-1870s, sold off copies of Owen's 1850s *Millenial Gazette* at half price.[67] When Reddalls died in 1875 and Harriet Law took over the editorship, she used the phrase 'social millennium' and praised Owen.[68]

Thus spiritualism was not unique in preserving something of the mix – which, for a time, had become associated with Owenism – of millenarianism and rationalism into the decades of the 'New Socialism' on either side of 1900. But it did do most towards this; and we shall see that spiritualists had various methods of preservation.

In the first place, though, why should spiritualism have been millennial? One persistent reason was that a belief which so disrupted most people's definition of reality was likely to shake their historical assumptions too. But this is not sufficient by itself. In addition, spiritualists needed no historian to remind them of their millenial origins. Generally, they claimed descent from mediaeval European and even earlier millenarians.[69] Again, many remembered David Richmond both for his impact in Keighley during the 1850s and for his lifelong enthusiasm for communities. Richmond (1816–91) settled back in Darlington as a shoemaker in 1862 and penned (as we shall see at the end of Chapter 6) unreadably ambitious millenarian visions.[70] Admittedly, these were 'not appreciated by spiritualists generally',[71] and Richmond himself became 'rather secluded during his last twenty years'.[72] But he had been locally prominent till then. And Joseph Dixon (1820–1903) his companion and fellow-vegetarian, and fellow-shoemaker, ended his days attending not only spiritualist, but also ILP, meetings.[73] Owen himself bulked large as spiritualism's first well-known convert. Burns emphasised this; later the *Two Worlds* and the kindred *Lyceum Banner* did the same, under headings such as 'A Socialist and a Spiritualist'.

Not that spiritualists' millenarian interest was a matter of merely keeping the Owenite memories alive. It also involved an interest in those sects – such as the Shakers[74] – which persisted with a communitarian way of life. Many members of these sects had, like Richmond, been through more than one phase of communitarianism.

Spiritualism also benefited from being strategically attractive to people of any reforming cast of mind. Its attractions varied. Hints of Owen's own version of spiritualist strategy (which we noted in Chapter 2) are audible from much later contexts. During 1892, a spiritualist spoke of 'the great . . . Labour Question . . . spreading like an epidemic over the land . . . People talked of the millenium which was going to be brought about by God himself. But [we say] the millenium can only be brought about by the Angels of God influencing humanity.'[75] And during the next decade, the *Two Worlds*, rejoicing at news of the 1905 revolution in Russia, could attribute it to the power of 'the angel message'.[76]

But this was only one version of spiritualist strategy. Equally from the time of its arrival, spiritualism offered to the politically disheartened something that present-day sociologists would call a 'failure mechanism'.[77] Not that the Owenites lacked their own explanation for failure: the effects of the bad old environment were still operative, closing the minds of the people against correct ideas. Rather – and this is central here – spiritualism offered to Owenites a flexibility which, arguably, they sorely needed: however many people managed to play truant from Owenite or secularist or socialist education here on earth, none could hope to do so in the next world. Then, spiritualists believed, we were all destined to 'endless progression'. Unlike Owen, most spiritualists probably leant towards this patient version. Owen's 'New Moral World' (another of his names for socialism) might arrive on earth, one century or the next; but for us, now, it would have to be restricted to the Summerland. This, in the words of a *Two Worlds* editorial, was 'where Socialism is already an accomplished fact'.[78] Given this assumption, not only was the millennium's timescale made more flexible, but the millennium itself was atomised or made piecemeal.

And this millennium was not left as an abstraction. As we shall see in Chapter 8, spiritualists possessed detailed conceptions of social relations and institutions in the Summerland. Via spiritualism, millenarianism echoed into almost any politics, from individualist to socialist. Of course, the worse the actual state of society on earth, the more it stunted people's characters and overtaxed the Summerland's system of re-education. Human nature, for spiritualists, required 'proper . . . environments in which to . . . reveal its innate . . . perfections'.[79] This could sharpen one's politics – as with one anonymous writer in *Human Nature*[80] who saw the feasts at which employers hobnobbed with employees as 'opiates to induce the victims to submit to further injury, and thus postpone the day of re-administration and retribution . . . for the life-destroying evils which prevail in the manufacturing districts'. Bitter or not, though, the more a spiritualist emphasised outside agency – the impact of spirits – the greater the risk of inevitabilism and political passivity: one could, logically at least, just sit back and merely enjoy denunciations of the bad existing society. Meanwhile the 'spirit' of Robert Owen's son and associate R. D. Owen could, *reportedly*, promise 'the new Jerusalem' as coming 'yet . . . though slower than I once thought it would . . . but it's better that the building be drained . . . before it's open for the occupancy of man. Steadily, surely the fabric is getting erected with durable materials.'[81]

Whether on earth or in the Summerland or both, the process would be a piecemeal, educational one. Late in 1879 a Manchester spiritualist, crossing Albert Square (the local speakers' corner) heard an orator attacking the lunacy laws and claiming to be the Messiah. This gave him lengthily to meditate:

> The . . . reconstruction of human society will not be brought about by the appearance of any special . . . messenger, . . . but rather by the insemination of pure and undefiled truth into the mind, which shall work out from as many centres as there are individuals. . . . And whosoever has this [interior enlightenment] developed within himself, to such the new Messiah has appeared in the form of a new life principle in his or her own nature, not in any individual outside.[82]

Ideas of millennial transformation popped up in various ways. 'For a second, I thought we were switched on to the millennium', joked one spiritualist during the 1900s.[83] More seriously, spiritualism could calm someone's millennially-toned socialism as powerfully during the 1890s as back in the 1850s. Reminiscing on his days as a non-spiritualist socialist, Isaac Pickthall felt he had to 'blush' at 'how rash' he had been: 'I was enthusiastic and almost believed myself a heaven-born prophet. I imagined, like Prometheus, I had stolen fire from heaven, and that the world – or at least . . . Stockport – would surrender to our frenzied glorification of the Socialist ideal . . . We set people thinking,' but 'Tweedledum and Tweedledee [Liberals and Tories] [were] still secure.'[84]

SPIRITUALISM AND THE LABOUR MOVEMENT

Millennialism was available to secularists. But it was an integral part of spiritualism – sometimes latent and atomised, sometimes manifest. We can now note that it was anything but foreign to spiritualist ILP-ers. How close were spiritualist ideas to ILP-type socialism? (I say 'type' because it was not exclusive to that organisation.) And how likely were spiritualists to feel at home in or near an ILP milieu?

It was quite easy to translate from ILP to spiritualist idiom. One ILP-er, James Swindlehurst (for whom see also below), could straightforwardly quote Keir Hardie from the *Labour Prophet* (the monthly of the Labour Churches) on 'the unseen forces that make for progress'. Hardie saw these things as acting 'with or without our co-operation, but . . . all the more effectually and speedily when we put ourselves into harmony with them, and become . . . the media through which they communicate themselves to our fellows'. This, Swindlehurst enthused, made excellent spiritualism: 'Yes, the "unseen forces" of the angel world are steadily working . . . to concentrate the thoughts of the time . . . Modern thought is fast permeating and thus becoming the controlling element.'[85] As with many other spiritualists, Swindlehurst's version of socialism was thoroughly moral and individualistic: 'the central fact of moral Socialism' would, he explained, 'spring from spiritualism' – viz: 'that individual effort is required before man can work out his social salvation'.[86] 'Socialism', one spiritualist explained during 1912

> cannot be regarded as a political party, but rather as a channel through which the ideals of a reformatory nature are finding expression. Politics is reform degenerated . . . Politics is of the flesh. Reform is of the spirit. Politics is the avenue through which all forms of reform are obliged to pass, and where they experience adulteration . . . almost beyond recognition.[87]

Not surprisingly, the *Two Worlds* defined socialism as 'true naturalism – justice, law, order and degree. . . . It should level up rather than pull down, and range all ['the varieties of the race'] into such harmony as will give to each his due share of human rights'.[88]

Thus, unlike Robert Owen during the late 1850s, most Victorian and Edwardian spiritualists normally saw moral change as necessarily slow. One London spiritualist, who saw socialism as 'part of spiritualism', imagined that socialism would 'probably take about five-million years' to come.[89] 'Keep on sowing', Isaac Pickthall exhorted his audience in Hulme Labour Hall, Manchester, 'somebody is sure to reap by and bye . . . That is all the more reason why our seed should be of the purest quality.'[90]

Uplifting, spiritual, moralistic and timeless: a socialism such as this would have been congenial to many a mid-Victorian plebeian radical. It encouraged either the preaching of the Word in the teeth of the existing Immoral World (as in Owenism or secularism) or a concentration on a specific aim while recognising its modesty (as in many political agitations during these decades). In either case, it emphasised that the lower orders (the excluded and the half-excluded) were, if anything, superior to those who patronised them, morally and therefore in respectability. The competition for respectability was, as recent writers have noted,[91] complicated by differences over how to define this crucial concept. And these differences could be avowed only partially. 'When I tell you', a spiritualist Northumbrian miner explained, while on strike during 1887,[92]

> that I have worked in the pits here for over thirty years . . .
> and am still without any capital, you will see that it is a case
> of resistance to the death. The master here . . . has accumulated
> a large fortune for himself and his heirs for ever. The grandson
> comes in for all who has never done a day's work in his life.
> But for all this,

he hastened to add, 'I am not a socialist in the present sense of the word': 'poverty and peace are better than riches,' so he would not 'exchange places with my employer'. Not surprisingly, in 1887, (the second consecutive year in which unemployed riots gave national notoriety to new marxist organisations, particularly the Social Democratic Federation), 'socialist' to him meant revolutionary.

Was the socialism of the ILP always so different? There was more than one version, though some were articulated more frequently than others.[93] The version to which the *Two Worlds* was closest was the most modest: the *Two Worlds*, like its predecessors, encouraged its readers to emphasise independence for both class and individual. Against the 'titled and wealthy class', reasoned one spiritualist socialist during 1902, 'we, men, cannot own any material thing or possession. The only possessions we can own are our character and our knowledge.'[94] 'Do the spirits teach Socialism?' wondered a *Two Worlds* editorial during 1897.[95] The answer was an emphatic yes, though (as we are discovering) the definition of socialism could hardly have been more watery. As 'two systems of philosophy devoted to the development of human brotherhood', 'Spiritualism and Socialism' were 'Fellow isms'. Both were 'happily unorthodox'. Both had 'the same enemies': wealth and priestcraft.[96]

Many spiritualists would have said the same about secularism.

For us, this underlines the extent to which late nineteenth-century plebeians, like their mid-century precursors, could change their political labels without altering their concepts. This should affect our attitude towards both the 'decline' of Owenism and the 'rise' of allegedly new socialisms with the SDF (from the 1880s) and the ILP (from the 1890s).

I have already pointed out the uneven regional pattern of spiritualism. This was shared by most plebeian movements. All our Victorian and Edwardian currents of plebeian independence – Owenism, secularism, the SDF, the ILP, the Labour Churches and the lower ends of Nonconformity – tended to be particularly strong in northern England, whereas only some (particularly the first three) were so in London. From the north, examples are plentiful of spiritualists adhering to one or more of these other movements or to other sympathetic agitations. I will note, first, some of those whose political allegiance (to SDF or ILP) is recorded with fewest complications. After these, I will mention four individuals in whom complex views are most traceable.

SDF-ers' appearances in the records are relatively rare. Readers may feel surprised that any SDF-ers – marxist and 'materialist' – should have had any trace of sympathy with spiritualism. Nonetheless, the oddest things can occur underneath labels: back in the early 1870s, George Sexton had managed, overlappingly, to be not only a recently converted Christian spiritualist (in contact, via his own mediumship, with the 'spirit' of Owen) but also a 'staunch' supporter of Karl Marx within the faction-ridden International Working Men's Association.[97] And the SDF's theoretical magazine, the *Social Democrat*, carried a full-scale feature on an 'international spiritualist conference' in 1898.[98] One Wandsworth (but ex-northern) spiritualist – who was himself sufficiently 'materialist' to feel suspicious of the Labour Churches as an attempt to suborn the labour movement for Christianity – had allegedly found 'the seeds of spiritualism . . . fast taking root' in the SDF when he joined in London. He gave the impression that his 'comrades' were sympathetic to spiritualism's ideals – 'so in harmony with their own'. Indeed, they were 'continually asking for more'.[99] (We have to assume they were not pulling his leg.)

But ILP sympathies were far more frequent. One Bolton spiritualist complained that 'in some places . . . some of the best workers [were] going over to Socialism' on the scale of 'a great

Will Phillips
Socialist. Edited the *Two Worlds* from 1899 to 1906, and ran his
own *Spiritual Quarterly Magazine* during 1902–04. Was another
of those North-English socialist spiritualists who were
particularly close to the atheist, J. W. Gott (see picture no. 17).
During one year alone, he claimed to have spoken at 48 socialist
meetings and nearly as many spiritualist ones, plus weddings
and funerals.

leakage in our movement'.[100] And among the most prominent was
Will Phillips, editor of the *Two Worlds* from 1899 to 1906 (and of
his own *Spiritual Quarterly Magazine*, 1902–4). He claimed during
one year to have spoken at 48 socialist meetings and nearly as
many spiritualist ones,[101] plus a number of weddings and funerals.
    Labour Churches were a particular challenge. 'A number of
spiritualists' had 'been attracted'. The informant thought this
'inevitable' – given, partly, that the two movements were so
akin.[102] The Labour Churches – not just the 1890s ILP at prayer,
for they became less and less theological – officially aimed to make
socialism and the labour movement into a moral crusade. By early
1894,[103] 'several' members of the Blackburn spiritualists'
committee were also on the local Labour Church's committee. Yet
the reporter was not very worried at this: 'Spiritualists will probably return to our cause or spiritualise the labour movement.'[104]

J. T. Ward
'Among the founders of the Independent Labour Party in
Blackburn' and prominent within it and as a spiritualist for 20
years. A healer. A director of the *Two Worlds*. Borough councillor
for 12 years.

Certainly, the *Bolton and District ILP Pioneer*[105] had contributions
from at least three spiritualists or what one might call 'spiritualis-
ants' within its seven thin issues. One contribution was a summary
of an address to the local Labour Church.

Generally, adherents of both movements were aware of an
overlap.[106] Just as non-socialist spiritualists could still show interest
in socialism, so could socialists spend time testing their scepticism
over spiritualism. 'Yanto', regular contributor to the ILP *Bradford
Labour Echo*, softened his attitude when he sat down with 'Sperrits',
as he called them, who proceeded to refute his pessimism over the
new general 'Workers' Union' (ancestor of today's Transport and

Mrs Peggy Ward
'never went to a dayschool', 'worked over 50 years . . . as a
cotton weaver and always enjoyed factory life. . . . She has the
pleasure . . . of knowing that every one of her children . . . are
ardent workers both in the spiritualist and labour movements.'
From this, we may imagine she took most pride in her locally
most famously ILP of her sons, J.T.

General) and snap-answered a string of queries such as 'Is the
revising of the local [ILP] constitution a good move?'[107]
    There were a number of partial 'overlappers'. The Bradford ILP-
er Margaret McMillan visited a local Lyceum and hoped out loud
that the School Board (where she was prominent) would adopt
lyceum marching and callisthenics.[108] She had already serialised
fiction in the *Two Worlds* – without, apparently, being spiritualist
herself. Allen Clarke, friend of Robert Blatchford the *Clarion*
editor, was another *Two Worlds* serial-author. He spent part of the
1890s moving quite publicly towards spiritualism. (One narrative
of his experiences in this field[109] was itself a reprint from the

C. Allen Clarke
Humorist, social investigator, journalist and Lancashire dialect
writer. Novelist of working–class struggle in past and present.
Began as a half-timer, errand-boy and pupil teacher. Socialist for
half a century: loathed 'the factory system' as obscene
ecologically let alone socially. Cyclist and rambler. Moved from
vague agnosticism to spiritualism after family tragedies and on
experience of his second wife's psychic powers.

Clarion.) Loosely again, Robert's brother Montague Blatchford
was willing enough to adjudicate the choirs of the North East
Lancashire Lyceums.[110] After our period, Robert himself was to
switch famously from his 'materialism' to spiritualism. But spiritualists had long found his 'altruism' and 'determinism' particularly
sympathetic, even during the years when he saw himself as a
champion of militant agnosticism. And he was quoted as sympathetic to spiritualism as early as 1901.[111] His rival strategist within the
ILP, Keir Hardie, was not vocal about spiritualism. Subsequently,
though, there has grown up a commonplace among biographers[112]
that he occasionally attended seances and that his religious beliefs
included a virtual acceptance of spiritualism. Coincidentally a
report, that the *Medium and Daybreak* quoted, of Keir Hardie's
attendance at a seance along with two other socialists (Frank Smith
and Bruce Wallace), had originally been published in a local newspaper on the same date as the number of the *Two Worlds* which
had reprinted a 'fair and impartial' treatment of spiritualism from
the *Clarion*.[113]

There were many less-known overlappers,[114] but I will concentrate on four whose complexities were particularly obvious. The
first, Ernest Marklew, is perhaps the most complex of all. Around

Ernest Marklew
'45 years an active spiritualist, . . . 40 . . . actively Socialist'. As
a child, worked on the land. Moved to a steelworks. By late
1890s, a largely self-educated SDF-er. Imprisoned for free speech
during 1906. Edited *The Medium* and wrote *The Sacrament of
Sex*. Later, exchanged a stall at Grimsby fish market for a seat in
the Commons. Psychometrist and inspirational speaker.

1900 he was an SDF-er. This we could again leave as simply
untypical, except that Marklew's main locus of activities was
Burnley, whose SDF had long been particularly reformist, unsectarian and (relative to most other northern SDF branches)
successful – in other words, particularly ILP-ish. During his last
four years (to 1939) Marklew was Labour MP for Colne Valley,
the seat which he had helped Victor Grayson, the rebel ILP-er, to

win in 1907 as 'the first Socialist MP'.[115] He was 'for 45 years an
active spiritualist . . . 40 years actively Socialist'. In the Commons,
Marklew was to defend unorthodox healing. 'All I am . . . and all
I hope for,' he was to declare, 'I owe to spiritualism.' Certainly
spiritualism is said to have remade his character so dramatically as
to convert his father.[116] He began work as a child – at first on the
land,[117] later moving to a steelworks. By the late 1890s, in his
twenties and largely self-educated, he was speaking powerfully for
the SDF.[118] He also claimed psychometric powers,[119] and 'inspirational assistance from the other side'[120] (whether on occasions
when he spoke for marxists we do not know). This did not save
him from spending 14 days of 1906 in jail for free speech at
Nelson, Lancs. His wife was later said to have been some sort of
'suffragette'.[121]

From 1904 to 1907, Marklew ran his own periodical the *Medium*
in Burnley, priced at a democratic halfpenny. It was socialist,
spiritualist, secularist and defiantly heterodox on just about everything. Never flourishing, it disappears even from Burnley Borough
Library after Marklew had advertised his forthcoming pamphlet
on 'the Sacrament of Sex'. (Although his publicity for it was
'calculated to shock prigs, prostitutes and parsons', the work itself
discussed sexuality mystically not physically.) Conceivably, this
may have helped to impoverish him.[122] At any rate, by 1911 he
had moved to Grimsby where he founded a Socialist party branch,
and eventually became a fish-merchant. In the aftermath of the
General Strike of 1926 he spoke for the Miners' Federation in a
public debate at Mansfield against the 'non-Political' or 'stooge'
breakaway union.[123] By the 1930s he was also a borough
councillor.

A particularly prominent ILP-er and spiritualist was Peter Lee
of Rochdale. He had edited the *Two Worlds* for about six months.[124]
He could also lecture on mediumship,[125] mesmerism and
geology,[126] and write dialect stories.[127] He was an ILP-er for nearly
20 years, and was prominent in the local *Labour News*. His eight
years on the local School Board were brought to a close (1900)
only when the SDF split the socialist vote, allegedly for his 'crime'
of behaving 'like a gentleman'. According to the 1898 *Labour
Annual*, Lee had been 'converted to Socialism during the 1893–4
coal strike'. A principled and therefore hard-pressed commercial

Peter Lee
Exchanged Anglicanism plus Toryism for spiritualism plus
Liberalism. 'Converted to socialism during the 1893–4 coal strike.'
Sometime editor of the *Two Worlds* and prominent on Rochdale
ILP's *Labour News*. On the School Board from 1892 to 1900.
Wrote dialect stories, and lectured on mediumship, mesmerism
and geology. Worked during much of his life as a commercial
traveller.

traveller, he had exchanged Anglicanism plus Toryism for spiritualism plus (at first) Liberalism. He died in 1908.[128]
   Another prominent ILP-er spiritualist during the 1890s was
James Swindlehurst. His father had been a Chartist and his grandfather one of the great pioneers of teetotalism (total abstinence
from alcohol). James continued these family traditions. For a time,
he was also a secularist. Further, before he became a socialist, his
main notoriety had been as an opponent of compulsory vaccination
(a thoroughly spiritualist stance, as we shall see). Eventually his
goods were seized and he and his family evicted. They slept out,
and his wife gave birth 'on the cold flags'.[129] He also suffered a

James Swindlehurst
Came from a Chartist and teetotal background. Formerly
secularist, he was, by 1877, speaking publicly for spiritualism. For
this (and perhaps for his trade unionism), James suffered
victimisation, distraint and imprisonment. His wife, after they
had been evicted for the same reasons, gave birth 'on the cold
flags'. James became a medium and locally prominent as both
spiritualist and socialist.

fortnight in prison on this issue. By the 1890s, he sat on the
executive of both the Spiritualist National Federation[130] and the
Lancashire and Cheshire ILP Federation. His oratory was much in
demand in Lancashire among spiritualists and socialists alike. He
was also a medium. During 1893, by now 'an ardent Socialist', he
stood 'against religious bigotry' for Preston Council. In his support
his wife mounted the platform to scotch rumours that he was a
freelover and a wife-beater.[131] But he still lost.

I could cite many further people who remained in or near many
movements. Seth Ackroyd would be one from an older generation.

Inglis and Hobsbawm have noted him as an 'ex-Wesleyan machine sawyer' and, during 1895, as secretary of Hull Labour Church.[132] By then, he seems to have been into 'phenomena'.[133] His first impact on the east coast may have been as a Free Thought lecturer 'on the sands at Cleethorpes [Summer 1892], his eccentric nature securing him audiences by his grotesque antics with a few sea shells'. As a young Wesleyan in Huddersfield he had led a number of his fellows into an open-minded study group, where his orthodoxy disintegrated into 'Liberal Christianity'. A Bradlaugh debate had begun his long association with the secularists. Though he never formally joined the Secular Society, he had chaired meetings for visiting secularist leaders. By 1890 he had become prominent in a lyceum. Apparently lyceum methods had 'entirely captured' him into spiritualism's orbit. Intellectually, he wished lyceum leaders to have the maximum grounding, and himself offered talks to his own Liberty Group (ages 16 and over) on 'Descartes . . . Spinoza, Berkeley, Shelley, Haeckel . . . Kant . . . Hamilton and . . . Spencer', also recommending literature, 'positive science' and comparative religion.[134] Near his seventieth year (1915), he was still a regular visitor to lyceums around Huddersfield and Halifax.

The last four individuals underline, more obviously than ever, that spiritualists' activities involved not only kinship with a few other isms, but also commitment to something at the foundations of plebeianness. This something is what I will discuss as 'democratic epistemology' in Chapter 6. But this should not be taken as implying that plebeian spiritualism had no kinship with non-plebeian. Rather, the two did overlap in their methods – as we shall see in section C.

B   Plebeian and non-plebeian

But before coming to overlaps in method during the next section, we need to establish *who* may have overlapped – in other words to see to what extent plebeian and non-plebeian spiritualists themselves had a distinguishable identity.

The 'phenomena' attributed to a medium were possibly – so far as I can tell – the same, irrespective of the social class of other participants at the seance. And highly 'successful' mediumship tended to boost the confidence of any spiritualists accepting such reports. Given these two aspects, mediumship sometimes held out to the medium the hope of social ascent. True, hope must frequently have been dashed. But some mediums did rise, securely or not; and these notably included some women.[135] My point here, though, is that – particularly if mediums' early practice had been predominantly among plebeians – they would usually find themselves in a somewhat unfamiliar ideological world when among non-plebeians. Here, they would have to tone down, not necessarily their language but often the heterodox abrasiveness of the theological views to which many of them had sometimes, implicitly or not, appealed. One such medium would surely have been James J. Morse who, as a 'trance medium' by late 1870, was sitting for the 'Dalston Association of Enquirers into Spiritualism' (President: Captain J. Watts).[136] As we shall soon see, Morse was so thoroughly a London plebeian that a respectable spiritualist quarterly could recommend his autobiography, eight years later, to 'who[m]ever would understand popular spiritualism in its strength and weakness'.[137] Some years later, on its side, the Dalston Association was to give entree for at least one newly arrived and still unknown American medium, 'among the most influential persons in English society'. Possibly, he was starry-eyed; but the point is merely that, had the gathering been plebeian, it would hardly have dazzled him.[138]

So far as one can tell, much early respectable spiritualism was London-centred. As remarked, the core practice of spiritualism was and is officially the seance. This can be a very private affair indeed. And given London's always exceptional size, there would have been at least as many difficulties for either contemporaries or historians in detecting unpublicised seances in London as elsewhere. During 'period[s] of spiritual dearth' between crazes for spiritualism, some spiritualists saw evidence of few regular seances taking place at all – Morse as late as the mid-1890s.[139] This, for him, was because spiritualism's intimate nature tended to keep it hidden except when attacks and controversies drew it into the public eye.

This fickleness aside, however, London spiritualism seems to have had the following rhythms. First, it tended repeatedly to know little and care less about the spiritualism of Northern England. Similarly, during spiritualism's first decade, the London-based and middle class *Spiritual Herald* bitterly attributed its own demise to a 'want of English manifestations, or want of English courage': there were, it explained, 'either . . . very few mediums in England, or . . . they are fearful of publicity'.[140] This editorialist seems not to have digested at any rate some of the advertisements in his own pages: J. G. H. Brown certainly possessed 'courage' whatever else, and the *Yorkshire Spiritual Telegraph* brimmed with evidence of the existence of mediums in its locality and beyond.[141] The problem was, rather, that London spiritualists remained for long frequently peripheral, while seeing themselves, as Londoners, as at the centre. Those two London spiritualists who can be exonerated from this accusation more than any other were, significantly, both plebeians: Morse and Burns. By contrast, as we shall also see, the great journalist W. T. Stead was, as late as the 1900s, to be uncharacteristically ill-informed about the bitterness of provincial plebeian spiritualists' hostility to Christianity: although himself a comparatively recent arrival from Northern England he was, as the Christian editor of (amongst other and more famous ventures) his own occult journal, a Londoner. True, London's very position as a magnet and entrepot meant that spiritualists who migrated to it were sometimes less ignorant. But Morse and Burns owed their exceptionality in this regard to their continual willingness to tour *away* from London. Indeed, as we will see later, Burns' willingness to base himself on provincial spiritualists was to help worsen his isolation from most other London spiritualists.

Second, there were of course plebeians in London who were spiritualist. The autobiography of one of the most prominent, Morse, mentions such people as already active by the late 1860s (and, one can imagine, earlier), and also suggests how mesmerism was becoming available among plebeians as operators, not only as subjects. Morse was born in 1849, the son of a London publican. Orphaned young and often starving, he was scratching a living by the age of 10. By 1868 he was working in a pub himself and was, he says,

in a fair way of becoming an atheist. The avocation I pursued was not calculated to remedy this tendency on my part. My reason revolted against the dogmas of eternal torment hereafter, and also against the doctrines of original sin and total depravity. Heaven was impossible to me, it seemed; and Hell

James J. Morse
Teenage orphan and starveling, was following his father's
footsteps as a barman when accidentally discovered spiritualist
doctrines. These revolutionised his life: he blundered into
mediumship and, steadied by his new-found temperance,
became a leading trance-speaker. Also prominent among
spiritualism's editors and pamphleteers. In his later years, he
(and/or his wife) ran London's only self-proclaimedly spiritualist
hotel.

> was too awful to think of. Was there another life? I knew
> not, but I hoped so.

But in the autumn of that year, he burst a button near Bishopsgate,
and called at a haberdashers' shop kept by the mother of the
spiritualist Unitarian, the Reverend J. P. Hopps. Finding Mrs
Hopps discussing spiritualism with another customer, he weighed
in sarcastically against her view. When he left the shop, however,
he was clutching some books she had lent him on the question,
including one by her son. These opened his mind and, when he
returned them to her, she gave him a Whitechapel address where
at least two mediums (a Mr Cogman and a Mr Woolnough) held
a meeting every Sunday. Morse went, but felt only 'disgust . . .
with the whole proceedings' up to the moment when he, to his
bewilderment and horror, found himself as if

> endowed with another personality, which for a period of three-
> quarters of an hour raised a most un-Sunday-like din . . . I
> shouted, I rolled around the room, I swore, and, as if to render
> my position more uncomfortable, I was perfectly conscious
> of all my gentlemanly actions! The more I tried not to do these
> things, the more perfectly were they accomplished!

When these antics subsided, he apologised to the medium-host –
the latter took it as all rather routine – and, furious with embarrassment, vowed to keep well away in future. He was, he recounts, 'in
a perfect quandary. Disbelieving spiritualism, not understanding
trance mediumship, I was utterly at a loss to account for the
phenomenon in my own person' and felt driven to 'the mortifying
conclusion that I . . . was becoming a fit subject for [the lunatic
asylum at] Colney Hatch.' Worse, at work the next day, his hand
began to be possessed by a spirit claiming to be his mother's and
wanting him to write out its messages. Terrified that he would
scandalise the whole pub and lose his job, he drove a bargain with
this spirit: he would do its bidding, but not during opening hours.
After some time spent in further uncertainty, he returned, despite
his earlier vows, to the Whitechapel meeting where – till then a
lad who had 'never before, to my knowledge, spoken consecu-
tively for ten minutes together on one subject' – he found himself
delivering an impromptu sermon of forty, on a randomly-chosen
text from the New Testament. His preaching over, his character
seemed to invert itself: 'I seemed transformed into a complete
blackguard.' Even after these further capers, he 'was still in doubt.
The thing seemed too ridiculous to believe as the work of spirits,
and yet it was far too real for me [not] to know I was not doing
it myself.' (His omission of one negative in this sentence may be
worth noting, or not.) His exhibitions at these Sunday seances
continued for more than a month. During these weeks, a new
acquaintance persuaded him that mesmerism was true; Morse
therefore tried to explain his own behaviour as somehow caused
by his being mesmerised unawares. He accepted a spiritualist explanation, only when he received what for him were proofs that his
interlocutors during his phases of abnormality were undoubtedly
his parents and no one else.

> I rejoiced at the discovery thus brought to me. All the love
> and affection for my parents, which had for so many years
> been buried or bound up, now burst forth. My father and my
> mother seemed to live anew before me, and from the depth
> of my soul aspirations of thankfulness rose up to the Cause of
> all being for the joy and the happiness thus conferred upon
> one so humble.'[142]

I have quoted Morse's account at such immense length, because – while some of its psychological burdens may belong in later chapters – it seems to state well many of the dilemmas faced by many an incipient medium from a non-spiritualist background, whose life-tensions had, up to the time of conversion, included bereavement, avowed despair over religion, self-consciously humble birth and morally decent aspirations. But such people's problems hardly lightened at this stage, and Morse's narrative includes not merely discoveries of his own power as medium, mesmeriser and healer, but also of further economic trials. In his case at least, these were worsened by his decision to escape from an impending adulthood as a publican: 'the continual influence of spiritualism' left him 'dissatisfied with my course of life and its surroundings'. He therefore resolved on 'getting into something better adapted to my new modes of thought'. Accordingly, he sought to become a clerk. The immediate result for him was nearly eight months of unemployment, during which he profited all he could from his new-found 'abstemiousness' and emerged, he claims, much the healthier. During this period, he developed not only his powers but also his contacts with spiritualists.

The result was engagements, one of these with the independently minded anti-vaccinator C. W. Pearce of Dalston. Pearce bought Morse a badly-needed suit of clothes and let him stay two months at his house as a sort of resident medium – not a unique arrangement around this time.[143] Morse was, like many mediums, relating to non-plebeians and plebeians in roughly equal measure. Not least among the latter was Burns, for whom he worked as 'assistant' (for a time, alongside another mediumistic friend) for three years at the Spiritual Institution – where Morse also held seances for some years. The Institution vastly accelerated his contactings: 'as there was no other . . . central depot in the metropolis, I had the opportunity of meeting . . . most of the prominent spiritualists and workers in England' plus, one can imagine, some from America. The two men found they agreed much in their views, and Morse also became 'deeply indebted to [Burns] for much useful physiological knowledge'.[144] They also toured together (Morse as trance-speaker – the field in which he became one of the most famous of his generation – and at least once with the added attraction of 'Dr J. R. Newton, the American healer' until the time, in 1872, when he felt able to launch out on his own career as a medium.

But for all Morse's understandable gratitude to Burns, we should not forget, as we have just heard him implying, that the latter was unique among plebeians and could obviously never hope to clothe or feed him for his mediumistic activities alone. (Burns may well have known difficulties doing the same for himself and his own family). Thus, in London, spiritualism's non-plebeian adherents were usually more visible. Here, we may distinguish two main categories – though usually with hindsight alone: we may call them stayers and visitors. Of course, we could probably make the same distinction in relation to almost any movement but, in relation to something so deviant (and, for believers, usually so heartwarming) as the spiritualist, it was particularly likely. For the same reasons, the distinction was particularly important in reinforcing the fluctuations in the movement's fortunes. More committed spiritualists might resent being on such a switchback but had difficulty in knowing how or when to lift the movement off it. After all, even in its 'arrival' in London's high society, spiritualism had had a faddish aspect. As we have seen, mesmerism had also tickled much of 'society' gorgeously during the 1830s and 1840s. The individual patterns of support or rejection for each successive fad were variable; but the social circles seldom were. We can gather the ambiguity of much of the motivation there from the memoirs of the wealthily-born homoeopath, Dr George Wyld (whom we met in mesmeric and alchemical contexts during the previous chapter). 'One day in 1854' and already a supporter of mesmerism, Wyld was buttonholed by 'an old mesmeric friend, who . . . said: "Have you seen anything of spiritualism?" to which I answered, "I know nothing about it, and I have taken no interest in the American stories about it;", on which my friend said: "You're wrong; take my advice and lose no time in informing yourself, for you will find Spiritualistic experiments infinitely more surprising than mesmeric experiments".'[145] Wyld therefore hastened to watch D. D. Home. 'Ever since', he recalled nearly fifty years later, his mind had 'been absorbed in the facts and theories of Spiritualism.'[146]

Thus admittedly, curiosity-seeking might sometimes blossom into lifelong commitment. But sometimes it remained superficial and therefore unreliable. Worst of all, faddists were liable to run for cover wherever a medium – particularly one who had sat for the rich and famous – was allegedly or actually exposed in fraud. This occurred more than once during the 1860s and 1870s.[147] As

Morse reminded a meeting of the rather respectable London Spiritualist Alliance during the mid-1890s,[148] the 'thirst for phenomena' had made this 'side of spiritualism . . . the sensation of society's drawing rooms'; but, when 'some fancied they smelled sulphur, [and] others cried humbug . . . society took fright.' Interestingly, the length and direction of flight were variable. On the one hand, after one such scare, even the L.S.A.'s predecessor, the British National Association of Spiritualists, is alleged to have tried to persuade two American spiritualists during the late 1870s to suppress any claim to communicate with spirits and to talk instead of 'exhibit[ing] only certain mental phenomena'.[149] On the other hand, while what we have seen Morse metaphorically calling 'sulphur' – i.e. the claim that spiritualism was anti-Christian – was certainly a frightening argument which all spiritualists and opponents had sooner or later to take a position about, a respectably nurtured thirst for novelty might occasionally make well-off spiritualists more tolerant than the less well-off. Certainly the same pair of American spiritualists received a far frostier welcome from Burns than from other London spiritualists. This was partly because of recent fraud cases: "'I have been directed by spirit influences to come to London'", J. W. Fletcher opened – no doubt in the tremulous way usual to him – to Burns on visiting him at 15 Southampton Row: "'Is there any work for me to do?" Mr. Burns briefly replied: "No. American mediums have ruined the cause here, and I wish none of them would ever set foot in England again."'[150] But it was partly also doctrinal. True, Burns and most American spiritualists – including this couple – held the same views on Christianity. But, as we have seen, what Burns seems increasingly to have abhorred (despite insinuations from respectables to the contrary) was the commitment of many of his American sisters and brothers to what he saw as free love.[151] Even at this nadir in his foreign relations, though, Burns remained quite happy not only to advise such dangerous visitors on where to stay but also, more significantly, to feed them a contact or two.[152]

Morse (and surely Burns too, once he had recovered his civility) did not see such panics as unmitigated disasters. Or at least, not in the long term. 'Spiritualism', Morse countered – for once, orating officially in a 'normal' state but still with somewhat ethereal chronology – was 'freed from its high class restraints . . . After the smiles of fashion were withdrawn, the inevitable democratisation of the movement set in and the new thing spread among the people.' This, we can appreciate, is a worthlessly watery narrative for England as a whole; and even for London, the list of meeting places which he proceeded to give suggests only the vaguest definition for his 'people'.[153]

But whatever the nature of this 'democratisation' in London (and we have now seen enough to nuance, even there, any 'from-above-downwards' model for the diffusion of the mediumistic practices), the spread of spiritualism among the respectable classes was complicated from about this time (the late 1870s) by a number of splits. Morse distinguished three; and he implied in relation to all of them an elite correlation. To him, 'the first noticeable cleavage' had been that which had produced the Society for Psychical Research.[154] While admitting that this Society's founders had objections to spiritualist practice which were to do with method, he still sneered that they 'resented being associated with those who they considered were not possessed of that fine critical sense which the case . . . demanded.' Consciously or not, this sneer was not simply anti-elite but anti-intellectual, and therefore alerts us to the methodological aspect discussed in the next section. He derided Theosophy, which came third and latest in his narrative of splits, in implicitly social terms also: as 'attractive to those formerly among us who found it "so much superior, you know, to Spiritualism!"'. In between, there had occurred his second 'cleavage'. This had been really more of a falling-away – and again on grounds inextricably social as well as ideological: it had 'undoubtedly' been

> caused by the disinclination upon the part of our more
> conservative adherents to be associated with that presentation
> of spiritualism . . . which appeared as an aggressive reform
> movement, adherence to which would bring them into
> conflict with their friends and neighbours upon religious, social
> and even political matters, if their names were associated with
> it.

Clearly, Morse was contrasting this with certain aspects of plebeian spiritualism. 'Today', he proclaimed, spiritualism had become 'publicly a question of the masses' – though 'privately . . . it is true', it still had 'its hold upon the classes'. Particularly during the

1890s, this distinction between the 'masses' and 'classes' was a favourite device of populist rhetoric among liberals and socialists, and its apparent ease may have helped make it slipperier. Morse, here at least, did not stop to imply so much as a social definition, but rushed on to give it a geographical: whereas spiritualism in London was, he felt, prone to 'ever-increasing apathy' – being 'sleepy because [without] . . . fighting to do', 'our brethren in the provinces were not slumbering'. He instanced their quantity: not only more than 130 'places outside of London' with weekly public meetings but also 60 venues for Lyceums. Qualitatively too he was impressed.

> They are people, in a great number of cases, who have
> exhausted orthodoxy and heterodoxy. . . . They . . . look
> upon spiritualism as a religio-philosophical system, and they
> are surely building up a reformed belief, may I call it, upon
> all matters concerning religion, philosophy, morals and
> immortality.

To them, 'Spiritualism appeal[ed] with all the force of a religion.'

As already noted, his contrast was one of geography more than of class. But there can be no doubt that he saw the one as implying the other, and that he was talking of the plebeian spiritualism discussed in this book. And the fact that Morse's contrast is geographical, underlines the weakness and ambiguity of London from the plebeian spiritualist point of view – all the more, given that Morse (quintessentially plebeian in his origins, as we have seen) must have known what he was talking about in this regard, given his very extensive travelling as a professional trance speaker up and down England. (This is one reason why he had identified another of the objections by spiritualism's 'more conservative adherents' as being to 'professionalism': he was anything but hostile to ordinary spiritualists' relying on their own or local mediumship but, once the invitations began to mount up, how else were mediums with aspirations to more than part-time activity, and without private income, to keep body and spirit together, or even to meet their travel-expenses?)

Whatever London's weaknesses within English spiritualism as a whole, however, the capital attracted and held many intellectuals, or middle-class ones at least. Partly for this reason, London spiritualism produced – if only proportionate to the apparent numbers of adherents – a deal of periodicals. Most of these, as we have seen, have a middle-class feel and most were theologically either orthodox or careful not to provoke people of orthodox views. Their separation from much of the plebeian spiritualism that was so much stronger in the provinces seems to have been clear to Morse, for one. Why else would he have gone out of his way, as we have seen, to contrast provincial spiritualism with metropolitan? Nor was this contrast a matter of rhetoric. Why else would he have bothered to give a basic definition of Lyceums ('Sunday schools called Lyceums') to the L.S.A.?[155]

Coincidentally, the editor of the periodical where Morse's address was printed provides a good instance of the ignorance among London-based journalists of the leading ideas of these spiritualists. W. T. Stead, already famous as founder of the *Review of Reviews* had now started the *Borderland* as its occult counterpart. The 'borderland' in question was of course that between 'science and superstition'.[156] Stead wished, in his words, to 'democratise the study of the spook'[157] along, particularly (or so he claimed), S.P.R. lines. For May 1895 in London, he organised a two-day conference of spiritualists[158] and invited the Lyceum pioneer Alfred Kitson to talk on the need for Lyceums. But he was reduced to intervening hurriedly from the chair after Kitson had read a bitter and sweeping attack against orthodox Christian doctrines. As Stead's whole aim during this decade was to build consensus among spiritualists and semi-spiritualists of every kind, we can hardly imagine he would have given Kitson his broadest-ever national platform had he known that the latter had always seen Lyceums' 'purpose' as 'deliver[ing] children from the false . . . doctrines which the Christian system existed to propagate.' True, Stead had, in *Borderland's* very first number, reprinted the latest *Two Worlds'* list of meeting-places – 'from which', as he noted, it would 'be seen . . . that the North is much more spiritualist than the South'.[159] Once again, though, even so energetic a journalist as he seems to have lived in a largely separate world from that of one of the chief ideologues of plebeian spiritualism.[160]

Nor was Kitson alone in at least some of his views: on the same occasion the 'statement which was received with more applause than any other made during the meeting, was a denial of the doctrine of the atonement'. This statement was attributed merely to 'a speaker', who 'maintain[ed] that we are all our own saviours.' Stead was reduced to replying, in print now, that all this amounted to 'more of a protest against a conventional misapprehension of Christian doctrine than Christian doctrine itself.' And this reply was more than merely belated: to call a misapprehension conventional was to admit that it remained widespread.

The gap between respectable and other spiritualisms is also visible in 1894 at the end of James Burns' life. During his last months he had been unable to afford even a pair of spectacles.[161] As we have seen, he had been the key spiritualist editor through three decades. But he was 'unfortunately not a businessman'[162]: as his main legacy to his sons (James and William) he left a tidy debt of no less than £887.[163] 'The spiritualists', Stead commented, had 'given very inadequate support to the work of one of their earliest pioneers.'[164] But what lent his phrase 'the' spiritualists its accuracy?

From the plebeian side, Burns had served his purpose in helping to catalyse spiritualism in the provinces. In this, as one 'crowded' memorial meeting in Blackburn was told, 'no [other] man could have done the good work he had accomplished'.[165] True, another of the preconditions for his effectiveness there had been a willingness to travel. During the 1860s for instance, he was often away from London for 'more than six months at a time'[166] – admittedly lecturing not just on spiritualism but also on vegetarianism, phrenology, education and other topics, but he never had seen himself as just a spiritualist. Without all this effort, his impact might have been merely that of one other inveterate spiritualist whom, incidentally, he outlasted by only a few months: Burns's commemoration of his old friend Hay Nisbet sounds like a self-description minus all the travelling. Nisbet had merely been 'one of the pioneer spiritualists of Glasgow, [who had] . . . printed much of the literature for a number of years'.[167] And Burns had not only done all this and travelled as well; he had also been the key organiser and speaker at a number of spiritualist conferences in Northern England during the middle and late 1860s.[168]

But the beneficiaries of his activism seem to have been slow to extricate him from the financial drawbacks of his London location. Obviously, in other words, this location meant, to a significant extent, isolation from his main base. Within a purely London context, his position was less secure. True, he might organise whole series of meetings,[169] as well as occasional ones for pres-

tigious visitors (as for Emma Hardinge Britten[170]); his 'undoubted
. . . tact and talent for gathering together large numbers of persons
whom no other spiritualist lecturer succeeds in reaching' might be
highly prized[171]; he might, as early as the 1870s, be patted on the
head as a 'veteran worker' in the cause; his bookshop and meeting-
room – grandly titled the 'Progressive Library and Spiritual Institution' – at No. 15 Southampton Row did last for many years.
But there were also undercurrents of mistrust. These were not
merely a matter of doctrinal disagreement – nor of stylistic, as
suggested in one respectable spiritualist's complaint that Burns's
language was coarse.[172] True, on one occasion, the disservices
which this or some other quality of Burns's was said to be doing
the cause seem to have been thought so dire, that the same respectable, allegedly, even offered him the princely temptation of £6 to
give up editing *Human Nature* (which Burns had, after all,
founded).[173] But, for many London spiritualists, style and even
doctrine were not the only matters of complaint. Morse – who,
all the more significantly, agreed with Burns on doctrine (as we
have seen) – formulated another ground for unease: why had
December 1878's 'annual effort in support' of Burns's 'Institution'
– '"Institution Week" as it is called' – have produced only a 'trifle
over £50'? Aside from 'bad trade and hard times' there was, 'as
the [spiritualist] movement grows, a disposition . . . to utilise
means at home, instead of sending away for purposes over which
no control [could] be exercised. Taxation without representation
. . . may suit the policy of an autocracy, but it is out of harmony
with modern spiritualism.'[174] Morse was also, apparently, hinting
that London spiritualists felt particularly doubtful over Burns's
activities outside the metropolis.

Doctrine, therefore, may have been the main, but was not the
only, reason why Burns was to remain, for most of the socially
more influential of London spiritualists, eccentric and undesirable
(however much respect he might sometimes be paid as an individual). And Morse himself – with whom there was so much
doctrinal agreement – seems sometimes to have been half a rival:
on the one hand, Burns sold Morse's autobiography[175]; on the
other, Morse founded at Uttoxeter a few months later his own
(possibly short-lived) 'Progressive Literature Agency' – a title
which Burns sometimes used for his own Institution.[176] More
broadly, Burns's bitter opposition during the mid-1870s to the

then incipient British National Association of Spiritualists had been attributed 'largely' by 'many people' to his fear of 'the effect of such a [development] on his business interests in the Spiritual Institution'. (As we have seen, he need not have worried.) And certainly when, in 1887, Kitson published the first *English Lyceum Manual*, Burns reacted bitterly.[177] Thus he reinforced his own isolation somewhat.

But this behaviour of his was surely predictable – would have been from any but some superhumanly 'evolved spirit' – given the pressures of pioneering in such a cause. For he had not lacked something to sacrifice: he could probably have had an easier life in some other role. His 'Cranial Psychology' was remembered into the 1890s[178] as having, some decades earlier at least, been the best available; and during the 1860s and maybe later, his lecture tours on 'Phrenology and Physiology' were apparently a 'great success, and made a great deal of money'. But such prospects, he had sacrificed; and he is said to have devoted 'the greater part of his earnings to the furtherance of the Spiritual Cause'. Hence, at least partly, his dying in debt. Nor was he ever a one-person-show: rather, he had perhaps the exhilaration – but perhaps increasingly the stress – of being the official head of a one-family-show. By the end, his two sons were heavily involved. And, from her marriage in 1860, his wife Annie would 'entirely' take charge of his 'bookselling business and library' while he had been away or on tour.[179] When, in the mid-1870s, during one of *Human Nature's* financial crises, the printers had refused to handle any more copy, Burns relates how, 'for many a Sunday', his 'family worked with me' – often for 36 hours at a stretch – to print this monthly themselves. 'Mrs. Burns being very mediumistic [she was already giving seances], set type under the influence of a printer in spirit life. We had so little type that we were often driven to the last letter. She would clairvoyantly see one that had got into the wrong box.'[180]

But if these decades of sacrifice of his own and others' comfort explain why spiritualist respectables might sometimes honour him verbally as an individual (and J. P. Hopps – as we have seen, a Unitarian minister – was to officiate at his funeral[181]), he remained, in their eyes, wrongheaded; and similarly, his bitter independence made him seem egocentric even to such a dogged brother as Morse.

True, not all better-off spiritualists were automatically or rigidly respectable (and, in the provinces, plebeians occasionally benefited from large donations). Nor, if we take spiritualist journalism, were all predominantly middle-class spiritualist periodicals exclusive towards plebeians and their heterodoxies. From the mid-1890s we have already met with W. T. Stead's *Borderland* – whose title, incidentally, Stead acknowledged to have been suggested by Morse.[182] Stead explicitly aimed to bridge some of the gaps between élite and non-élite interest in the occult, and said so at his customarily elegant length. But the point about his surprise at Kitson's oration – already noted – is clearly that he had underestimated just how much of a chasm there was. It was one thing for an individual Christian spiritualist – whether Unitarian as Hopps, or an Anglican clergyman such as ('M.A. Oxon') W. Stainton Moses, or Congregationalists such as Stead himself – to tone down or circumvent the abrasiveness of many in their respective denomination towards spiritualism. It was quite another, though, to sit through plebeian declarations of war against whatever was seen as Christianity. Against these, one needed at least to define one's beliefs, if not to measure blow with blow.

The size of the gap had also been indicated, some fifteen years earlier by another – otherwise, so far as one can tell, actually more successful – attempt to bridge it. This was a monthly called *Spiritual Notes*. It, too, was London-based. It tried hard both to be doctrinally open and to foster relations with Northern and other provincial spiritualists.[183] It allowed space to at least two plebeian spiritualists of established and growing reputation (Morse and E. W. Wallis, respectively) to spread their journalistic wings. Their forthcoming meetings were listed also and Morse, at least, was designated as holding the paper's 'agency for the Midland districts'.[184] The paper also regretted that the only would-be 'national' organisation of spiritualists, the British National Association of Spiritualists, was not only 'chiefly metropolitan' but also 'very "respectable"'. *Spiritual Notes* seem to have been associated, further, with an abortive attempt to start a spiritualist weekly which was to be impartial between different versions of spiritualism and, obviously, independent of Burns. The 26 signatories of the prospectus for its limited liability company include, on the one hand, some of the spiritualist Reverends mentioned above, plus Maurice Davies, D.D., and Burns's American friend J. M. Peebles and, on the other, men who were, or who were shortly to become, more identifiable as backers of plebeian spiritualist ventures (such as H. A. Kersey, the pioneer of lyceums in Newcastle and elsewhere[185]). Had *Spiritual Notes* – let alone this weekly – survived, then the shape, or at least the journalistic map, of English spiritualism would have developed somewhat differently. To accomplish this, *Spiritual Notes* would have had to have transferred its main springboard from the middle class of the metropolis to the plebeians of the provinces. But such a leap was obviously too much to attempt, despite the alliance with such as Morse and Wallis. Instead, the journal became increasingly entangled in the faction-ridden disintegration of the B.N.A.S. At least partly for this reason, it lasted half as long as Stead's later journal, in other words a mere two years or so. The main significance of *Spiritual Notes*, in other words is that – despite all its effort, backing and intelligence – its task proved impossible.

However bewildered or outraged non-spiritualists might be by spiritualists, no external pressure could fuse the latter together – even into a loose journalistic alliance. Into the early twentieth century, there remained too much to divide them.

C Method

From about the same period, though, they began to converge. One factor tending to bring them together was their shared method. Spiritualism – to revert to basics – was centered around alleged communication between the physically living and dead. Non-spiritualists viewed both the communication and the presence of one of its partners (the dead) as either non-existent or taboo. And as the 'spirits' involved were often those of one's nearest and dearest, the whole question groaned with emotion as well as with conceptual anxiety. For this and other reasons, the communication was extremely personal, and was impossible to replicate. Mediumship – the ability to facilitate it – was unpredictable in many senses. Its possession was hard to generalise about, though some recent research has argued some correlation between it – or at least 'spirit possession' – and membership of marginalised categories,[186] such as, in most societies (including that of England during my period) women. Its development was no less tricky; and often it seemed to wilt all too embarrassingly under strain. Thus, and above all, impersonal checks on its accuracy were hard to agree on: arguably, over-elaborate ones might increase the strain. Mediumship was a personal (or group) transaction. Believers might talk of 'tests' which they had set the medium and which the latter had 'passed' or 'successfully given'. But such talk could hardly be expected by itself to convince disbelievers,[187] though it may have sometimes. The best proof of the alleged pudding remained in the apparent eating.

Conceptually therefore, spiritualism was anarchic – or at least, as I have called it, atomistic – partly but very precisely because any other basis of proof was almost impossible to agree on. This atomism usually led to empiricism (in which, as we shall see in the next chapter, it correlated during our period with a democratic 'epistemology', or definition of knowledge). But it could also – not always incompatibly – lead to what we might call do-it-yourself universe-building (with materials pre-mixed to a varying extent). For this activity, the main preconditions were self-confidence, a certain level of obsessiveness, and perhaps a broad literacy[188]: we may recall J. G. H. Brown here. The main product was more or less new cosmologies which added to the general intellectual chaos, thereby helping to reinforce both empiricism and universe-building. From its side too, empiricism might also, of course, be no less of a reinforcement both of itself and of universe-building.

We have seen that Morse's sneers at the S.P.R. were tinged with anti-elitism. And this was typical of many other plebeian spiritualists' stance towards this Society. From a plebeian vantage-point, non-plebeian spiritualists succumbed all too easily to respectability – usually religious and sometimes, as here, intellectual. But the point is that these weaker, allegedly because haughtier, brothers and sisters were still sisters and brothers. Tidings of success or exposure amongst them elated or (as we saw with Burns) depressed the plebeians, however much the latter might view their own reactions as the stolider. In other words, spiritualists both respectable and plebeian shared in spiritualism certain attitudes about method. Morse's anti-respectable sneers embodied a social explanation of what he saw as methodologically wrong in the S.P.R. approach; and he could sneer – even though his hearers on this occasion were perhaps wholly respectable – precisely because he could know they were with him on method.

All spiritualists believed themselves to be based on 'facts' –

'phenomena' as we have seen them calling them. These were inherently the most successful, though not necessarily the most logical, argument for spiritualism.[189] Appeals via any particular superstructure of belief were – particularly for plebeians – secondary. Indeed they were optional and, for most, undesirable. This, as we have just seen, helped many plebeians to feel superior to respectables, whom they saw as limping after religious orthodoxies or else after pseudo-oriental cults such as Blavatsky's Theosophy. True, late-nineteenth-century plebeians might have felt humbler here, had they been mindful of, say, J. G. H. Brown's crystal! But, as just argued, their very emphasis on 'phenomena' helped avoid such old pitfalls. In a sense, everything was based, ultimately, on trust: trust in one's own 'experience' or in that of others whom one trusted. Whether a 'spirit' claimed to know details of one's life or even to have been formerly acquainted, one could 'test' it. If such tests were personally convincing, they were 'satisfactory'. By extension, once one had accepted the mediumistic process and a particular medium or mediums as satisfactory, then one could widen the range of one's 'spiritual' acquaintances and questions. Trust, in spiritualism, was based on 'facts'; but these, we might say, were based on trust. They were thus intuitive in the sense (amongst others) that they were, directly or indirectly, very personal. A 'fact'-based empiricism, intuition and 'common sense' consensus: all these were associated.

And these were the weapons with which spiritualists faced some perplexing questions and inconsistencies in both their two worlds. These were problems not merely *in* spiritualism but *for* it. Centrally, there was a need to explain why some mediums misbehaved or were seen, instantly or subsequently, to be lying or engaging in trickery. There were, as we noted, two competing answers here. One of these was that of Christian spiritualists: all spirits which appeared to contradict one's own theology were evil. Unfortunately for Christian spiritualists, prominent non-spiritualist Christians could often be heard saying similarly about even the most orthodox 'spirit', or even about phenomena in general. All – as Kitson ruefully quoted one Bishop[190] – emanated from the 'Powers of Evil'. Christian spiritualists found themselves on a narrow ledge between, on the one hand, non- or anti-Christian spiritualists and, on the other, Christian anti-spiritualists. The frequent touchiness between the two spiritualist tendencies is thus understandable. The alternative answer open to spiritualists was, of course, the 'progressionist' one embraced by the non-Christians: all spirits evolved from various levels and at various speeds. Some still enjoyed lying or playing tricks. More confusing still, the wittier of them often began by being demonstrably honest and serious.[191] Spiritualists tried to put a brave face on this: occasionally, they hoped that, while still in the flesh, they might even be able to help such spirits. And failing this, lying spirits retained, arguably, a more useful potential than they intended: their utterances, being lies, could at least afford glimpses of what at any rate their own, less evolved, regions of the next world were *not* like.[192] But why should such spirits not pepper their lies with truths? And anyway the problem then returned of how to sort reliably evolved spirits from the rest. And here an irrelevant if often plausible response was to blame the medium. What Morse (for example) called 'tricksy' ones were honest in their normal state but became dishonest when in a mediumistic one.[193]

Or possibly this response was not so irrelevant. As the medium Susan Gay put the argument, one aspect of spiritualism 'as a science' was that it hoped to be able to specify 'not only . . . the best conditions on our side, but all that affects our invisible friend on the other. The tone of our minds affects the spiritual atmosphere. . . . Our mental atmosphere is undoubtedly sufficiently tangible to spirits to attract or repel them.'[194] Thus, one might argue from her Newtonian metaphors, mercenary mediums or even cynical sitters attracted those spirits with whom they harmonised most or, in plain language, whom they deserved. At any rate, she was using for the cornerstone of her 'science' a very common excuse for failures in 'phenomena'. And she was anything but alone in this procedure. The *Medium and Daybreak* fervently applauded one reader's appeal for particularly careful recording of the conditions in those seances where unreliable phenomena had occurred: surely some useful common denominator would emerge?[195] In, they believed, intrepidly facing their problems, spiritualists liked to contrast themselves with something their opponents smeared them with: in Miss Gay's words, 'Conjuring never fail[ed]', whereas by contrast 'Christ himself could do "no mighty works" in Nazareth "because of their unbelief".'[196]

But to compare one's phenomena to those of Jesus (without a big H for Himself, or with) was to step into even larger problems.

Particularly if one claimed to have gone beyond areas where, as
the Rev. S. Moses put it, 'literal demonstration and analysis [were]
. . . becoming impossible' and to be advancing into 'the subtler
truths of spirit', one would find that 'the higher conceptions . . .
even elude[d] the hard limits of human language'.[197] In spiritualism,
perhaps not only the 'higher conceptions' and 'subtler truths'
escaped ordinary language: there was, rather, a lack of shared
language between believers and disbelievers.[198] As Burns wrote
during 1867, phenomena alone would – 'without collateral
agencies' (such as, for him, phrenology, mesmerism, 'anthropology' and other 'sciences of human nature' as he usually called
them) – be 'entirely unable to explain themselves'.[199] Otherwise,
as he warned a conventionful of spiritualists during the same year,
they themselves would become so 'crammed with the "ipse dixit"
of spirits' as to sink spiritualism 'into a degrading superstition'.[200]

This line had obviously never been enough for anti-spiritualists.
For all spiritualists, the opposing approach crystallised in the
S.P.R. during its early years in the 1880s. This, too, involved
claims to open-mindedness, to 'tests' and thus to 'science'. Only
the meaning of these words turned out – in the hands of most
S.P.R.-members – to be very different from what spiritualists
had expected. For spiritualists, their phenomena were tested and
attested facts, science was based on facts, therefore spiritualism
was scientific. But in contexts such as the S.P.R.'s, their facts were
(as Perry Williams has expressed it) 'dissected with an analytic
knife'. Most woundingly, 'the method of residues' was used; this
'classified cases [according to] the extent to which they could be
explained [via] existing knowledge instead of [via] what common
sense proclaimed them to be.' This of course involved treating 'the
details . . . in isolation without regard for their collective strength
and power of conviction'[201]; and so did the S.P.R.'s 'separation of
mental and physical phenomena, and [insistence] on . . . impersonal evidence'.[202] No wonder one middle-class spiritualist accused
such a researcher (as Williams gloriously quotes) of 'degenerat[ing]
into a hard, pitiless, self-glorifying intellectual sportsman, bent on
running his victim to earth, and then decorating himself with the
trophies of slaughter'.[203]

There was not, of course, much new in the definitions held by
the S.P.R. or attributed to it. The founders of this Society – many
of whom fervently hoped for proof of life after death[204] – were

merely spending years confronting problems which Wakley (whom we met in Chapter 4) had 'run to earth' far more summarily some half-a-century earlier. True, he had done this in relation to mesmerism, not directly to spiritualism. However, not only can we see the latter, here, as a cousin of spiritualism, but we also have Wakley's own word that he was concentrating on it merely because it happened to be the most fashionable current challenge to medical orthodoxy.[205] We have already seen that his fear of mesmerism had an imponderable aspect (i.e. that it would dissolve all barriers, etc.) and also that he was concerned to define, simultaneously, the medical profession and its area of competence. The second of these concerns is obviously part of the background to his war on non-professionals and their supporters, irrespective of social class.[206] But Wakley was not only upholding professional hierarchy as against social; he was also seeking to clothe orthodox medicine in the highest methodological pedigree.

Thus, one of his longest anti-mesmerist polemics was considerably taken up with worship of William Harvey, the seventeenth-century discoverer of the circulation of the blood. Wakley's act of worship included much wordy weeping at this ancestor's grave. And the grandeur of Harvey, for Wakley, lay not so much in what he had discovered as in the method he could be seen as having used: that of Francis Bacon, whom Wakley in a conventional way, saw as in his turn the founder of modern science as such. 'BACON described the method' – the 'inductive' – 'HARVEY executed the first great problem'.[207] Part of the inductive method (and Wakley had long trumpeted this) was what we might call suspicion and replicability: 'Dr. E. G. Jones, of Southampton, thinks it possible that in the recent experiments on the O'Keys' – where Wakley had, to his loud satisfaction, utterly unmasked them and therefore mesmerism as a whole –

'our judgement was biassed by a previous disbelief.' . . . We can only reply that a believer in mesmerism is evidently not the proper person to test its truth, and that it was our *duty* to employ such tests only as would be used by those who considered [mesmerism] to be wholly an imposition [i.e. fraud]. If the patients could not stand one kind of test they could not have stood another.[208]

Two years later he suggested with rougher inductiveness that Elli-otson should prove the existence of mesmeric force by putting some of his 'young women' into a railway carriage to see if they could make it move along the rails.[209] (Ironically, in his defence of replicability, Wakley was more of a genius as a polemicist than as a methodologist[210]: his *Lancet* was apparently happy to print one reader's claim that mesmeric patients exhibited all the *phrenological* symptoms of low cunning[211].)

As Wakley would no doubt have agreed, methodological allegiance was no automatic effect of broad social class alone. There is no necessary contradiction in middle- or upper-class people, as spiritualists, holding to an epistemology (or definition of knowl-edge) which I am about to define as democratic. But their very respectability helped make them into weaker sisters and brothers in their allegiance to this. And yet, had there not been this overlap in method, plebeian and respectable spiritualisms could not, by the end of my period, have so quietly begun – as we shall see during the conclusion – to converge.

Chapter 6 *Presence and problems of democratic epistemology*

A Introduction

The previous chapters have suggested, if nothing else, that plebeian spiritualism lay at an intersection between many currents of varying depth and compatibility. We will now see that it was one among a number of pursuits within overlapping plebeian milieux and that these pursuits usually correlated with a democratic epistemology – i.e. a definition of knowledge as open to anybody. I will also argue that democratic epistemology of almost any kind contributed to its own very broad defeat during, particularly, the century around 1900. Assuming that democratic epistemologies and democracy are, in the final analysis at least, vital to each other and that democratic epistemologies were, for varying reasons, decaying outside Britain too, then part of the irony of the twentieth century is that the same decades saw the winning (against whatever opposition) of formal democratic rights and often a flourishing of democratic ideologies on a scale utterly unprecedented in world history.

The last paragraph may appear odd on any number of levels. First, what could be less democratic than a phrase like 'democratic epistemology'? Is not a Greek root – to any Anglo-Saxon reader with her feet planted firmly (or stickily) in empirical ground – 'Greek' merely? Would she not be less scandalised by my phrase 'definition of knowledge', or by 'perception' or 'version' of it? My preference for the Greek is not because it gives us the longest-worded affliction that anyone, in their benighted ignorance, *never* imagined themselves to be suffering from, but simply because it is a single word, and can therefore modify to give 'epistemological' and – let us hope for the future – 'epistemologist'.

Second, to introduce so broad a discussion at so late a stage in a book may seem like not only changing our destination for Dublin but also – as the pseudo-Irish joke invites us to say – setting out from the wrong place. However, all we have really done so far is define our vehicle. We needed, surely, to concentrate on that; but here is where – perhaps our main or at least our broadest – argument really starts. Spiritualism did, as we shall see during this chapter, relate to what was surely the main democratic epistemology of the nineteenth century. By chance or not, spiritualism caricatured certain of the vices of this epistemology and was surely an indirect contributor to its undermining. However different any turn-of-the-twenty-first-century successor would have to be, there remain important (if negative) lessons for us in the matters discussed in this book.

The present section therefore attempts some further historical and analytical defining. As we have just seen in the previous chapter, spiritualism did lay claim to some (often disruptive) kinds of knowledge. Further, as we saw in earlier chapters, it involved something more flexible (if, in the end, perhaps no less repetitive) than already existing modes – such as millenarianism, whether Owen's or Brown's – of situating the mundane world in relation to one's personal experience of a supramundane one. And, as we are about to see during the present chapter, the decades around the mid-nineteenth century seem (at least from our sources) to have resounded with claims to the superiority of, in effect, democratic epistemology. Most relevant here, these claims frequently came from plebeian medical and other practitioners who related regularly to plebeian spiritualists (as well as overlapping with them sometimes).

In method, a democratic definition of knowledge – one, as we remember, in which knowledge should be accessible – tends, as we saw during the last chapter, very often towards empiricism. (In this connection, as we saw, spiritualism was typical in claiming to be founded on its 'facts' and 'tests'.) But there is nothing inevitable or universal about this tendency, however strong it often is: as we also saw, epistemology is distinct from method. Again, to define knowledge as open to anyone, does not logically mean going to an extreme and claiming that it is easy to understand. But in practice, it often does. Conversely, the dominance of elitist epistemologies during most of the twentieth century has depended on, among many things, two confusions: between frequent knottiness and eternal impenetrability for all but a few, and between complexity and unsummarisability.

Elitist epistemologies, in other words, derive further power from their confusion about their own naturalness and inevitability. Thereby they increase the difficulty of distinguishing when they are just not noticeably democratic from when they involve brazenly elitist assumptions. 'Democratic' (as we will see) is easy to exemplify from even the recent past, and 'elitist' is easy to formulate abstractly; but between these poles any typology is – like many another one with political dimensions – a matter of slipperily empirical argument.

Socially, the call for openness has negative aspects as well as positive. Negatively, it encourages a belief that – to paraphrase so many mid-nineteenth century statements of this view – when knowledge is 'mystified' and shut up in academies, it either wilts or turns out never to have been knowledge anyway, or even to have been 'one huge deception' or conspiracy.[1] Democratic epistemology, in other words, encourages suspicion of established intellectuals and professions. Thus, in his medical context, Samuel Thomson (founder of a system of 'Medical Botany' popular in America and Britain into our period) issued six rich words of defiance: 'don't poison me with your grammar'.[2] This suspicion should not always be automatically labelled anti-intellectual, let alone as against all use of even one's own intellect (though it sometimes was one or both of these). This is because, positively, it may interact with the intellectual stirrings of people of low status. Not that such strivings invariably encourage such an epistemology; but during the nineteenth and earlier centuries the two very often strengthened each other.

Any epistemology will of course interact, vitally or deadeningly, with the broader social and intellectual situation. Instances of such interaction from outside my period are many. One, is the 'Comenian fusion of Baconianism and Hermetic natural philosophy' which so appealed to some artisans around 1650 – partly, no doubt, because of its democratic epistemology: its 'great emphasis on the social and democratic possibilities of the new science'.[3] Again, there was no necessity for all this to be empiricist, though it was in fact empiricist for its time. (Indeed, the empiricist credentials of Baconianism are now said to have had certain ambiguities; and the empirical ones of Hermeticism were undoubtedly weaker still.)

Nowadays, when an epistemology is democratic it is usually

seen as eccentric, and we are encouraged to examine its social context (as in this chapter). But when it is elitist, it is often so taken for granted that any discussion of its sociopolitical roots is in danger of being taken as eccentric too: the complexities of modern knowledge are often seen as so overwhelming as to make such discussion irrelevant, and their institutional form is often talked of as if engendered directly by the knowledge itself – whereas, surely, institutions and their technologies and knowledge reinforce each other variably. But perhaps only from, roughly, the late nineteenth century have elitist epistemologies seemed self-evident so widely: hence the present chapter. Given that one common denominator between spiritualism and a number of other pursuits was a democratic epistemology, we are at last starting for Dublin from an excellent place. That others, with recognised vehicles and starting-points, have failed to set out before us is their problem more than ours.

Nowadays, elitist epistemologies seem correct in secular and 'scientific' terms alone. Previously, by contrast, almost any clash of epistemologies was, on all sides, fought partly in religious terms if not as part of a religious struggle: between, for example, Catholic or Anglican 'apostolic succession' versus a Puritan, Dissenting or low-church 'priesthood of all believers'. Another example is the fearful reaction against one aspect of the popular intellectual currents that seem to have welled up around 1650: against the 'philosophy of rude mechanicals' as Hill calls it.[4] This reaction reinforced both the triumph of the more sedate 'mechanical philosophy' via the Royal Society and, subsequently, the early-eighteenth-century deification of this philosophy in its Newtonian version as part of the broad Anglican underpinning of the social order.[5] Both triumph and deification involved an explicitly social definition of knowledge, one that was elitist – whatever the effort of non-elite enthusiasts of Newton. In the nineteenth and early twentieth centuries, as we have seen, spiritualism developed considerably on a terrain riven by religious chasms. And as we shall note later in this section, many plebeian opponents of religion seem to have assumed that, with religion on the run, no fresh hierarchical epistemology could develop.

In the previous chapter, I implied that spiritualism's personal and anarchic qualities made it particularly compatible with a democratic epistemology, and that the latter was held in common by both plebeian and non-plebeian adherents (where, at least, the latter did not revert to hierarchy via pseudo-oriental cults such as Theosophy). I also argued that, politically, most plebeian spiritualists seem to have tended consistently towards the left. But there is no need to claim the same for their respectable counterparts (whatever the significance of, say, Frank Podmore: S.P.R.-member, founding Fabian and pioneer historian of both Owenism and, as we have noted, spiritualism). In other words, a democratic epistemology does not necessarily enforce a democratic politics (however defined): though the 'demos', the people, may all be equal before the spirits, the herbs or the magnetic fluid, some persons may well be viewed as more equal than others in any mundane context. Spiritualism was hardly the only pursuit to lend itself to different or conflicting political views. We have already seen one example in British mesmerism during the nineteenth century; another, would be mesmerism in France during the years before 1789.[6]

Relatedly, a democratic epistemology – like any other – can lend itself to loudly confused class-political programmes, as in the often self-dissolvingly gaseous gestures towards it around 1968. Grimmer examples are China's alleged Great Proletarian Cultural Revolution (other than its official aims, or some of these) around the same years or, in the Russia of Stalin and Krushchev, the support among 'peasant-scientists' and others for Lysenko's 'agrobiology' and, potentially, for rewritings of sciences outside biology too. In both examples, the spontaneity of the support is obscured by a dogfight between would-be elites, by careerism and massive political terror[7]; in both, too, an avowed democratisation of knowledge turned out to mean its devastation.

But when something is misused, it is not necessarily refuted: on their side, elitists have often been too eager to blame demagogy on democracy. If absolute politics short-circuits anything (including epistemology) absolutely, so also does lack of politics. And epistemology remains inescapably political. In the area of political assumptions, its influence during the last hundred or more years has been underestimated. And this underestimate is becoming ever more harmful. For, everyone labours under some epistemological assumptions – just as, however unawares, everyone usually speaks prose. These involve some mix of judgments partly introspective (about one's own abilities) and partly objective (about the world and the knowledge in it outside one's own tiny brain). At any time, any person who is distanced from any particular body of knowledge which s/he has so much as vaguely heard of, has a stance towards it, however unreflective: for example, as to how attainable it is and as to how much, apart from this, it amounts to a waste of her/his own time, and perhaps of anybody else's too. Again, a person may claim, optimistically, that s/he already possesses it or some richer equivalent, or could, at least, have access to as much of it as necessary for some purpose. Many of the contrasts I would draw between my period on the one hand and our time on the other involve a decline – along dimensions such as those mentioned in the last sentence – of optimism, i.e. of individual or collective self-confidence. No doubt, my enumeration is pedantically solemnising the obvious.

But when the obvious is both important and unsaid, then the time may come for saying it in, let us hope, an historically informed way. Let the nineteenth-century democratic epistemologies discussed in this book be ever so foggy – and let the twentieth-century ones just instanced be ever so confused too (and far worse) – they do not in the slightest lessen the need, now, for democratic epistemologies. These are needed against both elitism and their own ally (or double?) which we can label Lysenkoism. At the moment – as into the generations around 1900 – elitist assumptions are the immediate problem (and by now perhaps not only in the West). They are no less oppressive – including of potential talent – for being (wrongly) seen as in the nature of modern things. (They can also be no less dangerous: we may imagine many a victim of almost any nineteenth-century version of medicine – particularly perhaps the orthodox – gurgling in agreement with, say, the children of radiation victims). Permutations and combinations of epistemological position are as much part of the background to our lives as the air we try to breathe; but the currently dominant ones have, at least till recently, been less disputed than some of their predecessors. Yet to this day they are constantly re-negotiated.

Let us take the arena of education. This is assumed – despite recent renewals in the adult sector – to occur during our first fifteen or twenty years. This assumption would have amazed and, even more, have dismayed those nineteenth-century plebeians who were autodidacts (persons who were making their education their own affair, irrespective of social superiors.) But the more stress we lay on our early years, the more we make them even more the epistemologically most active phase in our lives: a situation which renders all the more deadening the routine misapplication of – perhaps anyway questionable – theories such as Piaget's about child-logic (as a gradation of age-stages which a child cannot outpace, even when she clearly seems to have): Gradgrind inverted. Nowadays, we can watch many a child of identifiably active intellect 'negotiate' epistemologically with a vengance. More accurately, such children also undergo negotiation: are often licked into shape, or worn down and baffled, by much of the interaction of home, gender, class, ethnicity, media, teachers and contemporaries. (There's no need to discuss here how many children remain unidentified, but one factor keeping them so is perhaps their perception of the fate of many of those identified.) We can take anything from a minute to a professional lifetime to enumerate the results of such interaction (e.g. 'hidden curricula'); the point is that they usually discourage an active approach to knowledge, sometimes for the remainder of a person's life. And the only aspect of such bafflement I wish to mention here is the one most seldom mentioned, perhaps because seemingly inevitable. It is this: a lack of confidence that your knowledge is relevant to more than your private vanity and perhaps to a feeling of clutteredness in part of your brain. (What do you give to children who can sense they are heading for the scrapheap? – Let them eat *Spacewars* or *The World about Us*.) Put positively, what is lacking is a confidence that knowledge, once gained, may enable you to do, discover or help decide something important. However seldom nineteenth-century plebeian autodidacts were potentially in such a position (and, as we shall see soon, some were actually), we shall hardly find them believing invincibly in their own stupidity or rather – if it is 'rather' – in their own pointlessness or lack of qualification. Not them: on this score, they – or at any rate those who fill our sources – were decidedly optimistic.

One reason for their optimism may, with some, have been that – however great the social and political barriers against acquiring many types of knowledge – the situation was sometimes more open than today. We have only to think of very famous examples such as Faraday (1791–1867) – former starveling and bookbinder's apprentice – whose interest in science was nurtured in evening classes and whose career as a scientist was launched when, mostly through a chapter of accidents, he became personal assistant to Sir Humphrey Davy.[8] Examples remained available into the late nineteenth century of individual plebeian scientists being legitimated, locally or naturally, by their so-called superiors. (Also, in the powerful area of medicine, plebeian methods were often less lethal than those of many an established professional, as we shall see later.)

And there even continued to be one or two plebeians who became recognised leaders in a field. Most famously, though A. R. Wallace (whom we met – in this book at least – during Chapter 5A) was of impoverished gentle family, he had something of a craftsmanly formation, during which he became a life-long Owenite (he died in 1913). Had his fellow-FRSs borne this in mind, they might have been less puzzled by his left-wing politics, his anti-vaccinationism and his plebeian-type spiritualism. A recent historian has plausibly treated him as an import into the later nineteenth century from the 1840s,[9] and we might also see him as an import into prestigious scientific circles from the world of self-taught scientists. His particular route to eminence involved much specimen-hunting but no diploma-hunting, much jungle-fever but no exam-fever.

Further, for every Wallace there were many self-taught plebeian enthusiasts whom the established 'great' scientists (the Huxleys or Tyndalls – not least to the extent that their own epistemology was democratic) took seriously as local informants or even as fellow-scientists. (Of course, something that affected this was how a particular specialism managed to structure itself and its field.) Two examples would be Robert Dick (1811–1866), the walking and starving baker and geologist of Thurso in the north of Scotland and his fellow-Scot, Thomas Edwards, a poor shoemaker-naturalist who became an Associate of the Linnaean Society.[10]

Most numerous of all were a third category: those who might plausibly hope to become Robert Dicks in some field or other. At the local level, many such people might already enjoy some such reputation. The late E. Ledger of Lofthouse was said by a Christian writing to the atheist *National Reformer*[11] to be mourned by 'men of science from Leeds, Wakefield, Bradford and other towns'. A colliery storekeeper, he

was entirely a self-taught man. He possessed a more than

ordinary knowledge of the sciences, and was up in the general literature of the day. He had amassed a considerable number of books, mostly of a scientific nature, and his snug little sitting room had somewhat the appearance of a small museum of science and art [i.e. technology], being literally crammed.

Another writer, besides praising Ledger's 'sturdy adherence to Rationalism in all relations of life', reported that he had built 'electrical machines, Galvanic batteries, electrometers, thermometers, barometers and other apparatus'. He had also constructed a very good lathe and, at the time of his death, was assembling a microscope.

Quite possibly, there had also been E. Ledgers during the eighteenth century or even earlier. True, there were to be during ours too. But the point is that today an active approach is likelier to seem quixotic and that, though more or less self-taught plebeians are, mercifully, still with us, a plebeian autodidact culture is not; see Conclusion.

True, most of the socio-economic barriers which plebeians faced (from income, social milieu or flexibility of time, to accent, speech behaviour or body language) were appreciably higher than today. But what we might call the qualificational ones (the 'relevant' – as opposed to the symbolic, such as genteel acquaintance with Latin) were sometimes less rigid. Significantly, as we shall see in this chapter, they had started to become more so by, at any rate, the early nineteenth century. But to the extent that people still based their individual hopes on the Wallaces, Dicks or Ledgers, optimism would have been easier than today.

Here then, if I am remotely correct, is an undervalued aspect of our current situation. It can be approached very usefully, as in this book, via the conceptual culture of nineteenth- and early-twentieth-century plebeian autodidacts. Our approach is made by means, not merely of contrasts between 'then' and 'now', but also of an argument that the epistemological confusions which were normal within their culture had some small part in the genesis of those normal today. And for the study of the earlier confusions (which, in a small way, they reinforced), many nineteenth-century plebeian spiritualists provide caricaturally clear examples: hence directly this chapter and indirectly this book.

Let us, for one paragraph, make a 'then-versus-now' contrast between many plebeians' perceptions, in an epistemological context, of equality. When Burke labelled the mass of people a 'swinish multitude', his insult provoked generations of plebeians not merely to fury but also to laughter. During those generations, though, none would have imagined 'educational opportunity' to be remotely equal: the very phrase is presumably an anachronism. By contrast, since 1907 (to instance the date when the 'scholarship system' was officially inaugurated[12]), there have been claims that education either provides or will soon provide the equalising salve in an admittedly still unequal society. The more such claims are believed, the more the salve turns out to be salt, sprayed broadcast into very personal wounds: the more those educationally labelled as failures are encouraged to blame themselves (this quite apart from the impact, perhaps muffled or distorted, of educational theories). Even those 'failures' who remember that the level of an exam-hurdle varies locally and over time, can hardly help wishing that they, individually, had somehow jumped just that little bit higher. During at least the nineteenth century, by contrast, education was not simply, as today, something provided 'for' plebeians – though it increasingly was: by churches, charitable institutions and the state. It was also sometimes provided deliberately by them – directed both at children[13] and at adults. One thing that the upper and middle classes had long feared about the swinish multitude, in other words, was that swine are brainier than most farm animals (though, for all I know, Burke may have been referring to their, for him, lack of individuality or, Orwell-like, to their smell). What was feared was some plebeians' attempts to educate themselves independently: hence much middle-class support for rival institutions, such as Mechanics' Institutes. By plebeian strategists of reform, such education was often seen (as I have argued elsewhere[14]) as not merely aiding collective emancipation as well as individual, but often as the highroad to it.

Relatedly, we shall see shortly, the 'education' which many nineteenth-century plebeian autodidacts experienced would nowadays have been almost unrecognisable. For, as we shall soon discover via two very different men (S. T. Hall and David Richmond), it was often highly informal and thus overlapped very much with home and workplace as also with ideological involvements: the vicissitudes of plebeian life moved you into and out of more or less educative situations. Within the workplace (which sometimes was still the home also) it frequently involved a type of intellectual quickening which we can call the craftsmanly. This word happens to underline very conveniently the maleness of much of plebeian autodidact culture (something I could note, gesturally, via the autobiography of William Lovett[15]). This quality obviously circumscribed it, and may therefore in the long run have helped undermine it.

Of course, no one – then *or* now – would feel a thrill of recognition on being informed that they possess an epistemology. But we can see many nineteenth-century plebeian autodidacts as in thunderous revolt against hierarchical epistemologies. And they certainly recognised these, minus the word, as strengthening social hierarchy. Unfortunately, as we shall note four paragraphs from here, they seem to have believed science would not replace these with its own. Indirectly, they helped encourage most of their socialist successors from roughly the 1880s to the 1960s to assume an identity of interests – even, an identity – between socialism and 'science' or 'natural science'.[16] And this assumption has reverberated massively till now.

Plebeian spiritualism shared much or all of its epistemology with, on the one hand, non-plebeian spiritualists and, on the other, devotees – both plebeian and sometimes, as with Dr. J. J. Garth Wilkinson,[17] non-plebeian – of various pursuits, many of these partly or wholly in the area of medicine. This chapter and the next will centre frequently on this relationship. For the purposes of my argument, it is characterised by a non-event: that democratic epistemologists seldom theorised their epistemology, for they misread the trends optimistically.

To talk about a non-event is not necessarily to be anti-historical. This one is to be seen, most obviously, against a background of what we can retrospectively recognise as a steep rise in the esotericism of most sciences and of much of technology during the century or so around 1900. In the more immediate background, there also occurred a development which Wilkinson (in his Swedenborgian way) recognised as foreshadowing something like this broader rise: the raising of his own profession, the medical, to an eminence from which its legal powers (during the 1850s and for some decades after) exceeded its curative. I will expand on this clause during the next section. Wilkinson also came nearest to theorising in a democratic direction (though less democratic than some of his plebeian allies). But his theorising was anyway deeply idealist, thus increasingly quixotic.[18]

Perhaps, in other words, his solitariness and idealism symbolise how thoroughly those nineteenth-century democratic epistemologies we will examine were about to be outflanked by increasingly hierarchical sciences. For, as we shall see repeatedly, supporters of particular pursuits (spiritualist, herbalist, mesmeric and even, as I will explain during the next paragraph, secularist) continued concentrating on these — not surprisingly, given the hopes they entertained of them for recasting broad areas of knowledge — while using their own even wider claims for the democratic nature of knowledge as if these were mere propagandistic appendages.

Another exception, far larger than Wilkinson, was the 'infidel' or 'secularist' movement. It proves our rule far more broadly and at a more plebeian level than he (which means that it indirectly reinforced also the scientism of many succeeding generations of socialists). As its names suggest, it existed to fight what had, since time immemorial, indeed been the main direct source of intellectual hierarchy, that of priesthood. But by welcoming established scientists as allies in the 'conflict between religion and science'[19] the secularists helped, as we can now see, to sanctify a fresh intellectual hierarchy of an unprecedentedly secular kind. In the longest term, we can see this scientism (as we may call it) as independent plebeians' most fateful own-goal; yet it could hardly be more understandable in the light, not only of the immense age and (by the nineteenth century) clamour of this warfare, but also of many secularists' own experience or memories of being victimised — whether during their childhood or their teens or as adults or parents — for their religious questionings. Holyoake might smugly entitle his account of his own 1840's sufferings *The Last Trial for Atheism in England*; but he was repeatedly refuted before his death in 1905. And as late as 1922 another veteran, J. W. Gott — recently labelled by a police inspector 'a Socialist and Atheist of the worst type' — found the Lord Chief Justice and the Home Secretary overriding a jury's plea for clemency and confirming a sentence of nine months' hard labour for committing 'a most dangerous class of crime': blasphemy in Stratford Broadway, East London.[20]

True, very few of the plebeian participants in nineteenth-century pursuits other than secularism seem to have seen a need to think their democratic claims through. Again, a further impediment

J. W. Gott
'A Socialist and Atheist of the worst type', though many plebeian spiritualists found him sympathetic. Some socialists loathed his uproarious hammerings of humbug – particularly religious or ethical – or saw them as tactically disastrous. As a wholesaler, he employed many penniless or victimised comrades as his agents. He was thus a friend to many spiritualists (although not a Spiritualist himself).

would have been that, unlike any plebeian secularist and many an established scientist too, their stances on the primacy of Reason were various and sometimes vague. But persecution of rationalists in the name of Christianity along (as we saw during the previous chapter) with occasional persecution by rationalists of spiritualists as traitors to Reason – all this suffering was anything but an encouragement to anyone on any side to view scientism and irrationalism (each under whatever names) as twin dangers to be avoided equally. And some thinking-through would have been one of many absolute preconditions for any democratisation of the social structure of knowledge during our own century. In other words the way in which interests such as spiritualism were pursued by independently-minded plebeians helped make democratic epistemology ever more of a 'shattered alternative'[21] (so shattered, indeed, that today's Foucaultian perspectives of 'knowledge-power' are applied in ways that exclude the dimensions we are exploring here: a classic attempt to float above the socio-economic atmosphere).

To sum up so far. We began by noting how democratic epistemology does not necessarily involve an empiricist method but often tends to. Likewise, it does not necessarily go with an appeal to democratic politics but in fact often (as we saw in Chapter 5) does. We can, to remain summary for one more sentence label most nineteenth-century plebeian autodidacts as empiricist (though some, consistently or not, also liked to build their own cosmologies) and as democratic in their politics. Being mostly empiricists, many seem to have believed themselves to be continuing the work of scientific heroes such as Isaac Newton, but in other spheres (though, as we have seen in Newton's case, not altogether so 'other' as they could have known).

But of course, intellectual independence can be unstable, and some of those seeking to exercise it go questing off in unpredictable directions. One of many examples would be William Martin – 'Natural Philosopher, and Poet' or, later, 'Philosophical conqueror of all nations' of Wallsend-on-Tyne – a fundamentalist rhymester who offered a (so far as I can make out) abstract 'perpetual motion' or 'God and his spirit, the air' as the cause of all things. His three bugbears were Newton ('a knave and a deceiver' because, so he believed, irreligious), Owenites (whom he saw as the latter's disciples, because avowedly irreligious) and – established medical doctors ('a set of fops that take more delight in playing themselves with their gold watches and chains with fine rings on their fingers', than in curing). However resoundingly plebeian and democratic, he contrasts neatly with most of the plebeian autodidacts to be met with in at least this book, by being Anglican (though not Tory) in his politics. True, his Anglicanism had a populist tinge – he wanted anyone excluded from Parliament who was not 'in favour of God's poor people'. But he also intended all non-Christians to be excluded along with them; and he ended one of his longer pamphlets – entitled *The Christian Philosopher* – with the words 'God Save the King'. We may agree with J. F. C. Harrison that Martin was 'harmlessly mad', but however untypical his madness may have been of even any lunatics among plebeian autodidacts, he still, however inconsistently, combined certain of their beliefs with others they would have opposed – which is the point in mentioning him here.[22]

Of course – as we saw also with Brown – fundamentalism was not necessarily incompatible, either, with political radicalism: we have only to remember, once again, most millenarians (with obvious exceptions such as Southcott). Indeed, the inclusion of many Methodist ministers among the supporters of one of these pursuits, medical botany,[23] can serve to remind us that some of these were not necessarily incompatible with religious tradition-alism in the least. Wesley himself had famously pamphleteered for 'Primitive Physick', much of it herbal.[24] And this may have been one immediate reason why Holyoake, whom we have already noted attacking spiritualism, is said to have denounced medical botany too.[25] Conceivably another factor was precisely that he saw it as hostile to science. But for him as a secularist, ministers of religion were by definition hostile in this way. And one can hardly imagine that at least some secularists were not supporters of medical botany. A heresy in one field did often attract people who were already heretics (or becoming so) in another, particularly when such heresies emphasised – many a Methodist minister to the contrary – relying on one's own judgment in matters medical, intellectual or spiritual: in other words, were epistemologically parallel in an activist way. And medical botany will be our next area: it is an excellent one in which to sample the grandeur or poverty within democratic epistemology during our period. For impoverished it increasingly was – at least in relation to the situation. And maybe one aspect of this relative impoverishment was democratic epistemologists' tendency (an understandable one, given how embattled they were) to assume commitment or at least internal consensus.[26] For today, this aspect is troubling: those attempting to enforce some kinds of commitment find democratic epistemology a useful megaphone through which to shout at their opponents – though, for such as the Lysenkoites, a Stalinist state can surely come in even more useful. Many of our nineteenth-century democratic epistemologists were concerned mainly with medicine. Here, partly because patients are by definition suffering and anxious, rival commitments can spring up with pathetic ease. Perhaps this was one reason why plebeian activists of heterodox medicine so seldom theorised any aspects of what we would call their epistemology beyond the level of anti-elitist cliché: for nearly all of them, epistemology was strategically subsidiary to their medical truth, and truth would soon transform everything.

B   Incoherences of nineteenth-century democratic epistemologies: medical botany, S. T. Hall and others

By definition, this section is about medicine. If, as we have seen, the decades around 1860 saw the birth of plebeian spiritualism, they also saw unusually clear expressions of epistemological divergence. The central reason for this is that they saw *medical* discussion at its most polarised and, not least, class-polarised. I would be tempted to call this polarisation one of 'lay' versus securely 'professional', did that distinction not beg the central issue within these very discussions. Within them also, we can glimpse apparent possibilities – however distant then and seemingly remote now – of alternative social relations of knowledge. All this is not to forget the probability that medical 'life', for most Victorians, was dominated by polyclinicity (i.e. patients having doctors from different versions of medicine) to the limit of one's finances, and by more or less orthodox doctors who *might* be tolerant about both finance and medical doctrine.

At the cost of going over old ground, certain aspects of the mid-century context are worth summarising. In 1858, the medical profession (hardly more than a quarter century after covering itself in confusion over the 1832 cholera epidemic)[27] acquired the structure and powers which it has to this day. Indeed, from 1853, it enjoyed for some decades powers even greater than today, in relation to vaccination.[28] This at a time when bleeding, heroic dosing and even cruder tortures were still matters of sick-and death-bed experience, even for members of the House of Commons[29]; when antisepsis (under any name) was still mostly the music of the future; and when, partly as a result, the safety and advisability of vaccination were suspect even among the rank and file of orthodox medical practitioners such as – to take a provincial example – some of the self-selected members of the Bradford Medical Society during the 1870s.[30] To repeat, if ever the legal powers of orthodox medicine exceeded its curative, they did so around 1860.

Opponents of orthodoxy were encouraged – merely to take examples from mainly English-speaking lands – by the existence of at least one country, the USA, where 'free trade' in medical provision already existed and of another, Canada, where homoeopathy was raised to a status equal with allopathy's in the same period[31] when Britain, with the 1858 Act, was striding further towards monopoly. (And the Act was followed by attempts to strengthen and extend it). Descriptions of this opposition require that I define the word 'heterodox'. By heterodox I mean all those versions of medicine not favoured by those leaders of the profession recognised by most of the social and political establishment – those same leaders who now legally dominated the very self-definition of that profession as a whole. The best example of heterodoxy was the homoeopaths who, during this period, enjoyed a significant vogue among all classes (not least among the rich and titled), and who restricted their numbers to those who had legally qualified in the version of medicine which they themselves opposed as 'allopathic'.

The plebeians among the heterodox were fond of scorning such inconsistencies. At least one heterodox version of medicine – the botanic and its derivative schools – seems to have been overwhelmingly plebeian.[32] And one particularly important medical botanist, John Skelton, could make it his boast during the early 1850s that there was *not a single legally qualified member of the medical profession practicing . . . in England* as a medical botanist: all such practitioners 'belong[ed] to the working order, and their influence lies in their

numbers, poverty and faith'.[33] True, he had himself till recently
been 'a leader among the London Chartist shoemakers' – active as
a Chartist radical from the start – as well as an 'internationalist', an
'aggressive republican' and semi-socialist. But he was not merely
rhetorical in his identification of botanists with the working class.
One Kirkstall botanist told him that a meeting of supporters from
the West Riding was best fixed for the Christmas week – given
that, 'many of us only being working men', 'most of the villages
in this neighbourhood' had 'medico-botanic societies . . . too poor
to send delegates any distance'.[34] Other versions of medicine, such
(as we have seen) as the mesmeric, involved practitioners from all
classes, while hardly fusing them together.

Most or all these medical heterodoxies shared not only, often,
an epistemology but also certain medical assumptions. And these
assumptions may often, directly or not, have strengthened or been
strengthened by it. They included beliefs in what I will define as
the economy of nature and in returning to nature. They were also
holistic (i.e. they treated the patient and health or illth, the physical
and the psychological, as one single interactive entity). Perhaps
particularly important at this time, there was a particular concept
of disease. This concept may loosely be called contagionist (i.e. it
involved a belief that any kind of contact, direct or not, with a
sick person was enough to spread the sickness), and it often related
powerfully to assumptions which Chapter 4 defined as imponderable: the less traceable a substance, the more devastating or curative
its effect might be argued to be. 'It was a law of nature' proclaimed
one defender of mesmerism, hydropathy and homoeopathy (S. T.
Hall, whom we shall meet further in this chapter), 'that that which
was most subtle was also the most potent'.[35] Here J. J. Garth
Wilkinson provides a particularly good summary.[36] Another comes
from the semi-plebeian itinerant lecturer (and ultimately, like
Wilkinson, virtual spiritualist) John William Jackson, who lumped
'all' medical heterodoxy together as

> consist[ing] in a return to Nature. Homoeopathy reduces the
> drug dosage to vanishing point. Hydropathy, kinesipathy and
> mesmerism wholly ignore it. While all combine to reject the
> murderous lancet and the cruel blister. This is only saying, in
> other words, that the orthodox or established system is
> eminently analytical and disintegrative . . . It attacks the

disease through the patient, generally wounding the latter in the process of destroying the former. Strictly speaking, it is not a science of HEALTH. It is satisfied with combating *disease*; which under the most complex nomenclature, it seems to have exalted into a personal entity though [disease is] . . . simply a derangement of normal function.

However, Jackson went on to praise orthodoxy's refusal to become 'stupidly immutable': here he may have been aware of what I will argue was orthodoxy's greatest long-term advantage over its rivals – its cumulativeness[37]. All heterodoxies were in agreement with Jackson that allopathy was far too drastic in its remedies: it made no attempt to assist the suffering body and personality, but merely to bludgeon them physically. It was thus unnatural and therefore self-defeating. But what remedies did any of the heterodox propose?

Let us take our particularly plebeian heterodoxy. Medical botany[38] had long traditional antecedents but, as a self-conscious doctrine, it began around 1810 with the New Englander, Samuel Thomson, a poor, self-taught 'child of nature' (as his followers saw him) who, during his youth, had picked up his early botanic and medical knowledge from a local wise-woman and, directly or indirectly, from Red Indians. He had then tested this lore, to his satisfaction, on his own family[39]

In parentheses, we have, here already, at least six favourite botanic appeals: to allegedly immemorial tradition, to the natural person or noble savage, to locality, to experience, to learning by doing and to familial medication; further, within the latter, we still need to know far more about the balance of roles between female medicators and the plebeian father. Thomson's disciples saw him as the systematiser of a lore which had often been handed down in families[40] and was often female at least as much as male. And yet 'Thomsonians' and their mid-century successors seem, from the sources, to have been mainly men, whatever their revulsion at men functioning as midwives.[41]

As a system, medical botany was – as Pickstone has noted – 'like much popular medicine' 'essentially transatlantic'. This applies, though, only to its renewal or systematisation: its native British roots were considerable – as Skelton, for one, was aware (he was particularly emphatic on its long rootage in areas formerly remote from the metropolis, such as Yorkshire[42]). It 'arrived' in Britain during 1838 via the propaganda of two (we presume) unfairly named Americans, Dr Coffin and Mrs Pilling.[43] In Britain as in America, strict Thomsonianism was, by mid-century, eclipsed by the more flexible creed which came to call itself Eclecticism. 'As an Eclectic', wrote one who was also a mesmerist, 'I *choose*. In choosing, I try all things which are not manifestly opposed to reason.'[44] But Eclectics continued to revere Thomson as the greatest pioneer. The main difference was that Thomson had been against all medical education – indeed, one historian has blamed the American movement's decline (after 1839–42) on its spawning of colleges and professional structures which, allegedly, had the effect of separating it from its popular base[45] – while, in Britain at least, the Eclectics tried to be simultaneously (as we shall see) for a structure of training but against all exclusiveness, not least that of the Coffinites. This openness was self-reinforcing in numerous ways; many of Coffin's British disciples soon applied it against him and broke away. One of them was the avowed Eclectic, John Skelton. Eclecticism nonetheless continued many Thomsonian impulses – not least the emphasis on Nature and, for us even more important, on what we can call democratically mutual caring.

Before coming to the latter, some of the basics of botanic medical theory are relevant. One such is the emphasis on the body as a steam engine requiring the correct temperature and fuel. Pickstone relates this to artisan strivings for independence. He notes the overlaps, often considerable, between medical botany on the one hand and Nonconformity, temperance, steambathing and hydropathy on the other. Another such basic (if we pursue our hydraulic analogy) was an emphasis on the purity of the blood. This emphasis followed conceptually: it was not merely a reaction against orthodox medical practice. For a medical botanist, indeed, 'the blood is the life': everything depended on, not only its 'quantity' but also on what Skelton called its 'equalisation in circulation, and power to sustain itself when equalized'.[46]

The crucial importance of feeding to the blood the right ingredients brings us to the botanists' emphasis on what they sometimes themselves called the Economy of Nature.[47] This emphasised hierarchy in the natural sphere but equality in the human. The hierarchy, which had at all costs to be respected, was that which placed the vegetable kingdom between the mineral and animal kingdoms.

Medicines, therefore, which were derived from the mineral were too direct for the animal frame, and were thus poisonous. This principle, too, had its reactive aspect: against, here, the allopaths' resort to mercury and similar materials. But it was, again, more than a reaction: herbal and other vegetable remedies were seen as long predating the mineral perversion which most botanists viewed as only a few centuries old. Further, the Economy of Nature reinforced democracy among human beings. For, nature was an economy in the sense also of being balanced: every geographical area had certain local ailments *and* remedies. This had been known to our ancestors, and was still known among present day savages.[48] Thus, when botanists rhapsodised about the beauty of Nature, they were not merely following the literary fashion of the period. Rather, they themselves had also a Rousseauean strand – even where they mispelled the man's name.[49] This strand had a number of qualities. It was to some extent disintegrative for the movement: for example, however great the benefit of importing American books and ideas, it was limited by the need to find and research the local herbs. But in other ways it was not disintegrative: it might – or so one might believe – allow cumulative scientific advance. This was because botany was bound to be rootedly empiricist. 'Man', as Skelton sloganised, was *progressive in his nature*. When we say "progressive" we mean that he can only acquire knowledge through experience.'[50] The question whether this empiricism made plebeian medicine – and related pursuits – in fact as cumulative ('progressive') as Skelton believed, is one to which I will return: is my word 'sloganised' unjust to him? How self-defeatingly empiricist were those whom the orthodox had long scorned as 'mere empirics'?

At this stage, though, I wish merely to explore the democracy of this epistemology. Logically if not always in fact – and here is the rub – its core aspect was an alternative model of medication which I have called democratically mutual caring. In this, all humans were obliged to care for each other medically. Medicine, therefore, was a subject which 'all [should be] equally taught, and where the advantages and duties are mutual,'[51] in Skelton's words. Such mutuality might sometimes, admittedly, amount to no more than what would today be called meritocracy: education had to be 'applied to all men and women [no more than] according to their capacities'. But nonetheless, even this solution demanded the universalising of a medical education in which 'the minds best fitted by nature for becoming masters of the practice, may do so, for the general benefit of all'.[52] True again, the phrase 'best fitted' was almost a cliché of the mid Victorian period, and reminds us that, then as now, meritocracy excelled as a lubricant for journeys or amalgams between class consciousness and individual upward mobility. Again, though, democracy also involved both a way of doing medicine and a certain class consciousness. On the first, as Pickstone and others have pointed out, both Coffinite and other medical botanic societies were supposed to run their affairs by methods which we can recognise as incorporating the most democratic aspects of the labour-movement and plebeian-sectarian (most recently, popular-Methodist) tradition: office-holding was elective and often by rotation; each member reported at every meeting on cases, particularly on the uncertain ones, which he (or she?) had encountered. Admittedly – if this *is* an admission – one had to pass an exam before acquiring membership; but this exam was oral and in front of other members.[53] Medical botany was a democratic medicine also in the sense that, being done largely by spare-time amateurs, it was cheap: with its growth, there would, in the words of the chair-person at a tea party of Bradford Botanic Society, 'be less money to pay to the doctors . . . medical botany is good for the picket'.[54] Given that full democracy of medical knowledge could not be attained overnight, the medical relationship to be striven for was one in which the plebeian family retained, for an annual fee, a medical practitioner, whose main task should be, not to administer medicine, but to educate all members of the family in the laws of health.[55]

Meanwhile, plebeian supporters of any medical heterodoxy could agree with the hydropathic Dr T. L. Nichols that 'if doctors were paid by results, and in proportion to the health, and not to the sickness of their patients, there would not be one druggist [his and many others' term of abuse for orthodox medicator] where there is [sic] now a dozen'.[56] Altogether, lack of democracy in the relationship between professionals and outsiders was hard to separate from lack of democracy in that between doctor and patient; and from either direction, it encouraged the doctor to take risks with patients' lives and (often almost as speedily disastrous for plebeians) earning-power: an even more important sense in which they could see medical botany, along with other revolts

against medical orthodoxy's violence, as 'good for the pocket'.[57]
'Mankind have been too long in the habit of looking to doctors
for *orders* in regard to health. . . . This must be given up with the
three learned professions, and every man and woman become
qualified to think for themselves in all that concerns their present
and future welfare.'[58] Though these words came from the direction
of another presumably not very cheap 'hydropathic establishment'
– and though, to historians, they may smack of nostalgia for
what is now seen as the domination of eighteenth-century medical
relations by *moneyed* patients[59] – it was plebeians who, during the
mid-nineteenth century, would have had reason to feel the most
subjected to lethally disdainful styles of medical intervention.

And here, even 'style' in the literal sense was a powerful aspect.
Not only was many an allopathic doctor seen as having a bad
psychosomatic effect on his patients. He was sometimes seen as
deeply callous or even as actively malicious. And here we can
discern echoes even of vampire-beliefs. Thus one literarily-minded
York botanist, munching his lunch by a secluded stream during
an expedition in search of herbs (at home, even his 'barometer'
was 'a long straggling seaweed'), claimed to experience the sight
of the water in ways very different from those of the nature-poets
who were so familiar to him: he was, rather, overwhelmed by the
stream's 'cold, smooth, and placid face; methought it was a
surgeon of the old school that [sic] was looking upon me, cold
and smileless, having drawn almost the last drop of blood from
my veins, watching the struggles of expiring life.'[60] We should
never forget that the nickname 'leech' clung to allopaths into the
twentieth century, nor that no medical botanist yielded to any
homoeopath in accusing the medically orthodox of poisoning
anyone they could lay hands on. This poisoning might even be
seen as deliberate. In one imagined trial of that 'old woman [sic]
familiarly known as "Holy Allopathy" before Lord Chief Justice
Reason, in the Hall of Public Opinion', she – alongside her
'Accomplices' ('Dr Bolus, physician, and Mr Sawbones, surgeon')
– was arraigned for having 'knowingly and wilfully propagated a
system falsely called "Medical Science" by which, . . . more
human beings had been destroyed than by all . . . wars.'[61] This
particular writer believed the crime to have been going on for
'2,500 years'; Skelton (with his usual historiographical seriousness)
dated it to the irruption of Paracelsianism.[62] And he, at least, did

not necessarily see this poisoning as deliberate (and might, we can therefore imagine, feel uneasy at this writer's echoes – however rationalist – of trials for witchcraft). But this hardly made it less dire: he would have agreed with another botanic journalist that, if the human race had degenerated, allopathy was to blame. And the same journalist talked phallically of 'the fangs of that fell destroyer, the [medical] faculty'.[63] Not always consciously or directly, medical botanists did much to spread (and often, perhaps, to pioneer) the rhetorical association between vampirism and medical conspiracy, an association which as we will see was soon to become very powerful in the movement against vaccination (as, indirectly, in its sister-movement against the Contagious Diseases Acts). In this context, the *Eclectic Journal* was to agree with Skelton's tagging of vaccine as 'an untraceable poison' that would make 'our Anglo-Saxon race, . . . like the Sandwich Islanders, . . . generally diseased and deteriorated'.[64]

A plebeian class-consciousness was nourished whenever botanists glanced up the social pyramid towards their official opponents, whom they anyway viewed as mirror opposites of themselves. Thus, to revert to the economic aspect for a moment, officially established doctors were thought to have an interest in ill health: as Skelton alleged, 'a healthy population [was] a state of things above all else that the medical profession as it now stands must . . . guard against.'[65] The conclusion followed that professionalism in medicine amounted to a crime against humanity: 'To mystify, shut up in the schools, and make private property of that knowledge, which of all others ought to be universally taught, is a wrong the deepest and most injurious to society.'[66] This crime was inevitably a conspiracy: 'The so called science of medicine . . . [was] one huge deception . . . injurious to all.'[67]

Such injury went beyond the direct physical harm wrought during this period by so many allopathic medicines. It was, for botanists, inflicted even by respectable homoeopaths whose actual medicines were harmless. This was because the homoeopaths were seen as supporting the existing political and medical/social structure. They did not seem to have grasped the botanists' truth that 'exclusive teaching . . . [led] to general deficiency'.[68] Thus the homoeopaths' strategy was upside down: 'Had homoeopathy been good for much, . . . [it] would have gradually raised itself from the base. The foundation, like all great reforms, would have begun

with the people, and grown up with them.'[69] In fact even a 'great'
reform was too modest a phrase. 'What is the task which the
present age has to accomplish?', Skelton enquired. 'Nothing less
than to revolutionize the *present condition* of medical practice; not
reform it, for it cannot be reformed; but to take it down and
reconstruct it.'[70] In any case (as a botanist noted of a homoeopathic
deputation which had demanded government permission for
homoeopaths to practice on the troops at the Crimea), 'when
once the advocacy of reform gets into the hands of lords, dukes,
marquises, bankers etc., we calculate there is really very little
worth in it.' The unhappy homoeopaths were 'with but few exceptions [one of the more vocal of whom was Garth Wilkinson who
scorned the same deputation in similar terms[71]] . . . self-conceited,
highly genteel and legally qualified . . . there is *nothing vulgar* about
them.' By contrast (whatever analogies might and will be drawn
between homoeopaths and botanists in their medicine, in general
outlook and sometimes in politics), the botanists felt 'stronger in
[their] isolation' from respectable opinion, since they were the ones
'sustained by the principle of free thought and the masses'.[72] With
this populism went a confidence in ultimate success whose implicit
timelessness is reminiscent of the rhetoric of 'Moral Force' Chartism: botanists, according to the same writer, could rely on 'an
enlarged diffusion of knowledge, correct principles, and the public
will'. 'I desire', another botanist explained, 'a revolution in the
theory and practice of medicine . . . but a revolution wise, slow,
and sedate.'[73] Apparently, sedateness and democracy guaranteed
each other. Not surprisingly therefore, botanists were so hungry
for snobbish abuse from their opponents as sometimes to formulate
such abuse for them: 'These illiterate quacks – these uneducated,
vulgar, unscientific tailors, smiths, ploughmen, tinkers, weavers,
shoemakers, carpenters, and all the lot of hard-working miserable
plebeians called Medical Botanists', and so on.[74]

   Thus, although I have not myself found a profusion of sources
allowing insight into the actual class of medical botanists'
supporters, the movement's self-image was thoroughly plebeian –
as in the constant sneers against 'legally qualified, money made
and college-taught doctors'.[75] Often, it was directly working class,
as with one 'collier [of] some few years [back]', who was now
'a doctor, who could cure diseases whether he had studied in a
conventicle college, or the college of nature'.[76] To some extent,

even, medical botany was or became one of the many sectional or compartmentalised successor-movements to Chartism. And there were at least some direct overlaps between it and post-Chartist popular politics. One example is the trial during 1867 of Josiah Thomas, a teetotaller,[77] medical botanist and former assistant to Dr Coffin. Thomas had treated a young woman botanically and had then withdrawn from the case on discovering that she was in labour. The woman died after a subsequent visit by an orthodox surgeon who now formally accused Thomas of manslaughter. After hearing the prosecution evidence, the judge stopped the trial and acquitted the defendant, to applause from the public gallery. (The surgeon committed suicide soon after.) For us, this case's most important features are neither applause nor suicide but, firstly, that Thomas was defended – in this year of the second Reform Bill – by Ernest Jones (the greatest leader of late Chartism and, outside Parliament, of the campaign for political reform) and, secondly, that the chair-person at a meeting called to honour Thomas after the acquittal was Thomas's friend of more than twenty years, Joseph Cowen (lion of Newcastle and British republican radicalism) backed by his journalistic aide James Watson.[78]

So far I have been examining the epistemology of only one school of medicine. But the very fact that this school added or substituted the word 'Eclectic' in its name, underlines how chaotic the situation was. Anyone unwilling to accept the official medical fashion was, irrespective of their social origin, plunged into a cacophony of competition between, on the one hand, reductionisms and, on the other, attempted syntheses which themselves were at least in danger of adding to the cacophony. 'The art of healing became a passion with me,' one thoroughly autodidact handhealer remembered of his travails before he had produced his own synthesis: 'From one system of medicine I was led to look into another, and then another. I thus gained a certain amount of knowledge of Allopathy, Homoeopathy, and Hydropathy, to say nothing of Kinesco- and a host of other pathies. Without pretending to have gained a very exhaustive acquaintance with any of these systems, I nevertheless studied them sufficiently to be dissatisfied with the results they produced.'[79] As I said, this *pro*fusion existed round anyone starting out in pursuit of medical enlightenment. But the accompanying *con*fusion does not seem to have encouraged anyone to think-through their common epistemological position: as I have already argued, their optimism (about the significance of their particular pursuit or group of pursuits) would anyway hardly have confronted them with any need to think much through.

Thus when we read a later (1890s) spiritualist punning that 'spiritualism was democratic', in that it could be 'demonstrated to anyone',[80] we can at once make four comments. One is that all these pursuits claimed (as we saw with spiritualism) to be demonstrable to the unbiassed eye. A second, is that this confrontation of unadorned phenomenon – whether, say, herb, spirit, character-reading, telepathy, or cure – with naked eye (the sexism of my metaphor may somehow be appropriate) was expected to transform everything else. A third, is that this particular spiritualist's 'anyone' meant, for him as for most plebeians, the lowliest; but it also in fact included (as we have also seen) people of respectable class, too. And a fourth, is that (as again we have seen) people of the latter type tended to try and force a new belief or apparent discovery – however fundamental it might seem – into old professional and religious bottles. And this is one reason why this chapter, like most of this book, is overwhelmingly about plebeians. After all, the greater one's social respectability, the more one might risk losing when identified with heresy. One might lessen such risks in a number of ways: one might play down both the association with, in effect, a democratic epistemology – particularly with the latter's anti-hierarchical aspects – and the range of one's revolt (leaving most other medical disciplines in their place or even unruffled). Such risks anyway lessened themselves when the leaders of a particular heresy were identifiable (as those of homoeopathy and, at least during much of Elliotson's time, mesmerism) as themselves respectable.

True, fashionable support for homoeopathy and mesmerism only envenomed the orthodox further: Wakley, for one, was no lover of aristocracy in any context, and his *Lancet* warred year in, year out, against any weakening towards heterodoxy. And within the medical profession itself the level of bitterness could damage even the most prestigous (and usually orthodox) of would-be peacemakers. Thus when, in 1839, the medical editor, Sir John Forbes – himself no friend of mesmerism – had noted of what he dubbed the 'pseudo-sciences' that, 'though they have no truth *in* them they generally have some truth *under* them',[81] he was merely underlining the long-term perplexity among the franker medical practitioners of any social class at what we have called the problematic of imponderables. And yet (despite Forbes's being among the most revered medical writers of his day and a sometime physician to the Queen's household) his own august journal had, within a decade, to close because even so grudging an openness was shared by too few of his fellow-MDs.[82] Perhaps even more damaging than his willingness to give mesmerism something like a fair hearing, was his admission that allopathy was often more dangerous than homoeopathy, even where the latter was practised by unqualified people.[83] In other words, orthodox practitioners could be merciless to even the most occasional of internal dissenters as well as to external, and even the most august among the former had much to lose.

As we have seen, if there was one thing that even Elliotson could agree with Wakley upon, it was in loathing 'quacks' of the lowly kind (even if Wakley also saw Elliotson as one of the higher). To support medical botany publicly would have involved legally qualified medics in too many simultaneous sacrifices: in jettisoning too much of their training – and perhaps anyway of their intellectual and social self-respect. The distance between Herr Doktor Hahnemann (lowly-born though he had been) and say, plain Samuel Thomson – whose autobiography bristled with barbs against elite doctors as such – surely spoke for itself. (True, Garth Wilkinson more than once acknowledged, in writing, his debt to herbalists[84]; but the last accusation one could make against him would be of being necessarily typical in anything.) Worse, even had the individual healer or wonder-worker been granted some special place, the whole tribe of medical botanists would have been harder to accommodate: officially and brazenly, they claimed not to be exceptional or in any sense heroic healers but very ordinary persons who helped each other to cure in ways more (as we might say) supportive and collectivist than even the most regular and local meetings of legally qualified 'exclusives'. For such reasons, medical botany seems to have remained, even among those nineteenth-century pursuits associated with a democratic epistemology, a notably plebeian one (some of its Methodist ministers apart, maybe).

At this point, we will leave medical botany for a few pages and introduce Spencer T. (or 'Spencity'[85]) Hall. He illustrates some of the inadequacies of most of the democratic epistemologies of his time. He also illustrates how some of the pressures on many an unestablished medical practitioner – particularly with the cumulative impact of the 1858 Act – were contradictory and often stifling. Not that the number of such people – full- or part-time – necessarily declined into the twentieth century: one has only to remember the 1910 Report of the Committee on Unauthorised Medical Practice.[86]

Hall's intellectual formation had been almost caricaturally plebeian in its lack of emphasis on formal schooling. Indeed, the way in which he had learnt to read had a quality not only artisan but also well in accord with the emphasis, in 'progressive' educational theories of his era (as of ours), on learning actively. Hall was self-consciously a 'Sherwood Forester' and born of poor Quaker parents. His

> father, being a shoemaker, and having several tiers of last-rails in his workshop, got the alphabet printed in large and small characters, and had it pasted at intervals along the rails. As soon as I could begin to scramble about, on trying to walk by holding on these rails, the letters caught my eye; and so I learnt to read and walk together – thanks to the ingenuity of my father! I am free to attribute all my learning to this source; for although I never went to a charity school in my whole life, my whole education, books included, did not cost so much as a guinea. I began to work at seven years of age,[87]

winding cotton for stockingers. This would have been in 1819.[88] Later he worked as a compositor and subsequently as a journalist.[89] In 1885, one obituarist was thus accurate, if waffly, in seeing him as typical of 'self-made toilers in the world of letters'.[90]

Hall was autodidact not only in his social and intellectual origins but also in many of his attitudes. The latter had presumably existed long before 1841 when he embraced mesmerism, but without any doubt interacted positively with it. Methodologically, his attitude can best be called one of open empiricist flux. Thus he excused his inability to 'elaborate into a very definite system all those views which [had] dawned upon him at first' as 'only because his horizon has so constantly expanded – so much new experimental matter has been accumulated . . . One fact is worth a hundred reasons'.[91] This reinforced in him a nominalist attitude to all theory: it was, he wrote, 'of no consequence what a truth was called', so that 'the laws of Mesmerism, and a great deal else we have to do with [were] very much what we choose to make them'.[92] And this openness implied the existence of certain enemies. For Hall self-consciously belonged to 'a large, intelligent and earnest class of investigators who, belonging to no *caste*, have dared to be honest and avow their observations and discoveries in the face of all scepticism and derision'.[93] Caste was the inherent curse of all those men legally qualified or with letters after their names. Hall's own bogeymen included 'Mr Wakley and other scientific journalists of London' who, at this time, were attacking him by name and also mesmerism in general. As we have seen, Wakley was perhaps already allopathy's fiercest gladiator. Such men were, for Hall, mere 'Dictators to Nature'. By contrast, versions of knowledge such as his de-stooled the mighty 'exclusives' as he called them: 'experience has taught us that those who have had the most rigid scientific training, as it is called, have ever been the first to oppose and abuse, and the last to receive the knowledge of any new and grand development of our nature.'[94]

Nor did he stop at throwing down the epistemologically mighty: he at once exalted the meek. Hall, claiming experience of 'large popular audiences in the manufacturing towns of Yorkshire and Lancashire and other districts of the middle and north of England and Scotland', liked to 'contrast . . . the puerile bickerings so often attending experiments in exclusive circles generally' and particularly among 'the literary and scientific magnates of the day', with the 'immense volumes [that] might be filled with instances of the beneficial use of Mesmerism' among 'the common (that is, working) people, who' – 'particularly in the manufacturing towns' – 'obtained the elements of their knowledge from public lecturers'. 'Is the editor of the *Athenaeum* [who had recently joined in the attack on Mesmerism][95] – a specimen of 'mind among the spindles', or 'as hard and impervious to truth as the spindle itself?'.[96]

At this point I propose to silence Hall's eloquence for a moment, so as to note that from early in 1850 he was helping to manage a homoeopathic dispensary in Sunderland[97]; that he subsequently acted during an unstated period as 'coadjutor in general practice of Dr G. Dunn of Doncaster' (also a homoeopath)[98]; and that altogether he spent the last thirty or more years of his life (i.e. to 1885), working not as a phrenomesmerist but mainly as a self-styled homoeopath and sometime head of more than one hydropathic establishment in the Lake District.[99] Not that he dropped his propaganda for (in effect) democratic epistemology. In 1865, for example, he was claiming no less than Hippocrates himself for an autodidact – him having 'had no college to learn medicine in but that of Nature and Common Sense'.[100] His career highlights some of the hindrances in the environment of plebeian practitioners and also some of the weaknesses or insufficiencies within much plebeian epistemology. Already by January 1844, he was in Edinburgh in order – as he remembered with no more than a comma – 'to give a course of lectures, and to graduate for a medical degree'.[101] While his lectures attracted prominent intellectuals and were perhaps what attracted to him some friends willing and able to finance his studies at that University, he let this opportunity slip. This renunciation was to be one reason for the poverty of his later years: his medical degrees were not such as to make him 'legally qualified'. They came from Tübingen (probably purchased) and Cincinnati.[102] The latter was an Eclectic Medical College whose head, Dr J. R. Buchanan (see Chapter 4C), Hall was happy to own as his 'distinguished friend'.[103] At any rate, Hall continued to call himself a homoeopath and hydropath, doing so without legal qualification – and soon in an era when such qualification was to be ever more necessary. Subsequently he described his Edinburgh renunciation as resulting from principle:

> I had already the burden of one heterodox ism [i.e.
> Mesmerism], and an almost equally heterodox ology [i.e.
> Phrenology] to carry through the proposed curricula; and it
> was morally certain that if, in addition to these, the bulk of
> my belief were swelled with a pathy [i.e. homoeopathy] more
> heterodox than both of them together,

he would anyway fail the course.[104]

And he seems to have remained principled in this way. According to one probably close friend, his 'convictions relative to homoeopathy' prompted him to resist 'all the appeals of his friends to qualify himself allopathically, and thus secure a position which the law would recognise. Had he done this his career would have been a far easier one.'[105] In fact, he was to die in straitened circumstances. One of his sons – the future 'labour agitator', Nietz-schean and semi-syndicalist Leonard Hall (who seems himself to have been something of a boyhood autodidact in his father's extensive library) – had already, for financial or other reasons, catapulted himself into the working class at the age of 13 as a parcel-boy on the railways.[106] Indeed 'Spencity' seems always to have rated his own (and his family's) comfort lower than the pursuit of what he saw as truth. After all, he had discovered mesmerism only as a journalist sent to report on Monsieur la Fontaine's demonstrations of it, but one can hardly believe that his editor required him to attend – as Hall allegedly did – all 300 of these. Again, he was able to study 'mental and physiological science' more thoroughly for himself when he became 'resident governor of the Hollis Hospital at Sheffield': presumably a relatively sedate post. But, once he had almost casually discovered his own abilities as a lecturer, he embarked on what was later remembered sometimes as 'his "vital magnetism" crusade'.[107]

Both Hall's crusading and his activities as an author and lyricist brought him not only occasionally huge audiences but also august friendships: the phrenological Combe brothers – 'at whose table he met Liebig' – the philanthropist James Silk Buckingham and the early Christian Socialist John Minter Morgan. Most famously (and, for Wakley, infamously), he cured Harriet Martineau of a painful and long-standing ailment – or so both she and he claimed.[108] His lifelong friendship with Lord Morpeth (later the Earl of Carlisle and Lord Lieutenant of Ireland) originated with his Lordship's admiration for him, both literary and mesmeric. Again, his lyrics won him another noble friend in the shape of his Grace the Duke of Rutland. Relevantly here, during Hall's last months, 'a most extensive number' of 'representative men of all classes in Lancashire and other parts of England' petitioned the prime minister (Gladstone) and the Queen for a grant from 'the royal bounty'. But again, none of this warmth could, at the end, make more than £100 of headway against Hall's apparently much larger burden of debt. Somehow, amid all his verbal and (apparently) curative abilities, he had fallen between the elite and democratic stools.

And whatever mistakes of opportunism or, more likely in Hall's case, lack of it that he may have made, his care-worn end is, more important, indirect evidence of the incoherences of the epistemology he had once propagandised so clearly. Centrally, while it had the virtue of activism it remained, most damagingly, non-cumulative. It was active in the particularly democratic sense that, if practice equalised the practitioners, then their duty was fundamentally to get on with practising. 'Like virtue', declared Miss Chandos Leigh-Hunt – a non-plebeian mesmerist with an at least half-plebeian clientele – during the late 1870s, 'the power to Magnetise is in all and can be developed by all'.[109] Once this was 'recognised', she added 2½ years later, 'people would not rest contented [sic] until they could both magnetise and be magnetised . . . To discover from experience the exact extent of your power, and the class of persons you are able to control, it is necessary to make experiments, and carefully note their results.'[110] Spiritualists similarly (and, as we shall see in Chapter 7, Miss Leigh-Hunt was herself virtually or wholly such) cultivated an active approach to all techniques, including to their own: they preferred to 'become operatives, not mere subjects', as one of them proudly proclaimed.[111] This attitude, spiritualists believed, made them superior not merely to elite practitioners of any pursuit, but also to plebeian secularists. The latter were ridiculed for avoiding any practice at all. Thus, when Harriet Law, the secularist gladiator, attacked spiritualism – at a meeting (itself chaired by a spiritualist) in Darlington Mechanics' Hall during 1872, a correspondent of the *Medium and Daybreak* countered that secularism remained on the level of a 'sectarian religion, . . . ask[ing] us to believe or disbelieve; spiritualism', by contrast, 'simply asks men and women to gain knowledge by experiment'.[112] 'Our object', Burns had recently stated in *Human Nature*, 'is to individualise our readers, and challenge their powers of intellect, rather than to lead a sect of blind devotees.'[113].

And in the short term, all this empiricist activism may well have been highly invigorating. Its scorn of system strengthened and drew forth not merely an easy-going democracy but also, as the other side of the coin, a bitterness against any sect-like structure within or near science: against those intellectual monopolists – the 'men who' (in Hall's words) 'styled themselves B.L., M.R.C.S., M.D., LL.D., . . . and Omniscience'[114] – in other words, the professions as such. 'Spiritualism', one 'spirit' announced during 1890, 'is a science. The science of sciences, the Oxons, Cantabs,

F.R.S.'s, the Archbishops of Canterbury and York and all their tribal and non-expounders [sic] of "spiritual gifts" not withstanding.'[115] The spectacle of Burns, the former 14-hour-a-day gardener, trading abuse and innuendo with the litterateur and now respectable spiritualist William Howitt[116] would surely have excited Hall here.

But beyond the short term, the trouble was not merely, as we have noted, that from mid-century the 'Omniscients' (archbishops, surely, apart) were in the ascendant. There was also doubt – sometimes not simply faced but proudly proclaimed – about the cumulativeness and thus, we might imagine, about the coherence of these pursuits themselves. Strictly of course, these ambiguities flow directly from the methodological aspects discussed in the previous chapter; but they bedevilled all such pursuits so much, that they begin to seem inherent in almost any democratic epistemology during the nineteenth century and early twentieth.[117] And spiritualists in particular, simply by basing their more ambitious intellectual dreams consistently on their belief, contributed disproportionately to the eccentric image borne by so many of these pursuits (as we will see in section D).

'The facts reported by spiritualism', the *Medium and Daybreak*'s Darlington correspondent had exulted against Harriet Law, 'are not for the purpose of building up a system of belief, but to stimulate investigators to labour for similar results.'[118] But, without *some* 'system', how was similarity to be defined? 'The pyramid of knowledge' – according to an anonymous and uncontexted statement inserted in the *Lyceum Banner* during 1909 'is made up of little grains of information, little observations picked up everywhere'.[119] This metaphor was designed to encourage the humble picker-up of little grains, no doubt. But what persuaded them to accumulate into so definite a structure? The metaphor refuted itself – or so we can agree now. Altogether, not only esotericism and jargon were undermined by so granular a version of knowledge; no less undermined was coherence itself. The reach of theories was all too quickly global; the grasp of practice individual. Nineteenth-century heterodoxies were therefore rich in new beginnings and incipient grand syntheses, but poor in advances or even in agreed languages in which to measure them.

It was long-term problems of this nature that helped impel some devotees of these pursuits into actions or words that might, aware

or not, probe the limitations of their type of democratic epistemology. Thus, early on, Hall was identifying himself as a 'pioneer
and expositor, rather than a theorist',[120] and as 'a toiling artizan'
who 'exult[ed] . . . that the cottage is already beginning not to
imitate but to *emulate* the college, both in the acquisition and dissemination of learning, and that men [sic] who, in youth, could not avail
themselves even of the modest elements of scholastic education,
are passing the barriers of conventional prejudice.'[121] He was, one
may note, hardly bothering to extend his cottagers' emulative
'acquisition and dissemination' into actual accumulation 'of
learning': 'dissemination', apparently, meant assisting 'acquisition'
by other cottagers. Indeed one reason why so many – though, as
we have seen, by no means all – of his militantly empiricist and
democratic passages had come from the two mid-century decades,
is his still fresh memory of how pursuits such as his were appropri-
ated by opponents of various pre-existing syntheses. As he put it:
'When Phreno-Magnetism began to excite popular attention in
[Britain], its revelations were instantly seized upon by opinionists
of different schools, as grand corroborations of their own particular
views.' He instanced 'Churchmen', and also materialists such as
Engledue; again, the Owenites had first 'unhesitatingly received
the new theory . . . and cherished it with all imaginable fondness'
but had hurriedly dropped it in face of the argument (a convincing
one, he believed) that the existence of a phrenological faculty for
'worship' implied 'something above . . . to worship and to rely
upon'; and so on.[122] We can easily understand how Hall's support
for what I have called empiricist flux was further motivated in the
short term by an urgent need to avoid a chaos of rival incorpor-
ations. And yet he himself, for all his loud avoidance of generalisations, authored at least one notorious one himself during the
1840s – and much to Wakley's glee. This was his discovery, by
phrenomesmeric methods of course, that the phrenological faculties were more numerous than hitherto believed; that each faculty
had its own positive and negative magnetic poles; and that some
of his new ones were situated outside the brain itself, in places
such as the eyebrows and nostrils.[123]
    Further, he was not alone among plebeian researchers in his
manner of rebutting the sneers of, say, Wakley that they were
mere 'empirics': were not orthodox practitioners, Hall countered,
themselves 'divided, confused and contradictory', their publi-

cations 'always falling out tremendously with each other'? In short,
were they not, he italicised, a '*systemless* school'[124]? And Skelton,
for example, counter-attacked in the same way.[125]

We are back, in other words, at the crucial question, begged
by most democratic epistemologists during our period. Did their
epistemology necessarily imply alternative ways of medical practice? As we have seen, it did officially with medical botany at least.
But was the epistemology developed mainly as a rhetoric of anti-
professionalism? Hall, for one, repeatedly gravitated back towards
the latter, often in passages around those I have already quoted
from him.

> Ye who consider yourself of 'the higher walk of Mesmerists',
> tell me why a Yorkshire weaver or a Northamptonshire
> peasant has less right than you to participate in such knowledge.
> Do astronomers and botanists alone enjoy or receive
> instruction from the stars or flowers? Has none but the
> physician ever relieved pain? Do but priests smooth the
> deathbed pillow? . . . As [Jesus] came to teach that religion
> was not confined to the priests and pharisees, but belonged
> to the common people; so also he showed that the powers of
> nature were not alone in the hands of the magicians or men
> of science – of whom the exclusive doctors in our day, who
> blindly deny the use of Mesmerism whilst the people are
> curing each other of it, afford, perhaps, a distant semblance.[126]

Such rhetoric – which he shared very much with other plebeian
medics, most notably the medical botanists from Thomson on –
might jerk between, on one side, the rights of men (and sometimes
explicitly women) and, on the other, the doctrine of the priesthood
of all believers. But it concentrated on the right to medicate more
than on how to organise before and after such rights had been
won.

And this brings us to a possibility that could disrupt much of
the argument in this book about democratic epistemology: what
if the rhetoric we are listening to is not so much that of democrats
as of, say, medical vendors and exhibitors in fairground and street?
'Everyone their own Doctor' is a classic slogan of many 'quacks',
define them how we will.[127] True, the rhetorical convergences
are audible – partly because socially understandable: the nostrum-

monger needed to encourage the audience to medicate themselves (if only with her or his particular nostrum) and, from the other side, anyone without private income who wished to spend more than their spare time preaching one or more medical doctrines was in need of money to keep body and soul together – so why not by medical means? And often the balance of motivations may be hard to distinguish. Two of legion examples are Samuel Thomson and Dr Coffin: the Eclectics themselves suspected the latter somewhat; when Skelton identified (correctly, too) the proposition that 'that which is intended for all should be accessible to all' as one which 'I am sure no progressionist will dispute', he was deploying it during an attack, precisely, on what he saw as the commercialism of the Coffinites.[128] But the fairground mode (as we may call it) involved, when fully deployed, more than merely an appeal to democratically mutual care or to democratic epistemology – when, indeed, it focussed in the latter directions for very long. As we saw during Chapter 3 when scrutinising the rhetorical overlaps of a very different kind of practitioner, J. G. H. Brown (though he too, as we saw, developed a botanic sideline), the fairground mode also included elements entirely inconsistent with any kind of democratic appeal. And these elements are seldom or never to be met with in pursuits such as the ones under study here.

In addition, the emphasis on self-organisation and self-education was – however much it apparently needed reiterating – far more than mere rhetoric: a mere glance at, say, the late-1860s *Eclectic Journal* will suggest at least hundreds and possibly (as was sometimes claimed) thousands of people, particularly in Northern England, involved in such self-organisation. True again, there were indeed commercial pressures (as we shall see in Chapter 7). But in general, we would waste our time if we searched for some constantly central fairground practice concealed hypocritically behind a mask of democratic rhetoric.

More likely instead, the rhetoric was limping behind the practice (at least insofar as blueprints for self-organisation were implemented), in the following sense. To the extent that plebeian medics merely called for full trade in medical care, they were that much less likely to escape from progressive – or, rather, libertarian – middle-class influence. After all, the homoeopaths used a rhetoric of free trade (even if, often, only for themselves). Further, the third quarter of the nineteenth century saw a major growth in the ideological magnetism of a whole range of 'physical puritan' and other movements in which working-class libertarianism orbited, however eccentrically, around middle-class.[129] It is therefore symbolic how frequently plebeian medics, after teasing the homoeopaths, found themselves in alliance with them. And the magnetic field was far broader than homoeopathy or even than medicine. It would therefore have been surprising indeed, had medical botany and similar plebeian medical movements escaped such a wide pull: their epistemology – we might say, lacked coherence and therefore thrust.

It is true that medical botanists, in particular, were fond of scorning the sanitarian emphasis on drainage as both middle class (for playing down the importance of shorter working hours and better food) and allopathic (as a method for doctors, led by Wakley and his ilk, to engross ever more powers). But in general, plebeians were usually and perhaps increasingly drawn along in the wake of middle-class leaderships which talked the language of free trade. True again, there might be serious divergencies between middle-class and plebeian reformers – such as Walkowitz has uncovered within the movement against the C.D. Acts.[130] On the whole, though, the class interests of the two groups appeared to converge in free trade libertarianism. The power of the latter current amongst plebeians is attested by its also serving as the main mobilisatory appeal even for the other side: for defenders of pubs, prostitution (under new regulations or any or none), and of traditional rough morality in every area.[131]

Could plebeians have gone beyond this configuration of polarisations? And is the mere act of uttering such a question antihistorical? I would answer, firstly, that counter-factual enquiry is not necessarily anti-historical and, secondly, that there were at least one or two democratic epistemologists whose inconsistencies, however crippling, also suggest some awareness of the problem. Skelton, for one, expressed dissatisfaction with medical botanists' intellectual situation in this very context: the aim, he announced during 1854, should be

> not only to increase the stock of general 'knowledge'. Hitherto, our system and its truths have been felt in the effect of application, more than in the knowledge which our friends have had of its *philosophy* or *science*. This point must now be

passed, and *greater men* and *greater minds* must be connected
with us before we can expect to win the general assent of
mankind. [132]

Here, apparently, Skelton was bewailing the intellectual effects of
an empiricism which he shared (he too could poke fun at 'philosophical' inhibitions in medicine). [133] Yet he was proposing to miti-
gate these by – capturing some of his opponents' (admittedly less
empiricist) intellects. But how did he propose to lasso these? Only
a month later, within a discussion of agitations by plebeian medics
and, implicitly, of possible alliances between them and the unorthodox, he tried to answer;

> The hold which legitimate [i.e. established] Medical theories
> have upon the minds of men who are thinkers, is so partial
> that they but require to be properly appealed to in order to
> enlist their cooperation. . . . But it is from the thinkers among
> the people [autodidacts, as we would call them] that their
> attention must be called to it.

This optimism may appear confused. But Skelton was not alone
in apparently suffering from it at this time. Take J. F. White's
report of a deputation (also during 1854) to the great Free Trade
MP, John Bright, to present a botanic petition. True, deputation
and recipient seem to have harangued or disdained each other in a
very clear-cut way, as self-conscious representatives of the working
and middle classes. And yet White's own arguments in this very
context suggest a confused or vague strategy. On the one hand,
'all great Reforms originate with working men', so that 'we shall
soon be able to convince the middle class, . . . then they will take
it up and it will become popular'; on the other, 'only by seeing its
effects on the working class [would] the middle class . . . adopt
it.' Whatever White's precise politics had been during the previous
fifteen or so years, Skelton's had, as noted, been social-Chartist.
Even more relevant here, he had been a Chartist intellectual and
strategically radical – part of what Goodway calls a 'coterie which
included Thomas Cooper and Harney, John Skelton and [the later
spiritualist] Thomas Shorter' and, during the late 1840s, in agreement with Ernest Jones's identification of 'the middle classes [as]
. . . our greatest enemies'. [134] Apart, meantime, from Chartism's

decline as a national movement, one factor which may have confused his class strategy (if it now was) may have been a possible convergence between plebeian and some other unorthodox medics within the campaign against vaccination.

Any such convergence is worth some paragraphs. It would have occurred at a time when Skelton, at least, believed that not only was medical botany having a considerable impact,[135] but also that its opponents were split. As to the first, he claimed, however exaggeratedly, that 'not a single city, town or village but what numbers its disciples [of medical botany] more or less. They support two periodicals, and have numerous works upon the subject.'[136] (His 'more or less' may be a ploy to lump traditional herbalists together with Thomsonians and Eclectics.) We can add (as Skelton does not mention this) that there was from 1864 a National Association of Medical Herbalists which, we are told, 'many botanic societies, especially from the North and Midlands [of England], elected to join'.[137] Medical botanists also drew succour from the USA, which had, Skelton claimed, 'not less than *nine* Thomsonian Colleges in her principal towns and cities'.[138] Thus, the newly acquitted Josiah Thomas found himself presented, not merely with a purse of silver but also with an unsolicited honorary MD from the Eclectic Medical College of Pennsylvania, signed by J. R. Buchanan[139] (the psychometrical Eclectic whom we met during Chapter 4). Six of the latter's works were advertised within one particular issue of the *Eclectic Journal*.[140] During the same weeks, 'an immense quantity of American medical works, new as well as old', was being offered for sale to medical botanists at below the American price.[141] And Buchanan, at least, was apparently sending such works free: no wonder 'the Medical Reformers of America' were one of the toasts at the centenary dinner, got up in Leeds for Samuel Thomson by the 'British Medical Reform Association of Botanic and Eclectic Practitioners'.[142]

Second, however much medical botanists might scorn the more respectable heresies, they could not help sensing that divisions among respectables helped take some pressure off themselves: '*but* for [homoeopathy and hydropathy's] influence in dividing the strength of the profession', Skelton acknowledged, 'the medical botanist could never have attained his [current] position.'[143] To this extent, in other words, homoeopaths and botanists faced a common enemy in allopathy; and botanists acted to convert this position into an alliance. One can even imagine some of them as hoping that this alliance would help disunite their allies, or at least bring some of them round to botany. We have already noted Skelton's scorn for qualified homoeopaths' overall strategy, which he saw as inconsistent; but the main grounds of his confidence were to do with medical theory. He saw their doctrinal grounding on infinitesimal dosages, not as an imponderable strength but as logically self-defeating. What, he ironised, was 'the *millionth*, *billionth*, or *trillionth* part of a grain but "nothing", and yet doses of this "nothing" determine its success.' At this point he was, effectively, in agreement with allopaths; but not for long: Hahnemann remained, for him, 'a great reformer' for having 'reduced [also] the "killing art" of allopathy' itself 'to nothing', by leaving 'nature to itself and secur[ing] the first step in . . . medical reform by refusing to *destroy life*.'

Conceivably, in other words, at least a few medical botanists hoped to conduct homoeopaths a further 'step' or two along 'the great progress of [sic] medical reform'[144] by involving them in a common campaign. (Though, for campaigns, the very prestige of many elite homoeopaths would obviously be handy too). And this brings us, as promised, to anti-vaccination. Not that all homoeopaths turned against vaccination or did so simultaneously: for years, some tried to promote it via their own organisation.[145] At first, they objected with greater unanimity to Compulsion – a 'despotic', 'unwise and unjust means to gain a good end' as the monthly of the 'English Homoeopathic Association' put it. Similarly, even among medical botanists, there had at first been less than blanket hostility to vaccination. Thus, during 1852, Skelton had seen it as sometimes necessary for counteracting the effects of bad urban environment[146] and, the next year, listed Jenner next to Thomson as two innovators who had been ridiculed and misrepresented by upholders of the medical status quo[147] (ten years previously, the short-lived Owenite publication, *The Mesmerist*, had viewed Jenner in this way[148]); and shortly afterwards, also during 1853, a speaker at the formal opening of the York Medical Botanic Society spoke of Jenner as even 'glorious'.[149] But less than a year later, Skelton was warmly welcoming a denunciation of vaccination as such, by John Gibbs, a St Leonards hydropathist.[150] And certainly by the late 1860s (and quite possibly well before) Skelton and his son – also named John – were on the committee of the

Anti-Compulsory Vaccination League, alongside not only at least two spiritualists (Burns, and George Dornbusch) but also at least two homoeopaths, with one of whom (Dr C. T. Pearce) Skelton had clashed verbally and in print fifteen or so years previously.[151] Skelton also went on at least one deputation to the government alongside some homoeopaths both legally qualified and not (such as S. T. Hall). Hall claimed to have been fined for non-compliance,[152] (i.e. for refusing to let his child be vaccinated) and one of the Skeltons was to suffer similarly two years later.[153]

As hinted, the existence of any botanic hopes of incorporating other heterodox medicators via campaigning alliances remains pure speculation. And there is anyway harder evidence that others were already taking a lead. Back in 1858, as part of the fight against the passing of the Medical Act of that year, homoeopaths (or at least some, around their stronghold of Northampton) had begun to form a 'Medical Liberty League' to try and 'unite all classes, medical and non-medical', into 'an eclectic body, including not only homoeopathists only, but hydropathists, medical botanists, and any other, even mesmerists, yea, those who have no medical creed at all . . . to save the country from a *state medical priesthood.*' Pearce seems to have been the prime mover in this attempt. Its perspective of 'unit[ing] all classes' is visible in its financial appeal to both poor and rich: a modest one shilling per annum would entitle the former to receive all the League's publications, while a grand £5 from the latter would entitle them to sit on its Committee.[154]

In other words, botanists and many homoeopaths were already offering rival alliances on at least any issue of 'medical freedom' – all too understandably when, for example, 'the Medical Council to be appointed under the . . . [1858] Bill [was] to be empowered to publish a Pharmacopeia prescribing the legal preparations [of medicine], with their weights and measures.'[155] What else, during the immediately following years, brought them so frequently together? By far the most obvious factors were, firstly, the tighter enforcement of vaccination and, secondly, of the 1858 Act (followed by moves to tighten the latter further[156]). In this context, one local paper, the *Norwich Dispatch* was perhaps accurately vague in the way it associated the two strands: 'from the highest to the lowest . . ., Liberal ideas in the art of . . . healing have taken hold of the minds of the people, consequently the homoeopaths and

medical botanists come in for a share of the business.'[157] But above
all, what fuelled anti-vaccinationism were the emotions of fear and
outrage: the fear, constantly reiterated, was of infection with all
kinds of disease including the most serious[158]; the outrage was
partly political (against centralised interference with the rights of
free-born English people) and partly familial. The latter centred
on the source of the vaccine and should be seen as more than
merely middle-class snobbery stirred up into phobic proportions.
When Garth Wilkinson fulminated against compulsory vaccination
as 'communism of the blood', he may well have spoken to many
working-class people too. And here the *Eclectic Journal* – though
still, so late, prepared to concede that vaccination 'may, on
occasions [though very rare ones], be useful' – identified the main
fault of Compulsion as its 'reduc[ing] the respectable mechanic,
etc., to a level with paupers'.[159]

We are back, in other words, with the contradictions (and, as
historians have recently argued, not the straightforward reactionar-
iness) of mid-Victorian plebeian 'respectability', and thus of plebeian relations with other classes.[160] Here the *Journal* seems to have
seen medical botanists as particularly well placed to harness plebeian anger in ways that would compel respectable homoeopaths,
within an anti-vaccinationist alliance, to pay greater attention to
them and ultimately to botanic doctrine. Thus such alliances were
valuable – and Skelton's grumblings, quoted three paragraphs ago,
appear to confirm this – less in helping to fight vaccination
(however important such an aim) than in assisting the medical
'thinkers among the people' in convincing their respectable equivalents. Here (and in the abscence of whole programmes of research,
we are reduced to speculating), such strategies were undermined
by what seems to have been a simple dearth of Garth Wilkinsons,
willing to risk much of their social and intellectual privilege. The
likely reasons for such a dearth have already been mentioned. In
the long run, the *Norwich Dispatch*'s word 'Liberal' – with a politically capital 'L' – turned out to have indicated who would do the
more absorbing of whom, as we shall see soon.

Among plebeians one strategy which Skelton and many other
botanists pursued simultaneously with the propagandistic one just
discussed, was to formalise their facilities for training. True, further
strategies were also envisaged or attempted, such as directly

attracting middle- and even upper-class patients,[161] or setting up dispensaries to attract poorer ones (as also to help ensure purity in the medicines).[162] These two strategies were themselves associated – given, at least, that 'the cooperation of [locally] influential persons' was seen as 'essentially necessary' to the funding of dispensaries.[163] (And both were favourites with the homoeopaths, too, even though not all of the latter would have approved when a medical botanist went on to extol dispensaries as promoting popular self-reliance[164]). For us, though, the training-strategy is the most relevant: it was so close to the epistemological area that, to the extent it was in tension with medical botanists' democratic epistemology, it suggests further incoherences in the latter.

Particularly when criticising medical hierarchies, medical botanists had little difficulty in sounding negative about any formal training whatever. Thus Skelton on one such occasion rejected degrees, education, genius, good character (and even success in curing), and proclaimed, instead of all these, one resounding criterion: 'truth'.[165] Even more question-beggingly, he had spoken of medical botany as, 'being the truth, . . . accessable [sic] to all mankind.'[166] And yet during the very same year (1853) in which he made both these statements, the founding meeting of a National Medical Reform League (in London) adopted as the third of its 'Principles' the 'establish[ing of] a people's College, in which the subject of Medical Botany and the pathology of disease [would] be taught to all those who desire to avail themselves of such information.'[167] Whatever may have come of such hopes – and Skelton's son was running a 'School of Domestic Medicine' at 105 Great Russell St, Bloomsbury, London by May 1865[168] – their point for our argument is that at least some botanists continued to think in such terms.

For, as any training – whatever its degree of formality – involved an investment of time and effort, there was always a temptation to view even botanic practitioners, despite and even alongside declarations of (in effect) epistemological principle, as a category separate from their potential patients. Part of the motivation was itself institutional: by 1853, the executive of the new Friendly United Medical Botanic Sick and Burial Society intended to 'examine all candidates' wishing 'to practice the *Botanic System* under the society's sanction' and to 'grant diplomas to all if qualified'. True, 'the only qualification' turned out to be somewhat informal: 'skill in practice, honesty of purpose, faith in the [botanic] system and strict adherence to the general laws.'[169] And the whole venture (whatever became of it) suggests that, in the West Riding at least, medical botanists were experiencing discrimination – both as patients and attendants – precisely because of what they would have seen as their openness. But, by 1866, when the *Eclectic Journal and Medical Free Press* introduced itself for the first time, it spoke of the 'great need of [sic] a cheap Medical Journal, both for the people and the [Eclectic] profession'.[170] By that year there were indeed 'candidates for diplomas' who were 'presented for [oral] examination' at the B.M.R.A.'s third meeting (in Leeds).[171] Two years later, on the equivalent occasion in the same city, fifteen candidates were 'selected as eligible' (their addresses being as far afield as London and Scotland – one each – but with ten from Northern England, including two from Keighley).[172]

And this ordeal was no longer simply the informal (though for many perhaps no less intimidating) contest of botanic knowledge such as took place at the 'Bills o' Jacks' in front, we are told, of an audience of 'upwards of five thousand' botanists and their friends from 'Lancashire, Yorkshire, Cheshire and Derbyshire' during 1868.[173] Rather, there was a scheme afoot to found, in Leeds, an 'Eclectic School of Medicine'. This was intended to have an imposing (and, no doubt, all too necessary) syllabus: 'Anatomy and Surgery, Physiology, Theory and Practice, Materia Medica of Great Britain and America, Obstetrics, and Chemistry'. The latter was to 'receive special attention. . . . Since the discoveries of Liebig, in organic chemistry, the study seems to have been invested with deep and peculiar interest, and connected as it is with the study of physiology, it requires to be mastered.' Altogether (and, true to the metaphor in the last word) 'the School' would 'afford facilities to young gentlemen in the Midland Counties to acquire a medical education near home'.[174] Late in 1869, 'nearly forty gentlemen' were enrolled when the British Eclectic Medical College officially opened. Their identity is not given, nor is that of the 'lecturer' on this occasion who 'referred to the University [sic] of Pennsylvania and its connection with this college, to the Pharmacy Act [which, so it was feared, would force practitioners to, in effect, use only allopathic medicines], to the proposed New [sic] Medical Act, to the Vaccination Act, and many other subjects.'[175] Also unclear are the College's fees, rhythms of payment and of study, how far its intended curriculum was implemented and how long the whole undertaking survived. On the latter at any rate, we have a statement of Skelton's only the next month (that the College was not yet securely established but that he, at least, felt sure it soon would be): 'We regret', he wrote, 'that a movement has been started by a few members [of the B.M.R.A.] to obtain a Charter of Incorporation – this is premature; before . . . [this] can be obtained there must be a college and a dispensary in full operation, and we can only see a failure at present which would be avoided by a few years' delay.'[176] Something else we can deduce from this statement is, of course, that many supporters were feeling further pressure towards formalisation. We cannot tell whether or not they necessarily saw this as reinforcing any hierarchy (which it might tend to, though not necessarily).

Unfortunately, any such tendencies are impossible to weigh up, as even the basic outline of these educational efforts remains to be researched. All we can know is that certain trends seem inferrable. And, through an even thicker fog of our own ignorance, we can also discern the same combination of tendencies again during the 1890s. Near the start of this decade, a controversial healer with long and wide experience, David Younger, helped found a periodical called *The Light of Day* in alliance with a grandly titled 'British and International Association of Eclectic and Medical Botanists'.[177] The context of this development involved both a perceived legislative threat to medical botanists' right to practice and an attempt to found a 'Medico-Botanic College of Great Britain'.

Within a year, this College officially opened. Like its predecessor a generation previously, it was easily viewed as a rallying point in the strivings of medical botanists as a group. In other words, its purposes were political as well as educational: as 'Dr' (or sometimes 'Mr') Joseph Blacker emphasised from the College's building in the Fulham Road, 'WE ARE WITHIN EASY REACH OF PARLIAMENT'.[178] The organisational structure was a federal one. This, presumably, was intended to prevent the metropolitan flower losing the advantages of any provincial rootage: there were to be local 'centres' which would send representatives to the 'periodical meetings of the College Council' which would take place in London.[179]

The ambitiousness of such structures looks forward to the Labour College movement of two and more decades later and, more directly, back to the 'Knowledge Chartism' of fifty years earlier. We have already compared, among others, the followers of Coffin and particularly of Skelton to the supporters of Knowledge Chartism. As we have seen, Skelton had himself been a Chartist and he remained politically radical during the 1860s.[180] Even more directly, the *Light of Day* serialised some of the writings of his now 'late' son.[181] Nor was this the only link with the unorthodox past: David Younger – for whom the College was only one in a series of such initiatives[182] – vaunted more than once his claim to have met and (readers were supposed to deduce) learnt deeply from Dr Elliotson.[183]

Whatever the fate of this College – and by 1893 its address was on Stepney Green (i.e. a little further from the Palace of Westminster)[184] – its publicity, for what publicity is worth, leaves an ambiguous taste. On the one hand it smacks, to us encouragingly, of autodidacts – both formally (in its uneven spelling, for example) and, more seriously, in making provision, within its entrance-requirements, for the barely educated (to whom it offered 'supplementary help' to bring them up to its minimum-entrance-standard[185]), for part-time students (to whom it offered a 'Postal Tuition' scheme) and for persons of 'limited means' (who could pay for the latter 'by instalments'[186]). There were also attacks – equal in their bitterness to anything of the previous generation – on orthodox 'Medical Intolerants' or on 'Medical Despotism'. (The latter was now said to lurk also within the 'cool, airy, noiseless, systematically kept wards' of the 'National Hospitals'.[187])

On the other hand, though, there was more talk of medical botanists as a 'profession' than as, say, a cause. Most significantly, the blueprint in the *Light of Day* for the structure of such a profession involved not only exclusivity and monopoly (part of the minimum definition for many a legal incorporation) but also two tiers according to degree of training.[188] And the College's patrons included not only George Howell (who, as a Lib-Lab M.P., was at least of working-class origin and ambiguously reforming politics) but also one Lord (Clifton), 7 reverends, 3 solicitors and so on.[189] The College also attracted at least one donation (£100) of anything but plebeian size: the donor was none other than Younger himself, who may not have been motivated by generosity alone but also by proprietorial ambitions: he is certainly remembered for, fifteen or so years later, obtaining a charter to found, in London, a 'College of Safe Medicine' – this charter being exclusively to him in person.[190]

And ambiguity extends to Younger's very self-description: variably 'Dr', 'Professor' or 'the Magnetic and Botanic Family Physician'. The latter title was also that of one of his books (retailing at 10/6d[191]): the word 'family' in this context had long implied lay self-medication – potentially at the opposite extreme from professional pretensions. And once, at least, Younger attacked Paracelsus for having founded not merely allopathy but simply a school, i.e. any formalised version of medicine.[192]

Ambiguities such as these prompted Burns, for one, into a bristling re-statement of some of the fundamentals of what we would call democratic epistemology. He did this despite recommending Younger's remedies and reprinting the latter's writings from Younger's own penny-monthly *Magnetic and Botanic Journal*[193] – and also despite Younger seeing anyway his own methods of healing as involving mediumship.[194] Burns's response to what he, like us, saw as hankerings, among some herbalists, after hierarchies was to cling to the old ideals. 'But why', he commented on the case of a Mr Steel of Hetton (in County Durham) – during which the judge had ruled that herbalists should designate themselves 'MD (Botanic)' instead of the incipiently fraudulent 'MD (Bc)' – 'But why these assumptions of medical craft and diplomas?'[195] Similarly, when Younger publicised, via (amongst other channels) the *Medium and Daybreak*, an appeal against a threatened tightening of the law, Burns's reaction to both 'Allopathic [and] Herbal trades unions', as he dubbed them, was '"A plague on both your houses!" We can do without you!.' He reasoned that, despite the alarm of the more professionally (and in Younger's case professorially) minded of the botanists there was still so far 'no law to prevent us from helping one another in a medical way'. Rather 'the [proposed] law is to prevent all from trading on healing except that large party of traffickers who hold the monopoly. What is the remedy? To make a knowledge of health and natural medication so general that all will be able to heal themselves or one another.'[196]

Burns, as ever, was basing a whole strategy on mass self-education. He was well aware that this involved building an insti-

tutional structure. What he hoped, though, was that its beneficiaries would not let themselves grow away from other plebeians.
And this brings us to the largest and longest-lasting embodiment
of plebeian-controlled efforts in this direction during the decades
around 1900: the Lyceums.

C   Spiritualism's contribution: the Lyceums

Of course, Burns had always urged plebeians such as spiritualists
to generate their own educational institutions. As early as 1865 he
suggested the setting up of a 'People's University'. The headings
of its intended curriculum included

> 1. Physiology . . ., 2. Phrenology . . ., 3. Social Science . . .
> based upon the Nature of Man as unfolded in [Phrenology]
> . . .', for 'Social reform [could] only be attained by the
> enlightenment of individual minds . . . 4. Psychology . . . 5.
> Spiritualism, Immortality etc. . . . 6. Anthropology [mainly,
> it seems, about alleged hereditary divergences between 'races']
> . . . 7. Cosmology

– the latter taken as 'a branch of anthropological science', in that
it involved 'an Inquiry into the Origin and Development of Worlds
and their Inhabitants'[197] (a phrase which underlines the relevance of
our next section). And he revived the words 'People's University'
during his last months, and encouraged his readers to enrol themselves as its 'members'. As we have seen, Burns – as witness
his rather poky 'Spiritual Institution' – sometimes indulged in
grandiloquent titles. And this particular initiative seems to have
involved no more than a correspondence network. (Indeed the
phrase 'People's University' was picked up, to similarly slight
effect, shortly afterwards by the subversively 'Egoistic' *Eagle and
Serpent* – whose masthead mottoes included the Jacobin 'the Great
are Great only because we are on our knees. Let us rise!'[198]). But
whatever the institutional form, Burns was hardly alone among
spiritualists in demanding some facilities for regular training. Thus
the *Two Worlds* printed one wealthy man's appeal for the founding
of a 'Training College for Sensitives',[199] and the medium Mrs
Hardinge Britten demanded a 'College for Mediums' a year or

two later.[200] However, irrespective of Burns's involvement or, occasionally, lack of it, such initiatives seem to have led to little, at least during the nineteenth century.

More fruitfully, Burns is remembered for his advocacy of Lyceums. He had expounded the lyceum concept when inaugurating his *Human Nature*. Both then and during the early 1890s, though, he combined it with his 'People's University' scheme, which we have just examined. Its echoes of Knowledge Chartism are self-evident.[201] And, it was as a component in a combined scheme for adult and child education that Burns expressed the hope that 'a generation of Lyceum influence would completely change the aspect of society on Spiritual matters'.[202]

Thus the Lyceums were to be, not exclusively for children and young people, but mainly oriented towards them. During the late nineteenth and early twentieth centuries, many spiritualist parents would have felt pressures to let their children go to hostile Sunday schools. Lyceums aimed to avoid this at least[203] – just as Owenite Sunday schools had, as secularist ones did, and as socialist ones were to. Some lyceums were attempted during the 1860s and 1870s, but growth only began during the 1880s. By late 1910, the total registered membership of 120 lyceums was over 10,000.[204] Geographically, the weighting, as with the adult movement, was overwhelmingly towards the north with, in 1902, seven lyceums each in Bradford and Manchester-plus-Salford, and four each in Burnley and Sheffield: as many as in the whole of London. From 1890 there was also a penny-monthly, the *Lyceum Banner*,[205] which interchanged editors and writers (let alone opinions) with the *Two Worlds*. The main lyceum pioneer was Alfred Kitson, who was based at Sowerby Bridge and whom, during the vital early years, Burns backed journalistically and often in person.

The lyceums' chief distinctiveness was held to lie not in their doctrine, but in their methods: broadly, they tried to raise the children up to become another generation of plebeian self-educators: 'What a lyceum is not. . . . Its aim is not to make all members think alike [or] to curb . . . individuality.'[206] The approved methods were very much those associated with earlier

Mrs Hitchcock
Herself a medium, Mrs Hitchcock (born 1829) and her
stonemason husband were active in vegetarianism and
temperance as well as in spiritualism. Together they started
Britain's first Lyceum in 1867, in Nottingham.

'progressive' educators: variety, learning-by-doing-and-dancing,
no harshness. In the early nineteenth century, this had been pioneered partly by Owen but, for spiritualists, the direct author was
the American, A. J. Davis, who claimed that these methods were
only what he had observed at work already in the Summerland.[207]
A typical lyceum service was supposed to consist of alternating
recitations (spoken and musical), marching and gymnastics ('callisthenics'), followed by a lesson, usually on a scientific, practical
or moral topic. Particularly for drill, and for some lessons, the
members would be split into year 'Groups'. In all, Kitson hoped

Alfred Kitson
From boyhood, Kitson followed his father as a miner and hell-
fearing Primitive Methodist. Joyfully converted to spiritualism at
the age of 12. Father followed. Alfred had learnt to read and
write at Sunday school, and went on to become the main
practical pioneer of Spiritualist Lyceums and of many activities
around them. Followed in this by his daughter, Nellie. Firmly
anti-clerical.

'to develop the innate powers of the rising generation'.[208] 'We try
to conform to all natural laws', rhymed a prominent lyceumist:

> We do not approve of the cramped up class,
> Croaking 'Thus saith the Lord'
> 'and it came to pass.'[209]

As against the lyceum type of curriculum, there is abundant
evidence that traditional Sunday-school methods were at a disadvantage. One opponent reportedly complained that lyceum chil-

dren were 'allowed to run riot, allowed to the nearest sweetshop to buy sweets, to learn to march, etc.' It is significant that this opponent lumped the marching with the sweets as wretched 'training for the future!!'.[210]

Such permissiveness would, for many children, have been the lyceums' best aspect. Four children had 'been attending an Undenominational [i.e. Christian] school – which started at 9.0 and closed at 10.30, so they passed the rest of the morning at our Lyceum; but somehow their superiors got to know it and told the boys that they must give over going to the spiritualists or else go for good.' The upshot was 'four new scholars' for Shaw Lyceum.[211]

Wherever the parents stood in this case, there is at least one instance of a prominent spiritualist having first been drawn towards spiritualism via his 5-year-old daughter's preference for a lyceum.[212] Sometimes the children's enjoyment must have attracted recruits even too fast: 'the Sunday before Easter, we opened the lyceum with one boy and two girls. At Easter we had an attendance of 70; of the 70, five are from avowed spiritualists' families, eight from sympathisers' families, and the remainder are children these 13 have brought us, and who, in turn, are taking the news home and bringing their parents.'[213]

Of course, marching was also the secret of the success of the (orthodox Christian) Church Lads' Brigade and of the Boys' Brigade[214]; children's play may have been more or less violent than now during the Victorian and Edwardian decades, but it seems to have had more of the paradeground in it, and not necessarily because of adult encouragement alone. Lyceum marchings were supposed to have great variety and were often more like large dances. They probably (via Davis, perhaps) had more in them of Shaker ceremonial than of the Board-School regimentation which so many lyceumists must have experienced (or suffered) on most other days of the week. In the 1870s, Burns had linked this quality with a vaguely republican sneer at displays of patriotism: he reported of a royal procession which happened to have passed near the Spiritual Institution that it 'was simply a few carriages containing men and women, some of whom wore queer hats . . . It was not so exciting as a Children's Progressive Lyceum on the march [where] . . . there is no display except of that which may be participated in by all. The Royal Procession is based on the opposite principle, and hence, however . . . imposing the array of brute force . . ., it lacks that great essential of moral beauty which the Lyceum possesses.'[215]

Of course, it is hard to say how far the reality measured up to the ideal. But it is probable that it often did: for, the lyceums were the most organised aspect of plebeian spiritualism and, particularly in the 'honeycombed districts' of Lancashire and Yorkshire, many new groups could count on help from an elaborate network of visitors and speakers.

In the methods recommended for the lyceums, we can glimpse in its simplest form how plebeian spiritualism could reinforce interest not only in intellectual independence but also in physical independence, including medical. One spiritualist could even claim that 'spiritualists cared nothing about your souls: you cannot find them until you've found your bodies.'[216]

Outline Lesson for Senior Groups.
Moral Growth
The channels through which the mind is impressed: Seeing, hearing and feeling. Their location in the brain, their relative importance – the seat of criminal impulse – its control by development . . . the nature of the nervous system – sensory and motor; the nature, form and mechanism of the brain . . . all these lead up, by degrees, to that of self-knowledge, which is the first step to moral growth. Any standard book on Physiology and Phrenology will assist you to work up a useful lesson.
Outline Lesson for Junior Groups
Eating
What is eating? – Why should we chew our food? – Why sweets taste good but are bad to eat . . . Every Lyceum should have a fairsized blackboard.[217]

The more banal we find this outline, the more we underline how seriously plebeian spiritualists viewed self-help in the area of health. Here, as the previous section has shown, they were neither original nor alone. But they were the most durably organised and, they would have hoped, encyclopaedic proponents of an already existing plebeian approach.

Typically here, Burns's own entrance into spiritualism had

occurred by paths broader than those of 'phenomena' alone. We have seen how his sparetime activity as a travelling pamphlet-seller and advocate of temperance had brought him a job as a clerk at a temperance publishers. While working there, he had been detailed 'to attend to the importation' of American books on phrenology. Soon after, a work on mesmerism 'fell into my hands. I devoured it while walking on the street, going on a business errand. It explained to my mind many things I had been thinking of for years.' These two events formed the immediate prologue to his discovery of A. J. Davis's writings.[218] There is, therefore, no surprise that Kitson, as well as he, earned money at various times as travelling phrenologists; but, as we have seen, they were hardly pioneers in this.

Altogether, spiritualism was in a position to articulate most flexibly with plebeian concerns. One reason was that it benefited from its own lack of organisation. (The lyceums are, precisely, by far the biggest exception to this rule: they generated their own complex structure of regional and district meetings and 'plans', all clearly similar to those of the Nonconformity where many of their cadres had originated; but even here, a minority of Lyceums stayed aloof from the 'British Spiritualist Lyceum Union'.). Secondly, it harmonised with the intellectual effervescence of plebeian autodidact culture – another side of the deeper chaos we have been grappling with. And this means that it added to it: after all, as an at least potentially non- or anti-Christian religion based on 'phenomena', its novelty sometimes induced a feeling of intellectual nakedness followed by a search for cover either in one's own or in others' mix of intellectual specialisms. Thirdly, the Lyceums institutionalised this search.

And here plebeian spiritualists surpassed their secularist rivals. Among the latter, by contrast, programmes such as the Science classes at Bradlaugh's Hall of Science remained mere optional extras, however elaborate they were and however lavishly, therefore, they chimed with the official doctrine that knowledge was the great liberator. But there was a sentiment no less typically plebeian-spiritualist in the claim that 'Enlightenment brings self-reliance and a desire to question authority.'[219] And it is even more important that, for lyceums, breadth was obviously the stuff of their efforts.

Spiritualism itself, even at its core, could be seen as self-

education: 'Like most spirit-mediums,' Swindlehurst stated, 'I am
practically self-taught . . . Mediumship is to me an ever unfolding
university.'[220] Mediumistic abilities seemed to extend the reach of
human potential out of all recognition. This impelled many people
to try and extend their intellectual grasp to a similar extent. This
was one of the attractions in the thought of Andrew Jackson Davis.
Davis packaged spiritualism as a 'Harmonial Philosophy'. As
Burns put the position, 'no class of men required to know more
of human nature than spiritualists'.[221] 'All topics that are of interest
to man's well-being should be considered. Physiology, Phrenology, Temperance, Botany, Geology, Marriage, Mesmerism,
Art, History, Chemistry, Mediumship, Spirit Life, Music . . . and
there are elementary and advanced manuals on all such subjects.'
Here, in 1892, the *Lyceum Banner* was sketching out a curriculum
for 'Liberty Groups' (ages 16 and above).[222] Spiritualists, according
to themselves, yielded to no secularists in their emphasis on reason
and science. In their eyes, spiritualism simply extended the range
of the natural sciences into areas labelled supernatural, thereby also
'converting the supernatural into the natural'.[223] Similarly, from a
trance in the backwoods of upstate New York, there had issued
the thundering aphorism that 'the spirit of man is a pocket edition
of the great volume of Nature'. These words had been uttered
shortly before the birth of spiritualism and came, reportedly, from
the mouth of Davis, the semi-educated young man who was to
become spiritualism's pioneer guru.[224] Delusion or not, this feeling
of actually participating in the process of Science or of sciences
was inseparably part of spiritualism.

D   Spiritualism's contribution:
outlandishness; eccentricities

All the same, spiritualism clearly occupied a peculiar position in
relation to Reason (in any definition). And this was one factor
fundamentally impelling it into an extreme version of all the philosophical weaknesses which I have been arguing were associated
with these pursuits. We can glimpse the core of these weaknesses
via Burns's own account of his acceptance of spiritualism. This,
he emphasises (and here he contrasts markedly with, say, Morse),
took place 'quite independent of spirit phenomena', which he had

witnessed 'in previous years' and to which he had 'attached but little importance'. Rather, Davis's writings had triggered within him an ecstasy whose intellectual, mystical and democratic aspects fused together; his mind had become

> illuminated with a Light that is simply indescribable. It was literally a divine enthusiasm, a universal pouring out of light and knowledge on every conceivable subject necessary for man's spiritual . . . progress. There was no longer any need for intermediate persons to stand between the Human Soul and Divine Light. It had come to me freely and it was equally free to all. . . . There was no [sectarian] creed . . . needed. . . . All should follow the Light that came from within. . . . Men, as brothers, should be equally interested in one another's spiritual welfare, which would lead to a unity of interests in every other respect.[225]

Avowedly this type of revelation was an ongoing one and presupposed maximum involvement with all sciences of 'man'. But, science or not, the problem was that spiritualism laid claim not merely to mundane Reason, but also to something higher. Try as one might to see the latter, too, as amenable to reason, the fact remained that such stances were (and are) topheavy.

We can see this precisely in what adherents would at the time have seen as among spiritualism's contributions to various non-spiritualist sciences and disciplines. Spiritualism, by inherently claiming to possess peculiar sources of knowledge, generated no less peculiar intellectual ambitions. If personality survived death then so, presumably, did intellect (arguably, the latter might even be enhanced). Might spirits not condescend to assist fleshed researchers on, for example, history or natural history? The simplest answer was to try asking. Unfortunately for the ensuing discoveries, their excitable non-cumulativeness exemplifies, to a caricatural extreme, much of what I have been arguing in relation to these pursuits in general.

With intellectual ambitions given so unprecedently flexible a leash, plebeian spiritualism overlapped after all with revelation-mongerings of a not always conspicuously rationalist kind. In this connection, I will soon discuss David Richmond's visions; there was also 'Oahspe' 's *New Bible in the words of Jehovih and his Angel*

*Embassadors [sic]. A Secret History of the . . . past 24,000 Years,
together with . . . Revelations from the Second Resurrection, . . . in the
Thirty-Third Year of the Kosmon Era,* sole agent for Great Britain:
J. Burns'.[226] Even in their titles, such outpourings would sometimes have made, say, the Book of Mormon seem unadventurous
both as history and as prophecy.

Also forthcoming were 'spiritual' priority-disputes over
'discoveries' in the area of one or other science, sweepingly grand
theories of human history, and what seems sheer pseudo-transcen-
dental waffle on any topic or almost none. In any case, most
statements made under 'spiritual' influence were stylistically
coloured not only by transcendentalism and various kinds of evol-
utionism, but also by a much older vagueness associated, traditionally with the irrefutably ambiguous predictions of fortune-tellers.
Such statements were therefore inherently liable to be lauded for
prescience and reviled for plagiarism. No less a spiritualist than A.
J. Davis was reproached in this way by the author of a book
(published by Burns) entitled *Primeval [sic] Man: the Origin, Decline
and Restoration of the Race. Spiritual Revealings,* no less. Davis replied
gently that, as both he and his accuser had written under spirit
influence, neither could claim originality.[227]

Spiritualism's 'phenomena' – as summarised in the Spiritualist
Teachings 'given' to Mrs E. H. Britten and 'laid by her under the
Foundation Stone of the Spiritualist Temple, Oldham, Lancs . . .
April 9th 1887' – 'open[ed] up arenas of new research for science':
'being founded upon facts', 'it place[d] true religion on the basis
of science, and revitalize[d] science with all that [was] true and
practical in religion.'[228] This gives us a further sense of spiritualism's so-called 'naturalisation of the supernatural': the two might
perhaps be set so as to multiply each other. Unfortunately, in
spiritualist eyes, the prejudice of the established scientific
community against so revolutionary a basis of knowledge silenced
many 'spiritual' discoveries of new facts in natural science until
such time as the latter had caught up. Though Davis, in the year
(1846) when an 8th planet was discovered, had predicted – 'spiritually' or plain plausibly – the discovery of a 9th, he had to wait
until 1873 before even spiritualists felt able to trumpet this (still 57
years prematurely, as it turned out[229]). More portentously, Burns
claimed Professor Huxley's announcement of the existence of
'protoplasm' as the basic organic substance

contain[ed] nothing new, at least to those acquainted with the spiritualist philosophy. The first volume of *Human Nature*, even from the very first article, contained allusions to this view of organisation. Twenty years ago, [A.J.] Davis, in a state of clairvoyance, . . . declared that the first forms of life originated in deep sea bottoms, and that a gelatinous mud nurtured the first germs of organisation. [Recent] exploration of the Atlantic Ocean bottom . . . [had] brought to the surface from depths of from 5000 to 15,000 feet a slimy mud, which, after much examination by Professor Huxley and others was found identical with the description of the primary substance given by Davis.

Natural-scientific confirmation of spiritual insights was occurring. Burns claimed, 'daily'.[230] But, again unfortunately, neither Professor Huxley nor the contractors for the Atlantic cable were interested in spiritualist telegraphy.

Not that spiritualists saw the natural sciences alone as standing to benefit from the new insights. Occult phenomena would also, it was hoped, give privileged access for historical research too. After all, if J. W. Jackson could publish a book on *Ethnology and Phrenology as an Aid to the Historian*,[231] why could not spiritualists use their own methods to embark on analogous ventures? Thus Burns enthused over 'psychometrical' confirmation that Europeans, too, had had progenitors 'whom we might not be so ready to recognise': 'savage, huge and brawny . . . aboriginal' hunters.[232] But he also hoped for active confirmation directly from former cultures. Accordingly, he proposed that the third Convention of Spiritualists 'should delegate a commission of mediums and others, to hold *seances* in the catacombs within the pyramids of Egypt. Layard had made great discoveries in Nineveh. The pick and shovel had divulged much, but the more potent "sword of the spirit" would attain much greater achievements.' His audience were surely at their most sympathetic at this juncture: they were on an excursion to the Crystal Palace where some had gone to the socalled 'Egyptian Court' for this very purpose. Here, though, after not surprisingly attracting an unwelcome throng of onlookers, they had retreated to the gardens, were they were now gathered in 'a shady spot, flanked by blooming rhododendrons near a pool of water.' Immediately before Burns's speech, a spirit had promised that such investigations would 'enable mankind to arrive at many hidden facts respecting the history of former ages'; and, immediately after, 'it was stated by other speakers that such a mission to the Land of Egypt was already in contemplation.'[233] To spiritualists, all this might appear a daring application of their belief; to anti-spiritualists, it could amount only to an intellectual debauch.

Irrespective of whether these contemplations ever brought forth an expedition, attempts to rewrite history 'spiritually' were quite frequent. One of the most ambitious was the Glasgow medium, David Duguid's, autobiography of 'Hafed, Prince of Persia' which Burns and others reviewed and resumed at great length.[234] This 'spirit' was all the more exciting for having allegedly been contemporaneous with Jesus.

But however much they might boost sales, such extravaganzas were hardly likely to aid the accumulation of findings. And indeed, from some spiritualists and others, cumulativeness is something we would be wrong even to look for. Our psychometrical-botanic friend J. R. Buchanan, for example, believed that 'fifty or sixty years' previously, 'many of the so-called wonders that astonished the multitude today were . . . familiar to a more thoughtful class of investigators. How subjects deteriorate as they become vulgarised, traded upon, by those who take up, ready made, the researches that have been attained to by the serious and toilsome labour of others!' Not that he sought to stand progress on its head. Rather, he drew comfort from the thought that there were 'periodicities in all things, regulating the succession of changes through which mental phenomena pass in the course of years, similar to the career of annual vegetation in the course of days . . ., leaving a thin stratum of solid mud behind, deepening the basis of further growth.'[235] For him, cumulativeness existed but was imperceptible to the mortal eye: the main movements apparent were cyclical. He was prepared for others to discern 'periodicities' even longer than his 'sixty years', and to claim that their particular pursuit resurrected some traditional or even ancient forgotten wisdom. But, whatever one's chosen rhythm, it did not have to be that of a 'Professor Huxley'.

Again, 'spiritual' aids might allow posthumous flexibility to the doctrines of physically dead thinkers (as when, via Davis's mediumship, the 'translated' Swedenborg softened the doctrine of hell which he had taught when in the flesh[236]). Or they might also pronounce on human psychology.[237] Or they might, far more usefully and frequently assist healers, as we shall see in the next chapter.[238] But (except, often, in the latter area) no degree of interest or even plausibility could abolish the chasm between belief and disbelief in spirit contact.

In other words we are back with (to paraphrase an earlier remark) beginnings outnumbering continuations. Spiritualism was repeatedly in the position of offering unappreciated breakthroughs within or ahead of more orthodox areas of research, while the most constant sound emanating from its own was of simple repetition of spirit contact. Spiritualism thus shared a problem with phrenology, mesmerism and other areas of what Burns called 'Human Natural Science'.[239] This was (to paraphrase again) the contrast between the global reach of their theories and the individual grasp of their practice.

I have taken Hall or Skelton in order to explore what were probably the commonest logical problems of nineteenth-century democratic epistemology. We can now look at one person who will help us plumb the extremes of eccentricity (perhaps of lunacy, but that does not weaken the argument) which these problems could help trigger – extremes far beyond those we have just been charting.

As we shall see, David Richmond's intellect was nothing if not independent. And for us his first point of interest is that he exemplifies the economic underpinning of many a plebeian autodidact's intellectual independence by abilities as a craftsman and/or small trader.[240] His origins were themselves artisan-radical:

> I was born in January 1816. I attended the 'Methodist' Schools. My father was a linen weaver and [like so many in that trade at this time] of the Radical school, and, working in the shop with him and others, I became a reformer, and well remember the struggle for the passing of the Reform Bill and the election of the first Quaker member of Parliament. I resided in Leeds in 1836, where I joined teetotallism. In 1837 I settled in Bradford, where I became a Socialist or Owenite, and became very well acquainted with the Secularistic and liberal views of the time. In 1841 I became a Vegetarian and Sacred Socialist

David Richmond
Woolcomber, later shoemaker. Teetotal, vegetarian and
communitarian from around 1840, David emigrated to America
as an Owenite, but soon became a Shaker and then also a
spiritualist. In 1853, was spiritualism's first missionary to British
plebeians. Left the Shakers. Returned to his native Darlington,
where he penned turgid visions: 'while he stitched his boots, his
mind was wandering through eternity.'

> or 'Concordist,' and afterwards I resided in the Society [the
> 'Concordium'] at Ham House, Ham Common.[241]

He was obviously a roving spirit, for he had once walked from
Northern England to Penzance (Cornwall), keeping himself by
'working at his trade of a woolcomber . . . where he could find
occupation.' This had been when he had been still 'quite a young
man'. At this time his craftsmanly trampings already had a
religiously bookish aspect: he 'carried . . . a New Testament in his
pocket, and studied its pages'. And when – eventually, after (as

we saw in Chapter 1) his move to the USA (1842), his period as
a Shaker (1846) and his tribulations (to which I will come) during
the 1850s – he settled back in Darlington, he deliberately sought
something which might continue this combination.

His old trade of woolcombing was increasingly racked by mech-
anisation. So, as Richmond's closest obituarist reported him
saying, instead of returning to that,

> I came to my native town and settled down in this small street,
> and put up my sign as a shoemaker. [This would have been
> in 1862.] The poor people bring me their work. I do it. . . .
> They pay me when it's done. I have enough or to spare, for
> I don't require much. [He was still highly vegetarian.] My class
> of customers don't trouble themselves about my opinions, or
> leave me because of them, as a class higher in the social scale
> would do.

Further, he had been particular in his *choice* of craft: 'I chose shoe-
making because while it kept my hands busy it left my mind free.'
'While sitting day by day at his shoemakers bench, [he would]
reason of "righteousness, temperance and judgement to come".' In
other words, 'while he stitched his boots, his mind was wandering
through eternity.' Happily, 'all his work was thorough' – in boot-
stitching at least: arguably, more than a stitch was loose in his
methods as a visionary.

The latter quality is regrettable, for he was surely (so far as
decipherable) the grandest shoemaker-visionary since the death of
Jacob Boehme in 1624.[242] The pressures that may have developed
this quality in him (and not in many others from his background)
are of course hard to research; but some surmises can be hazarded
here. His early denominational history is unclear. But the facts
(already noted) that he had, during his childhood, seen the inside of
'the "Methodist" schools' and, during his youth, been an obsessive
consulter of the New Testament are pointers towards some early
preoccupation with prophecy. Not that this was so unusual either,
but, in addition, his leaving Ham Common for America is
explicitly linked by his biographer to 'advanced viewpoints
[finding] a more genial [sic] soil [there] than in England'.

There were also particular pressures impelling him into prophecy
during the 1850s. Early in the decade, he paid two visits to

England. As I explained during Chapter 1, he saw his 'mission' during these as a double one: spiritualist as well as, if not more than, Shaker. But of course, this was hardly how the Shakers were likely to see it. Richmond must presumably have foreseen or feared this from the start. In any case, he began having visions towards the end of his second stay in Britain (1853), and anxiety about his tensions with the Society of Shakers is one plausible-enough factor in this timing. Certainly, once his welcome from the Shakers had confirmed his fears, his visions intensified. And we can imagine that their persistence into his final few decades was guaranteed by the agony which immediately ensued on his quarrel with the Society: when he and his wife seceded, they had to go to law to recover custody of their 7-year-old son.[243] (The role of Richmond's wife – whom he had married in Bradford, probably during the early 1840s – is little mentioned, though she seems[244] to have been with him during his 1853 trip.) Richmond's religious-emotional miseries during these years may well, therefore, have pitched him deeper still into other worlds.

In his visions – or in those of them that reached print, at least – he figures less as a prophet in his own right than as a seer and recorder of alarums, ages and armageddons of truly cosmic proportions. He was 'according to his own statement in constant rapport with the spiritual world,' and this state seems to have lasted for the rest of his life.[245] It helps to account for his major (though, it seems, little-trumpeted) deviation from certainly most plebeian spiritualists: his implicit acceptance that the Bible was in some way literally true. This, no doubt, went with his search for a framework within which to situate his own mystical experiences: he was often reinterpreting the sacred books to suit these.[246]

Most saliently Richmond believed that 'the manifesting of the Godhead and the ending of time' had occurred in 1854[247] – to him at least. 'Ever since' this event, he explained, 'virtually to me, Time is no longer: so that millions of angels and millions of Spirits are as familiar to me as mortals in the Body.'[248] This 'manifesting' refers, presumably, to what others usually called the millennium. If so, then Richmond was in a minority among millenarians in being what is called 'pre-millennialist' – in expecting the Second Coming to precede the thousand-year rule of the saints. Pre-millennialists tended to rely less on human action and more on divine, than 'post-millennialists'.[249] If, as I have argued, spiritualists in effect atomised millenarian doctrine, then Richmond, as we shall see, did so with its pre-millennialist version. The result was extremism (of a kind) at the cosmic level, combined with quietism at the mundane. This may be one reason why so much of his writing seems, in an eschatological (i.e. end-of-the-world) sort of way, to jumble tenses as much as it does quotes from holy writ. And the extremism of his visionariness helped propel him to the periphery of the movement he had helped found. During, for example, the preparations for a conference of spiritualists (perhaps, one imagines, the 'national' 'convention of progressive spiritualists' held in Darlington during 1865), the organisers 'had an inkling of the mysterious nature of David's lucubrations, and managed to shelve [his offer of a paper]. "Oh, it doesn't matter," said the imperturbable David, "if you don't want to hear it, I'll go down and read it in the backyard. There are thousands (of spirits) who want to hear it."'[250] Such extremism, though, must occasionally have embarrassed one or two spiritualists – whatever their usual feelings of tolerance towards so harmless an eccentric: Richmond was merely multiplying or inflating their own between-worlds stance. Eccentric he might be, but who was developing this stance the more consistently?

One of its essential qualities was that, with Richmond at least, politics for this world too remained socialist, even though his earthly strategy dissolved. After his secession from the Shakers, 'he engaged . . . in other social movements in the States and visited the Fourierite Settlement in company with Mr Horace Greeley.' Again, after his final return to Darlington, he spoke to local spiritualists of the struggle between Cain and Abel as one between individualism and socialism; and he predicted (analogously to the late Robert Owen whom we heard in Chapter 2) that spiritual 'Manifestations' 'will Progress unto the Holy Communion in the Righteous Principle of Joint Ownership of the Land in the Principle of Cooperation'.[251] His associating of socialism with 'Communion' is parallel, incidentally, with that by an even later Owenite, the bilingual Welsh Mancunian, R. J. Derfel who, though in many ways secularist, filled many volumes with (English) rhymes that were mystical, if far more loosely than Richmond's heavy prose. There are also similarities with Edward Carpenter's *Towards Democracy*. (With neither Derfel nor Carpenter, though, do any parallels suggest an awareness of Richmond or by him of either of them.)[252]

In strategy, however, Richmond viewed any organisation broader than local as inappropriate for at least spiritualists.[253] Indeed his strategy was atomistic at an unusually fundamental level: he was reported as 'think [ing of] the unfolding of being in a practical life [as] the complete and God given work of man. Every step is thus a step of salvation. This process will accomplish the work of Societary Reform.'[254]

Thus his politics – his extremist quietism as we may call it – gave him some common ground with other plebeian radicals, though even here he had his unusual aspects. But his visions seem to have been as gaseously baffling to most of his contemporaries[255] as they remain to us. This left him orating much less to them than to himself; or rather, for claiming to have seen and talked with millions of spirits, he must often have been forced by the bemusement of people around him to carry on doing so – whether at his bench or 'in the backyard'. Locally, not only secularists seem to have joked, to his face, that he had 'seen God and killed the Devil'. He was even rumoured to have tried his hand, Red Sea-wise, at parting the waters of a local river – and, worse, to have claimed success. Thus 'to the common herd, of course, David was mad.' We may wish to join them. And even his closest obituarist, probably a full believer in spiritualism, hazarded the judgment that Richmond 'may have taken, in some cases, subjective impressions for objective realities'. Yet even among the autodidacts in 'the common herd' (hardly the best metaphor for them, surely), he still seems to have enjoyed a certain backhanded prestige in the area. 'There was nothing, said an old Secularist once, not derisively but admiringly, left for David to learn. He had weighed up all systems, moral and material, governmental and religious.' 'Though peculiar,' another spiritualist added, 'he was a man of great intellectual ambition and an acute dialectician.'[256]

However great Richmond's 'peculiarities', they were seen as still earning him a place at the outer edges of the broad world of plebeian autodidact progressives. We can therefore nod with at least one statement of his – made as he paused while narrating his visions to the Leeds 'Spiritual Church' during 1885. We can nod, not in agreement but in our understanding: both it and its outland-

ishness symbolise many of the problems of democratic epistemologies of the nineteenth-century type. 'I am not', Richmond stated,

> a person who can be led on by imagination, nor by deceptive
> performances. I am not a medium at all in the matter; but my
> development through all the phases and struggles of Reform
> has opened up as it were to me, in my Spiritual and Natural
> Senses, the order of Immortal Being. And this my status [sic]
> has continued – day by day and hour by hour.[257]

In the long run, sadly, so much the worse for this (nineteenth-
century?) range of democratic epistemologies. From 1853, we can
hear Skelton quoting Samuel Thomson's own quotation of the
famous protest: 'What can we reason, but from what we know?'[258]
But with our awareness (such as it is) of what established scientists
have achieved during the last two or three generations, we can
also interpret this protest, in numerous ways and at every stage of
the re-quotation, as a licence for anything from mysticism to a
refusal to trust any instrument or theory that one could not, if one
wished, make or comprehend by one's own dexterity and common
sense. Here too, in other words, we can sense the outflanking of
these democratic epistemologies. Thus, when we discuss epistemology even in our sense, we still need to define knowing.

Chapter 7   Healing

We have already, in passing, noted an overlap between plebeian and various more broadly heterodox healing-practices. Parts of the overlap were in method and epistemology – as defined during the last two chapters. The present chapter focusses firstly and mainly on the healing practice that was most specifically – though of course not exclusively – compatible with spiritualist belief: that of so-called spiritual healing. By this I mean any healing – mental or physical – which is said to benefit identifiably from the assistance of spirits of physically dead people. As we will see, such assistance was variously conceived as aiding anything from initial diagnosis, to final and in a sense seemingly just 'physical' aspects of curative treatment. In the chapter as a whole, I will allow certain individuals to seem to introduce themselves, along with their claims and problems, rather casually. My reason for this, is that presummary – let alone an opening glossary of terms – can sometimes overdomesticate the – to me at least – strangeness of the claims that are being summarised. This would be unhistorical.

'It is one of the joys of my life to see the revival of apostolic healing.' Henry Pitman, brother of the best-known of short-hand pioneers, was equally well-known during these years – the early 1870s – as an opponent of drink, meat eating, the Contagious Diseases Acts and vaccination. He was penning a testimony to Joseph Ashman whom we met earlier. Healers such as Ashman were, for Pitman, 'mediums in the hands of the Great Healer'. True, a metaphor is, by definition, interpretable at many levels of literalness. And the one just quoted has been applied in praise of most varieties of medicine, including the orthodox. But Pitman, in his next sentence, made the context of his own outburst very clear: 'the drug addiction is doomed'. For him, in other words, medical orthodoxy was yet another bugbear; and the occult would help rout it.[1] His testimony went on also to describe some of Ashman's methods of healing:

the magnetised flannel you sent was efficacious in congestion of the chest; and when you kindly came to see us, you at once discovered the place of weakness in the lungs, and gave further relief by your magnetic passes.

The methods which Ashman himself remembered using from the very start of his career as a healer were similar. In early 1870, while assisting a visiting American healer, he had asked the latter whether he 'could have the same power'. The healer had

said yes, and gave me one of his magnetised *cartes de visite*. Armed with this talisman, I ventured on my first endeavour to relieve pain. Seeing one day a cabman with a swollen face standing by a police court ready to prosecute a man who had assaulted him, I asked him if, on condition I healed him, he would forgive his adversary. He replied that he would, and we accordingly got into his cab together. Bringing out the magnetised *carte*, I told him to look at it, and at the same time made a few motions over the swelling with my hand. I then left him much better and returned in an hour's time, when I found him taking a glass of beer with his antagonist, whom he had forgiven.

Ashman's 'talisman', as we have seen him calling it himself, may evoke comparison with certain healing-practices in many continents as well as – a comparison Ashman himself would have seen as equally relevant – with nineteenth-century mesmerism. But he was soon to discover that such devices of physical linkage were dispensable for all healing except – as we have noted with the Pitman case – at a distance. Ashman's discovery was necessitated – after 'by some chance' he had lost the *carte* 'as also the magnetised paper' which his American teacher had sent him – when he turned out to 'possess the power [him]self'. On this occasion, he helped a cripple to walk, merely by 'plac[ing his] hand on [the sufferer's] foot and knee'.

As has no doubt become obvious already, we are not so far dealing with strictly spiritual healing. Ashman's interest here, is that, although he was 'heart and soul . . . a Spiritualist',[2] his curative methods – which seem to have involved hypnotism (as we might call it today) stroking, rubbing, breathing at or opposite the

site of affliction and, occasionally, what he called 'percussion' –
bore a rather broad contemporary kinship. Such breadth seems to
have been typical of many or most spiritual healers, as well as of
spiritualists who were also healers as of healers who were not
necessarily spiritualists. We will call such breadth 'eclectic' (this
time with a small 'e').

Ashman's own kinship was not only with mesmerism and
'animal magnetism', but also with the seemingly more mundane
'medical rubbing'. Joseph Ashman (1834–1882) was brought up in
a rural Suffolk environment. Here he was allegedly steeped in a
popular spiritualist and medical tradition of unstated age – 'a native
spiritualism . . ., in which he participated'. 'As a farming man,
[he] was successful in healing the ailments of horses and cattle.' As
for the ailments of humans, the local lack of medical men 'often
obliged [the poor] to trust to their own simple *materia medica*
(fortunately for themselves, perhaps . . .)'. Thus he often 'said that
he was by nature a spiritualist and a Healer.' These, for him, twin
bents eventually extruded him from his original environment for,
though only a farm labourer of some sort and already 'with a
young family', he 'left his toil that he might follow the Spirit'.[3]
True, he may also have been impelled by a more earthy dissatisfaction: he was never to forget how, 'in early life, . . . [when] in
service in the country, . . . his master used to flog him until . . .
he nearly cut him in two.'[4] But his restlessness had nonetheless a
religious aspect which can be measured by the fact that, by the
time of his arrival as a healer, he had 'dwelt in the tents of the
Mormonites', and had at some different time 'been one of the
Peculiar People'.[5] Apparently it was in spiritualism that he found
something approaching ecstasy:

> Spiritualism [was] so in harmony with the yearnings of my
> inmost soul, that a heavenly music (whose completeness is
> the guarantee of its perfection) dwells within my breast; and,
> in my own sensations, I seem to stand forth as a whole and
> unified nature.

He felt this unity with creation on any level, including the physical.
And there is more than coincidence that this purple passage of his
should have occurred during a printed discussion about healing:

Ashman believed his own ecstasy to be linked with his healing gifts.[6]

Ashman's career as a full-time healer was said to have been triggered in early 1870 when he saw an advertisement for the meetings of the American healer (and friend of James Burns), Dr Newton, printed in the main publication of the temperance movement.[7] The two men found themselves to be 'of a kindred' and 'understood one another' – to such an extent that, during the latter part of Newton's 1870 tour, they often worked together as a team.[8] Shortly after Newton's departure,[9] Ashman settled in London as a healer. His economic plight, which had presumably been increased by his religious wanderings, were not at first eased by this new departure; and only a timely fee from a wealthy spiritualist lady enabled him to bury one of his children.[10] When the Rev. Morris Davies visited Ashman's so-called 'Psychopathic Institution' during 1874, he found most of the patients to be plebeian and the institution's premises to be small and seedy. But Ashman himself seems to have combined in his appearance the respectable and plebeian modes with the prophetic: Davies found in him 'a short cheery-looking man, with long, straight flaxen hair flowing down over the shoulders of his black frock coat' and an accent of 'broad provincial dialect'.[11] During the next eight years, up to his death at the end of 1882, Ashman went 'up-market' in his premises (from Marylebone to Kensington), as in his dress and clientele – though, in the latter regard, he is still said to have never rebuffed 'the deserving poor'. Relatedly, overwork hastened his death.[12]

Such overtaxing of his 'immense vitality and great magnetic power'[13] would have been more than simply mental. For although Ashman called himself a healing 'medium', his method also retained echos of rural bone-setting in its frequent emphasis, already noted, on physical manipulation. In addition, Ashman employed two 'rubbers' to alleviate much of the physical effort necessary with most patients. Luckily too, he himself 'looked healthy enough to heal a sick rhinoceros' (according to Davies, at least[14]).

Sometimes, however, the successes of even such methods were and still are credited by other healers and by their patients to, at least in part, supernatural intervention. Even with Ashman, we have seen at least an allusion to this from his patient Pitman. And yet Ashman included such testimonials in a book whose main aim was patently not to publicise himself so much as to instruct anyone in his medical methods and to give a lengthy but in the end tentatively couched exposition of their possible physical and physiological foundations. In all this, his democratic assumptions were clear: 'Do all [people]', he asked himself, 'possess this power [to heal by his methods]? My answer is that I believe nearly all possess it in a greater or less degree, and that it is cultivable.'[15] '"For a healer"', he similarly harangued the Rev. Dr Davies, '"give me a man as can clean a window or scrub a floor. Christ himself when He chose those who were to be healers as well as preachers, chose fishermen, fine deep-chested men, depend upon it, Sir"', and he rapped upon his own sonorous lungs until they reverberated.'[16]

Ashman is an ethically straightforward introduction to a subtly unstable mixture, in this area during my period, of fundamental uncertainty about the foundations of the physical world (my 'problematic of imponderables'), an often amazed discovery of one's own powers, a caustically exoteric (or, as I have called it, epistemologically democratic) approach to medical knowledge, personal exhibitionism and, not least, a probably growing commercialism.

Spiritualism, as present-day students have often emphasised,[17] was and is a religion of healing – not only of the healing of the great divide between the physically dead and living (as we shall see in the next chapter), but also of the latter's ills and miseries. Perhaps, though, the word 'religion' has acquired too many connotations of hierarchy to be accurate here. For, the emphases on healing and on self-improvement were not dissociated aspects, but rather strengthened each other. Plebeian spiritualists, as we saw in earlier chapters, wished to democratise the occult, and would have seen the contradictions between these two words as no more than etymological. This wish was of a piece with their support for what I have called democratic medicine and democratic epistemology.

Here again, examples are actually more concise than a summary. I will begin with an autobiography, that of W. A. Jones (known as 'Rolandus') of Tredegar. Jones was the eldest of nine children,[18] and had very little education, beginning as a steelworker at the age of 8. This was to be his main livelihood until 1891 when, after 'many years' of daily 'twelve hours . . . [at] hard manual labour, two or three hours healing afterwards, and then a few hours study on mystical subjects', as well as on 'Physiology, Mesmerism,

Phrenology, etc.', he at last began to heal on a full-time basis. His main break in his previous routine had come during 1882–85 when unemployment had taken him to Bristol. In parenthesis, though, a major break had nearly come during 1881, when his abilities as a singer, violinist and composer had attracted at least one financial backer and would perhaps have opened a career in music, but for Rolandus's religious scruples against his likeliest employer, the Church of England.

With an allegedly so poor and principled background, Rolandus's interest for us is, first, that he awoke to the benefits of, simultaneously, literacy, unorthodox medicine and the occult; and, second, that these awakenings happened to begin just *before* bereavement had roused him into a hatred of medical orthodoxy. When he was 11 or 12, his dislike of books was transformed into a passion. For, he had begun 'pondering over my grandfather's . . . old works on Astrology, Herbalism, etc.'. His attention had 'centred chiefly on Culpepper's Herbal, which [grandfather] used to say was his Bible'. Although grandfather 'reprimanded' him 'for rummaging amongst his books', he gave him the Culpepper – that is to say, the originally (if, since, unevenly rewritten) seventeenth-century astrologico-botanic compendium – which the young Rolandus proceeded to learn off by heart, and which helped redouble his interest in astrology.

But about this time, these heady new interests were given tragic urgency:

> I had just turned twelve years when my little brother and sister had typhus fever. My little sister had it first. Of course the doctor was called in and prescribed for her. I watched her day by day. Up to this time I had never dreamt of inability on the part of doctors to cure disease; I placed confidence in them – as too many do now – supposing that innumerable discoveries had been made since Culpepper's time; consequently, I took for granted that doctors knew all about disease, and the exact *how* to cure it.
>
> But my little sister continued to grow worse; and here I began to get confused, for the teachings of the pulpit were crowding on my mind. I was a regular attendant at Chapel and Sunday School, and they taught that Jesus frequently called the little lambs to his fold, and I was obliged to submit in my

mind that my little sister would die after all. I could see the
hope growing fainter in my parents, but, somehow, a deep
impression had taken hold of me.

I could not possibly get myself to believe that it was God's
will that little children should die. I reasoned with myself that
the All-Wise intended every person to grow up to maturity,
and in case a young person died or suffered pain, I thought
surely some law, or laws, had been violated. This idea had
taken deep root in my mind; I could not possibly get over
and reject this conclusion. Therefore, the teachings of my
superiors I could not reconcile to my way of thinking.

One evening a special message was sent requesting the doctor
to come as soon as possible. He came in about half an hour,
and with (what appeared to me) provoking coolness and
indifference took her little hand, and said in a matter of fact
way: 'She is dying. She will last a few hours.' The impression
then made upon me I felt could never be erased from my
memory. In the intensity of my grief I went out, and child-
like my faith was strong, and I prayed that God would spare
my little sister, and not take her away. I thought, surely, he
would heed and answer my cry to him; but I was doomed to
disappointment. She passed away that night.

I cannot properly describe my feeling when it was announced
that she was gone. I was stupefied with amazement. I had felt
my faith sufficiently strong to remove mountains, and yet here
I was denied a simple favour. I did not rebel against religious
teachings; they were too profound for my understanding, but
with the knowledge I had of medical books which
contradicted one another, I soon came to the conclusion there
was something rotten in the state of (Denmark) doctorcraft.

Jones now 'determined at whatever cost to investigate and find
out' what, significantly, he italicised in the singular as 'the *cause* of
pain and disease'. For, with a rather autodidact confidence, he 'felt
certain that pain could be subdued and . . . that disease could be
eradicated, notwithstanding the utter ability of doctors to do so.'

The object of all my thoughts now, the one aim of my life,
was to obtain the 'Pearl of great Price' – Knowledge!
Accordingly, books on mystical subjects had a new charm to

me. Just after laying my little sister's body to rest, my brother
became very ill, and he too would have passed on under the
doctor's treatment. I well remember that my parents had no
hope for him from the first; they considered his case more
severe than my little sister's. But luckily, an acquaintance of
my father's came to the rescue and saved him. I was anxious
to know what means had been employed, and they informed
me that he had only manipulated his feet and legs – rubbed
them gently for a long while.

The little patient was unconscious, had been so all that day
previous to the stranger's interference; methinks I can see his
vacant stare and glassy eyes even now. Next day he had
changed marvellously; he became bright and lively towards
noon, and began to improve rapidly. What mighty remedy
had this working man applied? Had he dived into the
wonderfully learned Physiologies, and learnt great and valuable
secrets? Nothing of the kind. He had learned to use his own
faculties and powers, which learned doctors have not. I
afterwards learned that this man was no scholar, although he
could read fairly well; in physical strength, however, he was a
veritable Hercules.

I now became dreadfully in earnest, devouring all the books
that came in my way: Haller's Physiology, the Cyclopedia of
Practical Surgery, and a lot of minor medical books, all of
which only excited my disgust at the end; and after my
wearisome task I found myself acquainted with a redundant
technical verbiage without any solid basis. The ponderous
tomes, thundering with heavy words, are make-believe very
learned, but they are in reality not so, because they run into
the old moss-grown theories, constantly imperfect and false.

So many of the medical definitions seemed to him circular.
Physiologists, he believed he had found, could not 'understand
processes which explain themselves every day before their very
noses'.

Rolandus therefore 'found no resting place in medical books: so-
called Physiologists were treating upon the "House", and
completely misapprehended and ignored the "Tenant" . . . I had
not found the prize – Light on the sublime mystery, Man!' And it
was, he says, 'just here' that he 'stumbled across Mesmerism' with

a series of lectures by a black man, Henry Box Brown.[19] Jones
now read some books on this subject. He also met a 'Professor
of [i.e. travelling lecturer on] Mesmerism and Phrenology'. This
Professor instructed him not only in mesmerism's techniques but
also in its 'healing powers . . .; I was therefore prepared to tackle
disease'. However, 'things turned out in quite an unlooked-for
manner' – a manner most important in our context. For

> after magnetising some of my subjects, and getting them
> through a few experiments, especially Phreno-experiments,
> some of them began to behave themselves in a strange manner;
> in short, they appeared to me to change into another person,
> the voice, gestures, and general deportment became entirely
> different, and, in fact, they addressed me as other persons
> would do, sometimes giving names of persons scores of miles
> away, the number of house and name of town. I demagnetised
> them, and tried to restore them to their normal condition;
> sometimes I was unsuccessful, as on a few occasions it was
> nearly an hour before I could succeed in restoring them to a
> proper normal state.
> I read up a lot of matter relating to Mesmerism, although I
> could think of nothing in the various authors to throw light
> upon my difficulty. I was considerably puzzled, so I went over
> several books on the subject carefully, but oddly enough the
> books were all silent on this point.

Nonetheless, and to Rolandus's surprise, his Professor replied
that 'although it was rather a rare occurrence still spirits did sometimes take control of mesmerised subjects': 'this', Jones writes,

> was the date [1884] of my conversion to spiritualism, and I
> found that pulpit teachings which I had hitherto regarded as
> the 'very word of God', were the illogical conclusions of
> ignorant men; I found that our friends who had passed on
> were frequently (if not constantly) in our midst, and not in the
> 'lake of fire and brimstone' to be sport for the devil and his
> angels; nor in the orthodox heaven – a sort of circumscribed
> palace where the favoured few were singing psalms and
> waving palms. Even up to the time of writing I have proof
> that our departed friends are taking an active interest in our

affairs, and are busily engaged in our betterment and upliftment.

Jones also gives one detailed example of the manner of such engagement:

> In 1889 I attended a poor woman who was laid up with erysipelas. She was fifty years of age and in much pain. She was quite ignorant on religious subjects; could not read her own name . . . Her eyes were swollen and closed . . . I passed my hands over face and eyes for twenty minutes; the swelling was now going down, so she opened her eyes. After making a few longitudinal passes from head to feet, she went to sleep, and I then left her sleeping.
> Next evening I called again. When I entered the room she began telling me that as soon as I had left her the preceding day, a very fine lady had made her appearance, and immediately commenced making passes over her, just as I had done, but a little more rapidly. I then commenced operating, and could see her passing into a sleep. As soon as I had discontinued, she immediately spoke up, and described the spirit Mesmerist who had then appeared again. Pointing her out to me, I stepped aside, and the Operator from the other sphere succeeded me at once, and began making passes. I was informed that she repeated the magnetising the third time, but I considered further treatment on my part unnecessary, and the matter ended.
> The patient made a complete recovery.

In this long extract from his autobiography, we have heard Rolandus mentioning two types of relationship with spirits. Firstly, people could be possessed by the spirits of other people who were still physically alive; secondly, the sick could be cured by the spirits of people who were physically dead. Some other healers claimed more complicated relationships with spirits. Some believed their magnetism to be their own, but that spirit-help went towards the diagnosis.[20] Others claimed to have spirit-assistance during every stage of the treatment.[21]

At an untypical extreme, we can quote a series of spirit-relationships which one healer-woman, Chandos Leigh Hunt (whom we met during Chapter 6B), claimed as the factual basis[22] of her late-1880s spiritualist novel, entitled *Visibility Invisible and Invisibility Visible*. Admittedly, Chandos, as we shall see subsequently, was nothing if not a complex ideologue of healing. But there is little in this to either strengthen or weaken her novelistic veracity. Possibly strengthening it, indeed, is the novel's lack of purely novelistic attractions (despite a deal of tired-romantic huffings and puffings) and, even more, its being published by James Burns. It even carried an unmistakeable word-portrait of him, and also of Ashman. It would hardly have been published, I would therefore argue, had it seemed implausible (however untypical) to at least spiritualists.

The novel's plot revolves mainly around the dipsomania of a hitherto respectable father and the curative efforts of his daughter and of her fiancé, who are the heroine and hero. The latter accidentally discovers Burns's occult and reform bookshop, borrows a work on manual healing along with another work – this time in manuscript – on the techniques of 'animal magnetism' and, accidentally again, puts his beloved into trance. In this state she becomes – as the Burns-figure subsequently diagnoses to the bewildered hero – 'clairvoyant and . . . [sees] that her father . . . is in reality controlled by the undeveloped spirit of a drunkard'. This spirit's unabated craving for drink leaves him unreconciled to his dematerialised status – despite his having entered it via suicide. Our hero asks for help in 'get[ting] rid of this spirit'.[23] and a colleague of the Burns-figure replies 'if my [spirit-]guides could see [it] they could tell you what to do'. This colleague, a medium, then goes to the afflicted home. Here, with surely a certain sense of occasion, the father – or the victim, as I will call him, so as, to distinguish him from his deceased drunkard tormentor – is lying in a drunken stupor. The colleague at once puts himself into a state of spirit-possession: his 'frame became strangely convulsed and then very still. After remaining silent for a minute or so, he rose to his feet' – till at least this clause, these lines had been a classic description of this state – 'and spoke in a quiet, kind and firm voice which sounded strangely [unfamiliar]'. Meanwhile the hero has returned the beloved back to her, magnetic, trance. In this state – which, as in some of my previous examples, will not after all turn out to be all that different from the colleague's mediumistic one – she sees the medium's (white and pure) spirit-guide extract the bad drunkard spirit from the victim's stupefied body and put it into the body of the medium. The latter accordingly begins to behave drunkenly, but is calmed by the still entranced heroine aided both by the good spirit-guide and by another good spirit who later – and perhaps in too mundanely novelistic a fashion – turns out to be the drunkard's mother. The medium then – as I would describe it – acts out the drunkard's suicide. Thereby, the latter's spirit is prevailed upon to accept the care of his mother and thereby, in turn, to end his affliction of the victim. The medium and the heroine then simultaneously regain normal consciousness.[24]

For reasons already enumerated, I presume nearly all these spiritualist details to be among the non-novelistic features which Chandos claimed for her book – though whether most spiritualists would have accepted her assumption that people could influence each other while in different states (here, the mesmeric state and the mediumistic) is another question. But 'spiritual' methods were not the only ones which she – along with most other spiritual healers – respected and, many of them, used. To remain with Chandos for another paragraph. Her lecture-topics during the mid-1870s covered a, for us, confusing range of sometimes partly overlapping medical heterodoxies: 'the science of electro-biology', 'magnetism as it has been and as it is practised in other countries', 'developing mediumship' and vegetarianism.[25] She campaigned in print against vaccination, and also spoke and debated on it in various parts of the country.[26] During the same years, she practised mesmeric and magnetic healing, charging prices graded roughly according to the beneficiary's income. She also instructed in the same subject both personally and by post.[27] And this instruction had expanded, by the early 1880s, into a formal course of classes.[28] By the end of this decade, at least six of her pamphlets were in circulation, ranging from *Practical Instructions in . . . Organic Magnetism* – which was among the few works on the subject which Rolandus, for one, thought worth recommending[29] – to anti-vaccination to *Physianthropy; or the Home Cure and Eradication of Disease*[30] and *366 Vegetarian Menus and Beverages*. The last-named area seems to have become her main interest, so that, by 1899, when the *Labour Annual* (which was close to the Independent Labour Party) awarded her a biography, its one-word label for her was to be 'food reformer'.[31] But her widest impact had probably been as an inveterate opponent of orthodox medicine. In her novel, therefore, its only representative had been made into the villain.

Rolandus similarly, as well as using mesmerism, bathing and what he called 'magnetic massage' as his staple curative methods, identified as his best preventives moderate drinking and the eating of 'coarse, plain' and preferably vegetarian foods.[32] We have already noted him, from early on in his healing career, using phrenology in conjunction with mesmerism. This was something of a principle with him: he advised 'every aspirant' healer to 'read carefully' the phrenological classic, Combe's *Constitution of Man*, as well as the more recent work on *Physiology* by the phrenological Professor Fowler, whom he referred to approvingly as 'our Fourier'. Such healers were thus, as we have seen, eclectic in their practice as well as democratic in their theory.

An eclectic approach was, however, hardly incompatible with free competition. Not that something as personal as mediumship lent itself automatically to marketing. Many mediums, including healing ones, probably saw the latter as not only unnecessary but also degrading to their spirits. Neighbourly word-of-mouth was one thing; handbills and printed advertisements were another. But some mediums used publicity resoundingly, even charismatically. And with many another, mediumistic aspects became part of the mongrel routine, perhaps almost as old as the printing press, of medical mongering. Take the following, more or less randomly culled advertisements in the late-1880s spiritualist press:

> J.W. Owen, qualified Medical Herbalist . . . 102, George Street, Hyde, Manchester, Respectfully informs Spiritualists and Mediums that he is prepared to make up any medicine, recipe or medical prescription given through mediums or otherwise obtained, from pure Botanic Remedies, and . . . can also supply the Crude Herbs, Roots, Barks, etc., as the case may require.

This advertisement included testimonials from 'Mr. W. Johnson, the well-known trance medium, 148 Mottram Rd., Hyde' and from 'E. Gallagher, Medical Clairvoyant, Stockport'.[33] Owen's subsequent address dignified itself with the title of 'Hyde Botanic Dispensary and Herbal Medical Stores'. From here he sold seven proprietary medicines, including 'Owen's Blood Scavenger (Registered Trade Mark Number . . .)' and 'Owen's Hindoo Female Pills (Registered Trade Mark Number . . .)' which claimed to 'correct irregularities'. This latter phrase was the then standard euphemism with sellers of abortifacients, although, as Owen continued his patter for this particular medicine with a list of apparently innocent gynaecological properties, I may malign him. His claims for his own curative abilities were as broad as those for his medicines: he 'strictly carried out' 'curative Mesmerism, Massage, Magnetic Healing, and the Herbal System of Medicine'; he 'skilfully treated' 'wounds of every description', and he appealed multifariously to 'sufferers from Diseases of the Stomach, Liver, Lungs, Heart, Bowels, Kidneys, Nervous Diseases, Piles, Rheumatism, Impurities . . . of the Blood, Skin Affections, etc.'. Not least, 'healing at a distance, and Magnetised Water, Oils, Cotton, Pads and Medicines [were] sent to all parts of the Kingdom.'[34] Note how, grammatically and perhaps intentionally, the 'healing' was included in the list of items 'sent'. Given the particular range of these lists, any summary would have taken even longer than my quotation. The point is now amply made, however, that – in addition to so-called 'medical clairvoyance' and 'medical psychometry'[35] – which might or might not claim to benefit wholly or in part from the assistance of spirits – spiritual healing was not merely part of a wide range of heterodox medicines,[36] but was also necessarily situated sideways on to it. By or before around 1900, some of these were becoming ambitiously commercialised – as, all too 'patently' here, this J. W. Owen.[37] On the other hand, many practitioners would have remained part-time for many years: I have already noted Rolandus doing so for a long period. It is probably impossible to know whether a higher proportion of spiritual than of other healers began and sometimes continued without conscious commercial motives. Apparent spirit-contact could sometimes occur with the spirits of most flatteringly famous or enticing dignitaries; and this too could combine with possible charlatanry or perhaps commercial hyperbole. One example would be Robert Harper who, in at least 1874 and based in Wardour Street, Soho, was the medium for 'Dr John Hunter and Dr Mesmer' to 'be consulted upon all forms of illness and for slight surgery cases'[38] and, by 1890 and based in Glasgow,[39] was mediating the 'Curative Mesmerism' of unspecified 'Ancient Roman Women' who, 'connected electrically with [him, undertook] the cure of many diseases.'[40]

Not surprisingly, it was this possibly scandalous aspect of spiritualist healing which attracted the critics. However unrepresentative it was, though, the critics themselves underline how spiritual healing was one significant part of heterodox healing practices. This much can be gathered from the nationwide enquiry carried out during the late 1900s under government auspices, 'as to the Practice of Medicine and Surgery by unqualified persons in the United Kingdom'.[41] Admittedly dependence on the local Medical Officers of Health (the totality of these) rendered this source sketchy, extremely uneven and, of course, biased. But the extent both of heterodox medicine and the presence within it of spiritualist healing – sometimes, as I instanced with J. W. Owen, in close association with herbalism – are not in doubt.

From the start, at least some British spiritualists had known, or known of, an association between spiritualists and healing. True, if we can take one article in the February 1856 *Spiritual Herald* as typical, they recognised this 'power', 'gift' or 'healing virtue' as 'independent of creed' and as apparently 'travelling' between adherents of various denominations – from Catholics to Protestants to Irvingites to mesmerists (allegedly being already 'far less vigorous in many [among the latter] than . . . some years ago'). More important, though, it had now 'arrived at the spiritualists in America'. Here it was 'not occasional only, but resident in the mediums, who . . . meet with a success that can only find its parallel in apostolic times, and even in those the modern gift was not surpassed except in the persons of one or two individuals.' True again, it could fail even with spiritualists, but similar failures had been recorded even 'with the Apostles themselves'. And meanwhile the methods and backgrounds of some of the healers were strikingly various. As to the first, there was 'Charles Main [who] feels the diseases of the affected in his own person before he relieves them by imposition of hands.' As to the second, there was John Scott, a former atheist and Mississippi River pilot, whose house in St Louis was now 'filled daily with patients ready to be touched'.[42] If, we can say, American spiritualism had begun with certain features of a revival, it also had aspects – now and then, at least – of a healing revival. And at the national level in Britain, these aspects also surfaced occasionally – if only in at least some of the tours by American healers (of whom Dr Newton, as noted, was one).

However spasmodic, even or consistent the underlying rhythms of healing in Britain, though, spiritualists seem virtually always to have seen themselves as very much part of a broad medical heterodoxy. Thus we have seen spiritualist journals, both plebeian and not, acting as entrepots for discussions and advertisements in almost any area of heterodox curative theory and practice. Similarly, an early number of *Human Nature* could lengthily echo attacks ancient and modern on 'Drug Medication' as 'necessarily . . . an experimental and murderous art!'.[43]

In the medical field, spiritualists' perception of themselves as anything but isolated was correct: they did not pretend to be original – except as spiritualists – but formed part of a looser revolt. This revolt contrasts with the snobbery, both doctrinal and social, which had characterised most unorthodox physicians during the eighteenth century. But such qualities had, during the intervening generations, lost much of their advantage in the face of orthodoxy's tighter discipline both of itself and of the medical trades throughout Britain.[44]

The coming chapter will note how plebeian spiritualists were no less lacking in originality in relation to death – to an area where, more than in any other, their distinctiveness might have been expected to be at its most fundamental.

Chapter 8 Bridging the great divide

A Death without dying

Spiritualism, Morse explained while himself in trance, was 'really a method by which you are enabled to solve the problem of death without dying',[1] Christianity, he went on, had originally been an excellent bridge to the next world, but was now crumbling. The new bridge was spiritualism: 'if ['the church'] were to admit that communication *could* be received from [the next life], its occupation would be gone.'[2] Such claims might lead us to expect plebeian – which, as with Morse here, meant self-consciously post-Christian – spiritualism to be at its most distinctive in this area. As we will now see, though, the pattern was more interesting. The present section will be about deathbeds and funerals. Spiritualists were not alone in believing the human personality would survive death. But what did they understand by personality? The second section will attempt this tricky question, via an examination of spiritualists' emphasis on the interpenetration between this life and the next.

Discussion of people's uncertainties and inconsistencies can help highlight our own. Nowhere is this truer than when the people we are discussing are Victorians at and around the moment of death. Here, their attitudes and behaviour may seem remoter from us than from some pre-Victorian cultures. Here too, perhaps, we should question both our conception 'Victorian', and the normality of our own culture. Nowadays, researchers on contemporary Western modes of dying report plausibly on how death – particularly of the young – is treated as an unbearably anti-social (partly because uniquely final) act which must be negotiated either indirectly by means of mutual pretence[3] or, if directly, then most carefully.[4] By contrast, during at least my period, death was likelier to come younger and was – officially at least – negotiated oftener than today in terms of belief in personal continuity (pleasant or not) beyond the grave. Whether we accuse our spiritualists, in particular, of practising pleasant mutual pretences depends on our definition of reality.

Our paradigm of Victorian attitudes to death and bereavement would include the following features: close attention to the behaviour of both the dying and the bereaved; and expectation among people of all classes that funerals be as elaborate as money could buy: the drawing of blinds: a funeral industry at its most labour-intensive – employing not merely embalmers, undertakers and stonemasons, but also, for example, 'over 1500 people in the town of Whitby . . . making jet mourning jewelry'[5] – plus, less concentratedly, thousands of black-crape workers, carriage workers, fancy embroiderers[6] and professional mourners, some of these mutes with wands; an emphasis on death's awesomeness; finally, successive stages of mourning starting, of course, with the deepest.[7] This paradigm seems to have remained predominantly accurate. True, it was weakening: exactly when, why and how much is very difficult to say. But even where undermined, it surely retained considerable psychological power. What is clear is that spiritualism was part – fundamentally not a very distinct part – of a counter-trend. Another paradigm which poses similar problems in the same area and period is that of the predominance of hellfire orthodoxy within Victorian Christianity. Some historians have played variations on this; others have simply inverted it: as if the cooling of theologians' hells is to be seen as influencing instantly the theologies purveyed, away from the plusher parts of town, to or among ordinary people. Such easy arguments telescope a number of long-term processes. As these, at the level of any individual person, had a heavily psychological dimension, they were all the likelier to be reversed at critical junctures such as those to do with sickness and death. The same processes occurred anyway at different speeds. They may, quite possibly, have had their greatest overt impact among many plebeians from the 1900s only: why else the transports of excitement, from the mid 1900s, over the Rev. R. J. Campbell's New Theology whose novelty amounted to little more than a vaguely universalist optimism plus an I.L.P.-ish politics, the whole mixture yeasted with fashionably evolutionistic waffle[8]?

The present section will begin not with spiritualists but with secularists. As explained during chapter 5, plebeian spiritualism formed a 'triangle of tensions' with mostly low-church Christianity and with secularism – not merely because many such spiritualists had already experienced one or often both of the other two from the inside but also (among many other reasons) because so many of them remained culturally very close to secularism in particular. In the latter, we have an ism whose overlaps with plebeian spiritualism were, in the area of the present chapter, dwarfed by a polar disagreement as to the finality of death. Secularists believed in no eternity whatever, but were prepared to defy the orthodox hell in a rhetorically Faustian way. Mrs Maden of Stalybridge had been a Wesleyan Methodist schoolteacher. At 20 she married a secularist and soon became one herself. She founded a secularist Sunday school in Rochdale. When she died at 28, her local obituarist in the secularist weekly, the *National Reformer*, reported that she had 'died, as she lived, an unbeliever', adding: 'and if it be true that eternal torments must be her portion she only adds one link to the chain that binds us to the hell that is undeserved, in preference to the heaven that faith alone can win'.[9] In other words, the only heaven that true secularists would have consented to enter (in the unlikely event of its existing) would have been won by the efforts of their own intellect and character.

This was precisely what spiritualists claimed to offer, as we shall see later. In most cultures if not in all, death is self-evidently a crisis for all concerned. As I hinted at the start – and this was only consensus – Victorians watched each other with extra care around this type of crisis. The portents which they were attempting to decipher were to do with religious truth and social respectability. These two dimensions overlapped considerably. Officially at least, the first was the more important, particularly when the dying person was a secularist. Here, the stakes were infinite: on the one hand the snatching of a soul from the jaws of eternal hell, on the other the final triumph of intellectual honesty and personal independence. Clergy and other activists naturally redoubled their efforts to win over (which usually meant to win back) the dying person. Failing this, they could at least hope to extract some moral victory in the eyes of the neighbourhood – whether by issuing their own version of the deceased's last moments or by interfering with the funeral.'The evangelical proof text, "as the tree falls, so it shall lie"', argues Tom Laqueur, 'referred more to a demonstration on the deathbed of already apparent salvation than to a moment of genuine suspense.' Even were this uniformly true in the eyes of each denomination for its faithful adherents (and we must doubt even this[10]), it was frequently anything but true in relation to doctrinal outcasts such as secularists. For them, their opponents prolonged the late-mediaeval death-agony in which the last hours or moments of the dying 'infidel' became a kind of Last Judgment, with the Christians in the role of Judge (and therefore of executioner too).

At the deathbed, there are numerous examples of Christians hammering on doors and windows to be let in for the last hours or minutes of a former adherent. More often, they got in. John Cockburn of Scarborough, dying respected by friend and foe, 'when told that several ministers wished to see him, "Let them come", he said, "I am ready".' This obituarist, writing in the (atheist) *National Reformer*, implies that Cockburn saw his deathbed as a wrestling-arena, for he took care to mention that Cockburn had 'died, as he had lived, a consistent Freethinker'.[11] But many dying secularists tried to decline the contest: one secularist's 'sorrowing widow reports that when the clergymen wished to disturb [her late husband's] dying moments, he answered that they should have come when he was strong and well able to defend himself'.[12] However, if those surrounding the dying person were secularists, he or she was likelier to be undisturbed. 'Ten minutes before she – "a staunch secularist" – died, on being asked if she had any desire to see a priest (she was originally a Roman Catholic), she replied "No, no, they are all frauds and they know it!"' [13] Of course, such remarks were precisely those that secularists wanted to hear or read about. Remarks that someone had 'remained a free thinker to the last', were welcome clichés to secularist obituarists. Nonetheless the pressures were far greater from the side of the orthodox. That the latter still dominated overall can be seen as one reason for all the defiantly secularist obituary-writing. In other words, however resolutely secularists might lecture against 'the superstitions which develop [sic] the death scene in the various religions',[14] they were themselves forced, again and again, to re-enact (as much as their Christian foes) the surely basic superstition that the dying are gifted with a clearer perception of truth – at least when that perception accords with one's own belief. They were forced to do this for fear that the orthodox would concoct narratives of secularists' last dying moments. Admittedly the orthodox sometimes limited themselves to a spectator-role around the arena: 'Disputants of the efficacy of Secularism who were present when life ceased', the *National Reformer* was informed on one occasion, 'acknowledged frankly that no signs of fear of death were manifest.'[15] But this was exceptional. Since at least the deathbed of the plebeian freethinking hero Tom Paine, Christian propagandists had harped endlessly (and often, as in his case, mendaciously) on his feeling the fires of hell already at the foot of his bed. And into the twentieth century, secularists and spiritualists were having to refute similar lies in relation to the great secularist Bradlaugh (who had died in 1891).[16] Nor was this treatment confined to secularism's gurus. On the funeral of 'a working [Clerkenwell] shoemaker . . . [and] keen dialectician', the reporter noted 'lies . . . already circulating about his opinions during his illness'. One excellent refutation of such lies was a simple narrative of the deceased's last struggle with the Christians: 'a few hours before his death, he scribbled a few words', which were sent to Bradlaugh. 'In [them] he says he is pestered by the people of St. Albans Holborn, aided by his doctor, and begs of Mr. Bradlaugh to protect him against this annoyance, for he says "they seem determined to make me accept the creed and prayers of a church against which I have preached for thirty years".'[17]

The protection which this dying secularist begged from Bradlaugh was not consciously a supernatural one – however extravagantly Bradlaugh was hero-worshipped. Rather the dying man was fretting about the funeral. This was obviously going to be the next battleground, and Christian harrassment sometimes continued all the way to the grave. Both coincidentally and not, around this time, the *National Reformer* was opening a list of 'freethinkers willing to conduct funerals in their districts'.[18] Recently too, a speaker at the annual conference of Bradlaugh's National Secular Society had 'enquired how a Secularist, alone in his views, could ensure burial without religious rites', and Bradlaugh had 'answered that, in the case of anticipated difficulty, special directions would be sent if application were made'.[19] Not that it was new for secularists to be buried in a fashion appropriate to their beliefs; but, by the 1870s and 1880s, secularists had come to expect the benefits of membership in a permanent all-inclusive movement. While it is true that voluntary societies of many types were already participating conspicuously in their members' funerals, this participation was seldom if ever such a clear declaration of defiance from

conventional belief – a declaration which defied an even larger
number of conventional assumptions than had, say, masonic
ceremonies in late-eighteenth-century Catholic Europe. So more
than one leading secularist wrote a secular order of service. Such
orders were not meant to be punctiliously observed, but sought
merely to give guidance on what might be most appropriate to
say at particular stages. Thus Austin Holyoake's apparently
popular 1871 burial service began with eulogy for the dead person's
secularist virtues – independence, adherence to 'science and philosophy and . . . common sense', struggling against 'prejudice and
the results of misdirected education'. Next, lengthily, it laboured
the materialist view of death as personal annihilation: 'the penalty
of life is death . . . all on earth must part'. Via a far briefer conceit
about flowers (a device far more emphasised among spiritualists
and also many Christians, as we shall see), the service ended with
a third, or comfort-giving, stage: Man's

> 'hopes, like the . . . leaves of the forest, may wither and be
> blown about by the adverse winds of fate, but his efforts,
> springing from the fruitful soil of wise endeavour, will fructify
> the earth, from which will rise a blooming harvest of happy
> results to mankind. . . . The reward of a [good] . . . life is the
> conviction that our memory will be cherished.' But even
> now, rationalism rationed the comfort. 'This is the only
> immortality of which we know . . . Farewell, a long farewell!'
> End of service.[20]

The very reading of secularist services involved negotiating two
centres of opposition: unsympathetic relatives and the controllers
of local facilities for burial. The former enjoyed a peculiar advantage when, as was still usual, the laid-out and then coffined corpse
remained in the house till the day of the ceremony. Sometimes
this enabled them to frustrate the deceased's wishes altogether – as
when a Congregationalist widow persuaded her minister to bury
her secularist husband according to Congregationalist rites.[21]
Undertakers, where used, were a frequent problem – though, in
London, this was temporarily solved by one whose conversion to
secularism had soured his market-appeal to Christians.[22] Where,
by contrast, the family were sympathetic, their house might

provide the only place for going through the secular service before the coffin-lid was on.[23]

But it was the local burial authorities who seem to have raised the more frequent problem. The Church of England had long used its legal monopoly of rites of passage to harrass Nonconformists; in the later nineteenth century, clergy of most denominations tended to use similar powers against secularists. John Roper, a joiner by trade, a 'sober, careful and frugal liver' – a teetotaller, in fact, who had worked at the same Leeds firm for fifty years, and whose three sons were 'now in respectable . . . situations', died a secularist in 1864. He had to be buried in the Baptist graveyard. Here the Reverend Ashworth used control of the ceremony in order to preach a sermon which at least one local secularist found 'disgraceful and loathsome as well as disgusting'.[24] Control of burial facilities was the subject of occasional discussion in parliament, but the resultant legislation was not wholly to secularist advantage. Thus, at the funeral of one secularist who had, 'in spite of very great pressure, . . . remained firm to the end', the secular service, though 'very impressive . . ., had to take place in the public highway in consequence of the [law] not authorising any Secular address in a churchyard.'[25] Secularists' status, in other words, verged on that of pariahs. Sometimes this made them all the more grateful for small favours. Coincidentally printed only a few lines after the report just quoted, another secularist mentioned that, in his locality 'in wet and tempestuous weather, the Cemetery authorities permit the Secular service to be read within the Chapel'. He did not note what their rule was for when the weather was merely freezing.[26] It also made many of them quick to note acts of generosity – as when a Christian minister allowed the secular service to be read[27] (on at least one occasion, immediately after he had finished reading the Christian one),[28] or merely advised the secularist officiator,[29] or, exceptionally, when the Christian himself read the secular service.[30] (This Christian was Unitarian: generosity seems to have been most frequent from this denomination.) But the general secularist insecurity is underlined by the frequency with which they observed, of secular burials, that, for example, 'all [had] passed off remarkably well'.[31] Christian opposition intensified secularist hope that their own ceremonies should compare well with any competition. Accounts often stress features that might otherwise appear uncheckable, let alone anodyne – such as that 'every possible respect was paid to the service throughout'.[32]

Whatever the local balance of forces, a secular service amounted to a peculiarly public demonstration, requiring a general mobilisation of local supporters: 'It was unanimously resolved' by Chatham secularists on hearing that a member had expressed a last wish for a secular burial, 'that every member should be strongly urged to be present'.[33] Such mobilisation was, to repeat, nothing unusual among organisations – whether trade-union, political or religious.[34] But participants in a secularist ceremony would, oftener than those in others, have been flouting community and other local pressures. Outsiders seem to have agreed on the demonstration-aspect of the occasion: there are numerous remarks that spectators had been 'attracted chiefly by curiosity',[35] sometimes in hundreds. Attractions may have been added when the ceremony was taken by a sympathetic relative,[36] or sometimes by a woman.[37]

Thus a secularist death often presupposed moral courage from the dying person; similarly a secularist burial as often presumed a circle of friends prepared to prejudice good relations with customers and employers. And secularist behaviour at the grave-side was supposed, as we have seen, to be wordy but, even there, unflinchingly fact-facing.

In addition, a few relevant aspects are still obscure. The accounts are nearly always silent as to whether mourning was worn: black, after all, was the conventional way of marking the all-important 'respect' – for the deceased, for one's own grief, for the relatives and, surely, also, for respectability itself. On the other hand, we are told that only Annie Besant 'came in black and heavily veiled' to Bradlaugh's own funeral. Secularists did, as it happens, often share one practice with the spiritualists and others: the throwing of flowers on to the open grave by most participants.[38] 'They [the church] have his corpse – his mind was ours' – one secularist wrote of a friend whose wish for a secular burial had been frustrated.[39] Brave though this sentence was, its tenses had had to be twisted carefully, given that secularists did not believe in survival of death. With spiritualism, by contrast, the sense of defiance was not abstract, but triumphant. Spiritualists might, in their own way, have echoed one Christian's reply to G. J. Holyoake's question, 'Why should the Atheist fear to die?': 'Why should the Atheist care to live?'[40] Amid the clashings of Christian versus secularist modes of dignity and morbidity, spiritualism occupied a peculiar place. It claimed to prove that everyone would enjoy something no less pleasant and far more varied than the Christians' eternal life – not least those who, on earth, had witnessed to an entirely secular enlightenment.

It would be neat to be able to follow spiritualists in the same order as secularists – from deathbed to graveside. However, the nature of spiritualist beliefs forces us to vary the order. First of all, then, spiritualists were no less aware than secularists of the opposition offered by Christians at the time of death. But, for them, there was no death: only a 'transition'. This aspect of spiritualist belief comforted the dying as much as those surrounding them. Thus, the 'transition' of Mrs Richardson of South Shields was said to have been 'a grand specimen of a spiritualist deathbed. She left the body rejoicing in the knowledge that she could still remain near to those she loved, although separated from them physically. A friend who visited her said that her last moments were her best ones.' Another reason for this was 'the thought, that she would again be reunited with those she loved' – both those she was leaving now and those who had preceded her. This 'gave her a stimulus and a hope that could not be surpassed, notwithstanding all that Christians may say as regards happy deaths only occurring in the Christian belief.'[41] Whether or not Christians made such a point of watching spiritualist, as they did secularist, deathbeds, more are likely to have been present at the tea that was generally given before or after the funeral.[42] 'Spirits' occasionally returned this soon.

> At the close [of the tea], an affecting scene was enacted [sic], namely, the control of the medium by our dear friend whose body we had so recently laid low. He spoke in the old familiar tones, addressing the members of his own family circle, adjuring them not to weep for him; he was perfectly happy and had no desire to come back. The meeting was concluded by singing.'[43]

This example underlines certain features of spiritualist doctrine so obvious as to be too forgettable. Spiritualism denied the absoluteness of separation between bereaved and the dead. Although most spirits were supposed to need a certain time to recover from the 'transition' before communicating with those left behind, and although most of those spirits who had subsequently evolved to the higher spheres were thought to be less forthcoming than those on the initial levels of the Summerland, the fact remains that *any* alleged communication was a denial that the community (such as it was) had been sundered by death: the recently 'arisen' spirit proclaimed simultaneously its arrival in the community of spirits and the partial interpenetration of this community with the earthly community.[44] We may now savour the ambiguities – intentional or not – in the ending of a *Lyceum Banner* obituary for one 17-year-old lyceumist: 'May we soon realise her presence amongst us.'[45] Officially, spiritualist and non-spiritualist funerals thus addressed different problems. Officially, the former were indeed rituals of transition but not of separation. Although Christians always declare belief in the 'communion of saints', spiritualists were correct in seeing such declarations as vestigial compared with their own practice. Spiritualism thus enjoyed over Christianity a selling-point which the latter had once enjoyed over paganism: alleviation of death-fears. And yet, in practice within a non-spiritualist world, the difference in the ceremonies was more apparent than profound, as regards structure and often even the sentiment: it was, after all, members of 'his own family [séance] circle' whom the just buried and quoted Slaithwhite pioneer spiritualist 'adjur[ed] . . . not to weep'.

Of course, as far as appearances went, funerals were the best possible arena for proclaiming spiritualist beliefs. But among non-spiritualists too, the full 'Victorian' funeral seems to have generated quite a wide revulsion against both its atmosphere and its elaboration.

One random example would be homoeopathic allegations about distress caused to nervous people by the delivery of black-bordered envelopes.[46] More broadly emblematic, we find Dickens placing his own cultivation of deathscene emotions in *opposition* to funeral paraphernalia. He is quoted (also, suitably, in a spiritualist periodical) claiming to have contrived the death of Little Nell in order to 'substitute a garland of fresh flowers for the sculpted horrors which disgrace the tomb'.[47] (I will come back to the much-told Nell and to flowers later on.) Shortly, as it happens, after Dickens' death, spiritualists, Quakers and others formed a Mourning Reform Association (with a low annual subscription of

2s. a year). Its brief was economic and social as much as religious: in the words of some of its founders, they hoped to counter the belief 'that the only means of "showing respect for the dead", is to empty the already too slender purse of the living'.[48] There already existed an Anti-Mourning Association which used similar arguments (and seems to have been led by Swedenborgians).[49] Such agitations seem to have been part of an underlying late-Victorian reversal of the orthodox black funeral. Spiritualists – respectable as much as plebeian – had begun, early on, to practise their opposition to funeral orthodoxy. 'Crape', reported a spiritualist journal during 1868, 'was dispensed with, much to the evident discomfiture of the undertaker, who thought it would be a "bad thing for business" if the whole world were spiritualists.'[50]

In fact, whereas the influence of 'Mourning Reform' could make a funeral ceremony more optimistic than the theology sometimes purveyed by those officiating, the optimism of spiritualist doctrine had already gone much further: to the limits of the logical. Spiritualist funerals served not so much as a lonely defiance – as with their secularist counterpart – of a homogeneous set of Christian practices, but rather as an extreme of an optimistic and otherwise Christian counter-current. And spiritualism's central doctrinal optimism was an obvious aid here. In their practice, too, spiritualists went far beyond merely dispensing with crape. They went beyond singing songs and hearing speeches about their 'arisen' friend starting an improving life in the Summerland. After all, it is hard to imagine the members of Clapham Junction branch of the Amalgamated Society of Railway Servants being the only randomly interdenominational assemblage to be told, after a long Lib-Lab eulogy at the news of W. E. Gladstone's death, of the 'most striking coincidence that Mr. Gladstone should be called into the Great Unknown on Ascension Day, . . . [this being] a confirmation of his strong belief that this life is but the introduction to a higher life hereafter'.[51] Spiritualists also wore – not black – but white (while, of course, keeping within their means) and, as a minimum, had a white coffin. The latter was normal for all types of adherent – unlike in many Christian denominations which were more selective. But, as if all this were not dazzling enough, the spectacularity of spiritualists' funerals was enhanced beyond anything available to adherents of mere 'Mourning Reform', by an address given by a medium under 'control' or 'guidance' –

speaking, not necessarily more loudly, but sometimes in an unusual tone of voice. Admittedly, these addresses introduced an element of unpredictability into ceremonies which spiritualists often tried to regularise by publishing their own orders of service.[52] Although, at the graveside of one young Bacup woman, the spiritualist officiator is said to have 'conducted' what the *Lyceum Banner* called 'the last rites . . . in a very creditable manner', the paper also reports cryptically that 'the assemblage of about 200 people . . . were mystified by the address, which was given by [his] guides . . . and [which] has caused a great deal of talk in the town.'[53]

But the risk that something vaguely untoward would occur was usually more than outweighed by the demonstration-aspect. At one spiritualist funeral in Heywood cemetery, the address brought

> the Roman Catholic mourners from their worship, leaving the dead to take care of itself [sic] while they listened to the stirring words of the entranced medium. Even the gravedigger forgot his labours to watch the unusual proceedings . . . We hope these spiritualistic funerals will be taken advantage of wherever convenient to let the world see of what is our faith.[54]

So far, I have omitted one device that was almost central to spiritualist ceremonies: the use of flowers. Funerals were not the only rite of passage that spiritualists (like most denominations including, partially, the secularists) sought to claim for their own. There were also marriages and 'namings'. While floral decorations would have been common with virtually all denominations for the first, spiritualist 'namings' were not strictly christenings, and the use of 'flowers . . . instead of water' was said to be 'customary' at them.[55] But the symbolism of flowers was dwelt on most cloyingly at funerals. Here at some levels, spiritualists were at most only at an extreme of an established practice.[56] 'At the graveside' of one 16-year-old lyceumist, 'we sang "One sweet flower had drooped and faded"'.[57] The coffin was usually surrounded with masses of flowers, and flowers were usually thrown into the grave at the close of the ceremony: a classic gesture of separation. Here again, the preferred colour was white. (I will shortly revert to this, as also to the word 'sweet'.) 'By these pure white blossoms showered upon her body', announced James Burns, 'we signify our knowledge that a separation has been effected between Spirit and

Matter.'[58] This peroration was banal compared with one that had been heard a few months earlier, also at the funeral of a young woman spiritualist. Here, in the normal way, 'the coffin was interred amid a profusion of flowers thrown into the grave'. But here too, 'the guides' of Mr F. Sainsbury issued

> a tender appeal . . . not to give way to sorrow. They were returning to the earth the worn out body that belonged to it, not with the sorrowfully echoed words 'Earth to earth', but as a glorious flower that had seen the light of God shining upon it, they returned it to the ground strewed [sic] with emblems of purity, the flowers of the earth – flowers to flowers – that they might decay with the body. But the essence and perfume that sprang from the flowers was the emblem of the spirit that rose to the eternal Father and would go from height to height unto the perfect day.[59]

I am certainly not suggesting that Victorians originated the metaphor of sweetness. Nor am I a specialist in the symbolism of flowers. The point is merely that raptures of such a kind are far less often met with in accounts of the funerals of any male spiritualists, of any age. Further, we have just seen the metaphor of sweetness being paired, here, with one of decay. Some writers have already noted a 'delight in decay' as important in the Victorian conception of death. But other researchers argue that this delight was pre-Victorian and that Victorians, on the contrary, reacted against it.[60] In this area, once again, historians seem able to set up paradigms and then invert them all too neatly. We can perhaps imagine the adjective 'sweet' being used in a public address about a boy, but hardly that it could occur three times in one short excerpt from a funeral speech for a man – as it does from one part of the address at the funeral of an 18-year-old woman spiritualist.[61]

It may be that those speakers who – whether or not in 'trance' – emphasised the quality of sweetness were doing so with intentions partly theological. During at least the oration which I have just quoted, the speaker talked of God as 'our common mother and father'. This emphasis had occasionally been associated with plebeian spiritualism from the start. The writings of Andrew Jackson Davis are one example – though his preferred phrasing was of 'Father God and Mother Nature', viewed as one.[62] This god was seen as superior to the Christian deity: 'Great Spirit', as one medium addressed it when under alleged guidance from a 'translated' Red Indian, 'Soul of Love . . . to thee we come. Not to the paleface God, full of wrath and small [and] selfish things.'[63]

But whatever its occasional originality in theology, spiritualism gave an extra twist to a tangle of very earthly complexities: whiteness, innocence, childhood,[64] symbolism, sexuality. After all, in many Christian denominations too, whiteness – including a white funeral – officially denoted innocence or simply virginity. And again, all these straight reversals of Victorianism – the substitution of whiteness for blackness – suggest that underneath the official joy lay great tensions. At the mid-1900 gathering of Yorkshire spiritualists, two participants were killed by lightning and four injured.[65] Under this extreme shock, at least, those at the two funerals were said to have 'very generally' reverted to conventional black mourning. Shortly after, when the coroner's jury described the accident as 'a visitation of God', the *Two Worlds* sought to salvage spiritualist self-respect by branding these words as 'libel on the All Wise'.[66] This double aftermath (the funerals versus the journal's brave words) highlight the extent to which spiritualism may normally have demarcated the conscious and the unconscious of people who must often have remained more anguished about the ultimate questions of life and death than they liked to admit.

Like most present-day observers – snugly sub-Freudian in their modes of interpretation – I view some records of mediumship as affording unreliable but nonetheless tempting peeps towards the borderlands of what we loosely call the unconscious of at least certain people. In the present section we will begin with two apparently trivial examples. One occurs in the mid 1850s. A medium who had once been a Methodist but who no longer held an orthodox belief in hellfire, gave a communication from the spirit of John Wesley which was full of such warnings.[67] My second 'trivial' example has nothing to do with death. It comes from a trance-address given during 1890 by a 'veteran spiritualist lecturer and reformer'.[68] He began by contrasting the present society's 'monstrous inequality' with the 'royally scientific . . . moral communism of Nature'. He next mentioned what he called his 'panaceas'. These amounted to total nationalisation plus, as he put it, 'costless money'. Despite these ambitious demands, he humbly nominated Gladstone as 'the agent of progressive ideas; and whenever the ideas of the people shall have progressed to the point of practical unanimity, he is prepared to carry out the will of the people.' But next he became millenarian: 'The elemental signs of a coming revolution are all around. . . . The might of the Lord God of Hosts is apt to express itself anonymously, through the savage passions of a populace whose pent-up passions have made it mad.' Only (he calmed down again) 'social improvement' could ensure 'that the stream of moral instincts' could 'flow more freely'. Trivial or not, the tensions behind these two widely differing examples clearly arose from many years of anxiety: in the first case, about hell; in the second, about political violence and, possibly also, one's support for it.

This is not a reading by one lone historian. In the case of early nineteenth-century Methodism, other historians – themselves divided over Methodism's political effect – have commented on the thinly veiled sexuality of Methodist hymns and sermons. It has also been noted that many Methodist texts simply long for death.[69] On spiritualism, I would add merely that its adherents had a more complex attitude to death than their official beliefs might suggest, and that this did not necessarily weaken those beliefs.

One spiritualist editor could rapturise for nearly 150 words when he found a corpse laid out to look beautiful.[70] In the light of his description, which I will quote in full, statements such as Geoffrey Gorer's[71] – equating (alleged) Victorian tabooing of discussions about sex with widespread twentieth-century tabooing of discussions about death – appear too summary. Not that we should try to construct for ourselves some 'taboo-free ivory tower' (D. J. Enright's metaphor[72]). Rather the problem I am about to highlight is that, whatever we may wish, the erotic and deathly were hard to separate. Often, too, they may still be: when we insist (as here) on the strangeness of, say, 'Victorians' we may also be trying not to see what strangers we sometimes are to ourselves, even where differently.

J. J. Morse was describing, in the *Lyceum Banner* and in a column directed particularly at child readers, the burial of the 14-year-old daughter of spiritualist friends of his. He himself had taken her naming ceremony and, at the time he described, was about to take her funeral. 'Never', he sighed, would he

forget the sight when I viewed the body lying uncoffined, so beautiful and still in that wonderful sleep called death. The rich profusion of lovely hair, carefully combed out over her shoulders, the fair young form clothed in a beautiful white dress, the lower limbs encased in white silk stockings, and the feet in white kid slippers, a pretty evening cloak, of cream cashmere, edged with white swansdown, enveloping the upper portions of the body, and a delicate coral of lillies of the valley resting upon the pallid brow, the white and delicate hands, like purest alabaster, resting by her side, and a look of sweet peace upon every feature. It was a perfect picture of maiden grace, innocent sweetness, and restful composure, that utterly robbed 'death' of its terrors, and inspired the beholder with the tenderest emotions.[73]

Admittedly we will have noticed that, in the end, Morse's whole description bore for him a spiritualist moral. But the description's fullness underlines three aspects in which spiritualists were probably at a frank extreme of a contemporary consensus. This consensus we will soon examine in greater depth. One aspect is, not (as some writers would argue) the repressiveness but, to us, the strangeness of what we might call the libidinous economy which seems to have been dominant during Morse's time. This distance from us is more complex than Gorer's statement of it. A second, related, aspect can best be introduced by a question: could Morse have written, or would he have been printed had he written, about the corpse of a teenage boy in identical language? My argument here is at its most speculative, and runs as follows. Take what are said to have been the dominant nineteenth-century ideas about children and women: that the first are sexually innocent and that the second are sexually passive at any age (except for the immoral and 'unwomanly'). Add to these assumptions the sight – or, here as very often – the elaborately laid-out spectacle of a corpse which, outside Gothic fantasy, is passive by definition. And (whatever Morse's own conscious views about the dominant stereotype of feminity) an explosion of what we have heard him call 'the tenderest emotions' was the simplest result: innocent passivity received its apotheosis, not posthumously but prehumously.

This relates to a third aspect. Here, spiritualists were at least at an extreme of a Victorian consensus. The author who is seen as having done most to reinforce Victorians' strongest emotions towards death is, of course, Dickens – most famously in his contrivance of the deathbed of Little Nell in his *Old Curiosity Shop*.[74] Spiritualists treated Dickens as particularly sympathetic in these passages, and Morse could not possibly have been ignorant of them. While we can have no inkling as to whether or not he could have written his description without them, his very context resounded to them. And yet the strict similarities are a matter of only a few words ('beautiful', 'sleep', 'still', 'peace'), whereas the differences are significant. Morse was more self-conscious: he was describing what he called a 'picture' which, as we have noted, he saw as full of spiritualist symbolism. The central and longest part of his description was also the least Dickensian: a deliberate and physical detailing. Most of this was to do with the clothes. Here, he was not merely showing how the dead girl's parents had done everything they materially could for her corpse (something his young readers were perhaps expected to find reassuring). Rather, his description also reads more like parts of a conventional report of a wedding. This, though, involved a 'bride' whose conventional whiteness radiated from her inert body as well as from her dress: 'fair', 'pallid', 'white', 'alabaster'. Dickens, by contrast, distanced himself from his dead young girl's clothing: the only dress he mentioned was away from her body, which he had not yet brought his readers to, and he put this clothing into the hands of an old man half-insane with grief. On the other hand – and still consistently with my contrast – the old man strokes these clothes 'as fondly as if they had been living things', and goes on to try and warm the dead Nell's marble-cold hand in his; whereas Morse – painting his picture in conformity to a respectable wedding genre – says nothing about feel or touch.

Here we have a small and indirect measure – deviance from one powerfully available image – of the extent to which spiritualists could treat deathbeds and funerals as in many ways weddings. In addition, they believed that the family was held together by spirit-contact after bereavement and was reconstituted posthumously (statements to this effect are legion). Admittedly, as we will see when we discuss the Summerland, they did not see life after dying as identical with life after marrying. Nonetheless, as they very publicly brought funerals and marriages nearer to each other, the question arises how far this tendency was fundamentally nineteenth-century or spiritualist. To take only our best-known commentators, one thinks – with Mary Douglas – of St Francis's joyful welcome for 'Sister Death'[75] or – with E. P. Thompson – of early Methodists' onanistic longing for death.[76] Nor were (nor are) European cultures alone in allowing or encouraging a jumbling of different types of transition. The *Lyceum Banner* might formally headline the death of one spiritualist as 'his spiritual birth!'; but there were and are numberless instances from every continent of 'primitive' celebrations of death as a rebirth.

We have already entered an area in which our spiritualists' ideas about the next world and about the nature of the human personality that related to it and survived into it are central.

B   Summerland, self-control, human nature

The Summerland was itself obviously one of spiritualism's central ideas – and a far richer and more attractive one than the secularists' eternal nothingness, let alone the orthodox Christians' eternal hellfire. It was, not surprisingly, one which many spiritualists seem to have enjoyed elaborating. Partly as a result, though, it was one where, to caustic outsiders, they must have appeared no less loose or silly than when trying (as noted in chapter 5) to reunite natural or human history on the basis of 'spiritual' sources.

For a start, was the Summerland's very existence physical (however imponderably) and, if so, where was it? Into the twentieth century, views diverged even on this. Whether many spiritualists felt troubled by such divergences (and also, perhaps shifts of opinion) is hard to tell. On the one hand, one spiritualist could casually treat as a 'very patent fact, that heaven is a spiritual condition and not a geographic location'.[77] And the editor of a 1917 selection of A. J. Davis's writings could declare flatly that, whereas the latter's overall thought remained of profound interest, 'none' by 1917 either 'accept[ed] or denie[d] many of the actual details of his cosmology': in particular, 'no one' spoke 'of a rainbow belt among the star clouds of the Milky Way as the world of disembodied souls'. On the other hand, this editor – identified merely as 'a Doctor of Hermetic Science' – may have been neither British, plebeian nor spiritualist,[78] and s/he was being too sweeping. For, among plebeian spiritualists in Britain, Davis was still immensely and, it seems, very widely respected – and not simply as an ancestor: some of his works continued to be sold, discussed and, we may presume (given his often easy style), read.

And at least some leading plebeian spiritualists continued to argue the Summerlands's physical existence. Thus Kitson could write during 1920 of the 'Spirit spheres or zones' as enveloping the earth (though admittedly not fully spherical), with the spirits dwelling on the outer surfaces.[79] The 'spirit world proper', at least as expounded in a series of anonymous 'spirit communications' printed in the *Lyceum Banner* during and after 1913 consisted of

'a number of zones . . . surrounding and enriching the earth at varying altitudes, something after the manner of the rings or belts of Saturn. . . . These spheres are separated from each other by a space of above fifty miles.' They were 'maintained at their respective distances from each other and the earth as naturally as the various stratas of clouds float one above the other; only the spirit spheres do not float but are stationary over their respective portions of the earth, and participate in its rotating movements on its axis. But they are unlike the clouds inasmuch as they cannot be seen by those living on the spheres beneath them'.[80]

True, as we have seen, no spiritualists had to agree with any and every 'spirit communication': many such were printed with little stronger editorial endorsement than that they were 'interesting' or simply 'beautiful'.

But spiritualists were obviously prone to speculate in this area. Firstly, it related to what I have called the problematic of imponderables. Thus one spiritualist during 1917 could talk of these 'spheres' as 'belts of semi-material structure and substance' and also of a 'spirit counterpart' accompanying 'each physical planet': such 'spiritual [planetary] bodies' were likewise 'imperceptible to the normal eye . . . even with . . . the most powerful telescopes', though the time would 'come when the astronomers of earth . . . [would] discover the spirit planet or counterpart of Mars.' All this imponderability preserved also a vaguely Newtonian echo – as when the same 1917 writer talked of the 'whole structure from centre to circumference of this system of world being governed by the one law of energy and of attractive force'. Second and even vaguer, though, were what may have been echoes (however indirect) of Giordano Bruno – a hero with plebeian spiritualists and not only with secularists. An echo of Bruno's fascination with the existence of life on other worlds was possibly something we could have discerned in J. G. H. Brown during Chapter 3. (In addition, many conventional astronomers during our period were seriously discussing the likelihood of intelligent life on at least Mars[81]). Far more central to plebeian spiritualists, though, was A. J. Davis. Ironically here, he himself had poked fun at precisely the conception, just noted, of spiritual spheres for each planet as 'creating utter confusion in spiritual geography.' In its stead, he offered his own belief in physical life (for him, of a superior kind) on other planets, solar systems and galaxies. Most Brunonian of all, he posited a central sun for the whole cosmos. All this (particularly the latter, of course) allowed him to conceive of one colossal Summerland, with room for spirits from all the habitable places in the universe. Or rather, he did not simply – to spew my own words out – believe, let alone posit. He simply demanded of the cosmos that this be so: 'No, no; give me a sphere vast enough to infold [sic] all the relations of the innumerable worlds of the universe – a space commensurate with the grandeur and glory and vastness of that universe – a universal Summerland.'[82]

But if spiritualists seldom seem to have been unduly worried over their disagreements as to where the next sphere of life might actually lie, they were broadly in agreement as to what it was like: it was a morally structured hierarchy. Those spirits who had 'left the [physical] form' at a low moral level were condemned to begin their so-far neglected duty of working out their own salvation in the first sphere. This sphere was as unpleasant as they, for here they endangered both each other and sometimes those still physically alive. (Anthropologists have often remarked on the thousands of cultures which treat people, not least spirits, of borderline or 'liminal' status as threats; spiritualists were no exceptions here.) But work their salvation out these spirits did, with or without the aid of morally better people in both existences. For, apart from these spirits in the first sphere, those at higher moral levels were also more 'spiritual' and were thus able (though not always immediately willing) to see and influence those at a lower.[83] The next life thus formed a succession of levels whose summit was admittedly neither knowable in a direct way nor much bothered about. After physical death, we evolved upwards at our own speeds and in our own ways. Unpleasant though the first or lowest sphere was, the second was decidedly pleasanter[84]; and the Summerland itself – 'the beautiful region . . . where good people of all nations dwell together in love' formed (in Kitson's words) 'the third spirit zone'.[85] Here, life seems to have been warmly egalitarian, combining collective institutions and informal support-iveness with unique scope for individuality to spread its wings. Throughout the hierarchy, the central principle was affinity: 'like attracts its like'.[86] This principle was seen as operating on any scale: whether helping to reconstitute the family posthumously (on the no-nonsense assumption that its members had nearly always had a true affinity) or drawing together larger groupings which seem to have been like ideal versions of the Friendly Societies, Sisterhoods, Brotherhoods and other associations – 'voluntaristic', as historians like to call them – which were so important within the stabler regions of plebeian life during these decades.[87]

The same principle operated not only within spheres but also between them. And this is where we encounter among spiritualists a confusion, aware or not, as to the shape and thus the boundaries of human personality. Coherence in 'the' human personality is something which many people today pride themselves on refuting. The point, though, about our spiritualists is that they liked to defend the eternal self-reliance of the free-thinking individual, but were also proud to argue that s/he received assistance more constantly than would be believable to all but the most fervently religious non-spiritualists. In this dilemma – or at least tension – they may have been transposing to the cosmic scale an often very plebeian support for both individualism and solidarity – this much is easy to claim. In their own terms, the nub was the existence or otherwise, given influence from spirits, of free will. Or rather, in the terms of their and immediately preceding periods: in North America and North-West Europe, obsessions with involuntary loss of individual self-control were at least as old as Gothic fantasy. We have already met them during controversies over mesmerism (where, of course, the loss was often voluntary), and have noted the importance of such an – apparent – episode in bringing Rolan-dus's mesmerism towards spiritualism.

We can approach this aspect on the wings of guardian angels. These will allow us to weigh its importance for spiritualists. The

word angel did not, here, necessarily carry connotations of hierarchy, orthodoxy or, literally, of wings. Spiritualists liked to
remind themselves that the word had originally meant merely
'messenger'.[88] Every inhabitant of earth had such a spirit or angel.
Who were these? To one 15-year-old spiritualist, they were
people's 'own loved [and physically dead] friends'.[89] Writers of
spiritualist fiction or avowed semi-fiction thus had the opportunity
to cast such spirits as, for example, the mothers of the main protag-
onist[90] (as we saw in Chandos Leigh-Hunt's novel). Such guardian-
ship was evidently a somewhat time-consuming occupation: 'I
have been with you' – as one guardian spirit (via Kitson's twice
serialised story on the topic[91]) explained somewhat plaintively to
her young charge – 'throughout your life, including when you
were angry.'[92] But Kitson, when constructing the plot of his story,
was right in seeing no doctrinal need to push the girl's own mother
out of earth-life in order to provide a guardian. For, as another
spiritualist explained, 'every spirit who cares more for others than
for self – and all spirits will do so in time – has a work of some
kind to perform, a work of uplifting . . . one or more individuals
– spirits or mortals.'[93]

Such emphasis – constant, as we shall see and also deeply
emotional – on aid from superior spirits was bound to open the
door to uncertainties as to how responsible each individual was for
her or his salvation. Thus there was, for instance, little doctrinal
precision – however much geographical – in one spirit's explanation that

> the surface of each sphere . . . [rose] in large and extensive
> plateaux or tablelands, which were peopled by spirit men and
> women of varying degrees of spiritual unfoldment [an
> optimistic metaphor]. As they grow wiser and better,
> mastering the shortcomings of their earth life, they are able to
> ascend higher and higher until they are prepared to ascend to
> the next higher [sic] sphere. Of course, their progress is quick
> or slow according to the success of their efforts to perfect
> their lives.[94]

Attempts at greater clarity produced only inconsistency. On
the one hand, the orthodox religious doctrines whch spiritualists
scorned most were those which appeared to lessen individual

responsibility. Thus spiritualists often claimed to raise individual responsibility to a unique level. A remark by one 15-year-old girl provides a relatively mild specimen: 'According to some, a man may lead a wicked life and commit all kinds of wrong, yet if he repents before passing over he will escape his measure of punishment.'[95] The point, within the plebeian-spiritualist scheme, about such 'punishment' was that it never lacked 'measure': no one would suffer it eternally, or any longer than her or his own efforts necessitated. True, repentance and forgiveness – so important in any orthodox scheme of salvation – were not forgotten in the spiritualist either: 'We do not', one 'spirit' remarked, 'scorn [a] spirit for what it has been; we honour it for its efforts to advance and to grow into something better.'[96] But, unlike in orthodox schemes, physical death did not change the rules of the moral economy whatsoever. Kitson's fictional heroine (whom he imagined discovering her guardian angel and much besides) 'had often wished she was dead, when in her sullen moods, but now that she began to realise the stern reality of life's actions, she was pleased she still possessed a body, through which she could do her work.' 'Realise', her guardian angel admonished her, 'there is nothing lost, but everything has an effect which will meet us again sooner or later.' How lucky she was, as compared with most non-spiritualists who had 'not the benefit' of this 'knowledge [of] personal responsibility': 'nearly all of them are taught that someone else will accomplish the cleansing process for them.'[97] Aside from directly ethical discussions, mere experience of apparent contact with spirits was sometimes sufficient argument – as for one former Wesleyan – 'that this "life is what we make it"': accordingly, he soon came to accept spiritualism as 'the religion for thinking men and women'.[98] Not for nothing had Kitson overloaded the fictional rhythm of one of his stories in order to imagine a dying freethinker who, 'instead of being a lost soul, as her friends thought, . . . had earned a beautiful [place in the Summerland], by her good works and ready sympathy.'[99] Thus, all this can be seen as within a tradition of radical Protestantism; as J. M. Peebles (himself a universalist-Unitarian, as we have seen) summarised the position: 'We believe that salvation is of works rather than of faith or of grace, each earning the heaven that he inhabits in the next stage of existence.'[100]

On the other hand, though, there was ambiguity as to how self-sufficient each individual was or should be. After death, according to Kitson's fictionalised guardian spirit, moral 'reformation must be done by [sic] ourselves, by our own endeavours, assisted by prayer and the help of angel friends, who are ever ready to help the willing'.[101] This was more warming than consistent.

Thus there was elegance but also, we may agree, glibness in the medium Mrs Hardinge's answer to the question 'Why does a communication from a spirit bear evidence of the mind of the medium?', that 'the idea is the spirit's – the expression is the medium's'.[102] For she hardly clarified the boundary between idea and expression. Again, Burns yielded to no other adherent in (as we have seen) emphasising spiritualists' need to rely on themselves intellectually and morally. And yet even he could protest on one occasion that 'we are simply pointers on the dial of the clock – the internal motive power operating upon which is the spirit world.'[103]

His uncharacteristic clumsiness collided with a problem he normally negotiated forthrightly. Being major, the problem also recurred. We can take some examples from the *Lyceum Banner* – which, given the Lyceums' aim, was bound to emphasise education and self-education even more than most plebeian spiritualist journals. 'We have had' one Lyceum conductor protested accordingly,

> too much of 'the inspiration of the hour' by [sic] a good many
> speakers, and too little thinking, and with what results? Why!
> a hash of thoughts, with neither depth, nor even beauty. . . .
> Let's be more individualistic, think for ourselves; don't let's
> depend upon spirit friends to do our work. I don't wish to
> despise the help of our friends over the border, because I have
> a great deal to thank them for; but if they are to speak with
> effect and power, we must become thinkers and students
> ourselves.[104]

And the spirit of, appropriately, Ingersoll had, reportedly, expostulated 15 years earlier: 'who are you that you should for ever walk in leading-strings? Must . . . the ministering spirits do your thinking for you?'[105] He seems to have had much to warn against here: 'a band of bright spirits', Kitson – no less fierce a partisan of intellectual self-reliance than Burns – had his young heroine informed, 'hope to make use of your organism to make known to others what you are now learning.'[106] True, this did not necessarily imply that, as recipient, she was passive; but it might well be read in this sense. 'Often', a *Lyceum Banner* editorial[107] comforted bereaved parents, 'do [spirit children] come to visit', and 'to leave a token of their love by prompting some kind act or gentle word, that will carry joy and comfort to the heart of the recipient.'

For spiritualists, the problem of the autonomy and of the very unity or coherence of the individual personality was all the greater for occurring frequently – even, for mediums, routinely. As one Mancunian ex-secularist is said to have recounted of his medium-ship: 'though he is perfectly unconscious during the time he is speaking, the ideas he gives utterance to seem to come back upon him afterwards, for he will sometimes make a remark as new and receive the reply – "Oh! that's what you said last Sunday!"' All the less wonder that, when still a secularist, he had 'for 18 months . . . displayed signs of mediumship before he could be brought to believe that his mediumship was anything more than hallucination.'[108] 'As the constant dropping of water will wear away a stone', reasoned one spiritualist forty years later, 'so the continued influence of earnest spirits descending upon another will produce its results.'[109] Any stray Calvinist might have remarked that some stones were harder than others; but our spiritualist was trying to be encouraging. True, one could formulate some sort of balance between spiritual assistance – or, to hark back to Christian terminology, grace – and self-reliance.

But ultimately, any such balance was left to individual spirits or to those concerned with them: grace was delegated or democratised from the Godhead (conceived only vaguely, as we saw) to the mass of good spirits, thus making the situation flexible but also more convoluted.

Daily . . . many sinners . . . [become] determined to [be] worthy members of humanity. Therefore, though largely peopled with undeveloped unholy human beings, even the lowest depths of the spirit world are places of advancement, wherein are provided facilities and opportunities for the growth of their inhabitants, which conditions are seized upon as soon as the torpid minds centred there become sufficiently aroused under [stimulus from higher spirits].[110]

Spirits could also receive stimulus from people who were still 'in the body'. Overall, contact between the physically dead and living formed what we might call a routinely two-way ladder: 'those of you who . . . strive to do right, attract the good spirits to your side; they come to gain magnetic strength from your lives, which ennobles [sic] them to resist the friction of material conditions while pursuing their labours for others, and at the same time they impart a blessing of peace to your souls.'[111]

All this communion of dead and living was no doubt most warming. But the problems of dying and bereavement were not the only context in which spiritualists – in particular – were ambiguous between unified and disunified approaches to personality. An even more routine area was that of sleep. Spiritualists seem to have conceived of sleep as, in the words of one during 1894, 'a state of unconsciousness' whose 'main purpose' was 'to restore or build various parts of our bodies'.[112] And few of them would have disagreed with A. J. Davis that the 'phenomena of ordinary dreaming [were] traceable mainly to defective slumber, to impaired health, and to unresting thought.' True, even here, Davis could also list, more opaquely, 'the simultaneous and indiscriminate operation of the Will with the faculties of thought or reasoning' as well as 'the mere play of mental faculties under the influence of some distorting cause'. But anyway, all these led merely to that kind of dream which 'emanate[d] from the Earthland; the other [was] indeed from the land of Spirits'.[113]

Clearly, an 'unconsciousness' that *always* dulled the soul would have smacked embarrassingly of a physical domination over the mental! And relevantly here, some spiritualists continued to argue that the soul wandered from the body during sleep.[114] This could also have encouraged a view of dreaming, too, as soul-wandering. And, for explaining at least some spiritual phenomena, spiritualists certainly did discuss the theory of one of their Newcastle pioneers, Alderman T. P. Barkas, which posited occasional 'unconscious interference' by 'embodied spirits who [had] temporarily left their material home during sleep'.[115] This may sound particularly old-fashioned. Not that spiritualists were necessarily ignorant of wider doctrinal shifts. At least some of them could have read in the same journal and year as this last quote (1862) that the very assumption that the functions of sleep were primarily physical was 'now breaking down' and that '[G.H.] Lewes says it is wholly discredited'.[116] Nevertheless, into at least the 1920s, a spiritualist could remark in passing that it was 'known of course by many that people visit the spirit spheres during sleep', and that this applied particularly to disadvantaged children who received an educational boost from 'spirit children in a special building in [these] spheres'.[117] We need not bother to inquire whether such celestial bussing was as widely believed in: my point is merely that even this extravaganza was at most a variation on spiritualist assumptions about sleep and dreaming.[118] Thus Kitson could have his fictional guardian angel explain how 'she had been labouring a long time to bring about [a] spiritual consciousness during the sleep of [his heroine's] body'.[119] Though there are a number of types of apparent absence from normal consciousness, Kitson's story – rather as Chandos's (in Chapter 7) – tended to blur them into each other. But Chandos apart, whether the soul visited the spirit-world during sleep or (as in Kitson's story) played host, an assumption that sleep afforded privileged access to other worlds was far older and more world-wide than spiritualism. In these areas too, spiritualism was definitely more traditional than innovatory – not that spiritualists seem to have pretended otherwise.

And the same must be said about their definition of morality and of culture. Here, they seem to have shared another unoriginal assumption, one particularly powerful around this time. To summarise very sweepingly, culture and morality were defined as repression of 'base' instincts. This conflation was perhaps most widely available via such writers as Matthew Arnold. But an eloquent instance would be the attack on Bernard Shaw by Robert Blatchford[120] who, as we saw during Chapter 5, was the socialist ideologue most admired by many plebeian spiritualists (and who, relevantly here or not, later became one himself).

Most such spiritualists talked (so far as we can tell from our sources) as if the spiritual and the sexual were simply opposed. True, the leading activist whom we heard in Chapter 5 talking of 'Socialism and Spiritualism' as 'two Fellow Isms' might speak also of 'the aim of the Socialist and Spiritualist . . . alike' being 'to allow . . . nature free play to satisfy the cravings of her own creating in her own way', for 'Nature never creates a craving without supplying a means to satisfy it.'[121] But such (as we might call them) libertarian expressions usually remained abstract; and even on a level of abstraction, the same journal could during roughly the same period reprint without comment an argument from the major temperance paper, the *Alliance News*, to the effect that 'all virtue is cumulative. . . . Just as the power of the muscles grows with exercise.'[122] Not for nothing were many plebeian spiritualists, not least Burns, lifelong temperance militants. For them (we might at first imagine from our sources) to blur the sexual with the spiritual would have been comparable to surrendering to the demon drink simply because – 'Nature never creat[ing] a craving without . . .' etc. – that demon was there, lying in wait in so many of the nooks and crannies of plebeian life.

More broadly, the main enemy was not merely sexuality (though I will return later to at least Burns's fear of this), but anything describable as 'passion'. Thus Kitson could imagine a disgruntled guardian spirit complaining to a sometimes bad-tempered heroine, that this girl's 'disturbed nature gave . . . [mischievous spirits] a chance of drawing round you, and using their influence or power over you. . . . And so I had to wait near you until your passion had subsided.'[123] In other words, insofar as this life had any moral hierarchy, the latter's interlockings with that of the next were not only governed by the principle of affinity (omnipotent, as we saw, in the next) but were also distorted by 'passion' which acted as a malign force of gravity. As one spirit explained, disembodied but unevolved spirits found it as 'impossible to ascend to the upper [spheres] as it is for mortals to pierce the heavenly worlds with their material bodies; for as the physical keeps you down to earth, so the weight of passion keeps those spirits down.'[124] Readers of such journals (unlike some devotees of hermetic or otherwise elitist mysticisms) would presumably have taken the word 'passion' in its everyday sense – and it would probably have been uttered or transcribed in the same sense too.

Thus, both plebeian and respectable spiritualists might seem to have agreed that the sexual and the spiritual were opposed. Let J. H. Powell state this seeming consensus. British-born and a former working engineer, he had (as we saw during Chapter 5) considerable experience of the USA and felt he could emphasise to British readers that 'what is miscalled *free love*' – i.e. legally untrammelled choice of heterosexual partner by women and men – was 'a very small drop in the ocean' of even American spiritualism: 'doubtless', he conceded, 'there are some . . . in the mire, but the vast majority are mortally opposed'.[125] Nonetheless, 'the sins of one or two' spiritualists allowed opponents to smear spiritualism as a whole. And in their response to this risk, plebeian and respectable spiritualists tended to diverge from their underlying consensus about morality. Burns, in particular, went out of his way (we shall shortly see how exceptionally far) to be tolerant. For this, he endured some of the bitterest attacks ever made by respectable spiritualists on plebeian. The issue was partly religious (i.e. the old question of what to say about 'lying spirits'). But only partly. This is why we find Gerald Massey – former poet of London Chartism and contributor to G. J. Harney's *Red Republican*, but subsequently influenced (in politics, not in religion) by the Reverend Charles Kingsley and other class-conciliatory 'Christian Socialists' – riding alongside Christian spiritualists to rescue respectability.[126]

Always happy to parade his scorn for what he saw as hypocrisy, Burns had printed twenty-one pages about the life of Victoria Claflin Woodhull,[127] the American feminist, spiritualist, socialist and so-called free-lover. During the same year, he had also printed a pseudonymous letter imputing free-love origins to no less a figure than Jesus. Burns had not only greeted the writer of this letter – self-styled 'Another New Man' – as 'one of our most valued friends' but had also, on the editorial page, defended the latter's line, which was to ridicule Jesus and Free Love together.[128] When Massey wrote to express nausea, as a spiritualist, at this writer's 'cast up gobbit of the gross nastiness that used to be dished up by the Atheists', (though he himself yielded to none in hatred of orthodox Christianity) Burns jumped at the provocation. He 'heartily . . . thank[ed] God' for Atheists as the greatest champions of free speech. And he rounded in particular on the dogma of the virgin birth as 'a highly obnoxious lie' against God 'the All-Perfect'. This dogma constituted, for him, 'an obstacle to the progress of true and spiritual knowledge and human improvement'. This was because it involved 'erroneous and disgusting notions respecting the *causes* of spirituality in one man derived from his parentage'. It was 'erroneous' in, as we may say, using an elitist superstition about one person's unique procreation so as to undermine Burns's autodidact ideal of intellectual and spiritual self-improvement by each individual.

But it was 'disgusting', as we shall see soon, in involving procreation at all. For here Burns rounded on respectable 'Society' (his capital 'S') as 'one vast system of hypocrisy', in which 'the greatest gentleman is he who . . . can most effectually disguise his true character. Thousands of estimable young women have been sacrificed in wedlock before such a system of deception, and viler things, if possible, result outside that rite.'[129] Here, Burns was possibly voicing, in a spiritualist context, the growing revulsion among 'morally respectable' plebeians and others against the Contagious Diseases Acts. But he was attacking wider targets too.

And within a month, his anger and tolerance took him further when he printed, not merely a further effusion from the same 'Another New Man', but also one from the secularist Myles McSweeney. McSweeney, a bookseller and self-taught philologist, frequently lectured and, at least in the *National Reformer*, published prolifically on his decoding (as also did Massey on his) of Christian dogmas as disguised pagan myths. Here in Burns's weekly, he rambled philologically all over the question of 'the parentage of Jesus, and Free Love'. Any Christian reader intrepid enough to pursue him into his longer paragraphs would there have discovered the Virgin Mary related to the goddess Venus. To the article as a whole, Burns noted merely that he disagreed.[130] Admittedly he seems to have retained for many years a soft spot for McSweeney. (Conceivably, they may have sold secondhand books to each other.) But personal or other affinities were clearly not his main motive: for, during both this and later years, his pages remained open to other no less provocative views.

Thus these formed, in addition to differences over 'lying spirits', the second issue over which respectable (i.e. so often, during my period, interchangably Christian) spiritualists had, according to their criteria, more than sufficient ground for suspecting the moral propriety, not only of Burns, but of virtually any spiritualist who disagreed with them. When, for example, some spiritualists formed the British National Association of Spiritualists, the rage of the Christians was fuelled by a conformity broader than religious. Writing in their *Spiritual Magazine*, William Howitt argued that the expunging from the draft of the new Society's rules of 'all mention of sympathy with the teachings of the New Testament' (avowedly for the sake of mutual toleration), would lead not merely to theological and intellectual barbarism but also to what he called 'Free Loveism'. The BNAS had thereby – to allow him the luxuriance of his metaphors – 'blackened' spiritualism with 'the pestilential breath and reptile contact' of such 'apostles of the lowest regions' as Woodhull. She, he alleged, 'pronounce[d] the indulgence of unbridled sensuality the highest and noblest object of human nature'[131]: in other words, we might say, seemed to invert his repressiveness.

Such was the virulence of which spiritualist, as many other, upholders of sexual orthodoxy were capable. Yet Burns – even though he too considered Woodhull 'the high priestess' of a 'disgusting theory'[132] – was hardly to be the last plebeian spiritualist to risk the wrath of the conventional. As for positive disagreements in this area, though, the most we can say is that the plebeians seem seldom to have gone beyond tolerance towards heterodoxy and intolerance toward whatever they saw as hypocrisy. And here Burns's own views, however unusual they may have been, provide a good example of how far sexual orthodoxy could go within a plebeian spiritualist context.

Fundamentally, he shared the by then conventional view[133] of sexuality as a finite resource whose depletion – particularly in masturbation – threatened the individual's health. For example, he offered cut-price copies of the American Swedenborgian John Ellis's *Marriage and its Violations* and, warmly reviewing it, attacked both the obstruction by the medical profession of 'popular information' and 'the deadly vice peculiar to boys and girls', a vice which often produced 'almost irreparable injury'.[134] The two worst aspects of sexual indulgence seem, for him, to have been: firstly, that by allegedly harming health it harmed one of the preconditions for spiritual awareness and, secondly that, by awakening a sexual craving, it dulled the spiritual.

These latter metaphors are my summary. The thoroughness of Burns's opposing of the sexual to the spiritual can best be seen in his decades-long admiration for the American Shaker communities. In these, men and women lived together in large groups, but celibately to the point of regimentation – or, as Burns phrased it, 'under discipline, mingled to a certain extent in [sic] family life.'[135] Not that Burns applauded celibacy as a lifelong ideal. On the contrary, he scorned the Shaker refusal to 'beget children in case they defile their own precious souls': souls might have been the last topic on which Burns would have been expected to sneer. Yet he sneered too at the Shakers' broader 'aloof[ness] from the wicked world'.[136] He also found their theology distinctly senile for harking back so much to its early years, notably to its foundress, 'Mother Ann' Lee and, above all, for a suspicion – which went with this backwardlookingness – of further revelation from spirits. Doctrinally no less than physically, the Shakers were indeed ossifying.

Nonetheless, when the former British Owenite, and now Shaker elder Frederick W. Evans visited Britain in 1871 and 1887 (on what were, transparently, attempts to recruit adherents), Burns acted as his main British sponsor and, in the earlier year at least, accompanied him to some larger provincial meetings, at least one of which was under spiritualist auspices.[137] True, at least as presented by Evans (whom Lawrence Foster rightly calls a 'far from representative' figure[138]), Shakerism, like plebeian spiritualism, was rationalist and not merely mystical. 'That noble, wonderful man Thomas Paine', he wrote to Burns during the 1890s, had 'laid the foundations of the New Earth, as Ann Lee laid the foundations of the New Heavens.'[139] A creed based on these twin foundations would, as he wrote during the 1870s, 'break sectarianism, priestcraft, doctorcraft and every craft opposed to the true interests of humanity'[140]: in other words would, via a democratic epistemology, enjoy a broad compatibility with plebeian autodidact culture. Additionally though, Burns had his own reasons for hoping and believing that the Shaker community-ideal might have a swift demonstration-effect in Britain. These were sexual. 'He thought every man and woman should be a Shaker before they left the body; that is, they should attain a state of mind in which the generative nature was superseded by the regeneration of the spirit.' No less important, he demanded that celibacy not be allowed to remain a lonely state: more than once he claimed to know 'many excellent men and women who had no desire for married life, and lived in a state of isolation and spiritual barrenness'.[141]

Why they had 'no desire', he left entirely opaque. On other occasions, he seems to have believed, as did many others including spiritualists, that celibacy – because, he seems to have implied, it encouraged masturbation – undermined health. The last metaphor is not mine. Metaphor is, sadly or not, one of our main guides into the world of at least some spiritualists' sexuality. And I can best summarise the latter by quoting two metaphors, both of which were very frequently if indirectly echoed among both spiritualists and others, but whose importance – and very relation – to each other is uncertain.

Firstly, we have the declaration by a prominent American spiritualist Hudson Tuttle, requoted at least once in one of Burns's papers, that it was 'not desirable . . . to trample the desires. Far preferable to say to those terrible forces that hold us to organic existence, "So far as you subserve the development of my spirit, it is well; but trespass not one step further."'[142] True, there were many divergent implications here. There were also no fewer uncertainties, not least as to whether such 'forces' owed their 'hold' merely to fuelling the process of human reproduction (a kind of optimistic dualism or Manicheism) or whether, instead, the whole sentence assumed that, unless anchored by such 'terrible' forces, one's spirit would float smartly upwards into the Summerland or – more logically here – some sort of Nirvana. Secondly, the fact that 'the desires' were 'terrible' brings us to another metaphor. Here, Burns was trying to control his disgust at Woodhull: 'while we do not desire to throw mud' he temporised – but was instantly sucked into his own metaphor of basis: 'we should be equally careful not to seek a muddy foundation for the fair edifice of human progress.'[143] But if (to follow this metaphor) the foundations of his 'fair edifice' had themselves to be 'fair', what did they rest on in their turn? Presumably the edifice, foundations and all, should float above the mud: spiritualised or even dematerialised. After all, as Burns once emphasised during one discussion of Shakerism, 'the whole purpose of human life was to develop into the spiritual degree before leaving the body.'[144] Significantly, the original quotation from Tuttle had occurred only a few months previously and as part of an attack on Woodhull. The less Burns and others saw any tension between the two metaphors (of harnessing terrible forces and of founding on throwable mud) the more significant the confusion. There is something Manichean about him at least. He had been vegetarian since the age of 16 – still on his father's farm in 'that nursery of vegetarianism, the Land of Cakes'; he agitated for vegetarianism to the end of his life, and was said (by one vegetarian) to have hastened his death with a 'meagre diet'.[145]

But in the sexual area, our sources may magnify the confusions. Certainly we are told[146] that sexual dimensions can indeed be found or discerned in seance-reports from at least these decades – quite in addition to any 'sexual-political' quality of mediumship as offering to some women the chance to rise socially. All this helped both to charge and to confuse the question of whether children – conventionally presumed innocent – should be allowed to be mediums. Some spiritualist parents strongly believed they should be so allowed. One argument here was that mediumistic experience would cure the child of any fear of dying. The mother of one young visionary rejoiced that, to her daughter, 'death has no terrors. . . . She has left the body so often, that when the last time comes there will be no struggle – the home of the soul is a real home of delight to her, and the way through which she must enter it is nothing to dread!.'[147] Similarly, one Barrow-in-Furness Lyceumist wrote to the *Banner* as if, in more or less any lyceum, 'the spiritual is developed by being taught to cultivate thought and conscience and to develop [lyceumists'] mediumistic powers, such as clairvoyance, inspiration, etc., and being taught of the spiritual universe.'[148] And her essay had won first prize in a competition.

But such an attitude was rootedly opposed by some other spiritualists. They would have seen as highly risky the visit of an (adult) medium to give a demonstration-seance for the children of Mexborough lyceum.[149] One woman complained of the 'bitter opposition' she had 'at times . . . [met] with from those in authority [in spiritualist societies] who have some strange ideas of spiritualism, and regard its messages and teachings as being suitable to adults only.'[150] This may in part have been a repetition of the old refrain raised now and then by many a lyceum cadre that too many adults were apathetic about channelling their children into the movement: as a lyceum pioneer, Burns railed against this apathy for decades. But again, something more than mere slackness may sometimes have been at work. The conductor of one Burnley lyceum, also in a prize essay, attacked what he called 'an inclination' to be found

> in some quarters to allow children to sit in circles for the purpose of developing spiritual gifts. To my mind, no greater mistake could possibly be made, and I can only regret that all [spiritualist] societies don't set their faces against such a practice by declining to make such engagements with children.[151]

As the last phrase shows, children were not always left in the role of audience but were also brought out sometimes as semi-public mediums. Potentially, therefore, they were open to exploitation – psychological or possibly even commercial. And there would also be the further strains associated with practising something which the broader culture was at best violently ambiguous about. From whatever considerations, the same writer laid down 'the earliest time at which the child should be allowed to sit in a circle with adults for such a purpose should be at 15 or 16 years': till then, 'the whole period of the child's life should be devoted to the development of its physical and mental powers.'

Yet, twelve years later he would, presumably, have denounced West Yorkshire's District Visitor for casually recommending lyceums to follow the example of Slaithwaite where 'there is a circle held for Lyceumists one hour before the normal Lyceum session', leaving the question at least open as to whether younger lyceumists were rigidly barred at the door.[152] And he would surely have been horrified that the front page of one number of the *Lyceum Banner* during the same year should even mention, while biographising one Lyceum worthy, how, 'frequently' during her childhood, 'when [her] mother was out and did not return as promptly as the young folks considered she should, they would resort to the use of the stool, and ascertain from the number of tiltings when their mother would return, the information always being correct.'[153]

This whole disagreement needs viewing in a far broader context. True, any system of assumptions about human nature should alert people against overstraining adults, let alone children. After all, even were the latter's alleged innocence so total as to make them in some way preternaturally wise, we should still, presumably, oppose overstraining them – even if only so as not to damage their wisdom. And, for all I know, spiritualists may well have foreseen some sort of anti-spiritualist moral panic in which they would be denounced for exploiting children.

More centrally, though, did children have even less to fear from death than adults did? In other words, were they even innocent by definition? The main spiritualist answers here were not wholly unsophisticated but not wholly consistent either. Let us concentrate on the lyceums. As these existed primarily to educate younger people, they were hardly likely to define these as passive victims, but rather to try and stir them into active self-improvement. Nonetheless, Kitson was clear that spiritualism's central doctrine here took all those children 'free from serious wrongs or sins' straight to the Summerland, where they were 'soon freed from the bad effects of any evil surroundings in which they may have been born'.[154] In a situation where the fear of hellfire – even when resisted by parents or, increasingly, by leading clergymen – might, for all we know, still be met with from many Christians, including from many playmates in alleyway and schoolyard, assurances such as Kitson's provided part of spiritualism's doctrinal and psychological appeal to children as much as to parents. But this did not mean that childhood was a passive state. We have seen how spiritualist doctrines were peculiarly unrelenting in their demand for moral effort. Why else would Kitson have directed his spiritualist tale about spirit-homes in the Summerland at lyceumists? The story's whole point was that these homes 'indicat[ed] the nature of each act and motive' at every stage of their construction, because 'the daily actions of each individual on earth [gave] off that force which act[ed] on [these homes'] psychic powers.' True, Kitson was clear that the 'process of building the spirit home commence[d] when the person reache[d] the years of understanding'.[155] But the exact year was left vague: presumably it varied between individuals. Perhaps, too, it was better left vague – otherwise the motivation of the younger lyceumists would be endangered, thus causing problems for at least the adults. Certainly the age at which Kitson's fictional heroine was first favoured with a supernatural scolding (from, of course, her guardian angel) seems to have been somewhere below ten years and, at the opening of the tale, she was sternly informed she had 'already begun' to build her spiritual home – set in her spiritual garden which was itself choked, even more emblematically, with weeds.[156]

Spiritualists' uncertainties about child nature bring us back to those about human nature in general. In particular, those about childish 'innocence' return us to those about free will. On the whole, as we have seen, the most frequent plebeian spiritualist treatment – if only in print – of one's character was as a sort of muscle whose strength should be cultivated in ceaseless struggle against one's underlying impulses towards sensuousness. Many present-day readers will view all this retrospectively – if not anachronistically – via some Freud-derived concept of the unconscious.

   Here, to say that something was different from now, is not to deliver judgments on its value, such as that it should have been similar to now; and obviously one reason is that it could not have been. Nor should a discussion of why it could not have been be necessarily interpreted as implying that it should have been. The modern concept of the 'unconscious' would presumably have been unthinkable at the time; and we should hardly demand of plebeian spiritualists that they should have attempted to invent it unaided. In this area too, the plebeians were not conspicuously in advance of their respectable spiritualist and non-spiritualist betters, in awareness of broad intellectual developments. But nor were they behind them. Rather, their reception of these has a sometimes rebarbatively autodidact quality (not surprisingly). The researches of Charcot, for example, received some discussion. But, for Burns at least, their main lesson was their *un*originality. As he proclaimed on his front page, the Parisian professor 'only did what many equally competent men had done before him, some of them in a less conspicuous position, but that he should establish curative mesmerism in an orthodox hospital, and maintain a leading position therein for so many years' – this was immensely impressive. Institutionally, it was as if Charcot was succeeding where, in London more than a generation previously, Drs Elliotson and others had failed. Doctrinally, Burns – and he was not alone in this[157] – saw Charcot as Mesmer plagiarised and re-hashed. (It was as if he had forgotten the dispute between mesmerism and Braid's hypnotism.) And this to such an extent, that he filled the rest of a long article with nothing more original than a phrenological analysis of the Parisian's cranium from a reproduced photo-portrait.

This only underlines how inevitably bounded Burns was by his own standpoint as spokesperson of plebeian practitioners – all those people of 'less conspicuous position'. It also underlines how rich a museum of plebeian versions of various sciences his spiritualism was becoming. I say a 'museum' because, as we began to see during Chapter 6 and will see further during the conclusion, the century or so around 1900 saw these versions being left behind by non-plebeian ones.

Some plebeian spiritualists were at least aware of new conceptual trends. Take a term such as the 'subliminal self', developed from the 1880s by F. W. H. Myers and his circle.[158] And take Eldred Hallas, a former steelworker and Congregationalist lay-preacher, by now a spiritualist and later to be an official of the Municipal

Eldred Hallas
Former steelworker, spent many years as an activist of municipal
employees' unions, but had already gained experience as a preacher
for Congregationalism and subsequently spiritualism around
Bradford and Birmingham. City Councillor for 8 years, he
became a Coalition-Labour M.P. in 1918; but hurriedly
reintegrated himself into the labour movement. Philosophical
pamphleteer: 'too much . . . a philosopher to belong to any . . .
section'.

Employees' Union and right-wing Labour MP. Hallas announced
during 1906 that his studies in psychology had convinced him of
the operation of 'subliminal consciousness or mental exaltation'.
This, he felt, explained his ability – 'still, . . . at almost any time',
to 'enter into an abnormal condition and deliver speeches [which]
. . . some of my friends consider evidence of a genuine trance
condition and "spirit control".'[159] This declaration of his had been
triggered by the disappointment of one Liverpool workman, pen-
named 'Socialist', at repeated failures to obtain 'phenomena'. Hallas
responded: 'The number of intelligent men and women occupying
the same position as "Socialist" is constantly increasing.' And he
was not isolated in his uneasiness. For example, one lyceum's
syllabus included a discussion of the question, 'Are Spirit controls
only multipliers of the subconscious?'[160] True, the last word is
hardly likely to have contained even the faintest Freudian connotations.[161] After all, the 'subliminal self' occupied not only Freud's
terrain but also that of the occult, which is one way in which
that terrain was structured in a pre-Freudian way. Indeed, it was
dominant enough to be dignified with a one-column entry in the
1911 *Encyclopedia Britannica*. But Hallas, at least, was to remain
spiritualist (though less actively than before). Nor was there any
sign as to whether he saw his 'subliminal consciousness' as hinging
considerably on sexuality. And I cannot say whether Myers's
'subliminal self' would, in the long run, have allowed some
convergence between discussions about sexuality and the occult.

Nonetheless, the sexual asceticism of Burns and possibly of other
spiritualists was not merely a matter of rooted opposition to sensuality. Some more positive tendencies may also be dimly discern-
ible, relating perhaps – if only in part – to Burns's 'many excellent
men and women . . . liv[ing] in a state of isolation'. In preaching
the good news that death was merely a transition, spiritualism was
admittedly far from alone – any more, therefore, than it was
alone in providing rapturous accounts of deathbeds. Such accounts
mingled variously a number of elements: among many, an
impression of relief that one is not (often despite earlier doubts)
coming to a full stop, and sometimes that one is meeting one's
nearest and dearest. Sometimes the other people present claimed
to have participated in the same experiences, vicariously or not.
But in addition, spiritualism claimed to offer peculiar proofs –

more or less renewable – of continuity, often by reuniting the
bereaved with those they mourned: to prolong at least the more
optimistic of the emotions experienced before and around the
deathbed. Thus it spoke to longings which seem – and not merely
during my period – to have been widespread: for endless reunion
and in some senses interpenetration both between people and
between the physical and spiritual worlds. True, 'interpenetration'
may often be too sexual a word – or at least too directly so. Rather,
there was an aspect which might, at first sight, be called feminine
but which is better described as flaccid.[162]

Flaccidity relates, firstly and centrally, to mediumship. Was not
one of the synonyms for the word 'medium' the noun 'sensitive'?
A medium or sensitive, commented the interviewer of our Mancunian ex-secularist, 'is like an Aeolian harp, liable to be played upon
by every breeze.'[163] Such qualities were almost a caricature of those
conventionally imputed to the 'Victorian' female – just (as argued
in section A of this chapter) as the passivity of a corpse caricatured
the same qualities in a different and absolute way. Again, the
flowers – supposedly or actually so conspicuous in spiritualist and
other 'anti-mourning' funerals – combined both flaccidity and passivity. Another instance would be the way in which spirits were
pictured: disproportionately they were portrayed as female (usually
youngish) and in their shape, and particularly in their dress, undeniably flaccid. (Admittedly this was not surprising, given that the
materials had to be imponderable: people physically living were
sometimes referred to as still 'in the form'.)

Thus when some non-spiritualist children, watching a lyceum
demonstration, were allegedly overheard remarking that spiritualists 'believed that at death the women were angels and went to
heaven, and the men went to hell',[164] they may indeed have sensed
something at the core of spiritualism, however wildly at sea they
were over doctrine. For there is something female about the
Summerland. Or rather, the qualities and roles which seem most
often to have been associated with it were among those which –
then even more than today – were associated disproportionately
with femaleness. Thus probably most of the spirits spoken of,
particularly in spiritualism's fiction, were female. And this is overwhelmingly true of the helping, i.e. all of the good, spirits – if not
so overwhelmingly true of those (spirits as well as people still on
earth) who were helped. To some extent, this preference was even

doctrinal: Davis, at least, could observe boldly, in passing, that 'the numerous angel women as missionaries far exceed the men.'[165] It was almost – we might have concluded – as if, just as medium-ship licensed men as well as women to be pliant, sensitive and broadly 'feminine',[166] so physical death liberated women from their oppressions on earth. One lyceum (and socialist and trade-union) activist, notifying the *Banner* of his wife's death, could thus wish her – as 'her loved husband' – 'great happiness in the new freedom she possesses'[167]: unawares or not, a complicated choice of words. But if death liberated women even more than men (and often even perhaps from the most 'loved' of husbands – though this particular widower may have meant simply a 'liberation' from the physical 'form'), it liberated them into a 'spiritual' continuation of their role on earth. When, after my period, Mrs Kitson followed Alf and their daughter to the Summerland, the *Banner* rejoiced that 'Ma [Kitson]'s life mission of "mothering" the other two [Kitsons] can now be happily resumed.'[168] More commonly, death opened broader fields for the qualities traditionally imputed to women as helpers, carers and, if necessary, as beings who were always prepared to sacrifice their own immediate ease in order to do good to others. Since such helping and caring was – from the vantage-point of most spiritualists – their most relevant activity, it was often treated as if it were the main or only one – *in* the Summerland, and not merely between it and those lower regions on both sides of physical death. In other words, or so we might argue, however hegemonic on earth were the qualities needed by the 'great men of the world' (to quote one Lib-Lab trade-unionist), the hegemony tended to be reversed in the sky, and the male to be elided into the female.

But the last two paragraphs are probably too neat. To begin, as before, with mediumship. The male medium might have, or have needed to develop, certain 'female' qualities, but the mediumistic state seems sometimes to have licensed a woman to behave semi-publicly in unladylike ways – from assertive to sexually explicit. Nor were spirits invariably described in female ways. 'The whole appearance' of one newly arisen male spirit was imagined as not merely 'of peace and joy' but also as 'one of strength, of virility.' True, his 'form [was] draped in substance, fleecy and shining, robes of softest light and texture' – imponderably and thus flaccidly. But he as soon discovered his limbs '[to be] . . . free, well rounded and shapely'.[169] Altogether, all this may amount less to some simple deification of femaleness than, often, of evidence of yearnings to extricate oneself from firm (or, we can say, essentialist) divisions between absolutely 'female' and 'male' qualities. Whether such yearnings can be labelled straightforwardly hermaphroditic, homosexual or anything else, is peculiarly hard to say. (Relevantly here, Shakers interpreted Adams' original sin as sexual, and may have been interested in hermaphrodism.[170])

In sum, within a broader culture which remained officially Christian and death-discussing, plebeian spiritualism amounted to an extreme of the 'anti-mourning' revolt. Spiritualism as a whole spoke in unusually clear ways to a range of emotions which could be met throughout much of the culture. It may also provide windows – however frosted or oblique – on to emotions and needs which, at least during my period, were trickier to express and sometimes even to formulate. The main example noted here has been that spiritualism was hardly unique in its tension between unified and dis-unified conceptions of personality, and this tension related untidily to its official emphasis on self-education.

Conclusion

This book avoids taking plebeian spiritualism past the 1920s, for reasons not only specific but also much broader.

Specifically, though spiritualism may flourish today among people of most or all classes in Britain, a plebeian spiritualism does not leap distinctively to the eye – though some 'ethnic' near-equivalents certainly do. This position contrasts with my period. The first aspect of this contrast is that, during the latter, plebeian spiritualists were characterised by often bitter opposition to Christian orthodoxy, whereas non-plebeian ones tended either to defend the latter or to try and build bridges towards it. One aid to bridge-building was to try and soften orthodoxy itself, or at least its image. More relevantly, the same process was occurring (though at variable pace and with various timings) among many non-spiritualist Christians during the same period. (The previous chapter has mentioned one indication of this: the excitement around the 'New' Theology.) In other words, by around the second decade of the twentieth century, the main doctrinal division among spiritualists was becoming less urgent, potentially and often actually.

Second, the geographical shift interleaved with the doctrinal: by the interwar years, even the lyceums (once so overwhelmingly based in England's older industrial regions) seem to have been roughly as strong in the more suburban parts of the Home Counties. During the decade or so around 1920, some members of one social group which was growing particularly fast in these areas and which was likely to throw up additional plebeian intellectuals – young clerical workers and very junior 'professionals' – were stirred not by an orthodox revival (in contrast to many people of these and other categories within Wales and the Welsh diaspora) or by secularist disgust, but rather by the same New Theology. In this context, therefore, spiritualism would have been accepted as often as an accompaniment to an easing of orthodoxy as (to take, say, Kitson's area and generation) a product of bitter conflict with it.

Third and coincidentally but no less important, spiritualism's doctrinal homogenisation was, from late 1914, reinforced by World War and influenza-epidemic. These seem, by all accounts, to have spread interest in spiritualism enormously. True, in the long term, they did not necessarily stabilise or even strengthen what there was of a spiritualist movement. But they may possibly have diluted some of its plebeian aspects further: Sir Arthur Conan Doyle, Professor Sir Oliver Lodge or even Hannen Swaffer were hardly the kind of propagandist to reinforce such demarcations as non/plebeian.

But the lessening of plebeian distinctiveness within spiritualism is part of broader, more fundamental processes. True, Chapters 4 and 8 (as well as 5C) have suggested that some important aspects of plebeian spiritualism never had been distinctive from non-pleb-eian. But much of the rest of this book has argued that others, no less important, had indeed been so: in particular, self-reliance in matters doctrinal (a self-reliance very often as abrasive as that of the secularists though less negative) and a democratic epistem-ology. The self-reliance and the epistemology characterised the intellectual culture of self-taught plebeians in general, and were also reinforced by it. Thus they were all too likely to be sapped when it declined. This it surely did. We will now focus on this decline.

True, such underlying shifts are not precisely datable. And pleb-eian autodidacts still turn up occasionally nowadays. But a plebeian autodidact culture no longer exists and autodidacts, even (my impression is) in present-day London tend, culturally, to be as lonely as, say, Robert Dick was in Thurso during the 1860s – until, at least, they are absorbed into the existing political or adult-educational scenes. (The current worker-writers' movement may just prove to be the beginnings of an exception.) This pattern contrasts with the decades (or longer) up to the early twentieth century. Why, thus, the decline?

We need to define more carefully what declined. The plebeian autodidact culture of the nineteenth century may be relatively definable – in terms of identifiable groups (such as secularists – or spiritualists – and their predecessors in earlier movements), of less identifiable ones (such as local discussion and debating societies) and, particularly in smaller places, of individuals mostly far less conspicuous, if locally less isolated, than Dick. It could also be defined according to degrees of plebeian independence from social and educational 'betters': the building and maintaining of independent organisations and printing-presses, struggles against and sometimes within the Mechanics' Institutes, individuals' elation at occasional recognition from 'betters' (how deeply was any kind of 'culture' common between classes?) and disgust at philistinism from other plebeians: in a word, the not always consciously felt contest between pressures toward individual ascent and collective emancipation. Along all such dimensions, that century can be said to have had a plebeian autodidact culture.

The latter's decline relates to a number of economic and social factors: the industrial and other unrests of the period 1910–26 which reinforced support, notably among the rising generation of working-class activists, for less educationally based strategies: the downgrading, within the workplace and outside it, of the skilled (a strategic minority of whom had become, in many places, a key group within this culture); and what seems to have been an economic sapping of independent lecturing during the same fifteen or twenty years. All these strands intertwined: not least (as we shall see soon), epistemologically. They also intertwined politically: one result of the declining prestige of educationally based strategies was an increasingly direct politicisation of the institutions (such as the Labour College movement) of independently plebeian self-education. These became polarised between the Communist Party on the one hand and the TUC and Labour Party on the other. These two power-centres tended to enforce their often bitter rivalry on to local activists and anyway (rhetoric apart) to see any education of a broader-than-party nature as either dangerous or of secondary priority.[1]

The most important point is not so much that – under political, conceptual and socio-economic shocks – plebeian autodidact culture of a nineteenth-century type went the way of whatever plebeian intellectual cultures we may see as its predecessors but, rather, that it has still not been replaced. This present-day absence (or non-replacement) is the big novelty. True, it has had social dimensions: there must be something important, here, in the decline of upper-working-class strata relative to the rest of the working population, since these – like earlier intermediate groups

– were subject to socially, politically and intellectually divergent pressures which were particularly likely to incite some of them towards greater intellectual independence. But there is also one neglected aspect: the type of active, confident, democratic epistemology we have been studying has not been replaced either. 'Replace' is anyway far too neat a metaphor for a process that was both negative and positive. Here our terrain, whatever its potential, luxuriates with rank speculation which I am in great danger of adding to. Some of the factors in the more or less hidden epistemological history of twentieth-century Britain have had an impact on areas much wider than those formerly covered by plebeian autodidact culture. The latter, after all, directly involved no more than minorities (however strategic these may sometimes be argued to have been).

To begin with the negative. Recruitment to these minorities occurred via many routes, some of which became more attractive and negotiable, others less. Some of these were epistemological. True, during the nineteenth century as during any other, autodidacts may, overall, have helped intimidate more people than they attracted. Our sources may come disproportionately from the latter. The intimidation could occur whenever, for example, a meeting was experienced as unbearably wordy or an individual as crushingly knowledgeable. For every young William Lovett energised by an overwhelming sense of his own ignorance, how many young men (and, even less visibly, women) were driven into deeper inarticulacy by a feeling of some innate inferiority? Autodidacts may have acted not only as intellectual energisers but also, sometimes, as what we may call 'stupefiers'.

But during the last 70 years or so, by contrast, stupefaction – relative to helping to do, discover or decide something felt to be important – has become far more multiform. This hypothesis is worth expounding: even if soon exploded, it may help clear the air. It has to do with the valuations (no less powerful for usually being implicit and unintentional) which people distortedly or accurately received about their abilities. True, such reception – were it not particularly hard to research (partly because it might involve asking individuals to estimate themselves counter-factually) – would, very likely, reveal all manner of inconsistency and countercurrent. But one very important source of such valuations was, surely, the politics of what is sometimes called educational meritocracy, i.e. of discussions as to whether and how to structure the education-system so as to reward 'intelligent' effort. This issue was so argued over, that even the majority of people – who may never have bothered about it much – would have had their self-esteem influenced forcefully if indirectly by it.

As we are about (unoriginally) to note, this politics interacted in Britain with justifications of traditional or aristocratic education – more intricately than in, say, France where, from the 1790s to the 1980s, the interaction was more often one of frontal and bitter opposition. This contrast is, of course, a vivid aspect of the divergence in the class history of the two countries. In this context, the 1902 Education Act amounted to a triumph of Sir Robert Morant over, in effect, T. H. Huxley: of the tradition-minded current in the upper-middle class over the modernising. But in France also, meritocracy has recently been argued to have had a stupefying effect on most people. So the aspect most relevant in, presumably, both countries is, not the precise details of meritocratic politics as such, but rather their indirect effect both on the self-image of most people and on the assumptions of political left-wingers – on those people, in other words, whom we might at first sight have most expected to help generate further democratic epistemologies.

In nineteenth-century Britain, whatever the popular agitations over education, even the meanest general measures of meritocracy were far less enforced from below than seemingly granted from above, often sparingly (and sometimes even half-withdrawn on narrow grounds of cost, as via Lowe's 'Revised Code' with its depressing effect on the number of pupils qualifying for Queen's Scholarships). Alternatively, as from 1907, measures of meritocracy were bestowed (via the system of scholarships to grammar schools) as consolation for a continued failure, precisely, to move towards broader meritocracy within even the publicly funded educational system as a whole. This system remained aristocratically impregnated, or at least in awe of the public schools: the latter influenced the grammar schools and these were defined as having what the rest of the publicly funded system – whatever virtues it might allow locally – was officially programmed to lack.

And yet, of course, the sun (or was it – is it – the moon?) of meritocracy was soon to gild even this gentlemanly compromise. It rose – to confused bayings from some Labour MPs, among others – at angles likeliest to leave most people in obscurity. In

effect, it stupefyingly made inequality taste egalitarian, by justi-
fying aristocracies old or new in terms of the alleged 'unfitness' of
most people for whatever sorts of knowledge gave, or were seen
as giving, access to power. Such confusions affected many people
on the left – not least some of those (such as many working-class
ex-Grammar-School Labour MPs) who were defined as 'fit' – as
well as on the right. Thus both the Hadow and Norwood Committees, however politically different their origins and personnel –
adduced the existence of different innate types of mind which
happened to correspond to the various types of secondary school
which were evolving or which either Committee wished to
encourage. And, if the ease of such correspondence might be too
smooth to convince some cynics on the left, more[2] grew convinced
of the scientificity of various forms of intelligence-testing. True,
there remained room to argue that intelligence could be increased
by stimulation, and thus be made to puncture Norwood's grand
barriers – by promoting at least some pupils from among those
'incapable of a long series of connected steps', right up to the
dizzyingly high table of those who were 'interested in learning for
its own sake, [and] who can grasp an argument'.[3]

But the overwhelming tendency of these theories was, during
the depressed and disturbed three decades after the First World
War – into, in other words, the first generation of one-person,
one-vote – to disfranchise most people's intellects: as unable to
'grasp an argument'. If doctrines were able, disembodied, to
avenge themselves on each other, this would be innate ideas'
vengeance on the Enlightenment. True, meritocracy always has
been ambiguous between collective egalitarianism and its own
'fairer' elitism: phrenology, for example, had consorted with
either. And both phrenology and intelligence-testing claimed to be
scientific. But one advantage that I.Q.-testers such as Professor Sir
Cyril Burt enjoyed over any phrenological predecessor was that
science, around the interwar years, was more distanced than before
from ordinary people while enjoying at least as much prestige and
what I am about to define as relatively passive interest.

Not least on the left. And here we leave the negative aspects of
the non-replacement of democratic epistemology, and come to the
positive. The novelty (again, for Britain) was not merely that
working-class independent schools had by now been all but throt-
tled,[4] nor that organised radical adult-education was becoming

more or less as party-politicised as it had long been in some other European countries (as in the Germany of the SPD). The novelty also involved the image both of natural sciences and of natural scientists. The former no longer appeared (at the very least via some of their most widely discussed areas such as physics) to be distilled common sense. This situation would have scandalised many a plebeian autodidact such as those we have met: in the eyes of those who, in conformity with Austin Holyoake's 1871 burial service, were eulogised – as we heard during the last chapter – for their faithfulness to 'science . . . and common sense', any relativistic doubts might have seemed as obscenely trivial as dancing a quadrille at the graveside. And scientists were seen on the left as needing collectivist liberation precisely so as, in their turn, to help liberate ordinary people – from outside and partly, in effect, from above.[5] Nor were these the only factors tending to give science and scientists a remoter image among lay people. Plebeian (as other) activists now related to both far less than before via participatory pursuits: however silly we might find such 'sciences' as mesmerism or phrenology, they frequently encouraged participation: were relatively easy to become expert in. And at the opposite extreme, even the disputes among the 'greats' were more accessible to ordinary mortals during the nineteenth century (as over Evolution – whether logically or by analogy with familiar pastimes such as botany) than during the twentieth (as over relativity or quantum mechanics).

However, though participation and active understanding have, during the last seventy or so years, become less easy, this has not been the story with passive consumption. The packaging of snippets of knowledge grew far better – and often, admittedly, far less superficially descriptive – between the early mid-nineteenth and late-mid-twentieth centuries. Passive access as spectator or consumer is now available at the flick of a switch. Possibly the very improvement of such access has itself had the effect of making people's exclusion from active participation in knowledge seem an inevitable part of the nature of modern things. And if, from at least the 1970s, there was sometimes widespread cynicism about many sciences' apparent ireelevance or worse, there were fewer widespread ideas about how to affect the situation. Knowledge-consumerism does encourage interest and a kind of learning (which can sometimes be considerable), but it sooner or later devalues them. Thus it encourages a brittler and narrower kind of confidence than that among many plebeian autodidacts during the period of this book.

Although not all these developments were exactly simultaneous, they were sufficiently so to allow us to surmise that they helped inhibit the elaboration of some fresh democratic epistemology by, for example, those who believed themselves to be, as socialists, striving for an unparalleled deepening of democracy. The outlines of any such epistemology therefore remain unclear yet. True, by contrast, any attempts to revive such a minority configuration as a plebeian autodidact culture would be less an act of creation than of taxidermy. Thus a central challenge sounded to us by both the current situation and our plebeian autodidacts remains more than ever an epistemological one.

In any case, was the decline of plebeian autodidact culture really so unprecedented in Britain? Partly. Some of the features of what we have glimpsed during the nineteenth century were probably in existence during the eighteenth or seventeenth, though how consistently or intermittently is quite another question. True, continuity itself takes much defining, let alone proving. But the presence of such features during, say, the 1650s and perhaps (to, arguably, however small an extent) during subsequent generations brings the nineteenth and very early twentieth centuries closer to earlier ones than to the two post-(First) war generations. The novelty of our own time, in other words, may be, not that the epistemology and the intellectual culture we have been exploring declined, but that they have hardly been replaced: where, to date, are today's intellectual equivalent of the plebeians among the Lollards, Antinomians, millenarians and their nineteenth-century successors? In England we could, in this sense, be living through one of, or the, longest periods of non-replacement since the days of John Ball.

There may therefore be useful comparisons and contrasts to be drawn with periods of non-replacement in other, say European, societies. To take merely one geographical area (for whatever geography may be worth, over so long a period), we would need to examine not only the Waldensians and some seemingly eccentric millers and peasants[6] (all too distanced from us by labels such as 'late-mediaeval' or 'early-modern'), but also the plebeian intellectuals of early-twentieth-century Ferrara or Turin. Indeed, a democratic epistemology (whether directed against 'hireling' priests, legally qualified doctors, established professors or just the expensively educated) can go with anything from a virtually 'know-nothing' attitude toward intellectual discussion to a passionate engagement in it: it is not necessarily dependent, in other words, on an intellectual culture (or at least on a historiographically visible one) of autodidacts. And the 'plebeian' group can involve many kinds of alloying, alliance and balance between say, big or small peasants, millers, shopkeepers, artisans, skilled or unskilled factory workers or whatever. Certainly, where a culture of such a type persists, the epistemology – however hard to define or trace – is likely to be influenced by it. But both are obviously affected also by wider developments: the ways in which, say, French and German universities can intimidate those outside and inside them is surely influenced, to this day, by the nature and timing of the overthrow both of absolutism and of the organisation of society along estate lines.

Altogether, one way of describing the novelty, in Britain, of the period from around 1910 to the present is that a democratic epistemology and the intellectual culture with which it interacted – that of plebeian autodidacts – declined simultaneously (somewhat in tandem) and have not been replaced. A fresh democratic epistemology – whatever the risks – may be worth creating now.

To summarise a book in a few lines: the first four chapters began by examining not only the original ingredients of plebeian spiritualism but also (in much of Chapters 2 and 3) what it amounted to a reaction against. To a considerable extent, the resultant mix was a fresh brew. As both process and product, this had many aspects. One of these was political (e.g. Chapters 2, 3 and 5A). In addition, this spiritualism related powerfully – though not exclusively – to a slipperily 'imponderable' definition of matter (Chapter 4) and to a democratic approach to knowledge (Chapter 6). The latter, in its full version, was shared with overwhelmingly plebeian currents, the former found favour more widely. Only with this background could we recognise plebeian spiritualism as appealing to fears in areas wider than merely sickness and death – vitally important though these were too (Chapters 7 and 8) – where it was anyway less radical, in some ways, than its adherents liked to believe. But, in sharing certain epistemological and philosophical approaches – let alone in caricaturing them – plebeian spiritualism in the long run benefited neither itself nor them (Chapter 6). Partly as a result, it was to share, from the early twentieth century, in the decay of the social and intellectual world in which it had first been shaped and had once flourished.

Notes

(Places of publication include London, unless otherwise stated).

Chapter 1

1 GK. Nelson: *Spiritualism and Society*, 1969, p. 24. Nelson's is a pioneering work but vaguely footnoted.
2 E.g. Nelson, Part 1, particularly Chapter 1 and both parts of Chapters 3 and 4; R. Laurence Moore: *In Search of White Crows: Spiritualism, Parapsychology and American Culture*, 1977, New York, Part 1, particularly Chapter 1; Ruth Brandon: *The Spiritualists: the Passion for the Occult in the 19th and 20th centuries*, 1983, particularly Chapter 1.
3 Whitney Cross: *The Burnt-Over District: the Social and Intellectual History of Enthusiastic Religion in Western New York, 1800–50*, New York, 1965. See also Paul E. Johnson: *A Shopkeepers' Millenium: Society and Revivals in Rochester, New York, 1815–37*, New York, 1978.
4 Johnson, pp. 14, 120.
5 I am not hazarding a traditional sociological (or keenly Weberian/ Durkheimian) explanation for spiritualism's beginnings: it was more than just another Protestant revival. Useful hypotheses can be overworked. For some sociology, see Nelson.
6 Nelson, pp. 55f.
7 Samuel Thompson: *A Narrative of the Life and Medical Discoveries of Samuel Thompson; containing an account of his system of curing desease with vegetable medicine . . .*, 1825, 2nd edition.
8 As it had also in American: Poughkeepsie, the town which produced A. J. Davis (whom we shall meet soon) boasted a botanic infirmary and periodical – according to Wallace (cited at the end of this footnote). Articles include J. Pickstone: 'Medical Botany (Self-Help Medicine in Victorian England)' in *Manchester Literary and Philosophical Society, Memoirs and Proceedings*, vol. 118, 1975–6; F. J. Forman: 'The Worthington School and the Thompsonians' in *Bulletin of the History of Medicine*, vol. 21, 1947; A. Berman: 'The Thompsonian Movement and its relation to American Pharmacy and Medicine' in *Bulletin of the History of Medicine*, vol. 25, 1951; Dan J. Wallace's: 'Thompsonians, the People's Doctors' in *Clio Medica*, vol. 14, 1979–80, contains a bibliography so useful as to absolve me from trying to rival it.

9 Nelson, p. 45.
10 Nelson, p. 17.
11P. Linebaugh: 'And all the Atlantic mountains shook' in *Labor/le Travailleur*, summer 1983, no. 11; also 'Critique' by R. Sweeny and Linebaugh's reply, in: same, Fall 1984, no. 14.
12 See, e.g., Michael T. Taussig: *The Devil and Commodity Fetishism in South America*, 1980, Chapel Hill, N. Carolina, particularly pp. 41, 97.
13 Nelson, p. 64.
14 See much of Gwyn A. Williams: *Madoc, the Making of a Myth*, 1979, and his *The Search for Beulah Land*, 1980. More broadly, see H. N. Smith: *Virgin Land: the American West in Symbol and Myth*, 1950, Cambridge, Massachusetts; R. Nash: *Wildness and the American Mind*, 1967; A. Kolodny: *the Lay of the Land*, 1975, Chapel Hill.
15 E. D. Andrews, *The People called Shakers*, 1953, p. 224; J. M. Whitworth: *God's Blueprints, a sociological study of three utopian sects*, 1975; L. Foster: *Religion and Sexuality, three American Communal Experiments of the 19th Century*, 1981, particularly Part III.
16 According to the very polemical W. H. Reid (*The Infidel Societies of the Metropolis*, 1800, p. 54), this was merely an excuse invented for a failure to gain converts.
17 See J. F. C. Harrison, *The Second Coming: Popular Millenarianism, 1780–1850*, 1979, p. 169.
18 My main sources on Richmond are his *The Kingdom of God*, Glasgow, 1885, p. 8f. Also *HN*, 1.1.68, pp. 171–4; *M. and D.*, 1870, p. 143; 1882, p. 442. Obituaries in *TW*, vol. 4, 1891, p. 193; *M. and D.*, 20. and 27.2.91; *Northern Echo* (Darlington), 17.2.91. Article by R. Scott in *Darlington and Stockton Times*, 1.1.1966.
19 E.g. as main speaker at presentation of the portrait of another pioneer spiritualist: *M. and D.*, 1882, pp. 442f.
20 Joseph Rhodes: *Half a Century of Cooperation in Keighley*, 1911, p. 17. There is also a passing hint, from a few years after Richmond's visit, of a Shaker presence in the area: see *YST*, vol. 1, p. 20 – which I quote to other purposes below.
21 Rhodes.
22 A. Briggs, 'Industry and Politics in early 19th Century Keighley' in *Bradford Antiquary*, vol. 9 (new series, vol. 7), 1952, pp. 310f.
23 *Keighley News*, 13.9.1952, p. 6.
24 There is disagreement as to whether his father had been landlord of an inn (as claimed by the author of *Good Fellowship in Keighley*, 1923, p. 13) and repeated by Briggs (same article), or a grocer (as argued in *Keighley News*, same page).
25 *Keighley News*, same page.
26 E.g. Brandon, Nelson.
27 Logie Barrow: 'Socialism is Eternity: Plebeian Spiritualists, 1853–1913' in *History Workshop*, issue 9, spring 1980, particularly the first 20 lines of p. 40. Credit for kicking me back to the Keighley sources belongs to David Goodway, in correspondence during 1982–3.
28 Nelson, p. 91.

29 Nelson, p. 91.
30 Nelson, p. 89.
31 Nelson, p. 91, quoting F. Podmore: *Modern Spiritualism*, 1902 – but, as all too often in Nelson, without pagination.
32 Desirée Hirst: *Hidden Riches: Traditional Symbolism from the Renaissance to Blake*, 1964, p. 286; see also pp. 240–5 for what Hirst calls an eighteenth-century 'Baedecker's guide to mystical Britain'. See also S. Hutin: *Les Disciples anglais de Jacob Boehme aux 17ième et 18ième Siècles*, Paris, 1960.
33 *Keighley News*, 4.10.52, p. 8.
34 This phrase is a nuancing of Nelson's, p. 91.
35 *Westminster Review*, 1862, p. 89; quoted by Nelson, pp. 141f.
36 I was wrong to talk in my *History Workshop* article (p. 40; the article is referred to in note 27) of the *YST* simply 'mov[ing] to London' when it 'became the *British Spiritual Telegraph*'.
37 Anon: *Table Moving Extraordinary, by Robert Burns*, Keighley, 1853, 2nd edition. Also a leaflet by 'a private party, Bingley', dated 16.8.54. Both are in Keighley Public Library. For anti-spiritualist disgust at such 'miserable, worthless' and 'nursery-rhyme-like' verses being foisted on the great Robbie, see *Keighley Visitor and general advertiser: a Monthly Magazine of Instruction and Amusement, published under the Superintendence [sic] of the Temperance Society* ('3000 copies gratis!!'), No. 3, December 1853, pp. 14f; similarly No. 1, October 1853, p. 8.
38 *YST*, vol. 1, January 1856, p. 138.
39 *YST*, vol. II, p. 120.
40 Thus Volume I and much of II were 'Printed and Published by B[enjamin] Morrell, Keighley' or 'at the B.S.T. office, Keighley'. The latter phrase continued into the first five numbers of Volume III; but many later numbers, while directing 'communications' via Morrell, were printed by 'D[avid]. W. Weatherhead, Keighley', and the same phrases were juggled through subsequent numbers. On the other hand, much of Volumes II and III were also published in London by G. J. Holyoake (the famous martyr for free-thought), by F. Pitman (brother of the shorthand pioneer and himself probably a spiritualist) or by William Horsell (a vegetarian). The latter two operated from addresses in Paternoster Row, the centre of much of the London booktrade.
41 *BST*, vol. 1, p. 26.
42 *YST*, May 1855.
43 *BST*, vol. 1, p. 67.
44 *BST*, vol. 1, p. 67.
45 'Upwards' may possibly be an exaggeration: Ian Dewhirst talks of 'up to' 400 (Ian Dewhirst: *Robert Burns . . . and the Yorkshire Table Rappers* in *West Riding Magazine*, vol. IX, no. 8, September 1972, p. 33f).
46 *YST*, vol. 1, p. 31f.
47 *BST*, vol. 2, p. 98f. The medium is given as Mrs Jane Joan Preece of Dudley.
48 E.g. *YST*, vol. 1, p. 46.
49 *YST*, vol. 1, pp. 40f.

50 *YST*, vol. I, pp. 20f.
51 *BST*, vol. 3, pp. 48f. One 'John Garnett' was among the thirteen signatories to the pamphlet, *Table Moving Extraordinary*; referred to in note 37.
52 E.g. *YST*, 1856, pp. 200, 223f.
53 *YST*, October 1855, pp. 94–7.
54 May 1856, p. 186; April 1857, p. 15.
55 *YST*, vol. 2, pp. 133f.
56 *YST*, vol. 1, pp. 48f.
57 See most of Barbara Taylor: *Eve and the New Jerusalem*, 1983.
58 *YST*, vol. 2, pp. 133f. For what may amount to partial parallels during the early eighteenth century to mystical interest in machinery, see Hillel Schwartz: *The French Prophets*, 1980, University of California Press, p. 239.
59 See J. H. Gleason: *The Genesis of Russophobia in Great Britain*, 1950, Cambridge, Massachusetts; A. Briggs: 'David Urquhart and the West Riding Foreign Affairs Committees' in *Bradford Antiquary*, vol. 10 (new series vol. 8), 1962.
60 Briggs, same article, p. 203n; the 'B. Morrell' instanced by Briggs on p. 206 was not provably Benjamin.
61 *Keighley Visitor*, no. 2, November 1859, pp. 4f.
62 Joseph Rhodes: *Half-a-Century of Cooperation*, 1911, pp. 20f, 28.
63 *YST*, vol. 1, pp. 115f.
64 *YST*, vol. 1, pp. 128f, 139ff, 151ff, 163f, 175ff, 186f, 197ff, 209f, 221ff.
65 *YST*, vol. 1, pp. 115f.
66 *YST*, vol. 1, p. 175.
67 *YST*, vol. 1, p. 20.
68 *YST*, vol. 1, p. 4.

Chapter 2   Owenism and the millennium

1 On the Owenite educational milieu, see particularly E. Yeo: 'Culture and Constraint in Workingclass Movements' in E. Yeo, S. Yeo, eds: *Popular Culture and Class Conflict, 1590–1914*, Hassocks, 1981, particularly p. 161, 167; on the Owenites in general, the standard work remains J. F. C. Harrison: *Robert Owen and the Owenites in Britain and America, The Quest for the New Moral World*, 1969; the same author's *The Second Coming: Popular Millenarianism, 1780–1850*, 1979, occupies a similar eminence in its field.
2 R. Owen: *Outline of the Rational System of Society, Founded on Demonstrable Facts . . .* [over sixty words in the title altogether], 1841.
3 W. H. Oliver: *Owen in 1817: the Millenialist Moment*, in S. Pollard, J. Salt, eds, *Robert Owen, Prophet of the Poor*, 1971, pp. 172f.
4 R. Owen: *Robert Owen's Address to the Human Race on his 84th Birthday*, 1854, pp. 3f: Owen's opening words to the meeting.

5 R. Owen: *The Future of the Human Race*, 1853, pp. 21f.
6 Owen: *The Future*, p. 22f.
7 Owen: *The Future*, p. 9.
8 Owen: *The Future*, p. 27.
9 *Robert Owen's Millennial Gazette*, no. 11, 1.8.57, p. 127.
10 See particularly A. L. Morton: *The English Utopia*, 1978 edition, pp. 15–45, 275–85.
11 *ROMG*, no. 12, 1.10.57, pp. 9–15.
12 Oliver in Pollard and Salt, p. 169.
13 As, say, in Hyde during 1839, 'Chartists, Methodists, Socialists and many of the supporters of the Rev J. R. Stephens' *New Moral World*, 28.9.39., quoted by E. Yeo: 'Robert Owen and Radical Culture', in Pollard and Salt, p. 93.
14 *ROMG*, 1856, pp. 30ff.
15 R. Owen: *The Future of the Human Race*, p. 31.
16 Owen: *The Future*, p. 26.
17 E.g., Owen: *The Future*, p. 53.
18 E.g. Owen: *The Future*, p. 17; or as reported in the *Investigator*, vol. 2, p. 45: two different versions of what we might call technologism.
19 On this, see particularly W. H. Oliver in Pollard and Salt, or the same author's nearly identical chapter 8 of his: *Prophets and Millennialists: The Use of Biblical Prophecy in England from the 1790s to the 1840s*. Auckland University Press, 1978.
20 E.g. Oliver, p. 8; Owen's 84th-birthday *Address* (as in n. 4, above), p. 7; *ROMG* – Owen's, in the sense that he appears to have written or dictated most of it himself – number 1, 23.3.56, pp. 10f.
21 R. Owen: *The Future*, p. 37.
22 Owen: *The Future*, pp. 32f.
23 See the 131 pages of minutes of this event – which lasted for a fortnight – in *ROMG*, no. 11, 1.8.57.
24 *ROMG*, no. 5, 1.8.56, pp. 9–16.
25 *ROMG*, no. 10, 1.1.57, pp. 1–12.
26 *ROMG*, no. 1, 23.3.56, pp. 10f.
27 Similarly *ROMG*, no. 6, 1.7.56, pp. 28f.
28 *ROMG*, no. 6, pp. 28f.
29 *ROMG*, no. 6, p. 12.
30 As quoted in *Yorkshire Spiritual Telegraph*, 1855, pp. 94–7.
31 *ROMG*, no. 6, p. 28. For Spear's animated dynamo, see Nelson, p. 21.
32 *ROMG*, no. 6, p. 28f.
33 *ROMG*, no. 3, 1.5.56, p. 9.
34 *ROMG*, no. 3, p. 9.
35 Owen's 1816 *Address*, quoted Oliver, p. 181; Oliver is legitimately concerned to bring out the analogies between Owen and older millenarian conceptions, but I think he should relate his emphasis (for example, p. 190) closer to such quotes.
36 *ROMG*, no. '10A', 1.1.57, p. 10.
37 *ROMG*, no. 11, 1.8.57, p. 113; similarly p. 83.
38 *Two Worlds*, 3.5.89, pp. 297f, quoting the Middlesborough *North-*

Eastern Weekly Gazette, which I have not checked. For an instance of spiritualist awareness of affinity with Roman Catholics, see 'Prefatory' to volume 1 of the *Psychological Review*: 'a Catholic of any sincerity is a practical spiritualist'.

Chapter 3   Nottingham and Cabala

1 *YST*, vol. 1, p. 177.
2 See particularly Roy A. Church: *Economic and Social Change in a Midland Town: Victorian Nottingham 1815–1900*, 1966, particularly pp. 228 (e.g. for the 'Manchester' comparison) to 232.
3 For Brothers, see, notably, J. F. C. Harrison's *Second Coming* (as cited above) particularly chapter 4. Ben Jonson's *The Alchemist* is most relevant in Act 2, scenes 3 and 5. Not that millenarians such as Brothers were themselves without seventeenth-century echoes.
4 Keith Thomas: *Religion and the Decline of Magic: Studies in Popular Belief in 16th and 17th Century England*, 1971, particularly chapter 8.
5 E. S. Drake: *Directory of the Town and County of Nottingham*, 1860, p. 185.
6 J. G. H. Brown: *The Cause of the Present War*, 1855 (henceforth: *Cause*), p. 4.
7 By the end of the decade, it was total. See J. G. H. Brown: *Light of the World*, 1859 (a 97-word title, henceforth: *Light*), pp. 22, 28, for indications of this advancing disability and of some of its effects.
8 J. G. H. Brown: *Fulfilled Prophecies; or the passing signs of the end, as foretold in Ancient and Modern Prophecy; together with the future fate of India and the world; as described in modern divine revelation*, 1857 (from now on, *FP*), p. 3.
9 Harrison, p. 155. For the Muggletonians, see C. Hill, B. Reay, W. Lamont: *The World of the Muggletonians*, 1983: not that Muggletonian doctrine was directly compatible with spiritualist.
10 Harrison, pp. 110, 158, 203.
11 Harrison, pp. 160, 256 n. 47.
12 Quoted from James Epstein: 'Some Organisational and Cultural Aspects of Chartism in Nottingham', in James Epstein, Dorothy Thompson, editors: *The Chartist Experience, Studies in Working-class Radicalism and Culture, 1830–1860*, 1982, pp. 223, 232, 252, 259 respectively.
13 *The Scriptural Monthly Magazine, 1856*; *FP*.
14 Epstein, pp. 231, 235, 240; see also John Rowley's entry on James Sweet in Joyce Bellamy, John Saville, editors: *Dictionary of Labour Biography*, vol. 4, 1977.
15 Harrison, p. 203.
16 See one list of such in the *Community's Journal* (henceforth: *CJ*), pp. 22 f.
17 The titles (abbreviated) are: *The Community's Journal; or, standard of*

truth. Useful Knowledge, void [sic] of fiction . . .; the *Universal Magazine* (henceforth: *UM*); and *The General Record and Successive Review* (henceforth: *GR*) (confusingly, its pages are headed 'the community's record, and general review').

18 See, e.g., *CJ*, pp. 100 f; similarly 'A Member of the Nottingham Spiritual Circle': *A public lecture*, n.d. but 1859.

19 'Over 330': Brown: *Light*, p. 18. 'Gentlemen': *GR*, pp. 91 f, 176.

20 *GR*, p. 195. There was also one mention of a 'Dr. Julien Goldstein', with or via an address in Nottingham (*CJ*, pp. 21 f) but who seems not to figure in any local street directory that I have seen from this time.

21 *UM*, pp. 54 f.

22 *CJ*, pp. 5 f.

23 Ibid., preface to the volume, p. iii.

24 *GR*, p. 13.

25 *GR*, p. 49.

26 *GR*, p. 75.

27 *M. and D.*, 1.7.1870, pp. 101 f.

28 Brown: *The Scriptural Monthly Magazine* 1856–57; similarly much of J. G. H. Brown: *The Book of Life, or the Fields of Death*, 1859.

29 Advertisement for *SMM*, in J. G. H. Brown: *Important Relations from the spirits of Emmanuel Swedenborg, the Swedish Spiritualist; and Joseph Smith, the Mormon prophet; shewing the sacred and holy doctrines, as set forth by Swedenborg, whose errors are proved unimportant; the doctrines of Joseph Smith being proved hypocritical and delusive, resulting through worldly ambition; as declared in revelations from the spirits of both men, which are sanctioned and confirmed by the great Angel Gabriel*, 1857 (henceforth: *IR*), pp. 5f.

30 *Causes*, p. 14; *GR*, pp. 71, 174; *BL*, pp. 20f.

31 Editorial in *CJ*, pp. 89f.

32 *The Universal Magazine, or truthful recorder of passing events; containing history and politics, select varieties and amusing facts, anecdotes, historical sketches and other useful and amusing information* (1857–58), 9.1.1858, p. 80.

33 Ibid., pp. 105f.

34 The Angel Gabriel had earlier agreed that the periodisation in Brown's *On the Causes and Results of the Late War* had been incorrect, though not the substance (Brown: *A Message from the World of Spirits*, p. 139): a simple enough example of what sociologists call a 'failure-mechanism'.

35 E.g., *FP*, pp. 9, 14–21, 28f; *BL*, p. 91.

36 Also to unnamed Indians who had fixed the end of British rule for 100 years after Plassey (same page).

37 Editorial in *CJ*, pp. 89f. I say 'would have', because the editorial was not provably penned by Brown in person, though it was certainly under his direct influence.

28 *FP*, p. 29; similarly p. 39.

39 Ibid., pp. 40f; similarly, e.g., *BL*, pp. 40f, 77, 101f, 160f; *Light*, pp. 45–8.
40 *Causes*, pp. 8ff.
41 *SMM*, e.g., pp. 223–37; later quoted in *BL*, pp. 97–104.
42 *BL*, p. 162.
43 *Causes*. pp. 18f; similarly *FP*, pp. 53f. For a general treatment of more down-to-earth opinions about America during this and other decades, see H. Pelling: *America and the British Left*, 1956; Philip S. Foner: *British Labor and the American Civil War*, 1981.
44 E.g., *BL*, pp. 98f.
45 *FP*, p. 9.
46 *FP*, pp. 53f.
47 *Light*, p. 16.
48 *FP*, p. 32.
49 *Causes*, p. 3.
50 *BL*, p. 164.
51 *Universal Magazine*, author's preface to the serialisation, p. 2.
52 *Causes*, pp. 15f.
53 Short, anonymous item in *CJ*, 18.7.1857, p. 52.
54 Harrison, p. 183.
55 *FP*, p. 9.
56 *FP*, pp. 9, 34ff.
57 Editorial in *CJ*, pp. 41f.
58 *CJ*, pp. 8f; similarly pp. 30f; reprint of an Indian's letter to the *Northern Mail*, pp. 119–22; similarly *FP*, pp. 14,22.
59 *CJ*, pp. 120f.
60 *CJ*, pp. 107f, 120f, 168, 210f.
61 *CJ*, pp. 187f.
62 *CJ*, pp. 107f.
63 E.g., *Causes*, p. 2.
64 *Universal Magazine*, 6.2.1858, p. 103.
65 E.g., *UM*, pp. 41ff, 58f, 79f. The Poor Law had been a bitter topic in Nottingham (e.g. Church, chapter V); but Nottingham was hardly unusual in this respect.
66 See 'A military execution', in *CJ*, pp. 6ff, 15; by 'WP, late of the 76th Regiment and an eye-witness of the facts related'.
67 Brown: *A Message from the World of Spirits* . . ., pp. 233f (Typically, the title took up 101 words; so, henceforth: *Message*.)
68 *Causes*, p. 10ff, Rule 'IX'.
69 *Message*, p. 240.
70 *Message*, p. 235.
71 *Message*, p. 241f.
72 *Message*, p. 249.
73 *Message*, p. 237ff.
74 *Message*, p. 239.
75 *CJ*, pp. 5f.
76 *CJ*, pp. 259f.

77 CJ, p. 143, Notices to Correspondents (here, to 'J.J.' of Coventry): could this have been Goodwin Barmby himself?
78 CJ, pp. 5f: 'An address to members forming the community of the great organisation.'
79 CJ, p. 143; the command to 'keep aloof' occurs also in BL, p. 145.
80 Light, p. 8.
81 Message, p. 241.
82 CJ, pp. 89f.
83 UM, pp. 59f; similarly pp. 195f.
84 UM, pp. 195f.
85 UM, p. 105.
86 E.g., BL, pp. 13, 17; GR, p. 73.
87 BL, p. 148.
88 BL, p. 148; FP, pp. 3–10; GR, pp. 45f.
89 E.g., GR, pp. 179f.
90 GR, p. 42.
91 FP, p. 5.
92 At one stage, half of the Circle's members came from outside Nottingham: GR, p. 94.
93 GR, p. 101; similarly, p. 174.
94 GR, p. 136.
95 GR, p. 138. Relevantly or not – in the London of 1708 – the 'French prophets' had grouped themselves into 'tribes': Schwartz, (as in note 58 of chapter 1), p. 126.
96 Schwarz, pp. 136f; similarly BL, pp. 17f.
97 GR, p. 19.
98 GR, pp. 26, 124–43.
99 M. and D., 1.7.1870, p. 101.
100 E.g., 200 people in Quorndon, Leicestershire: Light, 2nd series, p. 5.
101 E.g., UM, pp. 59f.
102 CJ, volume preface, p. iii; for another allegation of pressure from all denominations wherever the Brown revelation had been proclaimed, see Light, p. 42.
103 Title of editorial, CJ, p. 25f.
104 Particularly by Gareth Stedman Jones: The Language of Chartism in Epstein, Thompson, eds. (see n. 12 above).
105 Editorial in CJ, pp. 25f.
106 E.g., BL, pp. 145, 222.
107 E.g., GR, pp. 173, 177f.
108 GR, pp. 178, 181.
109 Light, pp. 22f.
110 GR, p. 203.
111 UM, pp. 105f.
112 UM, p. 112.
113 UM, p. 128.
114 GR, p. 42.
115 UM, pp. 54f.
116 UM, p. 112.

117 *CJ*, pp. 20f, 37f, 123 and instalments between the last two.
118 *GR*, p. 179.
119 End of the text of Brown: *Charity, Rest and Freedom* . . ., 1856.
120 *M. and D.* (as in n. 99 above).
121 1861 census (kindly consulted for me by Mr. Stephen Best of Nottingham County Library, after the return of the microfilm from repairs: letter of 27th March 1984); *C. N. Wright's Nottingham and Suburban Directory*, 1858, 1862; E. S. Drake: *Directory of the Town and County of Nottingham*, 1860; *Light*, p. 18.
122 *GR*, p. 116.
123 E.g., *GR*, p. 172.
124 *GR*, p. 179.
125 *UM*, pp. 154f.
126 *M. and D.* (as in n. 99, above).
127 *BL*, pp. 197ff.
128 *CJ*, starting at pp. 23ff. See also the two learned lectures deposited in Nottingham Library; both were given at about this time, and one at least was by Stretton (though catalogued under Brown).
129 *Light*, pp. 22f; *GR*, p. 203.
130 C. Cooke: *Curiosities of Occult Literature*, 1863, p. 128. Cooke had 'corresponded for some time' with such a seer whose beliefs sound amazingly like Brown's, but who may in fact have been Brown himself. The latter possibility seems all the likelier, given that the man's prophecies were simply not coming true (Cooke, pp. 126f)! Relatedly, the only seer whom Cooke mentioned by name, a Mr. Hockley, was presumably the Mr. Hockley of Croydon whom 'G.B.' had mentioned in the *YST* of August 1856 (pp. 189ff) alongside Brown. If Cooke's unnamed seer really was Brown, then the fact that Cooke was almost prepared to finance the publication of one of the man's 300-page books sheds, possibly, some light on the kinds of finance Brown sought to tap from outside the ranks of his direct followers.
131 *M. and D.* (as in n. 99, above).
132 *YST*, August 1856, pp. 219f; Brown: *Message*, inside back cover; *UM*, pp. 11ff.
133 *GR*, p. 77, 84.
134 E.g., *Light*, 3rd series, p. 20.
135 E.g., *Light*, 1st series, pp. 43f.
136 *GR*, p. 87.
137 E.g., *BL*, p. 168.
138 *BL*, pp. 202f.
139 *GR*, p. 86.
140 *GR*, p. 117.
141 *GR*, p. 172; the move involved only a short distance: from Walker Street, Sneinton, to Great Alfred Street, Nottingham.
142 *GR*, p. 182. This is one of the very few occasions Mrs Brown is mentioned – or indeed any female adherent (though such are referred to generically, now and then, in passing).

143 *GR*, p. 203.
144 *UM*, pp. 54f.
145 E.g., *FP*, p. 37.
146 For fairground and other medicine-hawking, see Roy Porter: *The Language of Quackery* in P. Burke, R. Porter, eds: *The Social History of Language*, 1986.
147 The previous two paragraphs are based on pp. 3ff of Brown: *Cause*.
148 E.g., inside back cover of Part 6 of Brown's *Message from the World of Spirits*.
149 *Message*, Part 1, pp. 16f.
150 No copies of Brown's *Book of Knowledge or, the Medium's Guide* seem to have survived – in at least the British Library or Nottingham Library.
151 *Cause*, p. 5.
152 *Cause*, p. 5.
153 *BL*, p. 183.
154 These quotes from the *Book of Knowledge* (see n. 150, above) are based on *Light*, pp. 23f; and on an article in *YST*, June 1856, pp. 189ff, by 'G.B.' who, as argued above, may possibly have been Goodwin Barmby.
155 *GR*, p. 40.
156 *Message*, pp. 18f.
157 *UM*, pp. 105f.
158 *FP*, p. 3.
159 *FP*, p. 23.
160 *FP*, p. 3.
161 *BL*, p. 184, summarising his *Warning Message*.
162 *BL*, p. 183, summarising his *Book of Knowledge*.
163 *BL*, pp. 184ff, summarising his *Warning Message*.
164 For example, the title of his *Message from the world of spirits* claimed that the pamphlet 'mitigat[ed] the doctrine of eternal punishment'. Similarly p. 17 of same; *Light*, pp. 6ff; or 'J.G.H. Brown, medium': *IR*, p. 15 (a work in which the Swede was praised and the American denounced).
165 *Light*, p. 19; similarly *A collection of hymns and poems for the use of the . . . community of the great organisation . . .*, 1858, p. 4.
166 *IR*, pp. 10ff; *A Message*, pp. 22ff, 28ff; similarly 'W.W.' in *CJ*, pp. 20f.
167 *A Message*, pp. 28ff.
168 *Message*, pp. 13–19, particularly p. 15.
169 *Message*, p. 98.
170 *Message*, p. 15.
171 For Dee, see Peter J. French: *John Dee, the World of an Elizabethan Magus*, 1972, particularly pp. 28, 93, 109–25; also Frances A. Yates: *The Occult Philosophy in the Elizabethan Age*, 1979, pp. 74–93; and the same author's *Giordano Bruno and the Hermetic Tradition*, 1964, pp. 84–96, 148f; more distantly, see, e.g., D. P. Walker: *Spiritual and*

Demonic Magic from Ficino to Campanella, 1958, particularly, pp. 224–9.

172 *A Message*, p. 153 + n.

173 *Message*, inside back covers of Parts 6 and 8; inside front cover of the volume-binding of *CJ*, pp. 1857f.

174 See *CJ*, inside front cover.

175 B. Capp: *Astrology and the popular Press; English Almanacks, 1500–1800*, 1979.

176 J. F. C. Harrison's phrase: title of chapter 3 of his *Second Coming*. He too notes the popularity of almanacks (p. 61).

177 Harrison, pp. 49f.

178 This phrase refers to the so-called Lurianic cabala: see my references to Scholem below; also F. A. Yates: *The Occult Philosophy*, pp. 21, 209.

179 Among other works of Brown, Holyoake published *Charity, rest and freedom, in the reign of glory* . . ., 1856, *The Book of Knowledge* (subtitled *or how to become a medium*), 1857, *IR*, 1857, *A Message* . . ., 1856–70, also the *SMM*, 1856–57 and the *CJ*, 1857–58.

180 G. J. Holyoake: *Public Performances of the Dead, A Review of American Spiritualism*, 1865.

181 *UM*, pp. 154f.

182 *CJ*, p. 91; Turley's name is misprinted here, but corrected on p. 107.

183 *CJ*, pp. 106f.

184 W. Turley: *The Rescue of the Sabbath Day*, 1856. The 'rescue' was for the purposes of artisan self-education, and *from* the Sabbatarians.

185 Ibid., pp. 127f, 154, 171f.

186 *YST*, August 1856, pp. 219f.

187 *CJ*, pp. 90f.

188 *A Message* . . ., title page.

189 *UM*, p. 11. Did Morrell earn this (from Brown, unusual) accolade by being an Urquhartite (see chapter 1, p. 17)? After all, Brown – in his visionary way – yielded to no Urquhartite in his identification of Russia as the mainspring of world reaction.

190 *M. and D.* (as in n. 99 above).

191 W. H. Oliver: *Owen in 1817: the Millenial Moment*, in S. Pollard, J. Salt, eds.: *Robert Owen, Prophet of the Poor*, p. 187.

192 Apart from admitting that the membership had fluctuated: *M. and D.* (as in n. 99 above).

193 Francis Barrett, 'F.R.C.' (presumably a claim to be a Rosicrucian) . . .: *The Magus or celestial intelligence* (over 220 words in title). Barrett, on an astrological basis, had mixed cabalistic and talismanic magic (including crystal seership) with other kinds of natural and sympathetic magic of every conceivable description and for almost any purpose imaginable. Today's ideal reader, for him, would be an anthropologist well-versed in the late Renaissance.

194 *The Zoist* (for whose full title see next chapter), vol. 7, 1849f, pp. 66–72. This writer saw crystal seership, perhaps plausibly, as a form of self-hypnosis.

195 C. Cooke: *Curiosities of Occult Literature*, 1863, p. 127. Cooke was here described as 'late sollicitor to the astrometereological society'.

196 'Raphael' (a writer based at 79 St. Paul's Churchyard and, for this book, taking a long-dead writer's pseudonym): *The Art of Talismanic Magic: being Selections from the Works of Rabbi Solomon, Cornelius Agrippa, Francis Barrett, etc., etc.*, 1879.

197 Roy Porter: *The Language of Quackery*, in *Bulletin of the Society for the Social History of Medicine*, number 33, December 1983, p. 69.

198 Outside back cover of William Turley: *Modern Mysteries; or, Table-turning, Tapping and Tipping*, 1856, published by Holyoake.

199 See, e.g., *GR*, pp. 93f, 171f, 202, 207; *BL*, pp. 21, 100, 122f, 144, 148f.

200 *GR*, p. 42.

201 Church, particularly, pp. 76f, 362, 371. 'Possibly', though, 'there were some Jewish employees of Weinberg's lacemaking establishment in Nottingham' (H. Pollins: *Economic History of the Jews in England*, 1982, p. 128).

202 G. Scholem: *Sabbatai Sevi, the Mystical Messiah, 1626–76*, Princeton, 1973, which I have been unable to see. My sole window on to Scholem has been D. Biale: *Gershom Scholem, Kabbalah and Counter History*, Harvard, 1979 (on Zevi, see particularly pp. 149, 155–65).

203 G. Scholem: *Du Frankisme au Jacobinisme: la vie de Moses Dobruška*, 1981, Paris; also Biale, particularly pp. 163f.

204 Biale, pp. 127, 159. I am far too ignorant to know whether Scholem can remotely be called a history-of-ideas pedigree-plotter. But even if so, he seems to have refined gold out of base metal.

205 Compare – via Biale, p. 138 – Scholem's treatment of Abraham Cardozo.

206 I use this phrase because of its many meanings. One of these seems to occur in Scholem's contention that gnosticism was preserved within cabalism: Biale, pp. 113, 128–33, 137–41.

207 *CJ*, p. 143.

208 *YST*, June 1856, pp. 189ff, 193.

209 True, Barmby did not move to Halifax – i.e. near to Keighley – till 1858. Much of this sentence has, I hope, benefited from brief discussions with Barbara Taylor and Gustav Klaus during April 1984.

210 In *The Crisis* during 1833, as J. F. C. Harrison has recently reminded us (lecture to the Society for the Study of Labour History, 19 May 1984).

211 G. Stedman-Jones: *The Language of Chartism*, in J. Epstein, D. Thompson, eds., (as in note 12, above).

212 *BL*, p. 100.

Chapter 4   The problematic of imponderables

1 'At the turn of the nineteenth century', we are told, 'a leading feature of British intellectual life' was 'the weakness of the barriers between different forms of discourse' (L. S. Jacyna: *Immanence or Transcendence: Theories of Life and Organisation in Britain 1790–1835*, vol. 74, 1983, p. 312). Both Newton (1642–1727) and Darwin (1809–82) would have raised an eyebrow or two at the narrowness of this periodisation.

2 For one elegant summary of these two versions, see Trevor H. Levere: *Affinity and Matter: Elements of Chemical Philosophy*, 1971, p. 5.

3 Particularly by R. E. Schofield: *Mechanism and Materialism: British Natural Philosophy in an Age of Reason*, Princeton, 1970. But Schofield's version has anyway been criticised as too neat, as by J. McEvoy: 'Joseph Priestley, Natural Philosopher', in *Ambix*, vol. 15, 1968, or by P. M. Heimann, J. E. Maguire: 'Newtonian Forces and Lockean Powers: Concepts of Matter in 18th Century Thought', in *Historical Studies in the Physical Sciences*, vol. 3, 1971, particularly pp. 234f.

4 See particularly Levere, pp. 29–33, 122–31.

5 More than one Coleridge and more, even than one Davy (T. H. Levere: *Poetry, Realised in Nature: Samuel Taylor Coleridge and early 19th Century Science*, 1981) or eccentrically, one Reichenbach would have been needed for any transformation, particularly among non-specialists. In any case, the sources of Coleridge's thought were not all exactly new-fangled.

6 For a lightning summary of salient aspects of Hartley's two-volume 1791 *Observations on the Nature of Man, His Frame, His Duty, and His Expectations*, see Levere, pp. 9f. For Mesmer, see R. Darnton's entry on him in *Dictionary of Scientific Biography*.

7 As alleged, notably, in S. Schaffer: 'Natural philosophy' in G. S. Rousseau, R. Porter, eds: *The Ferment of Knowledge, Studies in the Historiography of 18th Century Science*, 1980, particularly pp. 55–8. One group who vociferously dissented from Newton were the mainly High Anglican followers of John Hutchinson. He saw Sir Isaac's teachings as tending towards denial of God. See C. B. Wilde: 'Hutchinsonian Natural Philosophy', in *History of Science*, vol. 18, 1980; the same author's riskier 'Matter and Spirit as Natural Symbols in 18th Century British Natural Philosophy' in *B.J.H.S.*, vol. 15, 1982; and Heimann and Maguire, as in note 3 above.

8 B. Martin's own italics during 1746, quoted in J. L. Heilbron: *Electricity in the 17th and 18th Centuries, A Study in Early Modern Physics*, 1979, University of California, pp. 55f.

9 Martin, p. 47.

10 Martin, p. 47.

11 Quaeries 17 to 24. I am following here the reading of R. S. Westfall:

Force in Newton's Physics: The Science of Dynamics in the 17th Century, 1971, p. 394.

12 'Embodied' and 'pretended to explain' are Westfall's phrases: p. 395.
13 Heilbron, p. 52; A. Thackray: *Atoms and Powers*, Harvard, 1970, p. 12.
14 As in Book 2 of the *Principia*.
15 Westfall, p. 396f.
16 Westfall, p. 398.
17 Particularly if the Jacobs are right: Margaret and J. R. Jacob: 'The Anglican Origins of Modern Science: the Meta-physics of the Whig Constitution', in *Isis*, vol. 71, 1980; M. Jacob: *The Newtonians and the English Revolution, 1689–1720*, Cornell, 1976, particularly introduction and chapters 5 and 6. That they are not, is argued, though on a narrow front, by N. H. Steneck: 'Greatrakes the Stroker: The Interpretations of Historians', in *Isis*, vol. 73, 1982, particularly pp. 176f. See also note 46 below. On a broader front, see G. C. Gibbs: 'The Radical Enlightenment', in *BJHS*, vol. 17, 1984.
18 For whom see Thackray, chapter 8.
19 B. Lautz: *The Doctrine of the Communion of Saints in Anglican Theology, 1833–1963*, Ottawa U.P., 1967, p. 181.
20 Westfall, pp. 398f; Heilbron, p. 72.
21 Thackray, p. 161.
22 Thackray's continual use of the adjective 'popular' is part of this blurring: Thackray, particularly chapter 8, entitled 'British Popular Newtonianism . . .', particularly pp. 234–8 – including note 5 and pp. 274f.
23 Thackray, p. 162.
24 Quoted Thackray, p. 53.
25 Henry Pemberton: *A View of Sir Isaac Newton's Philosophy*, quoted Thackray, p. 66.
26 Thackray, p. 67.
27 Heilbron, p. 70; Thackray, p. 161.
28 Heilbron, p. 53.
29 Isaac Newton: *Optics*, 4th edition, 1730, quoted P. M. Heimann: 'Nature is a Perpetual Worker: Newton's Aether and 18th Century Natural Philosophy', in *Ambix*, vol. 20, 1973, p. 3.
30 Quaery 31 to the 1706 edition of the *Optics*, quoted Thackray, p. 36.
31 Thackray, pp. 68f.
32 Van Marum, quoted in Heilbron, p. 71.
33 Heilbron's word, p. 73.
34 *The Zoist, a journal of cerebral physiology and mesmerism*, vol. II, 1853–4, p. 193n.
35 For Reichenbach, see *Dictionary of Scientific Biography*. German readers have Habacher's disentanglement: M. Habacher: *Auf der Suche nach dem 'Od' . . . in Clio Medica*, vol. 14, 1979, pp. 105–18.
36 *Zoist*, vol. 4, 1846–7, p. 125.
37 *Zoist*, vol. 4, pp. 255f.
38 *Zoist*, vol. 4, pp. 254–67.

39 Heilbron, p. 73.
40 See R. Cooter: *The Cultural Meaning of Popular Science: phrenology and the organisation of consent in 19th Century Britain*, 1985 (which I have not yet seen); R. Cooter: 'The Politics of Brain: Phrenology in Birmingham', in *Bulletin of the Society for the Social History of Medicine*, no. 32, June 1983; D. de Giustino: *The Conquest of Mind*, 1975; and the disputations between G. N. Cantor and S. Shapin on Edinburgh phrenology in *Annals of Science*, vol. 32, 1975.
41 See R. Darnton: *Mesmerism and the End of the Enlightenment in France*, Harvard, 1968.
42 Jacyna, (see note 1, above), particularly pp. 313f; de Giustino, particularly pp. 44–8, 94–8.
43 *Zoist*, vol. 9, 1851–2, pp. 197ff, commenting approvingly on a gloss by the *Calcutta Morning Chronicle* to this effect.
44 Contrary to Terry Parssinen: 'Professional Deviants and the History of Medicine: Medical Mesmerists in Victorian Britain', in R. Wallis, ed.: *On the Margins of Science: The Social Construction of Rejected Knowledge*, in *Sociological Review* Monograph 27, 1979, p. 106.
45 This and much of the following is based on 'I.L.E.' in the *Zoist*, vol 1, 1843–44, pp. 59–61, 72f, 85f.
46 Ibid.; also vol. 3, 1845–46, volume-frontispiece and pp. 98–102. For more recent discussions of Greatrakes, see N. H. Steneck: 'Greatrakes the Stroker', in *Isis*, vol. 73, 1982; and the counter-blast in J. R. Jacob: *Henry Stubbe, radical Protestantism and the early Enlightenment*, 1983, pp. 164–74. Jacob sees Stubbe's support of Greatrakes as, in effect, what I will define during Chapter 6a as epistemologically democratic (Jacob, pp. 50–63).
47 One of these had practised around Kennington 'about thirty years' previously (i.e. around 1813) and is unnamed; the other was 'a lady named Prescot' who had practised till recently at an address in Bloomsbury Sq. for many decades: 'I.L.E.' (see note 45), pp. 60f.
48 The *London Medical and Surgical Journal* during 1828, according to 'I.L.E.', pp. 60f; *Zoist*, vol. 1, pp. 85f, 89.
49 *Zoist*, vol. 1, p. 93.
50 *Zoist*, vol. 1, pp. 89f.
51 Parssinen, particularly pp. 110–15; Jon Palfreyman: 'Mesmerism and the English Medical Profession: A Study of Conflict', in *Ethics in Science and Medicine*, vol. 3, 1977.
52 *Zoist*, vol. 1, 1843–44, pp. 95–100. One of the main targets named was Spencer T. Hall, for whom see Chapter 6, below.
53 Indications of this can be culled from many sources including occasional allusions to august patients; e.g. the famous case of Harriet Martineau (vol. 3, 1845–46, pp. 86–96) who was soon to be mesmerising her servant-woman (vol. 4, 1846–47, pp. 267f); or Arthur Trevelyan (vol. 6, 1848–49; vol. 8, pp. 384–89); the lists of patrons and subscribers to the mesmeric infirmary in London (as, e.g., bound with vol. 6, 1848–9; vol. 8, 1850–1, pp. 203–11, 331f; vol. 9, 1851–2, pp. 122–44) – something which perturbed at least some prominent

physicians (vol. 4, 1846–7, pp. 596f) – and to its shorter-lived sister in Bristol (vol. 7, 1849–50, pp. 152–64; vol. 8, 1850–1, pp. 211–20; vol. 10, 1852–3, pp. 54, 228); or simply from denunciations of medical bigotry towards mesmerism, one of these being from no less than the Prince Consort (vol. 3, 1845–6, p. 88n).

54 All this comes, admittedly, from the same *Zoist* account, particularly pp. 89f.

55 Elliotson's summary, admittedly, followed by his italicised quotation, in: *Zoist*, vol. 4, 1846–7, p. 3.

56 As de Giustino (p. 95: see note) and others have noted, Elliotson was no meek lamb.

57 *Zoist*, vol. 3, 1845–6, pp. 316f.

58 *Zoist*, vol. 8, 1850–1, p. 212.

59 E.g. Rev. T. Pyne: *Vital Magnetism*, 1844; Rev. George Sandby: *Mesmerism and its Opponents*, 1844; Rev. W. Scoresby: *Zoistic Magnetism*, 1849; Rev. C. H. Townshend: *Facts in Mesmerism*, 1840, to *Mesmerism proved True*, 1854. For Elliotson's claims on clerical support generally, see *Zoist*, vol. 10, 1852–3, p. 311.

60 From clergymen to laymen, such as the redoubtable Charlotte Elizabeth Tonna: C. E. Tonna: *Mesmerism, a letter to Miss Martineau*, 1844 (British Museum catalogue: 1849), particularly pp. 4, 8; see also A. D. Farr: *Religious Opposition to Obstetric Anaesthesia: a Myth* (sic), in *Annals of Science*, vol. 40, 1983.

61 Minutes of the first Annual Meeting, *Zoist*, vol. 8, 1850–1, pp. 103–11; similarly vol. 9, pp. 122–44.

62 Minutes of the second Annual Meeting, vol. 8, 1850–1, pp. 211–20.

63 Vol. 10, 1852–3, p. 158n.

64 Same page; *Spiritual News*, vol. 1, 1870–1, p. 6.

65 Vol. 10, p. 311.

66 Vol. 13, 1855–6, p. 171.

67 Vol. 10, p. 311.

68 Vol. 12, 1854–5, pp. 212f. Elliotson had early on boasted of his friendship with Dickens (vol. 1, p. 49); see also Fred Kaplan: *Dickens and Mesmerism*, 1975, Princeton.

69 Vol. 12, pp. 108–11.

70 *Zoist*, vol. 13, 1855–6, pp. 195f. Mesmerism was occasionally assailed with allegations that its 'subjects' were always of lower social standing than its practitioners. (Similarly, for France, see the claim from 1818 that 'magnetism always works [socially] downwards, never upwards': quoted in H. F. Ellenberger: 'Mesmer and Puységur: From Magnetism to hypnotism' in *Psychoanalytic Review*, vol. 52, 1965, p. 294). For Britain and America this was incorrect: S. T. Hall (see chapter 6, below) was merely the most vocal British plebeian.

71 *Zoist*, vol. 13, p. 196.

72 I say 'may', because this is not, on the whole, the contention of Dr. Roger Jeffery's paper – on 'Indian Medicine and the State' given to the 1980 S.S.R.C. Symposium on *Concepts of Health and Disease: a*

Socio-Historical Perspective – which constitutes my nearest acquaintance with this topic.

73 See entry in the *D.N.B.*, which also lists entries on him in the *Zoist* and much else.

74 Though, even during Esdaile's rise, the doctors may have been marginally cooler than others: this is implied in *Zoist*, vol. 5, 1847–8, pp. 50–69.

75 *Zoist*, vol. 9, 1851–2, p. 314.

76 Elliotson seems to hint at this in: *Zoist*, vol. 10, 1852–3, p. 291; and there had at least been calls for government suppression, as by the editor of the *Spectator*, quoted in *Zoist*, vol. 4, 1846–7, p. 299f n.

77 George Wyld: *Notes of my Life*, 1903, p. 59.

78 But this healer, Thomas Capern – as 'sometime Secretary and Resident Superintendent of the London Mesmeric Infirmary' – had been a lowlier and far more persistent mesmerist. See Charles Isham, Bart: *Healing by the Hand and Will, exemplified by Mr Capern, during a residence at Lamport*, 1862 (published from Lamport Hall, Northampton), particularly p. 4. (Capern himself published two works on mesmerism). Isham had written to the *Zoist* once, at least: *Zoist*, vol. 9, 1851–2, pp. 54–60.

79 *Zoist*, vol. 9, p. 52.

80 His colleagues were, he felt, motivated by jealousy: many had howled at his earlier innovations – such as his introduction of the stethoscope – but had had to come round. The *Zoist* therefore carried more than one lengthy self-commiserating narrative from his pen (e.g. vol. 4, pp. 2f; vol. 6, pp. 213–37). Elliotson was also one initiator of the cliché in which mesmerists compared themselves to the seventeenth-century discoverer of the circulation of the blood, William Harvey. In Wakley, though, Elliotson had met his match in Harveyolatry.

81 Parssinen, in effect, notes this on p. 113 in his article (see note 44, above), but finds it less relevant to his article.

82 E.g. vol. 5, 1847–8, pp. 65f; vol. 6, p. 235; vol. 7, p. 307; vol. 9, p. 190fn.

83 Vol. 10, 1852–3, pp. 77f, quoting vol. 5, pp. 65f.

84 Reichenbach posited what he called 'odic force'. His choice of adjective – after the chief Nordic god – was understood by the *Zoist* as 'a personification of the elements of nature' (*Zoist*, vol. 9, 1851–2, p. 399n. See also the learned correspondence over etymology between Reichenbach and the Christian spiritualist, William Howitt, in the *Spiritual Magazine*, vol. 2, 1861, pp. 508–11, 556).

85 *London Medical Gazette*, 4.10.50, p. 585, also quoted briefly in *Zoist*, vol. 9, 1851–2, p. 375.

86 See Jacyna, same article (see note 1, above); P. F. Rehbock: *The Philosophical Naturalists: Themes in early 19th Century British Biology*, Madison, 1983.

87 These are actually, as we have seen, the words of the *Calcutta Morning Chronicle*, 5.11.50, but warmly quoted in the *Zoist*, vol. 9, pp. 197ff.

88 W. C. Engledue: *Cerebral Physiology and Materialism*, 1842, Watson (reprinted from the *Medical Times*), p. 10f.
89 E.g., *Zoist*, vol. 2, 1844–5, p. 269.
90 E.g. the 1842 lecture (see note 88), p. 15; or *Zoist*, vol. 9, 1851–2, pp. 215–23, 316–31.
91 1842 lecture, particularly pp. 17ff.
92 1842 lecture, p. 5.
93 1842 lecture, p. 20.
94 See numerous quotes in the *Zoist*, e.g. vol. 6, 1848–9, pp. 13–37, 233f; Elliotson's reply to Dr F. Hawkins' Harveian Oration, same vol., pp. 421f, quoting Wakley in *Lancet* of 4.11.48; vol. 8, p. 164, quoting *Medical Times* of 27.4.50; vol. 10, pp. 1f, quoting same 24.1.52; same vol., p. 92, quoting Robert Hull, M.D., via *London Medical Gazette* of 21.11.51. For panic-mongering direct, see, e.g., *Lancet*, vol. 9, i (15.12.38), pp. 450f.
95 *Medical Times*, 24.1.52., quoted *Zoist*, vol. 10, 1852–3, pp. 1f.
96 For what might, at first sight, seem an attempt, by an anonymous contemporary, to intensify such panic, see: 'An eye witness: a *full discovery* of the strange practices of *Dr Elliotson* On the bodies of his *female patients!* at his house, in Conduit St, Hanover Square, with all the secret *experiments he makes upon them*, and the *Curious Postures they are put into while sitting or standing, when awake or asleep* . . . fully divulged! etc, etc, etc', 1842. In fact, though, the prurient title and internal subheadings packaged a sober description of Elliotson's beliefs and practices. The pamphlet is surely a tongue-in-cheek defence. Elliotson was able also to point to incidents of sexual misuse of ether or chloroform (e.g. *Zoist*, vol. 7, 1849–50, pp. 40ffn).
97 Dr James Johnson in *Medico-Chirurgical Review*, 1838, p. 365, quoted *Zoist*, vol. 7, 1849–50, pp. 40ffn.
98 As early as 1836, Wakley had disapproved of mesmerism's tendency towards what he called 'the supernatural'. This, for him, guaranteed its uselessness even more firmly than it once had alchemy's: *Lancet*, 1836, ii, pp. 836–40.
99 *Lancet*, 1846, ii, p. 52. Ether, by contrast, was safe: e.g., same 1847, i, pp. 436f. Yet, around the latter year, rumours were circulating (and not merely via the *Zoist*) that ether could arouse female sexuality: J. A. Shepherd: *Simpson and Syme at Edinburgh*, 1969, p. 81.
100 *Lancet*, 1846, i, p. 688.
101 *Lancet*, 1836, ii, pp. 905f.
102 Herbert Mayo (Senior Surgeon at the Middlesex Hospital, and late Professor of Anatomy and Physiology at King's College London), writing to the *London Medical Gazette* and reprinted in *Lancet*, 1837, ii, pp. 811ff.
103 *Medium and Daybreak*, 10.7.91, pp. 434f, where parts of his eve-of-twentieth-century prophecy seem like something out of the more feminist 1830s.
104 Unsigned: *Physical Puritanism*, in *The Westminster Review*, new series, volume 1, January–April 1852. See also B. Harrison: '"A world of

which we have no conception": Liberalism and the English Temperance Press, 1830–72', in *Victorian Studies*, vol. 13, 1969, pp. 151f; and for the 'provincial, dissenting and popular' character of this press: ibid., p. 142.

105 I have benefited particularly here from discussions with Ms Ginny Smith and Ms Ruth Richardson, both of whose doctoral theses are eagerly awaited.

106 Entries on 'Buchanan' and 'Psychometry' in Norman Blunsdon, ed: *Popular Dictionary of Spiritualism*, 1962.

107 *Zoist*, vol. 3, 1845–6, pp. 482n–485n. Buchanan was still recounting some of his 1841 experiments more than thirty years later: see A. R. Wallace, J. R. Buchanan, D. Lyman, E. Sargent: *The Psycho-Physiological Sciences and their Assailants*, Boston, 1878, p. 71. (Here, Buchanan's contribution was an expansion of an article of his in the *Popular Science Monthly* edited by Prof. W. J. Youmans). I am grateful to Dr Roger Cooter for mentioning this source.

108 Quoted in the *Zoist* with almost gleeful frequency.

109 Quoted in same, vol. 6, pp. 402f, quoting *London Medical Gazette* 19.6.46.

110 E.g. *Zoist*, vol. 10, 1852–3, pp. 1f, quoting *Medical Times* of 24.1.52. Significant of a possible hardening of positions, the *Zoist* had once spoken of the *Medical Times* as 'the only medical journal which has advocated our cause' (*Zoist*, vol. 2, 1844–5, p. 285).

111 As over Elliotson's giving the 1846 Harveian Oration at the Royal College of Physicians in which he advocated mesmerism (*Zoist*, vol. 4, 1846–7, p. 291; vol. 6, pp. 399–405); or from the 1848 Orator, Dr F. Hawkins (ibid., pp. 213–37); into 1851, Wakley was still fuming about the 1846 invitation (*Zoist*, vol. 9, 1851–2, pp. 248f), possibly because another respectable organisation, the Royal Medical and Chirurgical Society, accepted at about this time Elliotson's gift of a bust of himself for its library (ibid., p. 265).

112 Another, would be Dr William Gregory, F.R.S.E., M.R.I.A., Professor of Chemistry at the University of Edinburgh, who translated one edition of Reichenbach (*Zoist*, vol. 4, 1846–7, pp. 104–24, 227–84; vol. 8, pp. 430–5; vol. 9, pp. 201–6, 215–23) and who accepted both mesmerism and clairvoyance (for the latter: ibid., vol. 9, pp. 422ff; vol. 10, p. 224). The translator of the other edition was Ashburner.

113 As Parssinen has argued (same article, particularly pp. 111–15). The last quotation is from his p. 114.

114 See, e.g., R. S. Westfall: 'The Influence of Alchemy on Newton', in M. P. Hanen et al., eds: *Science, Pseudo-Science and Society*, 1980, Waterloo Ontario; B. J. T. Dobbs: *The Foundations of Newton's Alchemy, or 'the Hunting of the Green Lyon'*, 1975, particularly p. 233; or the contributions by Westfall, Casini and Hall to M. L. Righini Bonelli, W. R. Shea, eds: *Reason, Experiment and Mysticism in the Scientific Revolution*, 1975. See also Frances Yates: 'Did Newton

connect his mathematics and alchemy?' in (London) *Times Higher Educational Supplement*, 18.3.77., p. 13.

115 So much so, that at least two mid-nineteenth-century writers doubted whether *physical* 'transmutation' had ever been the aim of true alchemists (as reported by A. B. Waite in his 1888 preface to Barrett's *Lives of the Alchemystical Philosophers*, pp. 9–27). At least three secondary sources speak baldly of 'the last of the alchemists' during these decades. J. H. S. Green, in *Discovery*, January 1961, and A. C. Cameron, in *Notes and Records of the Royal Society*, October 1951, identify this beleaguered dodo as James Price; P. Davidson, in *The Theosophist*, June 1884, as Kellerman. Ellic Howe (in *Raphael, or the Royal Merchant*, 1964, pp. 12ff) speaks of an early nineteenth-century balloonist who attempted transmutation. Otherwise, my own source for all these is Alan Pritchard: *Alchemy: A Bibliography of English-Language Writings*, 1980, where there is a relative dearth of nineteenth-century titles, other than those of an antiquarian stamp. Also mainly antiquarian, was the short-lived monthly, *Light and Life. An Unsectarian Magazine of Mystic Light*, 1886.

116 G. Wyld, p. 59, his emphasis.

117 Or, if we adopt Désirée Hirst's perspective of a circum-eighteenth-century shipwreck of an occult tradition within which alchemy and much else had once moved, then Wyld and Dove were clinging to divergent spars from the great wreck. (D. Hirst: *Hidden Riches: Traditional Symbolism from the Renaissance to Blake*, 1964, particularly pp. 292ff).

118 D. C. Gooding, in *Annals of Science*, vol. 40, 1983, p. 212, reviewing G. N. Cantor, M. J. S. Hodge, eds: *Conceptions of Ether: Studies in the History of Ether, 1740–1900*, 1981.

119 B. Wynne: 'Natural Knowledge and Social Context: Cambridge physicians and the luminiferous ether', in B. Barnes, S. Shapin, eds: *Natural Order: Historical Studies of Scientific Culture*, 1978, New York, p. 215.

120 D. B. Wilson: 'The Thought of the late Victorian Physicists: Oliver Lodge's Ethereal Body', in *Victorian Studies*, vol. 15, 1971; and at a cruder level, for some of Lodge's spiritualising (including in the socialist press), L. J. W. Barrow, same thesis, pp. 211f, and *Clarion*, 3.1.08. Conceivably, he may have been echoing the broader work of Balfour Stewart and P. G. Tait: *The Unseen Universe: or Physical Speculations on a Future State* (2nd edition, 1875); see P. M. Heimann: *The Unseen Universe*: Physics and the Philosophy of Nature in Victorian Britain, in *BJHS*, vol. 6, 1972, particularly p. 76f.

121 J. H. Powell: *William Denton, the Geologist and Radical*, 1870, Boston, pp. 13–16.

122 *H.N.*, 1.9.68., pp. 456f, quoting *Morning Post* of 3.8.68.

123 *L.B.*, January 1894, p. 15.

124 'Rolandus' in *M. and D.*, 3890, p. 290f.

125 E.g., randomly, John Rutherford (later a prolific article-writer for the *Lyceum Banner*) speaking in Gateshead, and quoted from the

Gateshead Observer in *H.N.*, 1.6.68., p. 286; two letters in the *Greenwich Free Press* of 8. and 22.5.58. (preserved in Keighley Library) from 'William Carpenter, Curative Mesmerist'; Dr Joseph Dixon, an Owenite sympathiser and, later, homoeopath and translator of Adolphe Thiers's *History of the French Revolution* (*Light*, 1890, vol. 10, p. 82); Robt Cooper of Eastbourne, the wealthy spiritualist publisher (*Two Worlds Portrait Album*, p. 32); John C. Macdonald of Manchester (ibid., p. 35), M. Wallace who, with his wife, was one of the earliest public mediums in London (ibid., p. 30). And so on.

126 J. Coates of Liverpool, in the *Spiritualist*, 27.7.77.

Chapter 5

1 This is the main theme of G. K. Nelson: *Spiritualism and Society*, 1969.

2 TW, 1895, vol. 8, p. 676.

3 Invitation to his 1857 Millennial Congress, in: *YST*, 16.4.1857.

4 Even J. F. C. Harrison (*Robert Owen and the Owenites in Britain and America: The Quest for a New Moral World*), treats the 1871 Owen centenary celebrations as some sort of finale. On the other hand, see his warning (p. 249) that a movement's 'most enduring aspects' are 'not always' institutions, but rather 'the mental attitudes associated with it.' Links between millenarianism and rationalism would hardly astonish researchers such as Scholem. (See notes 202 and 203 of chapter 3.)

5 E.g. No. 6, p. 1, 1st (unsigned) article; no. 9, p. 29: 'd'esprit': 'Spiritualism versus Orthodoxy.'

6 No relation of the Owenite Robert Cooper, for whom see *Dictionary of Labour Biography*.

7 No. 118, 1.10.1866, p. 209: 'Valedictory'.

8 'A. and J. Burns', the 'J.' being presumably James Burns whom we shall meet immediately below, and the 'A.' his wife Annie: 31.3.1866, pp. 99–102.

9 *Spiritual Times*, 6.1.1866, p. 4.

10 *Spiritual Times*, first page of first issue.

11 J. H. Powell: *Life Incidents and Poetic Pictures*, 1865.

12 *Spiritual Magazine*, 1861, pp. 145–53.

13 I owe this point to Ms Alex Owen.

14 *SM*, 1867, pp. 337ff, 434–7. See also F. Podmore: *Modern Spiritualism: A History and a Criticism*, 1902, vol. 2, p. 166. For Thomas Shorter (with whom the *Spiritual Magazine* was much associated), see his *Confessions of a Truthseeker*, 1899, and *Later Autumn Leaves*, 1896.

15 S. E. Gay: *J.W. Fletcher, Clairvoyant. A biographical sketch*, 1883, pp. 19f.

16 *M. and D.*, 4.5.1894, pp. 273–6.

17 Ibid., 14.11.1883, 18.7.1884, 83.1895, p. 151; *M. and D.*, Burns memorial number, 22.3.1895.
18 Note for non-Americans: Andrew Jackson, soon to be U.S. President, was already a democratic hero in the year (1826) of Davis's birth. Davis's names do accurately indicate his early political environment.
19 *M. and D.*, 13.12.1872.
20 Podmore, *Modern Spiritualism*, p. 165.
21 *HN*, 1.4.1870.
22 As does Nelson, *Spiritualism*, as noted.
23 Or so Burns claims, in relation to Liverpool during the 1860s: *M. and D.*, 4.5.1894, pp. 273–6.
24 *TV*, 18.11.1887.
25 See the characteristic Address reprinted in *HN*, vol. 1, 1867, pp. 330–5.
26 See Burns in *M. and D.*, 17.6.1892, pp. 385ff.
27 *TW*, 1889, vol. 2, p. 485.
28 See the 50 or so headings of the contents of his twopenny talk, 'Spiritualism, the Bible and Tabernacle Preachers' in *M. and D.*, 22.7.1881, p. 459.
29 *M. and D.*, 1886, p. 639; *TW*, 1904, vol. 17, p. 80; 1902, vol. 15, p. 33: a front page. During 1899 it ran a seven-part Ingersoll article.
30 *TW*, 1904, p. 317.
31 *TW*, 1890, vol. 3, p. 287, unsigned, on 'Mrs. Besant on Theosophy and Spiritualism'.
32 *TW*, 1894, vol. 7, p. 28.
33 *TW*, 1902, vol. 15, p. 99.
34 *M. and D.*, 4 and 11.2.1881. The secularist convert was J. Holmes. The discussion was chaired, hostilely, by Leicester's leading secularist Josiah Gimson.
35 *NR*, 21.9.1873; *M. and D.*, 18.9.1874, p. 591; *HN*, 1874, p. 435, where there is also a vivid description of a plebeian Stockport seance.
36 Charles Bradlaugh versus James Burns, *Spiritualism*, 1872.
37 *TW*, 1891, vol. 4, pp. 225f; *M. and D.*, 6.2.1891, pp. 81–4; 20.2.1891, p. 121.
38 *TW*, 1908, vol. 21, p. 490.
39 G. J. Holyoake, *Public Performances of the Dead, a Review of American Spiritualism*, 1865.
40 Frank M. Turner, *Between Science and Religion*, Yale 1974, chapter 4.
41 South London Secular Society, reported in the *NR*, 26.7. to 23.8.1874 inclusive.
42 *NR*, 2.12.1866.
43 *SC*, 1875, vol. 4, p. 190.
44 Reddalls, *NR*, 5.9.1875; others: G. W. Moore, manager of the Hall of Science Club and Institute, London, *NR*, 15.10.187&. Notoriously, at the time, Messrs Cook and Maskelyne conjured in refutation of spiritualism. They were themselves countered by Sexton, *HN*, 1869, p. 307; *SM*, July 1873, pp. 327ff.

45 E.g. *SC*, 1871, vol. 1, pp. 4, 57f, 77f, 198; more than 16 entries in vol. 3, etc.
46 *NR*, 25.5.1873. Reddalls himself was based in Nottingham.
47 *M. and D.*, 1875, pp. 683, 493.
48 Bradlaugh v. Burns, same debate.
49 *NR*, 8.10.1871 in the regular column – usually unsigned – headed 'Our Crowded Table'.
50 *M. and D.*, 1872, pp. 24–9; *CS*, February 1874, pp. 22f.
51 For Barker see E. Royle, *Victorian Infidels*, 1974, particularly pp. 276–82. For Besant, see D. W. Nethercott, *The First Four Lives of Annie Besant*, 1961.
52 *NR*, 11.7.1875. The applicant was not named.
53 *NR*, 8.10.1871, 'Crowded Table'.
54 *NR*, 15.10.1876.
55 *M. and D.*, 7.3.1873, p. 113.
56 Bradlaugh's arguments against idealism were usually themselves made on an idealistic terrain. Or so I have argued elsewhere. L. J. W. Barrow, 'The Socialism of Robert Blatchford and the "Clarion" Newspaper, 1889–1914', London Ph.D. 1975, pp. 126–9.
57 *NR*, 26.3.1865.
58 For a surely excellent treatment of Smith, see J. Saville, 'J.E. Smith and the Owenite Movement, 1833–34', in S. Pollard, J. Salt, eds: *Robert Owen, Prophet of the Poor*, 1971. He was being remembered as late as 1895 (admittedly by Thomas Shorter: *M. and D.*, 1895, p. 188).
59 *NR*, 24.4.1870, Smith's summary: 5.1.1868.
60 *NR*, 2.8.1868, 27.9.1867, 5.1.1868.
61 *NR*, 3.11.1867, 1.12.1867, 9.1.1870.
62 Notably Smith's 'Divine Drama', which Bedingfield thought 'wonderful'; *NR*, 26.12.1869.
63 E.g., one of Smith's early mentors, Edward Irving; *NR*, 10.11.1867.
64 '"Shepherd" Smith, as the editor of the *National Reformer* may be aware, was by the religious world considered a wicked infidel' (*NR*, 1.9.1867).
65 Most frequently to Harriet Martineau's friend, the former mesmerist, Henry G. Atkinson.
66 *SC*, 1876, vol. 5, p. 119. Bedingfield sometimes used the pen names of 'B.T.W.R.' or 'R.B.'.
67 *SC*, 1878, vol. 7, p. 266 etc.; vol. 9, p. 211 etc.
68 *SC*, 1876, vol. 5, pp. 1, 225.
69 Many more knew that these had been reported in other times and continents. Thomas Shorter had set these out as early as 1864: 'Thomas Brevior': *The Two Worlds*.
70 E.g. *HN*, 1.1.1868, pp. 171–4; but particularly D. Richmond, *The Kingdom of God*, Glasgow 1885.
71 *TW*, 1891, vol. 4, p. 193.
72 *TW*, 1891, vol. 4, p. 193.
73 *TW*, 1903, vol. 16, p. 527; article by R. Scarr in *Darlington and Stockton Times*, 1.1.1966; obituary in same, 12.9.1903.

74 See the two visits by the English-born ex-Owenite, now Shaker elder, Frederick Evans, *HN*, 1871, pp. 459–64; *M. and D.*, 1887, pp. 376, 409, 426f. On both occasions Evans was accompanied by Burns's (and after the latter's death the *Two Worlds's*) friend, the American spiritualist Dr. J. M. Peebles. For another Shaker elder of similar experience see *M. and D.*, 1891, pp. 1ff, 43. For the significance of these contacts for Burns, see Chapter 8, section B.

75 *TW*, 1892, vol. 5, p. 1.

76 *TW*, 1905, vol. 18, p. 62.

77 E.g. L. Festinger, H. W. Riechen, S. Schechter, *When Prophecy Fails*, Minnesota 1956: pioneer 'cognitive dissonants'.

78 *TW*, 1897, vol. 10, p. 780.

79 George Young's 1908 presidential address to the Spiritualist National Union, *The Spiritualist Attitude towards Established Institutions and Progressive Movements*.

80 *HN*, vol. 1, 1867, pp. 109–13.

81 *TW*, 1893, vol. 6, pp. 543f.

82 *M. and D.*, 1879, vol. 10, pp. 477, 613–16. Admittedly the writer (Wm Oxley of Higher Broughton) is untypical in some ways, and was to publish a book on *Modern Messiahs and Wonder Workers* in 1899: obituary in *TW*, 1905, vol. 18, p. 355; also *M. and D.*, 1885, pp. 1ff, 25–8; and historical series in *M. and D.*, during most of 1888–89.

83 *TW*, 1907, vol. 20, p. 572.

84 *TW*, 1898, vol. 11, p. 51.

85 *TW*, 1892, vol. 4, pp. 507–8.

86 *TW*, 1895, vol. 8, p. 61.

87 *TW*, 1912, vol. 25, pp. 316, 342.

88 *TW*, 1888, vol. 1, pp. 450f.

89 *TW*, 1908, vol. 21, p. 280.

90 *TW*, 1898, vol. 11, pp. 33, 51, 61.

91 Clearest of all; Geoff Crossick: *An Artisan Elite in Victorian England: Kentish London 1840–80*, 1978.

92 First issue of the *TW*, 18.11.1887.

93 For Blatchford's version versus Hardie's, see Barrow (as note 56) section III.

94 *TW*, 1902, vol. 15, p. 164, his emphasis.

95 *TW*, 1897, vol. 10, p. 780.

96 *TW*, 1896, vol. 9, p. 660.

97 H. Collins, C. Abramsky, *Karl Marx and the British Labour Movement*, 1965, pp. 242, 260, 263f. *CS*, 1873, vol. 3, pp 99ff.

98 August, 1898.

99 *TW*, 1893, vol. 6, p. 572. He also claimed to have found many spiritualists at the Zürich congress of the Socialist International – as did another writer at the same International's London and Paris meetings, *TW*, 1902, vol. 15, p. 212. It would be interesting to know how many of these alleged spiritualists – if they really were such – also claimed to be marxists, i.e. 'materialists'.

100 *TW*, 1909, vol. 22, p. 516.
101 *TW*, 1909, vol. 22, p. 441.
102 *TW*, 1893, vol. 6, p. 552.
103 *TW*, 1894, vol. 7, p. 148.
104 It would be interesting to know more on the subsequent history of these two 'kindred' organisations in Blackburn.
105 This paper 'Pioneered' through 1895 only.
106 See, e.g. *Clarion*, 7.7.1894, 'Answers' column, to a 'Romanian Socialist'; *TW*, 1896, vol. 9, p. 660.
107 *Bradford Labour Echo*, 8.10.1898. The paper was edited by Alderman Fred Jowett, the Labour Church and Socialist pioneer.
108 *LB*, 1900, vol. 10, p. 88.
109 *TW*, 1898, vol. 11, p. 9.
110 *LB*, 1906, vol. 16, p. 251.
111 *TW*, 1901, vol. 14, p. 325. Some years earlier he had given an interview to the same paper, vol. 6, pp. 582f. For a prominent spiritualist welcoming Blatchford's determinism, see George Young, *TW*, 1904, vol. 17, p. 681.
112 W. Stewart, *Life of Keir Hardie*, 1921, p. 70; Kenneth O. Morgan, *Keir Hardie*, 1975, pp. 46, 57; Iain Mclean, *Keir Hardie*, 1975, p. 165; Fred Reid, *Keir Hardie: The Making of a Socialist*, 1978, p. 171.
113 *M. and D.*, 1893, p. 507, quoting the *Stratford Herald*, 21.7.1893 (a year that is not extant in the British Museum's run of this paper); *TW*, 21.7.1893, p. 348.
114 Such as Hanson Hey (see *Halifax Labour News*, 10.7 and 21.8.1909; *Keighley Labour Journal*, 24.12.1894; *TW*, 1909, vol. 22, p. 456; *LB*, 1892, vol. 2, pp. 114f; April 1903; 1905, p. 2; 1908, p. 139); G. H. Bibbings (see *LB*, 1905, vol. 15, p. 123); J. T. Ward of Blackburn (see, *TW*'s volume-indexes for vols 12, 1899; 15, 1902; 20, 1907; 26, 1913; 32, 1919; also the *Two Worlds Portrait Album*, 1897[?]); Isaac Pickthall (see Fabian Society *Lecture List* for 1892; *LB*, 1908, vol. 18, p. 28); John Marston (see *LB*, May 1915, vol. 28); Thomas Edwards (see, the [ILP] *Stockport Times*, 29.12.1893; *LB*, 1898, vol. 8, p. 33; *TW*, 1907, vol. 20, p. 319). The last three were all from Stockport.
115 For one version of Grayson, see all of R. Groves, *The Strange Case of Victor Grayson*, 1975 (also for a photo of Marklew).
116 *TW*, 1939, vol. 52.
117 *Grimsby Evening Telegraph*, 15.6.1839. I am extremely grateful to Mr. E. H. Travitt of Grimsby Borough Library for this and other information on Marklew in Grimsby.
118 *Grimsby News*, 17.5.1829.
119 *TW*, 1897, vol. 10, p. 328.
120 *TW*, 1898, vol. 11, p. 38.
121 Information to author from Mr. Travitt, 6.10.1971.
122 Apart from his leaving Burnley, a curious suggestion of this is that in 1911 Marklew visited Germany under, by all indications, Tory auspices, and attacked Free Trade when he returned (while still using Marxist terminology). His attack – *On the Spot in Germany, a Socialist*

Reply to Ramsay Macdonald, M.P. – was published by the 'Enemies of the Red Flag', Hammersmith, London, in 1911. Later, during the Great War, he was among those urging workers to enlist.

123 See transcription (in Huddersfield Borough Library) of debate between Marklew and J. A. Seddon, at Mansfield, held on 10 March 1927. Seddon, a former TUC chairman and wartime nationalist-socialist, was speaking for the 'yellow' union. The whole of Marklew's first-round oration was historical, mostly late-medieval.

124 *TW*, 1898, vol. 11, p. 8.

125 *TW*, 1898, vol. 11, p. 26.

126 *TW*, 1899, vol. 12, p. 3.

127 Obituary, *TW*, 1908, vol. 21.

128 *LB*, 1908, vol. 18, p. 28.

129 This occurred during 1877; *TW*, 1895, vol. 8, p. 61; see also *M. and D.*, 1885, p. 716; 1887, pp. 689f. A more recent instance of a working-class spiritualist (who was probably also, as Swindlehurst was to become, a socialist) suffering imprisonment over vaccination, is mentioned in *TW*, 1902, vol. 15, p. 506.

130 Sometime secretary. *LB*, 1898, vol. 8, p. 92.

131 *TW*, vol. 44, 1931, p. 537.

132 K. S. Inglis, *The Churches and the Working Classes in Victorian England*, 1963, p. 228; E. J. Hobsbawm, *Primitive Rebels*, 1959, pp. 144, 149.

133 *LB*, December 1915, vol. 25, for this and subsequent information. Also *Labour Prophet*, May 1895; *LB*, April 1891, vol. 1.

134 *LB*, 1909, vol. 19, p. 185.

135 For whom see an eagerly awaited Sussex D.Phil. thesis from Ms Alex Owen.

136 *Spiritual News*, vol. I, 1, 1.12.1970, p. 2.

137 *Psychological Review*, vol. I, 1878–9, pp. 182f.

138 Susan E. Gay: *John William Fletcher, Clairvoyant. A biographical sketch*, 1883, p. 55. But this book was written at an emotional moment in Fletcher's career (he had returned to America to avoid a prison-sentence, while his wife-biographer had remained in Britain to face hers). And even the same passage may exaggerate: Fletcher's 'position socially and professionally' during his halcyon years had not 'been attained by no other medium in England': his fellow-American, D. D. Home, at least, had preceded him.

139 Text of Morse's lecture to the London Spiritualist Alliance, in *Borderland*, 1893–4, pp. 252f.

140 *Spiritual Herald*, 1856, vol. 1, no. 6, pp. 207, 202f.

141 Advertisements in same, e.g. respectively: outside back cover of No. 3, April 1856; outside back covers of No. 1, February 1856 and of No. 2, March 1856.

142 J. J. Morse: *Leaves from my Life*, 1877, Chapter II, i.e. pp. 7–16.

143 Information from Alex Owen.

144 Morse, as note 142, Chapter 3, i.e. pp. 16–23.

145 George Wyld: *Notes of my Life*, 1903, p. 61.

146 Wyld, p. 122.

147 See, e.g., R. Brandon: *The Spiritualists*, e.g. pp. 110–13.
148 *Borderland*, 1893–4, vol. I, pp. 252f.
149 S. E. Gay, as above, pp. 49f.
150 Gay, p. 39.
151 Gay, p. 19f.
152 Gay, p. 87. or one contact at least: S. E. Gay herself.
153 *Borderland*, 1893–4, vol. I, pp. 252f.
154 For the S.P.R., see particularly Alan Gauld; *the Founders of Psychical Research*, 1968; F. M. Turner; *Between Science and Religion*, 1974, chapter 5: R. L. Moore: *In Search of White Crows*, 1977, pp. 138f, 147ff; Janet Oppenheim: *The Other World: Spiritualism and Psychical Research in England, 1850–1914*, 1985 (which I have not yet seen).
155 *Borderland*, 1893–4, vol. I, pp. 252f.
156 E.g. advertisement in *Spiritual Review*, April 1895, no. 1, inside back cover.
157 *Borderland*, 1893–4, vol. I, no. 1, p. 7.
158 *Spiritual Review*, 1895, p. 11.
159 *Borderland*, 1893–4, vol. I, no. 1, p. 7.
160 A. Kitson in *Borderland*, 1895, p. 236.
161 *Light*, 1895, vol. 15, p. 2.
162 *Light*, 1895, vol. 15, p. 2.
163 Itemised and defiantly headed 'who is really liable?' in *M. and D.*, 1894, p. 175; also 1895, p. 297; or, e.g., *Spiritual Review*, 1895, p. 64.
164 *Borderland*, vol. 2, 1895, p. 198.
165 *TW*, vol. 8, p. 165.
166 *M. and D.*, memorial supplement to 22.3.95., pp. 2f.
167 *M. and D.*, 1894, p. 491.
168 *S.M.*, 1868, p. 475; G. K. Nelson, pp. 100f.
169 For example at Doughty Hall: e.g. *Spiritual Notes*, May 1879, p. 46.
170 In late 1870 at the Cambridge Hall, Newman St, Oxford St: *Spiritual News*, December 1870, p. 2: 'got up chiefly by Mr. Burns'.
171 *Spiritual Notes*, same page.
172 Benjamin Coleman, in *CS*, 1871, pp. 60ff.
173 *CS*, 1871, p. 72f.
174 *Spiritual Notes*, February 1879, p. 99.
175 *Spiritual Notes*, July 1878, pp. 14f.
176 *Spiritual Notes*, outside back cover of December 1878.
177 Nelson, pp. 104, 178.
178 *Spiritual Review*, 1896, p. 278.
179 *M. and D.*, 1895, memorial number, p. 2.
180 *M. and D.*, 1894, pp. 273–6.
181 *M. and D.*, 1895, p. 22.
182 *Borderland*, vol. I, no. 1, 1893, p. 9.
183 See lists of addresses of secretaries of spiritualist societies and groups in its July 1878 issue, p. 12: approximately 15 Northern and 6 London.
184 Same number, p. 6.
185 See Nelson, p. 178. Also prospectus, bound with the British

Museum's 1878–80 volume of *Spiritual Notes*. Kersey had tried to interest the BNAS in starting a weekly spiritualist paper in 1880: ibid., June 1880, p. 302.

186 E.g., I. M. Lewis: *Ecstatic Religions*, 1971.

187 This, with what follows, is particularly indebted to discussions and correspondence with Dr Perry Williams and to an early perusal of those parts of his Cambridge doctoral thesis that he kindly made available. I have not altogether followed his categorisation, but remain deeply indebted to its stimulus. J. P. Williams: 'The Making of Victorian Psychical Research: an Intellectual Elite's Approach to the Spiritual World' (Cambridge Ph.D., 1984).

188 For two nowadays rightly famous instances from outside our place and period, see the scintillating and controversial books by Carlo Ginzburg: *The Cheese and the Worms: the Cosmos of a Sixteenth-Century Miller*, 1980; and *The Night Battles: Witchcraft and Agrarian Cults in the Sixteenth and Seventeenth Centuries*, 1983.

189 Perry Williams, thesis, p. 240ff is particulerly good here.

190 Of Salford, *LB*, 1908, vol. 18, p. 174.

191 E.g., *HN*, 1868, p. 162.

192 E.g., letter from 'W.A.', *HN*, 1867, pp. 599–602.

193 Letter to *CS*, 1871, vol. 1, pp. 71f.

194 S. E. Gay: *Spiritualistic Sanity*, 1879, p. 10.

195 H. Williams Jones, *M. and D.*, 1872, pp. 479f.

196 Gay, p. 10.

197 'M.A. (Oxon)', i.e. the Reverend W. Stainton Moses: *Spirit Identity*, 1879, p. 14.

198 I owe this point to Dr Perry Williams (see n. 187).

199 *HN*, September 1867, p. 329; also quoted in the Burns obituary-number of the *M. and D.*, 1895, p. 4.

200 *HN*, 1867, p. 333, quoted also in same number of *M. and D.*

201 Williams, p. 265.

202 Williams, p. 271.

203 Williams, p. 271.

204 F. M. Turner: *Between Science and Religion*, 1974, Chapter 5.

205 *Lancet*, 1842–3, 1, p. 686.

206 E.g., *Lancet*, 1846, 1, pp. 687–91, and many other pages.

207 Same pages, editorial of 20.4.46, emphasis in original. This was hardly the first of Wakley's editorials triggered by the news that Elliotson was to give the Harveian Oration – the arch-pariah defiling the great totem – but it was the purplest and most ambitious. The news had first been mentioned on p. 608 of the same volume.

208 *Lancet*, 1838–9, vol. 9, 1, pp. 34f, emphasis in original.

209 *Lancet*, 1840–1, 2, pp. 897–900.

210 His lions of induction included not only the today questionable Galileo, Kepler and Newton, but also 'the great French philosopher M. Comte': *Lancet*, 1846–7, pp. 687–91, emphasis in original.

211 *Lancet*, 1843–44, 1, p. 577.

Chapter 6   Presence and problems of democratic epistemology

1 Opening Propositions in Dr. *Skelton's Botanic Record and Herbal*, 1852, p. 71; similarly the Thomsonian medical botanist, Dr Stevens: *Medical Reform or Physiological and Botanic Practice for the People*, 1847, p. iv.
2 Quoted in *Eclectic Journal and Medical Free Press*, 1866, vol. 1, p. 271.
3 C. Hill: *The World Turned Upside Down*, 1975, Penguin edition, p. 288; similarly pp. 163f and Chapter 15 throughout.
4 C. Hill: *Intellectual Origins of the English Revolution*, 1965, p. 66, 127.
5 I.e. of the 'Latitudinarian' Anglican: I am relying here on the controversial M. C. Jacob: *The Newtonians and the English Revolution, 1688–1720*, 1976, particularly Chapters 4 and 5.
6 R. Darnton: *Mesmerism and the End of the Enlightenment in France*, Harvard, 1968.
7 See, e.g., D. Lecourt: *Proletarian Science?*, 1977; Zh. Medvedev: *The Rise and Fall of T.D. Lysenko*, Columbia, 1969; D. Joravsky: *The Lysenko Affair*, Harvard, 1970; Mark Popovsky: *The Vavilov Affair*, 1985 (which I have not yet seen).
8 See, for example, *The Dictionary of Scientific Biography*.
9 Frank M. Turner: *Between Science and Religion*, 1974, Chapter 4.
10 Samuel Smiles: *Robert Dick, Baker, of Thurso: Geologist and Botanist*, 1878; *D.N.B.* entries on Dick and Smiles himself; Smiles: *Life of a Scotch Naturalist: Thomas Edwards, Associate of the Linnaean Society*, 1879.
11 *National Reformer*, 6.8.1864.
12 For background see, e.g., much of B. Simon: *Education and the Labour Movement*, 1965.
13 See Phil Gardner: *The Lost Elementary Schools of England: The People's Education*, 1984.
14 L. Barrow: 'Determinism and Environmentalism in Socialist Thought', in R. Samuel, G. Stedman Jones, eds: *Culture, Ideology and Politics*, 1982/83.
15 W. Lovett: *The Life and Struggles of William Lovett in Pursuit of Bread, Knowledge and Freedom*, 1876, p. 37, 39.
16 See, e.g., G. Werskey: *The Visible College, a collective biography of British scientists and socialists of the 1930s*, 1978.
17 L. Barrow: 'Imponderable Liberator: J.J. Garth Wilkinson', in R. Cooter, ed.: *Alternatives: Essays in the Social History of Irregular Medicine* (forthcoming). A far more prominent homoeopath, Dr John Epps, supported at least Knowledge Chartism and the fight against medical jargon (E. Epps, ed.: *Diary of the late John Epps, M.D.*, Edin., 1875, pp. 321, 326; 307ff).
18 Barrow, 'Imponderable Liberator'.
19 This 'Conflict' perspective was anyway inadequate to describe even the religious impact of Darwin. See James R. Moore: *The Post-Darwinian Controversies: A Study of the Protestant Struggle to Come to*

Terms with Darwin in Britain and America, 1870–1900, 1979. I am grateful to Niall Martin for alerting me to this book.

20 G. J. Holyoake: *The Last Trial for Atheism in England*, 1871. For Gott, see Edward Royle: *Radicals, Secularists and Republicans: Popular Freethought in Britain, 1866–1915*, 1980, particularly Chapter 14; E. Pack: *The Trial and Imprisonment of J. W. Gott for Blasphemy*, Bradford, 1911; *Labour Annual*, 1900; *Truthseeker*, Bradford; *Eagle and Serpent*, Leeds; *Times*, 19.7.1918; 22.11., 8. + 10.12.1921; 17. + 31.1.1922. Admittedly Gott and the authorities had had a long history of provocation and persecution.

21 Title of a research-project at the University of Bremen. See P. Weindling: 'Shattered Alternatives in Medicine. A Review Essay' in *History Workshop*, issue 16, 1983.

22 E.g. William Martin: *Short Outline of the Philosopher's Life . . .*, 1833, p. 56; *The Northumberland Bard or the Downfall of all false Philosophy*, 1839, p. 31; *The Christian Philosopher: an Exposure of a New System Of Irreligion . . . Promulgated by Robert Owen, Esq., whose Doctrine proves him to be the child of the Devil, and is here exploded*, 1839; twenty-five other publications by Martin in the British Museum catalogue. See also Thomas Balston: *The Life of Jonathan Martin, incendiary of York Minster, with some account of William and Richard Martin*, 1945, pp. 1f, 115ff, 127, 130, 135; J. F. C. Harrison: *The Second Coming*, pp. 12, 24, 261. In however garbled a fashion, William may partly have been echoing the Hutchinsonians: see C. B. Wilde articles cited in note 7 of Chapter 4.

23 J. V. Pickstone: 'Medical Botany' in *Proceedings of the Manchester Literary and Philosophical Society*, 1976–77, vol. 119.

24 John Wesley: *Primitive Physick*, 1st edition 1747, 27th 1814, revised editions in 1832 and 1846.

25 Holyoake also compared medical botany to spiritualism: Dr. *Skelton's Botanic Record*, 1853, pp. 222f; see also pp. 230f.

26 I owe the germination of this point to Reinhold Zech.

27 In the words of the – hardly radical – *Annual Register* for 1832: 'the cholera left the medical men as it had found them – confirmed in most opposite opinions, or in total ignorance as to its nature, its cure, and the course of its origination, if endemic – or the mode of transmission if it were infectious' (quoted in P. Vaughan: *Doctors' Commons*, 1959, p. 36.) See also, e.g., R. J. Morris: *Cholera 1832*, 1978; M. Pelling: *Cholera, Fever and English Medicine, 1825–65*, 1978; M. J. Durey: *The Return of the Plague*, 1979; J. H. Young: *The Toadstool Millionaires*, 1961, Princeton, p. 56.

For a later tragi-comic (and admittedly medico-botanic) description of orthodox and clerical incompetence during the 1850s cholera outbreak in and around Middlesborough, see: *Dr. Skelton's Botanic Record and Family Herbal* (henceforth *SBR*), 1852–55 (years bound in one volume in BM copy), pp. 510f.

28 See R. M. McLeod: *Medico-Legal Issues in Victorian Medical Care* in *Medical History*, X, 1966; 'Law, Medicine and Public Opinion: Public

Resistance to Compulsory Health Legislation, 1870–1907', in *Public Law*, 1967, no volume number.

29 An example would be the at least partially fatal drugging and – by today's Latin-American standards – torturing of Augustus Stafford, MP, during 1857. See *Daily News*, 20.11.1857, verbatim of the inquest, quoted to predictable effect in the *Homoeopathic Record*, late 1857, pp. 29f and January 1858, pp. 41–5, 50.

30 David Goyder, MD: *History of the first 25 years of the Bradford Medico-Chirugical Society from May 1863 to June 1888*, 1888, Bradford, p. 23. Admittedly the provaccinationists seem to have predominated (relevantly or not, Goyder was among them); but the antis included the Society's president and also Dr John Henry Bell, who deservedly figures in 'heroic' approaches to medical history as the isolator of anthrax (till then known rather fatalistically as 'wool-sorters' disease').

31 USA: many secondary sources, e.g.: H. L. Coulter: *Divided Legacy, a History of the Schism in Medical Thought*, volume 3; *Science and Ethics in American Medicine, 1800–1914*, 1973, throughout; R. H. Shryock: *Medicine and Society in America, 1760–1860*, 1960, particularly pp. 140–46; Canada: *Homoeopathic Record* June 1859, vol. 4, pp. 145f.

32 True, there was a venerable Medical Botanic Society of London (founded, according to Skelton – who was surely the nineteenth century's historian of medical botany by far the widest-read in primary sources – by Sir Hans Sloane), presided over around 1850 by the Earl of Stanhope: *S.B.R.*, 1854–5, p. 484; *Eclectic Journal and Medical Free Press*, 1866, p. 271. But, for homoeopathy's far broader aristocratic support, see, e.g. bazaar-advertisement in *Homoeopathic Record*, April 1858, p. 120.

33 J. Skelton: *A Plea for the Botanic Practice of Medicine*, 1853, p. 199, his emphasis. Similarly *SBR*, 1852, p. 1.

34 Skelton as shoemaker militant: Dorothy Thompson: *The Chartists*, 1984, p. 186, also p. 332; his associated involvements and ideas: David Goodway: *London Chartism, 1838–48*, 1982, pp. 39f; David Jones: *Chartism and the Chartists*, 1975, pp. 164, 170. Kirkstall: *SBR*, p. 128.

35 S. T. Hall in *Homoeopathic Record*, March 1856, pp. 73f.

36 see L. Barrow: 'an Imponderable Liberator: J. J. Garth Wilkinson', in R. Cooter, ed.: *Alternatives: Essays in the Social History of Irregular Medicine*, forthcoming.

37 *HN*, 1867, p. 469, his emphasis. He also praised orthodox anatomy and – unlike many heterodox spokespeople – surgery.

38 Samuel Thomson: *Narrative of the Life and Medical Discoveries of Samuel Thomson*, 2nd edition, 1825, Boston (henceforth: *Narrative*). See also: J. Pickstone: 'Medical Botany (Self-Help Medicine in Victorian England)', in *Manchester Literary and Philosophical Society, Memoirs and Proceedings*, 1975–6, vol. 48. Other articles and papers on Medical Botany include: Dan J. Wallace: 'Thomsonians, the People's Doctors' in *Clio Medica*, 1979–80, vol. 14 (contains a most useful bibliography); J. Forman: 'The Worthington School and Thomsonianism' in *Bulletin of the History of Medicine*, 1947, vol. 21; Alex Berman: 'The Thom-

sonian Movement and its Relation to American Pharmacy and Medicine' in *Bulletin of the History of Medicine*, 1951, vol. 25 (a double
article); also R. L. Numbers' paper (which I have been unable to see)
in G. B. Risse, R. L. Numbers, J. W. Leavitt, eds: *Medicine without
Doctors: Home Health Care in American History*, New York, 1977.

39 For another claim of (partial) Red Indian maternity, see Dr. Coffin's
speech at the Nottingham Medical Botanic Soirée. This occasion also
provides an instance of the cliché about Thomson being a 'child of
nature': *SBR*, 1853, pp. 367f.

40 *A Plea*, pp. 49ff.

41 *EJ*, 1869, p. 274. Similarly *Botanic Eclectic Review*, 1856, p. 88; *SBR*,
1853, p. 311: principles of the National Medical Reform League. See
also Mary Chamberlain: *Old Wives' Tales: Their History, Remedies and
Spells*, 1981, particularly chapters 4–6. By contrast, erroneously or
not, at least one supporter of medical botany described his golden
age as one in which 'every father of a family [had been] his family's
own physician.' (David Irvine, in *SBR*, pp. 123ff).

42 E.g., *A Plea*, pp. 62f: in the early seventeenth century, Skelton
claimed, medical botany remained strong, 'particularly in those counties far beyond the reach of the great struggle [over Paracelsianism]
in the metropolis and cities of Europe; hence it is that Yorkshire was
the last to relinquish what had so long been transmitted from generation to generation. If you ever want to find out old *Botanic Records*,
go into Yorkshire; and if there are any anywhere, it is there' (his
emphasis). Skelton, we must note here, came from Plymouth. His
historiography would repay evaluation. His geography is confirmed
in, e.g., F. B. Smith: *The People's Health, 1830–1910*, 1979, pp. 168,
340.

43 Pickstone (as in note 38).

44 A. R. Gassion of Sunderland, *EJ*, 1866, pp. 174f.

45 Wallace (as in note 38).

46 *SBR*, p. 7. Also on botanic and eclectic disease-theory, see: ibid.,
pp. 34f, 47, 198. For an instance of the steam-engine analogy, see
what Skelton reprinted as Thomson's 'far-famed *Chapter of Life and
Motion*', in his *A Plea*, p. 174.

47 E.g., J. Skelton: *Family Medical Advisor*, 1852, Leeds, pp. 7–10.

48 See, e.g., *FMA*, p. 22; J. Skelton, senior: *The Science and Practice of
Medicine*, 1904 edition, preface to the 1871 edition, pp. 17ff; *SBR*,
pp. 34f, 44f, 61f, 131, 154, 261f.

49 As 'Rousseau': *SBR*, pp. 124f.

50 *SBR*, p. 322.

51 *SBR*, pp. 26ff.

52 *SBR*, pp. 26ff.

53 See, e.g., *SBR*, pp. 79f, 166ff, 170–6.

54 *SBR*, pp. 12–15.

55 E.g., *EJ*, 1866, pp. 81ff.

56 Dr T. L. Nichols in *HN*, 1873, pp. 426f. For Nichols and his Fourierite wife Mary Gove, see B. Aspinwall: 'Social Catholicism and

Health: Dr. and Mrs. Thomas Low Nichols in Britain', in W. J. Shiels, ed.: *The Church and Healing* (*Studies in Church History*, vol. 19), 1982.

57 This was certainly argued, on their side, by the homoeopaths: e.g., *Notes of a New Truth*, April 1856, p. 38.

58 Dr Archibald Hunter ('Medical director' of the 'Bridge of Allan Hydropathic Establishment'): *The Vaccination Question*, in *HM*, 1867, pp. 448ff.

59 N. Jewson: 'Medical Knowledge and the Patronage System in Eighteenth-Century England', in *Sociology*, 1974, vol. 8.

60 Robert Heppell, *SBR*, pp. 120f.

61 *EJ*, 1868, pp. 3f.

62 E.g., *FMA*, pp. 14, 24.

63 Dr Turnbull of Cheltenham, in his *Botanic Eclectic Review*, May 1856, pp. 81–6.

64 *EJ*, July 1869, pp. 287–91. Conversely, the wryness of F. B. Smith's remark that 'the progress of Coffinism [his sweeping word for herbalism] can be followed through the numerous inquests on its clients' may tip the balance further in favour of orthodoxy than he intends (to judge from his next few lines): F. B. Smith: same (see note 42 above), pp. 34f. In any sense, inquests are anything but impartial sources, particularly perhaps during this period.

65 *SBR*, p. 7.

66 *SBR*, pp. 34f.

67 *SBR*, p. 7.

68 *SBR*, pp. 26ff: this remark did *not* refer directly to homoeopathy.

69 *SBR*, pp. 587ff.

70 *A Plea*, p. 111, emphasis in original.

71 J. J. G. Wilkinson: *War, Cholera and the Ministry of Health*, 1854.

72 *SBR*, pp. 587ff.

73 Dr Thornton, in *SBR*, p. 34.

74 *SBR*, pp. 115–19; genuinely from an opponent's pen, see *The Lancet*, 10.12.1853, when blaming the Dunk Street cholera outbreak on Coffinites.

75 Letter from John Hamilton of Old Basford, in *SBR*, 1852, pp. 61f.

76 *EJ*, 1868–9, vol. 2, pp. 245ff.

77 *EJ*, 1867, vol. 1, pp. 252f.

78 *EJ*, 1867, vol. 1, pp. 242–8 (quoting *Newcastle Daily Chronicle*, 27.2.1867), pp. 283, 317f, 378, 380 (quoting same paper).

79 Joseph Ashman: *Psychotherapy or the True Healing Art*, 1874, pp. 1f.

80 *TW*, 1891, vol. 4, p. 65.

81 *British and Foreign Medical Review*, 1839, vol. 8, p. 495; confirmed in *DNB*.

82 *British and Foreign Medical Review*, July–October 1847, vol. 24, postscript, particularly p. 494.

83 See Forbes's unusual warmth for F. F. Sankey's argument to this effect: *BFMR*, ibid., pp. 215f.

84 Clement J. Wilkinson: *J.J. Garth Wilkinson. A Memoir of his Life with*

a selection from his letters, 1911, p. 252 (letter of 30.12.1852 to Henry James, senior), similarly pp. 250f.

85 A. Watson: *A Newspaperman's Memories*, 1925, pp. 22f.

86 *Report as to the Practice of Medicine and Surgery by Unqualified Persons in the U.K.*, 1910, preface, 1907, by Sir Almeric Fitzroy of the Privy Council Office (His Majesty's Stationery Office): a voluminous source, even though bureaucratic, uneven and brazenly biased.

87 Reprinted from *Glasgow Examiner*, 5.10.1844: *Memoir of S. T. Hall*, p. 6.

88 *DNB*. Also quoted in obituary in *Blackpool Herald*, 1.5.1885, p. 6.

89 Obituary in *Blackpool Times and Fylde Observer*, 29.4.1885.

90 *Blackpool Gazette*, 1.5.1885, p. 5.

91 'Advertisement' to *Phreno-Magnet and Mirror of Nature: A Record of Fact, Experiments and Discoveries in Phrenology, Magnetism, etc.* edited by S. Hall, lecturer in Phrenopathy, Feb.–Dec. 1843, pp. 18f, quoting *Manchester Guardian*, 22.2.1843, p. 291.

92 *PMMN*, Dec. 1843, p. 291.

93 *PMMN*, p. 321, his emphasis.

94 *PMMN*, pp. 322f.

95 See R. K. Webb: *Harriet Martineau*, 1966, p. 231.

96 S. T. Hall: *Mesmeric Experiences*, 1845, pp. 6f, 20–6, 85.

97 S. T. Hall, *Homoeopathy: A Testimony*, 1851, Doncaster, p. 11.

98 Same page.

99 *DNB*.

100 S. T. Hall: *Homoeopathy and Hydropathy: their Harmony and Efficacy in Practice*, 1865, p. 8. Botanists claimed Hippocrates similarly.

101 S. T. Hall: *Homoeopathy, a Testimony*, p. 5.

102 *DNB*.

103 S. T. Hall: *Biographical Sketches of Remarkable People*, 1873, p. 278.

104 S. T. Hall: *Homoeopathy, a Testimony*, pp. 8f.

105 *Blackpool Herald*, 1.5.85, p. 6.

106 For Leonard Hall, see *Labour Annual*, 1901; J. B. Smethurst: *Leonard Hall, Journalist Extraordinary*, in *Eccles and District History Society Lectures*, 1972–3 (cyclostyled); L. J. W. Barrow: 'The Socialism of Robert Blatchford and the "Clarion" Newspaper, 1889–1918', (London D.Phil., 1975).

107 This paragraph and much of the surrounding ones are based on S. T. Hall's obituaries, instanced in notes 71–3 above, plus those in the *Manchester Guardian*, 28. + 30.4.1885.

108 R. K. Webb: *Harriet Martineau*, 1966, pp. 226–31; S. T. Hall: *Mesmeric Experiences*, 18, p. 63–75; and, for Hall's presence in Newcastle around this time, *Newcastle Chronicle*, 28.5., 8 + 22.6.1884.

109 *M. and D.*, 28.2.1879.

110 *M. and D.*, 19.8.1881, pp. 570f.

111 J. Rutherford of Roker, to Gateshead spiritualists, *M. and D.*, 1892, vol. 23, pp. 259f.

112 Unsigned, in *M. and D.*, 1872, pp. 232f. The chairperson was not David Richmond (whom we will meet again soon), but a Mr Hodge.

113 Volume preface to vol. 4 of *HN*, 1870.
114 *PMMN*, pp. xif.
115 *TW*, 1890, vol. 3, pp. 326f.
116 As late as *HN*, 2.5.1870, pp. 228f.
117 I say 'almost', because Dietzgenism may be a different muddle. See S. Macintyre: *A Proletarian Science: Marxism in Britain, 1917–33*, 1980, particularly pp. 129–40; J. Rée: *Proletarian Philosophers: Problems in Socialist Culture in Britain, 1900–1940*, 1984, particularly Chapter 3.
118 *M. and D.*, 1872, pp. 232f.
119 *LB*, 1909, vol. 9, p. 136.
120 S. T. Hall: *Mesmeric Experiences*, 1845: preface signed from the hardly plebeian-sounding address of '59 Pall Mall, London'.
121 S. T. Hall: *A Forester's Offering*, 1841, preface, p. 3, his emphasis.
122 *PMMN*, vol. 1, no. 4, May 1843; for the Owenites' craze for phreno-mesmerism, see R. Cooter: *The Cultural Meaning of Popular Science: Phrenology and the Organisation of Consent in 19th-century Britain*, 1984, Chapter 8.
123 *Glasgow Examiner*, 5.10.1844, *Memoir of S. T. Hall*, p. 13.
124 S. T. Hall: *Homoeopathy, a Testimony*, 1851, p. 12.
125 *A Plea*, p. 110.
126 S. T. Hall: *Mesmeric Experiences*, pp. 23–6.
127 C. J. S. Thompson: *The Quacks of Old London*, 1928, p. 135. See also Eric Jameson: *The Natural History of Quackery*, 1961. I have benefited considerably, from Roy Porter: 'The Language of Quackery' (cyclo-styled paper, October 1983).
128 *SBR*, 1852, pp. 49–53.
129 See, e.g., B. Harrison: *Drink and the Victorians*, 1971, particularly pp. 26, 161f.
130 J. Walkowitz: *Prostitution and Victorian Society*, 1981, throughout.
131 Harrison; N. Longmate: *The Waterdrinkers*, 1968.
132 *SBR*, p. 235.
133 *SBR*, 3.7.1852, p. 33ff.
134 *SBR*, pp. 347ff, 394; Jones (see note 34, above), p. 145; Goodway (see same note), p. 282, n. 81.
135 One way of measuring part of this, might be via Friendly Society sources. For one indication that these Societies were calling on medical botanists as well as on homoeopaths and allopaths, see J. H. Blunt, M.D., of Northampton (a homoeopathic stronghold) in *EJ*, 1866, pp. 232f.
136 *A Plea*, p. 199.
137 However, our source is a loosely brief centennial history in a 1964 edition of the *Herbal Practitioner* celebrating the centenary of the (since 1945) National *Institute* of Medical Herbalists. The Whiggism – or at least, after-the-event gradualism – of this history contrasts sadly with the far lengthier, more concrete and complex (partly because more embattled) histories penned by Skelton himself, roughly 100 years previously. He obviously had the greater interest in herbalism's

historic legitimacy as against the comparatively recent irruption of allopathy.

138 *A Plea*, same page, his emphasis.
139 *EJ*, 1868, pp. 32f; an earlier issue had reprinted the report of the Eclectic Medical Society of the State of Pennsylvania, a Society over which Buchanan presided: *EJ*, 1866, pp. 79f.
140 E.g., outside-front-cover of June 1869.
141 *EJ*, 1869, p. 262.
142 *EJ*, 1869, pp. 299, 301–8.
143 *A Plea*, p. 437, his emphasis.
144 *A Plea*, pp. 126f.
145 For 'the Royal Jennerian and London Vaccine Institution' – which was bitterly hostile to the government-funded National Vaccine Institute – see, e.g. *Notes of a New Truth*, February 1856, pp. 19–24; May 1856, p. 50; February 1857, pp. 202ff; March 1862, pp. 790–5; June 1863, p. 90.
146 *FMA*, p. 64.
147 *SBR*, 1853, pp. 266–77.
148 *The Mesmerist*, 13.5.1843, pp. 1–4.
149 *SBR*, 1853, pp. 298–301: Robert Heppell.
150 *SBR*, 1853, Sept 1854, pp. 449–53; similarly Gibbs: ibid., p. 549.
151 *EJ*, 1868–9, vol. 2, pp. 66, 192; *SBR*, 1853, pp. 218ff.
152 *EJ*, 1867, p. 255, plus statement against vaccination, by S. T. Hall, 6 pages later.
153 *EJ*, July 1869, pp. 287–91.
154 *Homoeopathic Record*, February 1858, pp. 65f. Similarly *Notes of a New Truth*, December 1858, pp. 165f.
155 *Homoeopathic Record*, same month, p. 66.
156 E.g., *Homoeopathic Record*, 1869, pp. 301–8: speech by Dr. Turnbull.
157 *Norwich Dispatch*, 2.8.1865, quoted *EJ*, 1866, pp. 67f.
158 Skelton was detailing this only a few pages after conditionally supporting vaccination: *FMA*, p. 69.
159 *EJ*, 1869, p. 251.
160 See, e.g., G. Crossick: *An Artisan Elite in mid-Victorian London*, 1978; G. Crossick, ed: *The Lower Middle Class in Britain, 1870–1914*, 1976; G. Crossick, H. G. Haupt, eds: *Shopkeepers and Master Artisans in 19th Century Europe*, 1984; R. Q. Gray: *The Labour Aristocracy in 19th-century Edinburgh*, 1976.
161 Middle: as claimed by a Colne supporter: *SBR*, 1852, p. 87; upper: if only as claimed by Coffin (for one of the principal attendants upon Prince Albert): ibid., pp. 367f.
162 E.g. *EJ*, 1866, pp. 13f; inside front cover of August.
163 *EJ*, 1866, p. 62.
164 *EJ*, 1866, p. 62.
165 *SBR*, 1853, p. 214.
166 Skelton: *A Plea*, p. 233.
167 *SBR*, 1853, pp. 311f.
168 See, in the British Museum, the ornamental one-page Address,

presented to him along with 'a Tea Urn' by his pupils during that month.

169 *SBR*, 1853, pp. 166ff, 170–6; 266–77; by 1854, the Society numbered nearly 200 'brethren': p. 324.

170 *EJ*, Introduction, 1.1.66. 'Alongside': see the volume-preface: 'we have made as little use of technical terms as possible, and aim to simplify rather than mystify the theory and practice of medicine.'

171 *EJ*, 1866, pp. 183–6.

172 *EJ*, 1869, p. 299.

173 *EJ*, 1869, vol. 2, pp. 121f.

174 *EJ*, 1867, pp. 202f, 229.

175 *EJ*, 1869, pp. 347ff.

176 *EJ*, 1869, p. 363.

177 *Light of Day*, July 1891, p. 12.

178 *Light of Day*, pp. 51, 75.

179 *Light of Day*, p. 127.

180 Dorothy Thompson (see n. 34 above), p. 332. For 'Knowledge Chartism', see n. 201, below. For one Swedenborgian, herbalist and O'Connorite (James Scholefield) see: ibid., pp. 168f, and report by Tom Sharratt, in *Guardian*, London, 21.12.1981, p. 3.

181 The serialisation began on page 55–60 of same.

182 He was heavily involved in most efforts during these years for medical botany's defence and promotion, from the College to a 'handhealing hospital' (*M. and D.*, 1894, p. 292), to the 'Eclectic Publishing Company' (whose Annual Meeting he attended during at least 1885: *Light*, 1885, vol. 5, p. 199), to a defence-fund for persecuted botanists (*M. and D.*, 1894, p. 429).

183 E.g. *Light of Day*, pp. 84f, 95.

184 *M. and D.*, 1893, pp. 214f.

185 *Light of Day*, pp. 39f.

186 *Light of Day*, p. 126.

187 *Light of Day*, pp. 6f.

188 *Light of Day*, p. 39.

189 Outside front cover of *Light of Day*, July 1892, no. 8.

190 National Institute of Medical Herbalists, Centennial history in *Herbal Practitioner*, 1964: see note 137, above.

191 E.g. various advertisements in *LB*, 1893, vol. 3, no date being given for the book.

192 *LB*, 1894, vol. 4, pp. 99ff, reproduced from Younger's *Magnet and Botanic Journal*.

193 *M. and D.*, 1854, p. 743.

194 E.g. *Light*, 1881, vol. 1, p. 291; 1882, pp. 41, 51. The lengthiest source for Younger is *M. and D.*, 1887, pp. 801ff (including portrait) and same, 1893, p. 665. Younger also spoke at the memorial meeting for Burns: same, 1895, pp. 103, 73.

195 *M. and D.*, 1894, p. 393.

196 *M. and D.*, 1894, p. 429.

197 *M. and D.*, 1895, Burns memorial number, p. 12.

198 One of the enrollers in *this* 'People's University' was Leonard Hall: *Eagle and Serpent*, No. 4, September 1898.
199 *TW*, 28.7.1893; reprinted in *Borderland*, 1893, vol. 1, pp. 152f.
200 *Borderland*, 1895, vol. 2, pp. 354f, quoting the weekly *Light*.
201 For 'Knowledge Chartism' see, directly Wm Lovett, J. Collins: *Chartism, a New Organisation of the People*, 1840; 1969 re-edition, Leeds, preface by Asa Briggs.
202 *HN*, 1867, vol. 1, pp. 330–5; *M. and D.*, 22.3.1895, supplement p. 12.
203 E.g. Alfred Kitson, *LB*, 1900, vol. 10, p. 137.
204 Figures from *LB*. They were inflated by the inclusion of four colonial lyceums. On the other hand, the lyceums' own registrations were more than once argued to have erred in the opposite direction.
205 Replacing a nine-month old *Spiritualist Lyceum Magazine*.
206 *LB*, March 1898, vol. 8, p. 44.
207 A. J. Davis, *The Children's Progressive Lyceum, a Manual*, English edition, 1875.
208 *LB*, November 1890, vol. 1.
209 *LB*, 1908, vol. 18, pp. 97f.
210 Quoted on p. 74 of the *Spiritualist Lyceum Magazine*.
211 *LB*, 1898, vol. 8, p. 27. 'Attractiveness', as a growing obsession among many denominations during the late nineteenth century (see S. Yeo, *Religion and Voluntary Organisation in Crisis*, 1976), often clashed with official doctrine.
212 *LB*, May 1915, vol. 25, John Marston of Stockport, for whom see note 119.
213 *LB*, 1899, vol. 9, p. 81: Plymouth. Within three years, this lyceum was mostly run by former scholars: *LB*, 1902, p. 103.
214 See Hugh Cunningham, *The Volunteer Force, A Social and Political History, 1859–1908*, 1975, and John Springhall, *Youth, Empire and Society: British Youth Movements, 1883–1940*, 1977.
215 *M. and D.*, 1.3.1872.
216 *TW*, 1888, vol. 1, p. 15. The speaker was W. Johnson of Hyde. Similarly, ibid., 1894, vol. 7, p. 108.
217 *L.B.*, 1898, vol. 8, p. 27.
218 *M. and D.*, 4.5.1894, p. 273–6.
219 Reuben Webb, in *LB*, March 1903, vol. 13.
220 *TW*, 1895, vol. 8, p. 61.
221 *HN*, 1867, vol. 1, pp. 330–5.
222 *LB*, May 1892, vol. 2, p. 107.
223 *TW*, 1888, vol. 1, p. 542. This may be the origin of F. Podmore's 1908 book title, *The Naturalisation of the Supernatural*.
224 For an important and balanced treatment of American spiritualism, see R. Laurence Moore, *In Search of White Crows. Spiritualism, Parapsychology and American Culture*, 1978. Part 1 and Chapter 9. For a reworking of Davis's role in the origination of spiritualism, see A. A. Walsh, 'A Note on the Origin of "Modern" Spiritualism', *Journal for the History of Medicine and Allied Sciences*, vol. 28, April 1973.

225 *M. and D.*, 4.5.1894, pp. 273–6.
226 Same, 6.4.1883, p. 222; 25.5.83, p. 334.
227 *HN*, 1868, pp. 321f, 408–11. The accuser was Miss J. Fawcett, whose book had been published in 1864. Its pages 233–4 had allegedly been plagiarised into pages 65–6 of Davis's *Arabula*, published 3 years later.
228 *TW*, 1890, vol. 3, pp. 326f.
229 *HN*, 1873, pp. 411f. Uranus, in the mundane astronomical way, was discovered in 1846, and Pluto in 1930.
230 *HN*, 1.4.1869, pp. 222f.
231 J. W. Jackson: *Ethnology and Phrenology as an Aid to the Historian*, 1863.
232 *HN*, 1.4.1870, pp. 191f.
233 *HN*, 2.7.1867, pp. 253f.
234 E.g., same, 1876, pp. 163–80 – mentioning also a puzzled but positive review in the orthodox *Glasgow Christian News* of 19.2.1876. See also an enthusiastic review in the *St James's Magazine*, September 1876.
235 Quoted by an unnamed writer (Burns?) in the *M. and D.*, 10.7.1891, p. 434.
236 Referred to in *HN*, January 1877, p. 48.
237 T. P. Barkas: *Original Researches in Psychology*, in *HN*, 1870, pp. 517–27. For Barkas's doctrine of dreams as soul-wandering, see Chapter 8, below.
238 As the spirits of Drs Mesmer and Hunter, according to an advertisement in the *M. and D.* of 2.1.1874, vol. 5, p. 15; 27.3.1874, p. 207.
239 *M. and D.*, 5.3.1892, vol. 23, p. 150.
240 I have already listed some of my main sources on Richmond, in note 18 to Chapter 1, above.
241 David Richmond: *The Kingdom of God*, Glasgow, 1885, p. 8.
242 For shoemakers' broader ideological tradition internationally, see E. J. Hobsbawm, Joan Scott: *Political Shoemakers*, in *Past and Present*, no. 89, 1980; nationally, during the 1840s, Dorothy Thompson, same (as in note 34, above), pp. 179–87, 278f; and locally, David Goodway: *London Chartism, 1838–1848*, 1982, pp. 159–69.
243 This was hardly the first such contest that the Shakers had been involved in: see J. F. C. Harrison: *The Second Coming*. p. 170.
244 But his jumbling of the words 'I' and 'we' in the same 1885 account of his 1853 visit may, alternatively, indicate his brother Thomas who was also with him on the same trip: *M. and D.*, 1882, pp. 443f.
245 *M. and D.*, 1891, pp. 130ff. The most accessible extant of Richmond's visions comes from 1885: D. Richmond: *the Kingdom of God*, as in note 70 of Chapter 5.
246 See, e.g., much of the same pamphlet; or the method he used in *M. and D.*, 1889, p. 93.
247 *Kingdom of God*, p. 4.
248 *Kingdom of God*, p. 10.
249 See particularly Harrison: *Second Coming*, p. 4.
250 *M. and D.*, 1891, pp. 130ff.
251 D. Richmond: *The Brotherhood of Man*, in *HN*, 1.4.1868, pp. 171–4.
252 For Derfel, see L. Barrow: 'A Monoglot Sais looks at Wales's Greatest

Owenite' (unpublished paper, 1981); for Carpenter, see particularly
S. Rowbotham, J. Weeks: *Socialism and the New Life*, 1977; and S.
Rowbotham: 'In Search of Carpenter' in *History Workshop*, no. 3,
1977.

253 *M. and D.*, 21.8.1874, pp. 529f, though there were also additional
tactical factors at this time.
254 Quoted in *HN*, 1867, p. 862.
255 As, e.g., to the editor of the *Christian Spiritualist*: *C.S.*, 1871, vol. 1,
p. 32.
256 *TW*, vol. 4, p. 193.
257 *The Kingdom of God*, pp. 9f.
258 *A Plea*, p. 176, quoting Samuel Thomson's 'Chapter of Life and
Motion.'

Chapter 7   Healing

1 Joseph Ashman: *Psychopathic Healing*, 1874, p. 43, Testimonial number
1.
2 Obituary in *Medium and Daybreak*, vol. 14, 1883, p. 5.
3 Ibid.
4 Dr Maurice Davies: 'A Psychopathic Institution', in: *Medium and
Daybreak*, vol. 9, 1874, pp. 694f, reproduced from the *Sun*.
5 Ashman obituary, as note 2.
6 See discussion in *Medium and Daybreak* with Mr Alfred Ginders, in all
the four issues of September 1871, particularly p. 319.
7 Ashman, *Psychopathic Healing*, preface.
8 Ashman obituary, as note 2.
9 Which probably occurred as early as April 1870: see notice by F. R.
Young in *Medium and Daybreak*, vol. 5, 1870, p. 21.
10 As note 2. The spiritualist was 'Miss Makdougall Gregory'.
11 Davies.
12 In 1883, as note 2.
13 *Christian Spiritualist*, 1874, p. 141.
14 Davies.
15 Ashman, *Psychopathic Healing*, p. iv.
16 Davies.
17 E.g., V. Skultans: *Intimacy and Ritual*, 1974, throughout.
18 Sources for the section on Jones are: auto/biographies in *Medium and
Daybreak*, vol. 29, 1894, pp. 65ff, 275ff (includes portrait), 277ff, 316f.
19 Conceivably the famous escaped slave (hence the middle name).
20 E.g. 'Madame Louise of New York', noted in *Human Nature*, vol. 7,
1873, p. 47.
21 E.g. Mrs Davidson: *Human Nature*, ibid.
22 *Visibility Invisible and Invisibility Visible*, 1888; subtitled *A New Year
Story Founded on Fact*; and similar claim in preface.
23 *Visibility*, pp. 45.57.

24 *Visibility*, pp. 58–65.
25 *M. and D.*, vol. 10, 1875, pp. 71, 92, 316, 172, respectively.
26 *M. and D.*, vol. 11, 1976, p. 364. The second and enlarged edition of her *Facts on Vaccination* was stated to be in the press for publication by Burns during September 1876 (vol. 11, p. 590). Text of her lecture at Marylebone: vol. 11, p. 428. Debating: vol. 12, 1877, p. 140. She subsequently joined a select band of dignitaries as a vice president of the South London Anti-Vaccination Society (Report of the latter's annual meeting, in same, vol. 14, 1879, p. 43).
27 *M. and D.*, vol. 11, 1876, p. 495; vol. 12, 1877, p. 431.
28 *M. and D.*, vol. 16, 1881, p. 640.
29 *M. and D.*, vol. 23, 1888, p. 825; Rolandus: same year, pp. 290f.
30 Her *Physianthropy* was much enthused over in the spiritual lyceums, *Lyceum Banner*, vol. 4, 1894, p. 15.
31 *Labour Annual and Reformers' Year Book*, 1899, pp. 165f: includes photograph. See also obituary in *Light*, 9.4.1927, p. 175.
32 *M. and D.*, 4 + 18. May 1894.
33 *Two Worlds*, 2.12.1887, p. 47: a 3/4-column advertisement (I have homogenised the printing and capitalisation in these extracts).
34 *TW*, 9.11.1888, p. iii.
35 E.g., *TW*, 4.4.1890, p. iii: Mrs. Burchell.
36 See, for example, the list of W. J. Leeder in: *TW*, 7.4.1899, p. 231.
37 For a shorter but equally wide list see: *TW*, 5.4.1889, p. iii: Mr. Wakefield. For another, this time surely offering arbortifacients, see: ibid., 7.4.1877, p. 232: Prof. J. R. de Ross; or Mrs. Goldsborough's medicines: ibid., 2.12.1887, p. 47.
38 *Medium and Daybreak*, 2.1.1874, p. 15, small advertisement. Harper seems to have been working alongside a Mrs Empson, who contributed 'Clairvoyant examination for diagnosis of disease'.
39 Though as late as 1887 he was still based in London – though no longer in the centre – whence he was offering instruction in 'the Science of Curing Diseases by Somnambulic [sic] Medicine': *Two Worlds*, 2.12.1887, p. 47.
40 *TW*, 4.4.1890, p. iii.
41 *Report on the Practice of Medicine and Surgery by unqualified persons in the United Kingdom*, 1910, section on England, throughout. I owe thanks to Dr Roger Cooter for alerting me to this basic and tantalising source.
42 *Spiritual Herald*, volume 1, February 1856, pp. 12f; see also pp. 58f.
43 *HN*, volume 1, 1867, pp. 471–83; similarly, Dr. Trall of New York – a well-known American heterodox medicator (same, 1868, pp. 227f). From the side of the *Christian Spiritualist*, see one utterly average advertisement during 1874 (volume 4, p. 32) for 'Miss Godfrey, Curative Mesmerist and Rubber, and Medical Clairvoyant of 161 Hampstead Rd.'.
44 Roy Porter: *Before the Fringe* (paper to conference on *Medical Orthodoxy, Medical Fringe*, February 1985, Wellcome Institute, London); Ivan Waddington: *The Medical Profession in the Industrial Revolution*, Dublin, 1984.

Chapter 8   Bridging the great divide

1 J. J. Morse: *Practical Occultism: a course of lectures through the Trance Mediumship* (preface by W. E. Coleman), editions of 1888 and 1925, p. 12.
2 J. J. Morse: *What of the dead? An address delivered . . . in the trance state,* . . . 1873, pp. 2–5.
3 Outstandingly, Elizabeth Kübler-Ross: *On Death and Dying,* 1970, particularly p. 37; and Myra Bluebond-Langner: *The Private Worlds of Dying Children,* 1978, Princeton, particularly pp. 228–33.
4 See much of the rest of Kübler-Ross.
5 T. Laqueur: 'Bodies, Death and Pauper Funerals' in *Representation,* vol. I, no. 1, February 1983, p. 114.
6 See the description of the Ecclesiastical Art Exhibition, mounted in connection with the 1887 Church Congress, in *M. and D.,* 1877, p. 699.
7 See J. S. Curl: *The Victorian Celebration of Death,* 1972, Newton Abbot; E. V. Gillan: *Victorian Cemetery Art,* 1972 (entirely confined to part of the USA, however); Lou Taylor: *Mourning Dress, A Costume and Social History,* 1983. See also the hilarious conversation reproduced by Henry Mayhew during 1865, in D. J. Enright, ed: *The Oxford Book of Death,* 1983, p. 117.
8 See Barrow, same thesis, pp. 263f. Of theologians, a good treatment is G. Rowell: *Hell and the Victorians,* 1974.
9 Laqueur, p. 125.
10 Ariès is more circumspect: 'the ritual solemnity of the deathbed . . . persisted into the nineteenth century': P. Ariès: *Western Attitudes towards Death from the Middle Ages to the Present,* London edition of 1976, pp. 33–8.
11 *NR,* 1886, p. 266.
12 *NR,* 1884, p. 302: William Wilshaw.
13 *NR,* 1886, later pagination p. 157: Life of J. Allman.
14 A. R. Andrews, lecture to Paddington secularists, *NR,* 1886, p. 334.
15 *NR,* 1887, late p. 78: Mark Jackson of Brighouse.
16 For such a refutation by spiritualists, see *TW,* 1908, vol. 21, p. 490.
17 *NR,* 1886, late p. 62: John Charles Paul.
18 *NR,* 1886, p. 135.
19 *NR,* 1886, p. 411.
20 A. Holyoake: *Secular Ceremonies. A Burial Service,* 1871, throughout.
21 *NR,* 11.9.70, p. 172.
22 W. J. Antill, obituary, *NR,* 27.4.79.
23 E.g., *NR,* 1886, late p. 376; *NR,* 5.5.78: Oldham secularist before a Church of England burial.
24 *NR,* 17.9.64, pp. 426f.
25 *NR,* 1884, late p. 382.
26 *NR,* 1884, p. 382, Salford.
27 E.g., *NR,* 1886, late pp. 366, 375.

28 *NR*, 10.6.77: Brighton.
29 *NR*, 1886, p. 190.
30 *NR*, 28.9.77.
31 *NR*, 1887, late p. 270: Wigan; similarly same year, p. 286: Balls Pond (London).
32 *NR*, 1885, late p. 254: Portsmouth.
33 *NR*, 1886, p. 45.
34 Laqueur, particularly pp. 117ff.
35 *NR*, 21.1.83, p. 45: Northampton. Similarly, 5.2.88: Sunderland.
36 Such as the grandfather of two young sons of the manager of Leicester's Secular Club: *NR*, 1887, p. 221.
37 Such as Mrs Harriet Law: *NR*, 22.5.70; or, more often, Mrs Besant who also wrote a service of her own.
38 *NR*, 1.7.77: Heckmondwyke; D. Tribe: *President, Charles Bradlaugh*, 1971, pp. 289ff.
39 *NR*, 1885, late p. 174.
40 Frank Curzon: *The Gift of Life*, 1853, p. 11. (A reply to G. J. Holyoake's much re-published *The Logic of Death*, 1851.)
41 *M. and D.*, 1887, p. 172.
42 For this custom's generality, at least in mid-nineteenth century West Yorkshire, see Joseph Gutteridge: *Lights and Shadows in the Life of an Artisan*, 1893, p. 218.
43 *TW*, vol. 1 (end of 1887), p. 42; similarly *M. and D.*, 1874, p. 697; ibid., 39.1.81, p. 40; *LB*, 1894, p. 184.
44 For examples of non-European ceremonies with a semi-spiritualist content, and for general discussion of stages of separation, see much of the now venerable A. van Gennep: *Les Rites de Passage*, Paris, 1907; and R. Huntington and P. Metcalf: *Celebrations of Death: The Anthropology of Mortuary Ritual*, 1979.
45 *LB*, 1907, vol. 17, p. 119. There are less ambiguous declarations to the same effect in: ibid., 1911, vol. 21, pp. 52, 136.
46 *Notes of a New Truth*, August 1859, p. 290; January 1860, p. 380.
47 *HN*, 1871, pp. 408ff.
48 *M. and D.*, 12.11.75, p. 723; see also 'Mr. John or Jacob Bright, M.P.' recommending Quaker simplicity: ibid., 1875, p. 526; similarly: *SM*, 1870, pp. 28f.
49 The Association had been founded in 1866: see the back cover of: Mrs. Hume-Rothery: *Anti-Mourning, a lecture against the anti-Christian custom of wearing mourning for the dead*, 2nd revised edition, 1876. The author wrote as a Swedenborgian and her publisher was the Swedenborgian James Speirs. The Association's secretary was her husband, the Reverend William.
50 *SM*, 1868, p. 527.
51 Brother N. Wilson of the Clapham Junction Branch of the Amalgamated Society of Railway Servants, quoted in: *Railway Review*, 27.5.98, p. 2.
52 See, e.g., D. W. Weatherhead: *A Burial Service for the Use of Spiritual-*

ists and others, printed by the author, Keighley, n.d. but – on typographical grounds – quite possibly 1850s.
53 *LB*, 1893, vol. 3, p. 106: 'Mr. Smith' of Brighouse, at funeral of Miss Amelia Ingham. 'Young': aged 31.
54 *M. and D.*, 1881, p. 40; similarly: 21.8.74, p. 530. *LB*, 1901, p. 22.
55 *LB*, 1898, p. 113.
56 See Gillan (as note 7) pp. 116–25.
57 Lancaster: *M. and D.*, 1889, p. 663.
58 *M. and D.*, 1888, p. 690.
59 *M. and D.*, 1888, p. 396: funeral of Miss Annie Wilkinson of Foleshill.
60 Curl, pp. 22f; conversation with Ms Ruth Richardson, December 1979. For pre-Victorian, see, e.g. Rev. J. Churchill: *The Transplanted Flower*, 1817 (a sermon on the death of his daughter). In general, see Nicolette Scourse: *The Victorians and their Flowers*, 1983, particularly pp. 47–58.
61 *M. and D.*, 1875, p. 391. The speaker, Robert Harper, used 'sweetness' twice and 'sweet' once.
62 A. J. Davis: *History and Philosophy of Evil*, 1858, p. 87; *The Children's Progressive Lyceum*, 'c.1875', p. 2. God as both Mother and Father was also a Shaker concept.
63 *LB*, 1896, p. 113.
64 Even Lyceums were linked to death, given that their activities were supposed, from Davis on, to prefigure life in the Summerland. For this, see J. Ashworth, quoting Davis, in *LB*, 1894, p. 163; President of the British Spiritualist Lyceum Union in: *LB*, 1898, pp. 89f.
65 As a sociological sampler, lightning may be more random than representative. But, for what it may be worth, the victims included a woolcomber (a spiritualist for nearly twenty years), a mill-operative, a mechanic, an insurance-agent, (all from Bradford, the insuranceman the secretary of the Yorkshire Union of Spiritualists), a headwarehouseman from Laisterdyke and a master-tailor from Little Horton.
66 *TW*, 1901, vol. 14, p. 510; *LB*, 1901, p. 94.
67 *YST*, May 1855. As a Swedenborgian, the medium would, admittedly, have believed in hell, but probably not eternal, and certainly not of an orthodox kind.
68 *TW*, 1890, vol. 3, pp. 33f.
69 E.g., E. P. Thompson: *The Making of the English Working Class*, 1963, pp. 40, 368, 373.
70 J. J. Morse in the *LB*, 1892, vol. 2, pp. 56f.
71 G. Gorer: *Death, Grief and Mourning in Contemporary Britain*, quoted in Enright (see note 7), p. 103.
72 Enright, p. xiii.
73 Enright, the column was 'Aunt Editha's'.
74 Charles Dickens: *The Old Curiosity Shop*, 1st published 1841, Chapters 71 and 72 (particularly, in the Pelican pagination, pp. 637, 648–55).
75 Mary Douglas: *Purity and Danger*, 1966, p. 178.
76 E. P. Thompson, pp. 40, 368, 373.
77 H. T. Wharlow: *What are Angels?*, *LB*, 1915, p. 24.

78 A Doctor of Hermetic Science, ed: *The Harmonial Philosophy, A Compendium and Digest of the Works of A. J. Davis, the Seer of Poughkeepsie*, 1917, p. x.
79 *LB*, 1920, p. 46.
80 Ibid., 1913, p. 150; similarly during a long series via an American medium, same, 1917, p. 172, entitled 'Life and Labour in the Spirit Spheres'.
81 During 1855, indeed, the 'Astronomer to the Honourable East India Company' believed it 'probable that some of the known planets are inhabited, not very improbable that all of them are': W. S. Jacob, F.R.A.S.: *A few more words on the Plurality of Worlds*, 1855, p. 43. See also J. H. Brooke: *Natural Theology and the Plurality of Worlds: Observations on the Brewster-Whewell Debate*, in *Annals of Science*, vol. 34, 1977; W. C. Heffernan: *The Singularity of our Inhabited World: William Whewell and A. R. Wallace in Dissent*, in *Journal of the History of Ideas*, vol. 39, 1978; dispute between same and N. S. Hetherington in same, vol. 42, 1981.
82 A. J. Davis: *A Stellar Key to the Summerland*, 1868, New York, pp. 155f.
83 E.g., *LB*, 1915, p. 182; or 1920, p. 46.
84 *LB*, 1913, pp. 118, 151.
85 *LB*, 1920, p. 101.
86 E.g., Kitson in same, 1891, pp. 25–8.
87 See, e.g., S. Yeo: *Religion and Voluntary Organisation in Crisis*, 1976.
88 E.g., *LB*, 1915, p. 125.
89 *LB*, 1910, p. 108.
90 E.g., *LB*, 1914, p. 52.
91 *LB*, from November 1890 and July 1903.
92 *LB*, 1891, pp. 25–8.
93 *LB*, 1914, p. 137.
94 *LB*, 1913, p. 150.
95 *LB*, 1910, p. 108.
96 *LB*, 1914, p. 84.
97 *LB*, 1891, pp. 25–8.
98 *LB*, 1917, p. 41.
99 *LB*, 1891, p. 164.
100 *LB*, 1899, p. 11.
101 *LB*, 1891, pp. 25–8.
102 *HN*, 1.4.1868, p. 171.
103 *M. and D.*, 13.12.1872, p. 496.
104 *LB*, 1906, pp. 235f.
105 *LB*, 1900, *Spiritual Review*, p. 20.
106 *LB*, 1891, p. 27.
107 *LB*, 1902, p. 104; similarly 1892, pp. 4f.
108 *HN*, 1874, p. 434.
109 *LB*, 1914, p. 98.
110 *LB*, 1915, p. 110.
111 *LB*, 1915, p. 71.

112 *LB*, 1894, p. 119.
113 A. J. Davis: *The Great Harmonia*, vol. 3, *The Self*, 1858, p. 314.
114 Discussion at a Mutual Improvement Class of Nottingham spiritual-
    ists: *HN*, 1869, p. 638; fictional story accepting the hypothesis uncriti-
    cally: *HN*, 1871, p. 139.
115 *SM*, 1862, p. 92. Positive review of Thomas F. Barkas: *Outlines of
    Ten Years' Investigations of the Phenomena of Spiritualism*, 1862, in:
    ibid., 1862, pp. 284f. Barkas's theory rested on acceptance of Baron
    Reichenback's 'odyle force' or imponderable fluid. (Barkas: ibid.,
    particularly pp. 21f, 81f).
116 *SM*, 1862, pp. 30–5.
117 *LB*, 1922, vol. 33, p. 124.
118 So, again in the 1920s, a Liverpool lyceumist could write an article
    on 'the Communion of Man with God during Sleep': *LB*, 1925,
    p. 111. But, by 1928, see also a Battersea lyceumist's disagreement
    with the theory of soul-wandering: *LB*, 1928, p. 35.
119 *LB*, 1890, vol. 1, p. 4.
120 See L. J. W. Barrow, same thesis, pp. 243–7.
121 *TW*, 1907, p. 712.
123 *LB*, 1890, pp. 25–8.
124 *LB*, 1915, p. 182.
125 J. H. Powell in *HN*, 1867, pp. 599–602.
126 For Massey, see, e.g., Dorothy Thompson, pp. 195, 310; *DNB*, 1912
    Supplement.
127 *HN*, 1872, pp. 22–42.
128 *M. and D.*, 23.7.1872, p. 66
129 *M. and D.*, 1.3.1872, pp. 78f.
130 Ibid., 22.3.1872, p. 103. Massey, in his time uniquely or not, saw
    myth as originating as a primitive sign-language, and as having
    become literal belief only with Christianity: see, most accessibly,
    'C.C.''s preface to the 1925 secularist re-edition of his 1887 *The
    Historical Jesus and the Mythical Christ*.
131 *SM*, 1874, pp. 459–69. Howitt had earlier adduced milder reasons
    for steering clear of the proposed Association: ibid., p. 142.
132 *HN*, 1872, pp. 431f.
133 See, most accessibly V. Skultans: *English Madness: Ideas on Insanity,
    1580–1890*, 1979, pp. 69–76.
134 *HN*, 1869, pp. 586ff.
135 *M. and D.*, 1891, vol. 22, p. 3.
136 Ibid., 1889, pp. 67f.
137 *HN*, 1871, pp. 459–64; *M. and D.*, 1887, pp. 426f.
138 L. Foster: *Religion and Sexuality*, 1981, p. 268.
139 *M. and D.*, 1893, p. 11.
140 Quoted *HN*, 1876, p. 406.
141 *M. and D.*, 1887, pp. 426f; almost verbatim: ibid., 1891, p. 3.
142 *HN*, 1876, p. 182.
143 *HN*, 1872, p. 239; similarly pp. 278ff.
144 *M. and D.*, 1887, pp. 426f.

145 In 1890, Burns started his own fortnightly, the 2-page *Vegetarian Advocate*. Given that, as a young Hampton Court gardener, he was already a vegetarian of some years' standing, the question is less urgent as to any possible influences on him from any remnants of J. P. Greaves's community at Ham Common. For Burns's vegetarian aspect, see vegetarian obituaries to him, quoted in *M. and D.*, 8.3.1895, p. 151.
146 Particularly by Ms Alex Owen.
147 *LB*, 1904, p. 23.
148 *LB*, 1894, p. 102.
149 *LB*, 1904, p. 206.
150 *LB*, 1899, p. 169.
151 *LB*, 1898, pp. 83f.
152 *LB*, 1910, p. 79.
153 *LB*, p. 1.
154 *LB*, 1920, p. 46.
155 *LB*, 1913, p. 180; similarly, e.g., 1910, pp. 139, 188.
156 *LB*, 1891, p. 48.
157 See, e.g., F. M. Turner: *Between Science and Religion*, 1974, Yale, particularly Chapter 5.
159 *TW*, 1906, vol. 19, p. 601. For other biographical details on Hallas, see the *Dictionary of Labour Biography*, vol. 2, and obituary in *TW*, 23.7.1926, p. 431. Hallas had also been arguing prominently for socialism since the late 1890s. In 1906, he left Yorkshire for Birmingham 'as a lecturer at the Ethical [formerly 'Spiritualist'] Church.' In 1916, he spoke at the funeral of Leonard Hall (*Clarion*, 7.6.16). He was 'right-wing' within the Labour spectrum to the extent of being, at first, a Lloyd-Georgeite 'National Labour' MP.
160 Pendleton syllabus: *LB*, 1908, p. 118.
161 The first paper in Britain on Freud – by the (patriotic) S.D.F.er, Dr. David Eder – was read in 1911, with infamously negative results. See S. Hynes: *The Edwardian Turn of Mind*, 1968, p. 164.
162 The following three paragraphs (or more) are immensely indebted to a discussion with Alex Owen during March 1983, shortly before her untimely emigration. Whether I have learnt as much from it as I need is for her to judge.
163 *HN*, 1874, p. 435.
164 *LB*, 1894, p. 36; similarly 1905, p. 107.
165 A. J. Davis: *The Diakka*, 1873, p. 13.
166 Here, despite my next paragraph, there is great contrast with at least two or three then well-known tales by Bulwer (Lord) Lytton. In his *Zanoni* and *A Strange Story* – and to a lesser extent in his *Falkland* – Lytton's occult apparatus seems so crushing, that one might almost dub him as occult novelist. For my period he was surely one, if not the, most available. Alhough he himself seems to have surely believed in spirit-contact, he seems concerned to construct an overwhelmingly male-dominated occult tradition (from, e.g., Simon Forman to the alleged Rosicrucians, plus much pseudo-orientalism). Even his spirits

sound, not so much flaccid as, if anything, phallic, in that they 'contracted or expanded, like the folds of a serpent' (*Zanoni*, Book 4, Chapter 7). I do not mean that all his female characters were devoid of occult gifts but, rather, that the dominant characteristic in most of them was impressionability, and that the one most gifted in this direction turns out also to be the most impressionable (Lilian in *Strange Story*). (I was first alerted to the basic fact of Lytton's occult dimension by Rosemary Jackson.)

167 *LB*, 1912, p. 12.
168 *LB*, 1934, pp. 20f, 26.
169 *LB*, 1920, p. 139.
170 L. Foster: *Religion and Sexuality*, 1981, pp. 46f. Hermaphrodism: S. Hutin: *les Disciples Anglais de Jacob Boehme*, Paris, 1960, p. 122.

Conclusion

1 See S. Macintyre: *A Proletarian Science: Marxism in Britain, 1917–33*, 1980; J. Rée: *Proletarian Philosophers: Problems in Socialist Culture in Britain, 1900–1940*, 1984; T. Putnam: 'Proletarian Science?', in *Radical Science Journal*, no. 13, 1983. Also two books by leading participants: W. W. Craik: *The Central Labour College, 1909–29*, 1964; J. P. M. Millar: *The Central Labour College*, 1978 edition.
2 Though, as Gillian Sutherland has found, seldom evenly: Gillian Sutherland: *Ability, Merit and Measurement, Mental Testing and English Education, 1880–1940*, 1984.
3 *Report of the Consultative Committee*, 1943, p. 3, quoted in H. C. Barnard: *A History of English Education from 1760*, 1971 edition, p. 264.
4 See Phil Gardner: *The Lost Elementary Schools of Victorian England*, 1984, pp. 211–42, 276ff.
5 Somewhat analogously, the former public school-master Victor Gollancz has been 'interpreted' as intending his Left Book Club to create 'an alternative middleclass leadership for the Left': G. McCullough: *Teachers and Missionaries: the Left Book Club as an educational agency*, in *History of Education*, vol. 14, 1985, p. 152.
6 C. Ginzburg: *The Cheese and the Worms: The Cosmos of a 16th Century Miller*, 1980; *The Night Battles: Witchcraft and Agrarian Cults in the 16th and 17th Centuries*, 1983.

(No attempt is made here to distinguish between individuals who were alive at the time, and alleged spirits)